D0282386

# RELATIONSHIPS

# A Study in Human Behavior

*Helen Gum Westlake*

*GINN AND COMPANY*
**A XEROX COMPANY**

The drawings on the following pages are reprinted with permission from *The Saturday Evening Post:* 2, 6, 12, 41, 53, 56,
64, 65, 73, 87, 89, 115, 128, 129, 160, 163, 184, 185, 193,
204, 230, 232, 240, 243, 256, 260, 282, 283, 293, 294, 295,
301, 302, 307, 309, 318, 329, 348, 349, 359, 375, 390, 391,
393, 402, 403.

Illustrations are by Richard Noyes and Milton Johnson.

# Dedication

*To my husband, Don, our daughter, Dawn, and my parents,*
*Mr. and Mrs. Cecil L. Gum*

# Acknowledgements

As author of this book, I would like to thank the many people who made it possible. My chief indebtedness is to my husband for his constant encouragement, his sagacious counsel, and his willingness to subordinate his leisure time interests to constructively criticize the manuscript.

Our daughter, Dawn, was equally helpful, but in an entirely different way. As a happy and alert child, she provided entertainment, diversion, and an excuse to take a walk on the days when the writing was most difficult. Many of Dawn's pictures appear in the book and her antics help to illustrate the manuscript.

For the opportunity to borrow books for indefinite periods and for advice in the procurement of uncommon resources, I wish to thank the East Leyden High School librarian, Miss Nellie Stickle, and Superintendent, Dr. David Byrne.

I am grateful for the aid and advice of the Ginn editorial and production staffs. The book would have been impossible without their assistance.

Last but not least, I would like to recognize the insight that students over the last seventeen years have given me. I sincerely hope that they learned as much as they taught.

*Helen Gum Westlake*

# Preface

This book seeks to bring the principles of behavior to students in such a way that they can perform their vital tasks of relating to their fellow men more intelligently. A study in human behavior must be drawn from a vast body of research and theory. The fields of psychology, sociology, anthropology, biology, physiology, philosophy, religion, and education must be studied for essential principles. In *Relationships : A Study in Human Behavior,* the focus is on the individual as he strives to understand himself, his relations with others, his future interrelationships in marriage, and the subsequent intra-relationships of his family and society.

The speed with which change is taking place in our culture and the complexities of society make it imperative for young adults to study the various aspects of individual and family relationships. Young people now study the individual subject matter fields, but the facts from these fields must be related to each other and given focus so that they deal more realistically and more significantly with the actual problems today's young adults face.

No matter what interest, intellect, training, or family background a person has had, his success, satisfaction, and growth toward maturity will depend upon his ability to relate to others. The young doctor who graduates from medical school *magna cum laude* but who cannot gain the confidence of his patients is a professional failure. The scientist who is unable to relate to his peers proves himself ineffective in joint research. The lathe operator who dismembers himself because he is worried about home relationships is a hazard to his employer and to himself. The young mother who expects from her child a type of behavior that he cannot master until he reaches a future stage of development is distressed in her role. People in all walks of life need an understanding of the basic principles that function in their relationships.

This textbook is designed to give the student facts on both sides of a question. It is planned to provide definitive direction in the form of value guidance which is both practical enough and idealistic enough to be readily acceptable to modern young people. There is no insistence upon reciting threadbare platitudes and inapplicable moralizations. Instead, the student is challenged to focus on the principles, the research, and the validity of those behaviors which tend to strengthen individuals and families and to openly oppose those behaviors which tend to weaken individuals and families.

If a study of behavior is going to affect the lives of the students, it must be dynamic enough to produce change. Two useful concepts of change are that change is motion from one equilibrium in behavior to another and that change is always the introduction of deviation. As people try to communicate, build relationships, and work with one another, all kinds of interactions are going on at once. There is never a *status quo.* Human behavior is never static; it is always dynamic. The critical task for the young adult who is trying to understand himself and others and who is trying to bring about change is to find some way to perceive and be sensitive to the dynamics that are already in operation.

The student who begins to internalize the various reasons for a certain behavior and then acts in a way that is contradictory to the norms of current behavior becomes a deviant in his culture. The moment change effort begins, someone, someplace, is required to be deviant. This book strives to make young people think, so that they will deviate from the statistics dealing with illegitimacy, pre-marital relations, divorce, emotional illness, and suicide.

In change situations, the most urgent task is to build a valid communication system. This is not the creation of a common language system, for people can communicate without a common language. A valid communication system is a system of behavior that enables people to somehow say what their feelings really are, what it is that they really wish to share, and what it is that they must share in order to function. Building valid communication is finding a way to release people to say what they have to say, to feel what they really feel, and to share their thoughts and feelings with someone else.

With this task of communication in mind, Unit One stresses the need for self-realization. As the young adult grapples with his ideas and those of others, he will be able to confront himself and others with his ideas. To develop lasting relationships, a person must learn to communicate. One does not learn this by chance; one learns it by being given the task of spelling out feelings and intentions and being willing to engage in the risk of communicating these to another person. The textbook is written to introduce students to many viewpoints and to give him the techniques to be able to explain and defend his considered viewpoint.

This provides an additional thought regarding the dynamics of change: the formation of trust. A key element in trust is behavior which is predictable in the ability to accept other people and to communicate to them their acceptance. Further, it is the giving to other people the sense of being received, heard, and welcomed into one's existence without the desire or need to change them. Understanding ourselves in relation to others demands a look at our levels of acceptance. Acceptance means a real confronting of the feelings of other individuals.

Since there is no change without relationships, Units Two, Three, and Four all deal with growth toward the understanding, acceptance, and building of relationships. The building of relationships is difficult, but absolutely essential—thus, *Relationships: A Study in Human Behavior.*

# Contents

## Unit 1    *Understanding Ourselves*

| | | |
|---|---|---|
| 1 | Our Basic Needs | 2 |
| 2 | Personality Development | 12 |
| 3 | Character Development | 27 |
| 4 | Growth Toward Maturity | 41 |
| 5 | Mental Health—Mental Illness | 53 |
| 6 | Adjustments to Frustrations | 64 |
| 7 | Defense Mechanisms | 73 |
| 8 | Attitude Analysis | 87 |
| 9 | Religion | 95 |
| 10 | Philosophy | 107 |
| 11 | A Personal Philosophy of Life | 115 |

## Unit 2    *Understanding Ourselves in Relation to Others*

| | | |
|---|---|---|
| 12 | Parent-Sibling Relations in Late Adolescence | 128 |
| 13 | Sibling Relationships in the Family | 139 |
| 14 | Relationships Outside the Family | 148 |
| 15 | Relationships Between Attitudes in Youth and Old Age | 160 |
| 16 | Love-Infatuation Relationships | 172 |
| 17 | Relationship Between Attraction and Dating | 184 |

| 18 | Relationship Between Sex Codes and Morality | 193 |
| 19 | The Deviate | 204 |

## Unit 3 Understanding Ourselves in the Interrelationship of Marriage

| 20 | The Age for Marriage | 220 |
| 21 | Mate Selection and Marriage Plans | 230 |
| 22 | Role Expectation in Marriage | 240 |
| 23 | Career versus Marriage; Career and Marriage | 256 |
| 24 | Financial Values and Goals in Marriage | 270 |
| 25 | Happy and Unhappy Marriages | 282 |
| 26 | The Family and Crises | 293 |
| 27 | The Unmarried | 306 |

## Unit 4 Understanding Ourselves in the Intra-Relationships of the Family

| 28 | Reproduction | 318 |
| 29 | Family Planning | 329 |
| 30 | Involuntary Childlessness | 338 |
| 31 | A Birthright | 348 |
| 32 | Needs of Babies | 359 |
| 33 | Characteristics of Ages and Stages | 375 |
| 34 | Fears of Children | 390 |
| 35 | Discipline | 402 |
| 36 | For All Mankind | 411 |

# Unit 1
# Understanding Ourselves

"... *milk, bread, salt and get yourself an ice-cream cone.
Now I'll repeat that.* In the order of their importance —*milk,
bread, salt and get yourself ...*"

# 1
# Our Basic Needs

Basic to the understanding of ourselves and others is an understanding of
our basic needs. Ted Key, the creator of the cartoon "Hazel," has produced
a ludicrous situation by having Hazel emphasize the order of importance
that would be unnatural to the little shopper.

There is a universal and irreversible pattern of human development. It is universal in that all people regardless of race, creed, or culture develop the same basic needs, and irreversible because once one has grown through one stage of development to another stage, he cannot return to the former stage naturally. Human development encompasses all processes of change, both in the body itself (structure) and in its behavior (function) from conception through old age. To understand human development, one must study the basic human needs.

The basic physiological needs or wants include satisfaction of hunger and thirst, self-preservation, satisfaction or sublimation of sexual drives, growth, and activity. These physiological needs have been variously called biological needs, tissue needs, and life-maintaining needs. Whatever one chooses to call them, however, these needs must be satisfied at a minimal level at least, in order for the human being to live. Thus, they will take precedence over the psychological needs.

The basic psychological needs stem from the mind's requirements for love, esteem, and safety. Psychological wants or drives include the following: security (gained through belonging), sense of worth, approval; new experiences, adventure, fun, excitement; recognition, status; love, abiding sense of loving and being loved; religion; a philosophy of life.

## PHYSIOLOGICAL AND PSYCHOLOGICAL BEHAVIOR PATTERNS

Needs are basic in man's total make-up, but their expression and satisfaction develop many complicated patterns of behavior. Both physiological and psychological needs and the methods and objects through which we satisfy these needs can be observed in our characteristic way of acting, our behavior. Behavior serves a useful function when it is directed toward the goals that will fulfill our basic human needs. Behavior, however, will vary depending on the strength and intensity of the needs, the nature of the goals, and the availability of socially-approved outlets for satisfying our needs.

Behavior patterns in satisfying our basic needs are culturally determined, socially directed, and goal-oriented. Behavior may also be directed by intelligence, emotion, and age, plus learned responses and conditioning.

## NEEDS AND INTERACTION

A need has been defined as an *electro-chemical process of some sort which is inwardly felt as the force of a desire and which tends to propel thought and action in a certain direction.* This definition of a need makes

3

it applicable to all creatures that have a central nervous system. However, the needs of human beings are more numerous and considerably more complex than those of the lower animals. Human needs, particularly the psychological needs, are often neglected because of the complications of their interactions.

When an individual's state of equilibrium has been disturbed in some respect because of hunger, anger, rejection, or some other factor, he will endeavor to respond in the direction of establishing a new state of equilibrium; that is, to secure food, overcome an obstacle, or gain acceptance. How he does this will be determined by the interaction of the many forces diagramed below.

Interaction means the mutual or reciprocal action or influence that the many factors in the shaded area have upon each other. For example, a high-school boy may attend a prom on a June evening when the temperature is in the 80's outdoors. However, he appears wearing a jacket and tie. He is miserable as he dances in his prom attire, but social etiquette demands that men wear a jacket and tie to such a formal function. The psychological need to be accepted takes precedence over the physical need to maintain a comfortable body temperature. The social conditioning of the young

## INTERACTION

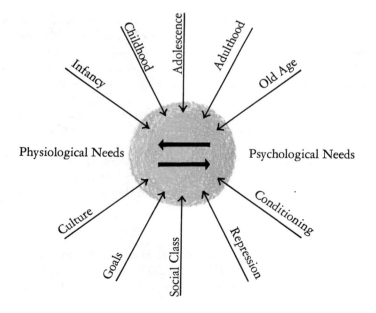

man is interacting with the conflict between his physiological and psychological needs.

## NEEDS AND GOALS

Goals can alter a person's response to the basic needs particularly if an individual's personal goals reinforce cultural, professional, and particular social class goals. We see this in young people who may delay marriage or close personal attachments and who may live at a sub-standard monetary level in order to reach a long-term goal. The young scientist, for example, must put in many years of study and work before he will be capable of doing basic research. The attainment of the doctor of philosophy degree may involve prolonged frustration that is alleviated by a succession of sub-goals, such as passing a series of courses or fulfilling other necessary requirements. If we can see ourselves progressing toward a goal, we can bear waiting to achieve it. In other cases, a person may be consistently thwarted in reaching a distant goal, no matter how hard he has worked toward it and this frustration may result in strong emotional disturbances. At times, these may be so severe that they affect one's physical health, thus emphasizing the interaction between physiological and the psychological needs.

## NEED TO NEED-REDUCTION

Needs, then, are internal tensions that we seek to resolve. The behavior sequences that they initiate end when the needs are satisfied or reduced. In many cases, the sequence from need to need-reduction is clearly understood: we are hungry; we eat; we are no longer hungry. After a certain length of time, the need will reappear and, most probably, we shall resort to the same sequence of behavior to satisfy it. However, in other cases, a person may not be so certain of the way to meet his needs. To begin with, he may not understand or be able to identify his needs. He may be aware only of a certain restlessness that drives him into various forms of trial-and-error behavior. One way of behaving may reduce his tensions and he is then likely to repeat it if his restlessness recurs. This is the case with a child who needs love but who is unaware of his need or of ways to satisfy it. He may resort to attention-getting behavior that only invites further rejection rather than the love he so badly needs.

## CULTURAL AND INDIVIDUAL NEEDS

In addition to our universal human needs, each culture has created individual cultural needs. In our own culture, the value of individualism is

assumed. We feel that the child must have his own distinct identity, his own toys, and his own room. Anyone observing a two- or three-year-old child quickly recognizes that this need is culturally imposed and not basic. The toddler wants to be where the family members are, and no matter how well decorated his own room is he prefers the area around his mother's feet. The mother has the cultural need for privacy so she rewards the child for putting away his own toys and staying in his own room, and reprimands him when he encroaches on her time, her friends, or her possessions.

Now the child grows up needing time to himself, a room of his own, freedom of choice, freedom to plan his own time and his own life. He will tolerate no interference and no encroachment. He will spend his wealth installing private bathrooms in his house, buying a private car, a private beach, and a private yacht, which he will then people with his privately chosen society. The need for privacy is an imperative one in our society, especially our middle class society. Because our culture values privacy so highly, it becomes one of our culturally derived psychological needs in adulthood.

Each individual has his own ways of ranking, or order, of needs after the minimal requirements are reached. This individual order determines his behavior. It is not only difficult to understand other people's ways of behavior; it is very difficult to understand our own actions when we think about them. This is because our needs vary from time to time as our desires and ambitions change. A particular combination of needs may collect to reach a goal. Let's look at an example of the collection of needs as they affected the life of Mary T. Mary's mother died when she was twelve years old. Her mother was a gay, easygoing person who liked people at their face value. Mary was put in the custody of her paternal grandmother who was very strict and very concerned with her status in the community. Mary missed the gaiety, love, and approval of her mother. She needed approval, love, and a sense of security. The only way she could gain approval from her grandmother was to follow her strict rules and to succeed. Thus, Mary studied to the exclusion of all other school activities. She graduated valedictorian of her class. Her constant study and success pleased her grandmother. This substitution of needs helped her reach an academic goal, but the real goal she pursued was acceptance and approval from her grandmother.

A goal that may motivate us when we are young may have very little motivational value for us when we are older. For example, a junior-high girl may practice long hours to learn the techniques required of a cheerleader. Fifteen years later she may be completely disgusted with anyone who would waste time with such an unimportant goal. As needs are met, our goals change.

## ADJUSTIVE AND MALADJUSTIVE BEHAVIOR

On the other hand, if we can identify our need, but have no idea what to do about it, other complications arise. This can happen when an adolescent awakens to an awareness of the sexual desire but finds all avenues of satisfaction closed to him by the dictums of our moral code. As a result of the restlessness created by this tension, he may discover masturbation, and if it aids in reducing his tension he may resort to it again when his restlessness returns. This masturbatory behavior may be "adjustive" from a physiological point of view. In general, the adjustive value of certain forms of behavior may be questioned if they create new problems for the individual.

In another sense the term "adjustive" refers to the solution of a problem while the term "maladjustive" indicates that only a symptom has been treated, leaving the core of the problem untouched. Adjustive and maladjustive behavior may both result in need-reduction. The difference is that maladjustive behavior does not really resolve the need. It is merely a tem-

7

porary expedient and actually may impede complete satisfaction. The following example will illustrate this. A young man, new to a college, desperately seeks companionship. But he is socially awkward, and although he has had many opportunities to meet people he has been unable to establish any satisfactory relationships. He tries various ways of coping with his need, including denying it, saying that he does not really care for people. He spends an evening reading. The book is interesting, and he becomes so absorbed in it that for a while he is quite content. But his need is reduced only temporarily. Losing himself in his reading and withdrawing from all social situations prevents him from acquiring those social skills that would enable him to make friends and thus prevent the recurrence of this problem in the future.

## BASIC PRINCIPLES OF HUMAN BEHAVIOR

Here, in summary, are some principles of human behavior. They should provide guidance as we search to understand our basic needs and ourselves. The ideas presented here will appear again and again throughout the book.

1. All human behavior is motivated by needs. We behave in order to adjust to these needs or to remove or satisfy them.

2. Rarely are these needs easily satisfied or thoroughly acceptable to us. Rather they are frustrated by conditions in our environment or in our minds which block our satisfaction of them. In other words, conflict is inevitable.

3. When conflicts occur, the behavior that involves the least possible resistance from whatever source, be it personal, family, friends, or society, is often selected. This selection is made whether it is appropriate for our overall and long-term development or not.

4. The way we perceive our needs or motives and the situations that satisfy or fail to satisfy them are related to parts of our total experience, past and present.

Maslow classified our basic needs into a rank of five categories.[1] His listing goes from the most basic to the least basic. That is, man must first satisfy his physiological needs, then his safety needs and so on before he can develop to his maximum potential. Maslow's five categories follow:

1. Physiological needs (hunger, thirst, etc.)

2. Safety needs (protection from harm or injury)

---

[1] A. H. Maslow, "A Theory of Human Motivation," *Psychological Review*, Vol. 50 (1943), pp. 370–396.

3. Love needs (affection, warmth, sense of belonging)

4. Esteem needs (self-respect, social approval, etc.)

5. Self-actualization (achieving maximum development of one's potentialities)

Until physiological needs have been gratified or reduced to a reasonable minimum, the individual's behavior will be organized primarily in terms of these needs. He will sacrifice safety, love, esteem, or self-actualization in order to satisfy them. Thus, it becomes apparent that one cannot preach about a sense of self-respect and social approval to people who are hungry and fearful.

For all people, the maintenance of life, that is, self-preservation, is basic. After this primary consideration has been taken care of, man is concerned with reproduction and continuation of the race. The third level of need centers around association with other people. Then, in the fourth step, man deals with curiosity, or the necessity of manipulating materials, ideas, and other factors in the environment.

In our culture and stage of civilization, most of us have met, at least at a minimal level, the first two groups of needs. Thus, we have the entire spectrum of needs and drives pressing for expression.

## TO PROMOTE UNDERSTANDING OF THIS CHAPTER

1. Define the following terms:

| interaction | behavior | adjustive |
| culture | self-actualization | maladjustive |
| conditioning | need | goal |

2. Do the social conditions under which we live here have an important effect on our sense of need and values? Explain your answer.

3. Is it possible for more than one drive, or need, to be active in man at the same time? Give an example that explains your answer.

4. There are a number of conditions that people in our society try to avoid because they are in direct conflict with needs. Identify the needs which are involved in avoiding the following: (a) loneliness; (b) poverty and want; (c) threatening situations; (d) inferiority feelings.

5. Consider the reasons why behavior patterns differ in individuals. In terms of those reasons, show how behavior might differ in winning satisfaction for the sense of worth.

9

6. What basic psychological needs are expressed in the following quote from Addison, "The grand essentials to happiness in this life are something to do, something to love, and something to hope for?"

7. The basic psychological needs are these:
   a. Security (emotional and economic)
   b. Sense of worth (attention, prestige, recognition)
   c. Mutually agreeable interactions with others (companionship, friendship, love)
   d. Variety and new experience (adventure)
   e. Freedom and independence
   f. Religion and a philosophy of life
   g. A measure of conformity
   h. Need to care for others

To what basic needs do the following ads appeal? Toward which ones does each seem to be especially directed? Write the letter of the need in front of the quotation from each advertisement.

( )   1. Three out of four people prefer Honeywell Controls.

( )   2. The man who thinks for himself knows. Viceroy has a thinking man's filter, etc.

( )   3. Change the look of your bedroom every time you change your sheets. (Spring Knight sheets)

( )   4. This is Charter Oak Paneling. It looks like a million!

( )   5. Trust your car to the man who wears the star. (Texaco)

( )   6. Should you be looking for a business of your own? Tired of the routine? Feel like a spoke in someone else's wheel of fortune? Want to build your own pyramid? Become an authorized Rambler dealer!

( )   7. Explore the flavor of nine countries with nine new ideas from Knorr Soups and Premium Saltines.

( )   8. Keep hospitality in your kitchen. Keep a cupboard full of cans. (National Steel Corp.)

( )   9. Something wonderful happens when you take time to remember. (Gibson Greeting Cards)

( )  10. Every woman alive wants Chanel Number Five.

( )  11. Woven together by telephone—the words of love and life.

( )  12. Never a dull diet! For a Sego dieter, the next meal can be a tempting change.

10

( ) 13. Put'em on your table. Put $1.00 in your purse. New **Ribs-in-a-Can.** (Armour)

( ) 14. Gold Medal gives you a feeling of confidence.

( ) 15. In most *modern* homes you'll find Honeywell Controls.

( ) 16. Handy phones make happy homes.

( ) 17. People like you like Sunnybrook (whiskey).

( ) 18. Build his future on a more solid basis with this Metropolitan service. (Metropolitan Life Insurance)

( ) 19. Now it's Pepsi for those who think young.

( ) 20. Behind every Burlington House drapery are the best dressed windows in town.

## SUPPLEMENTARY READING

BERGLER, EDMUND, *Tensions Can be Reduced to Nuisances.* Liveright Publishing Corp., New York, 1960.

LEE, DOROTHY, *Freedom and Culture.* Prentice-Hall, Inc., Englewood Cliffs, N.J., 1959.

LEHNER, GEORGE, and KUBE, ELLA, *The Dynamics of Personal Adjustment.* Prentice-Hall, Inc., Englewood Cliffs, N.J., 1955.

MASLOW, ABRAHAM H., "A Theory of Human Motivation." *Psychological Review,* Vol. 50 (1943), pp. 375–396.

MEAD, MARGARET, *Sex and Temperament.* William Morrow and Co., Inc., New York, 1935.

SORENSON, HERBERT, and MALM, MARGUERITE, *Psychology for Living.* McGraw-Hill, Inc., New York, 1964.

TUSSING, LYLE, *Psychology for Better Living.* John Wiley & Sons, Inc., New York, 1959.

Amos Sewell © 1953 The Curtis Publishing Company

2

Personality Development

Amos Sewell's drawing of the children's party is a study in personality development. The adults and the children show a variety of reactions to the empty ice cream container. The response and adjustment that an individual makes to any particular situation is a function of his personality.

12

Master Tee-shirt is not going to be concerned until he investigates. The little Miss with the braided hair remains optimistic. Miss Bangs, however, is voicing her concern without waiting for any investigation or explanation. Her counterpart across the table thinks that he had better eat before someone mentions a quality called sharing. Each individual in the picture perceives the situation differently. Each of us who views the picture will also respond differently. We may identify with one reaction pictured and question another. How we view it is determined by our past experiences and our present reactions which in turn will influence our future responses. There are many definitions of personality and many theories on the development of personalities. To investigate personality development is the task of this chapter. Perhaps, after you study it, you can turn back to Sewell's picture and suggest some theories or types that are portrayed by his artistry.

## PERSONALITY VERSUS POPULARITY

In everyday usage, "She has a nice personality" implies that the girl is an attractive and pleasant person. And "He has a tremendous personality" may suggest that he is the most popular boy in the school. These examples of everyday usage confuse personality with popularity. The dictionary tells us that to be popular is to be pleasing to people in general, to be loved and approved by people. Popularity can be a part of one's personality and the many parts of personality can contribute to popularity, but the terms are not synonymous.

Actually, personality is difficult to define, and psychologists differ somewhat in their definitions. Engle says, "Personality is the unique or individual pattern of a person's life. It is the fundamental organization of an individual's characteristic adjustment to his environment. Total adjustment includes the individual's characteristic attitudes toward others, his habits of thought and ways of expression, his interests and ambitions, his plan of life, and his attitude toward life in general."[1] It is an error to think of personality as one quality that some persons have and others lack. Everyone has some sort of a pattern of life and therefore everyone has a personality.

Gordon Allport's definition of personality might be capsulated by this statement: "Personality is the dynamic organization within the individual of those psycho-physical systems that determine the unique adjustment to the environment."

The term "dynamic" in this definition calls attention to the active and changing nature of the developmental process and to the continual inter-

[1] T. L. Engle, *Psychology* (New York, Harcourt, Brace and World, Inc., 1964), p. 147.

13

action of the constituent parts of personality. Emphasis on the organizational aspects recognizes the patterned nature of these components. This pattern accounts for the individual's essentially similar approaches to different environmental situations and also to his specific individuality. The term "psychophysical systems" in Allport's definition calls attention to the unity of the physical and psychological processes and specifically rejects the common tendency to think of the "mind" and "body" as separate parts.

For the social scientist, personality is the sum total of all that a person is. Personality is the combination of traits, habits, values, and tendencies that make an individual uniquely himself.

If personality is the entire self, it is a mistake to think that personality means just the ability to attract others. It really means everything about a person—his interests, habits, cheerfulness, kindness or thoughtlessness, tastes, likes and dislikes, ability and inability to get along with people and so on.

Thus, personality is what a person is, psychologically and physically. When you consider this you will realize how important it is to understand the self. Only through understanding the self can one understand others.

## THE SELF THEORY

Of the concepts that relate to personality, the self is most easily understood, for everyone possesses an image or idea of what he is like. The self is the person as he is known to that person; it is that part of his own personality which the individual is aware of through his knowledge, beliefs, impressions, and sensations; it is his image of himself as a physical and social being, or what he believes he should be like. This image is so highly valued that in some instances survival itself is valued less than the maintenance of a self-concept that has honor, family pride or national pride as an important part.

The self includes not only the person's beliefs about his own characteristics but also what he wishes to represent of himself to others and what he believes he should be. We will consider these interrelated subselves as the personal self, the social self, and the ideal self. The *personal self* is the image the person possesses of himself as a physical and social entity. As a result of the individual's developmental experiences, it becomes a highly organized system of attitudes, beliefs, impressions, habits, and values. The *social self* is not identical with either the social stimulus value which a person possesses or the sum total of his social skills; rather, it represents his perception, attitudes, and feelings about himself in relation to other persons. The *ideal self* is the image the person has of what he wishes to become. See the illustration on the opposite page.

14

First there is the personal self which is the existing self; second, the social self which is that part of the self that works for our acceptance by others; third, the ideal self which may be thought of as that part of the self which maintains the goals, aspirations, and the best thoughts about one's self as an individual. In order for a person to obtain adjustment and stability, it is necessary for these three selves to be pulled together and to be superimposed upon each other. If this type of closeness and integration can be maintained within the individual, he becomes adjusted and is satisfied with his total self.

The case of Carolyn A. is illustrative of a person whose personal self, ideal self, and social self are pulling against each other. Her standards are kept in a logic-tight compartment that makes up her ideal self. When crises arise in Carolyn's relations with other people, her social self cannot use these moral standards because she hasn't translated them into operation. Her standards are idealistic and relatively immodifiable. Thus her ideal self is in great conflict with her personal and social selves.

Carolyn is the youngest member and the only girl of a family of good, solid reputation. She is very close to her father who is a minister. Discovering early in life that it was neither difficult to secure his favor nor at times to receive individual attention and privileges, Carolyn accepted all her father's standards without question. Following her father's wishes, she readily accepted religious instruction. Her religious experiences in both childhood and adolescence within this religious environment were genuine.

Despite her position as the favorite of the children in the home, she became a hanger-on in the neighborhood group. She developed the habits and attitudes of the group, which were incompatible with some of her religious training. The two patterns of behavior were never compared. When she was with the gang, she lost herself in the group's pranks, but when she was with her father, she was his "good little girl." It was not until she reached college that she became clearly conscious of how strong were her tendencies to violate the standards of sexual behavior indicated at home and how weak her efforts seemed to be to live up to what she thought was right. It was puzzling to her that moral standards could be so clearly defined when she considered them at home and yet so vague and ineffectual for her when she was with people whom she considered immoral.

At no time did Carolyn think through the whole problem. She thought that since she paid allegiance to morals and ethics, they should function at all times. Religion to her was like a rabbit's foot or talisman that should work automatically. She didn't realize that in order for a code to function, it must be dominant in attitudes and behavior. She often became depressed, particularly when she was unable to repress the memory of her shortcomings and failures.

Carolyn had not been able to correlate her three selves. Since she had been sheltered all her life and allowed to follow her own pleasures in the family, she superficially accepted a code of standards without actually internalizing them. Furthermore, she carried this same pattern of behavior to her other relationships outside the family. The moral standards of her ideal self were principally verbal and were never associated in thought or action with events of her daily life, yet her social behavior was influenced depending upon her associates at any given moment. Her personal self struggled between her social and ideal selves and she began to dislike strongly her misbehavior and eventually everyone who behaved similarly. After a breach, she plunged fervently into her moralistic rituals. This was obviously a means of escape from her guilt. There was no attempt on her part to discover and understand the source of or motivation for her behavior or to accept it as a vital part of her personality with which she must ultimately deal. Rather Carolyn thought that if she vigorously denied and repressed it, her misbehavior would cease to exist. She certainly did not question the standards of her father or her ability to live up to them. Carolyn was a person divided into three selves floundering in a sea harboring both her father's immovable standards and her own violent passions.

16

## FREUD'S THEORY

One man interested in the development and levels of the self was an Austrian psychiatrist named Sigmund Freud (1856–1939). Freud's work led to the theory and techniques of psychoanalysis. Although psychoanalysis is primarily thought of as a method of therapy for emotionally-disturbed people, it is more broadly a scientific method of observing certain mental and emotional phenomena. On the basis of observations made by the methods used in psychoanalysis, a body of knowledge has been collected that helps explain personality development.

The following five points define some of Freud's major contributions relative to the development of personality:

1. Early childhood experiences influence psychological development. Freud pointed out that the experiences of the child during infancy and early childhood have a significant effect upon psychological development. He provided a technique whereby experiences of the early years, which seemingly have been forgotten, can be recalled.

2. Human behavior is influenced by irrational or unreasonable motives as well as rational or reasonable ones.

3. Behavior is multidetermined. This suggests that any specific behavior may be explained by a number of different combinations of motives and causes.

4. There are different levels of conscious awareness. In light of this, Freud pointed out that people may be quite unaware of the origins of their behavior. He introduced the term "unconscious" to account for a person's lack of awareness—his forgetting of experiences that may continue to have effects upon his behavior.

5. Psychological equilibrium is maintained through the use of the "mechanisms of defense." In its efforts to maintain a state of minimal conflict among its components and to minimize the anxiety it experiences, the personality employs certain protective and defensive techniques. These mechanisms of defense are also called mental dynamisms. Some of the common mental mechanisms such as compensation, conversion, displacement, idealization, identification, rationalization, and projection are discussed in Chapter 7.

These five points are accepted within the fields of psychiatry and psychology with a minimum of controversy, and the concepts of the id, ego, and superego are generally recognized as having value in describing complex psychological processes.

In the development of the ego concept of self, Freud felt that the individual acts in two ways: in relation to the environment and in relation to himself in satisfying his basic needs. Freud then departmentalized the individual's thinking into three component parts: the id, the superego, and the ego.

The id became the generating source and also a reservoir for satisfying infantile, instinctual, basic wants. It created the desire within the individual to have food, sex, and bodily needs satisfied immediately. This creates a tremendous power within the organism and when the basic needs cannot be expressed, tension is created.

Freud described the superego as the internal watchdog or the conscience of the individual. This force is continually exerting pressure to uphold the values that have been learned early in childhood from parents and teachers—the social values and the rights and wrongs developed from the relationship of the individual to his environment. The superego tries to make the individual conform to the cultural pattern with its mores and regulations so that there will not be punishment resulting from his actions. The superego controls behavior by making the individual prejudge his behavior.

The ego was considered by Freud to be an integrating mechanism within the individual that accepts the instinctual demands of the id on the one hand and the culturally and conscientiously accepted regulations of the superego on the other. The ego is in constant contact with the environmental situation (the real world); thus, it takes on an even greater function because it is then regulating the forces between the id and the superego and also the relationship of these two forces to the external conditions. Actually, the ego acts as a judge which determines how the person and his personality can best survive.

The meaning of the term superego was expanded in time to also include two other concepts: the ego-ideal and the idealized image. The ego-ideal is a person's "right" behavior, which was developed through praise and punishment when he was a child. The idealized image is the desire of the superego not to submit to the id or ego but to make the world over in its own image—a complete striving for perfection. The superego thus takes on two functions: one is the warning of the ego not to submit to the basic drives; the other deals with social aspirations, ideals, and the highest goals of human beings.

The student may ask, "Where are these things or forces located? Where do they come from?" These problems are never clearly resolved in Freud's writings. He always wrote of these factors as almost "physical" forces or "mind areas." To better see these forces in action, let us grossly exaggerate and simplify the interaction within the individual.

Suppose an individual is watching a child walking down the street with an ice cream cone. The id might say to the person, "You're hungry. It would be a pleasant experience to have ice cream. Take it away from the kid. You're bigger than he is."

But the superego would say, "No, maybe the child's mother will come along and call a policeman and you will get in trouble. You will be punished if you do this thing."

The ego stands between the id and the superego and will try to resolve this conflict of getting something to satisfy the body while not getting into trouble with the outside environment. It does fairly well under certain circumstances. For example, in this simplified case it might say, "Well, I could satisfy this desire to eat by taking a dime from my pocket and buying an ice cream cone. I (the ego) will satisfy the id. I will also satisfy the superego by not being punished or getting into trouble."

Fundamentally, the id represents the basic drives of man—the striving within himself for protection, pleasure, comfort, the fulfillment of wants without considering how they may be obtained or restrained from the outside.

The superego is the result of the restraints that are put on man's desire to be accepted by others, to gain the approval of others through his actions and to attain recognition and status in society. The superego is also the result of the moral teachings and the fundamental religious and philosophical doctrines thoroughly instilled into the moral fiber of an individual. Only by abiding by all of the rules and regulations that society, culture, and conscience have imposed upon him can the individual gain these desired results in life.

The ego evaluates whether it is more advantageous to gain the comfort and pleasure in addition to the survival of the organism or whether it is more advantageous to obtain the recognition and status from the environmental cultural group. If man becomes excessively concerned in satisfying his id, he becomes self-centered and selfish with a minimum of concern for others. On the other hand, if he acts to exclusively satisfy the superego, he may live in a constant state of anxiety or tenseness because he fears not being able to satisfy cultural standards or the others' ideals which may be varied and inconsistent. As he lives in fear of not being accepted, his behavior may become distorted and others around him may feel he is not acting appropriately. This in turn affects the person and a circular response is developed. The ideal personality maintains a balance between the id and the superego so that there is concern for the survival and comfort of the organism combined with an adequate amount of consideration for the other humans in the environment and concern for fitting into a social environment.

## SHELDON'S THEORY

*W. H. Sheldon* (1889–    ), an American who has done medical and psychological research, has developed a theory of personality types based on body types. He has classified man into three distinct types: endomorphic, mesomorphic, and ectomorphic. A study was made from measurements of thousands of photographs of male bodies. He concluded that the physique could be identified through the three main bodily components, one of which is more greatly developed in each type: the fatty, fisceral component, endomorphy; the muscular and body component, mesomorphy; the "skin and nerves" component, ectomorphy.

Although Sheldon's studies showed a high correlation between body build and temperament, other critics were not able to establish as high a correlation. They presented evidence to show that nutritional differences, ill health, and dietary factors can make changes in physical types. Sheldon then modified his concept to allow for these changes. Since the value of this type of classification is that it is a simple, rapid method of finding a clue to an individual's personality, these modifications limit its usefulness.

We have said that the physical factors are not, in themselves, an index of behavior. However, there are some physical characteristics that do pro-

mote certain types of behavior. For example, a fat man may have established patterns of behavior that do not require quick movement of which he is incapable. Such a threatening situation as getting into a fist fight may be resolved more successfully for him if he treats it in a humorous manner or passes it off as if it did not exist. Thus, the physical limitation that involves the lack of mobility of large bulk and slow physical response may produce an easygoing good humor as the best defense.

The deer runs when in danger, the turtle pulls in its head because it cannot run, and the chameleon changes its color to match its environment. The defense patterns are developed according to the varying circumstances in the environment and, consequently, certain personality traits are exemplified not only under threatening circumstances, but also as expected behavior.

## JUNG'S THEORY

*Carl G. Jung* (1865–1961), Swiss psychologist, believed that all people can be divided into two types, the extrovert and the introvert. Extrovert means to turn outward; introvert means to turn inward. Jung believed that each of us has both tendencies but that in each of us one tendency predominates.

The extrovert is the person who turns out to the world about him. He loves to be with people and lets others know of his feelings and thoughts. Since he values things, activities with people, and a feeling of importance, he tends to be actively engaged with people, things, and activities around him.

The introvert is the person who likes to take a little of the world inside to think about. He likes to be alone or with people whom he knows well. Keeping his feelings and thoughts much to himself, he values ideas, imaginations, dreams, and feelings. Much of his activity takes place in his thinking, dreaming, and imagining.

Jung did not think of one type or the other as being the more desirable. They are different, that is all. There is much that is of value about the extrovert, and likewise, there is much that is of value about the introvert. There are both well-adjusted and poorly-adjusted people in each group.

Many psychologists do not believe that people can be labeled as either extroverts or introverts, but rather that people have some of the characteristics of both and perhaps should be called ambiverts (ambi meaning both).

We should also make clear that these same terms, introvert and extrovert, are sometimes used in another way—that is, to describe a person's adjustment to his environment. In this second meaning, it is not so desir-

21

able to be called an introvert, for the term thus used means that you turn away from people because of feelings of inferiority. In this "adjustment" sense, it is desirable to be called an extrovert, for the term thus used means that you can turn your attention away from yourself and enjoy wholesome activities with others.

However, as Jung used the terms, introvert means that there is great interest in the world of the mind and extrovert means that there is great interest in the external world.

## ADLER'S THEORY

*Alfred Adler* (1870–1937), an Austrian psychiatrist, felt that the source of determinism[2] for a person was his will to power. This, he believed, was the primary motive of a man. Adler saw the will to excel in social, economic and sexual competition as the paramount considerations in men's lives. Failure to excel in these basic areas, Adler asserted, led to an inferiority complex which in turn was responsible for people's manifold efforts to compensate for their defeats. According to Adler, personality development progressed along a road paved with evidence of either personal superiority or inferiority.

## FACTORS AFFECTING PERSONALITY DEVELOPMENT

There are three main factors that affect personality development. These are the atmosphere of the home, the discipline of the individual, and the adult models. A positive home atmosphere leads towards individual initiative and a learning attitude, and away from anxiety, conflict, defense, and escape. Family, friends, school, neighborhood, past experiences, future plans, and so forth affect what a person is and what he may become. Each person is different. Even in the same family, each child has a unique position in relation to other family members. Each person has his own experiences, involving particular people, places, and things that are unlike any other person's experiences. The total of his reactions to all of his unique experiences shapes his personality.

The home atmosphere is probably one of the most influential factors in personality development. In this atmosphere conditions are present which stimulate personality growth. A favorable developmental climate includes: (1) affection that gives security, (2) discipline that is consistent

---

[2] Determinism as used here means that nothing in the individual's emotional or mental life results from chance but rather from specific causes or forces known or unknown.

and results in learning, and (3) parents or older individuals who are models for a positive identification and sources of standards and understanding when difficulties arise.

Your personality is a positive force in your development if it makes you happy, makes your associates happy, and is an asset to society. In other words, your personality can be said to be a good one if you are likable, successful in most of your undertakings, and honest and responsible, and if you have many wholesome ways of enjoying life, if your emotions are usually pleasant for you and pleasant for others, and if you meet your troubles and disappointments courageously.

## DEVELOPING AND IMPROVING PERSONALITY

The question of whether personality can be improved perplexes some people. They argue, "If personality is a reflection of my inner self, if it represents me, there is not much I can do about it. After all, if it is my nature to act in a certain way, I must accept it and let it go at that."

It is true that if you are tall or short or have big ears, you cannot change these physical characteristics. They are part of you. Being tall does not mean that you must stoop to appear shorter. Your big ears do not bother others as much as they bother you. The more you look at them the larger they seem. It would be wiser to concentrate on and develop other aspects of your personality. Emotional habits, such as a quick temper, irritability, and shyness are parts of your personality which can be changed. Since you were not born with these traits, you must have acquired them, and habit patterns can be altered.

Everything wants to exist as it is. A chair, because it is a chair, remains in its original form. A cat wants to act like a cat, and you want to be you. If anything or anyone prevents you from acting as you are, you try to overcome the obstacle. You also try to prevent change, even though it may be good for you, because of the existence of certain patterns of behavior. It has been said that if anything affects your eye, you have it removed; if anything affects your mind, you just put up with it. This may not be entirely true; you may have become accustomed to your likes, dislikes, and idiosyncracies. Do not feel too bad if you want to remain as you are. There is some rigidity in everyone.

There are four essential steps in the process of personality improvement and correction: (1) *realization* of the *need* for improvement, (2) *strong desire* for improvement, (3) *analysis* or stocktaking of one's strong and weak points, and (4) a systematic *plan* for improvement.

Personality improvement cannot be neatly rounded out in six weeks or a semester. It is something that should continue indefinitely. None of us will

23

ever be perfect. There always will be something more to be accomplished. It is true that you may be able to virtually remake yourself in three months of concentrated effort. You may be so changed and improved that friends who have not seen you during that time will hardly recognize you. However, without the strictest self-discipline and continued effort you may slip back into your old ways, especially if those old ways represent habits of many years' standing.

## CLASSIFICATION AND IMPROVEMENT OF PERSONALITY TRAITS

The personality traits that characterize each individual fall into a number of broad classifications:

1. *Physical appearance:* the individual's posture, body build and size, complexion, hair and eyes, facial expression, and appropriateness and condition of clothes

2. *Intellectual accomplishments:* the individual's range of ideas, the way he talks and the things he talks about, his quickness of mind, and ability to judge values

3. *Emotional adjustment:* what an individual likes and dislikes, whether he is aggressive or docile, how he responds when things get a bit difficult, whether he is usually calm and self-reliant, how quickly he gets angry, whether he can take a joke, whether he has a sense of humor, and so on

4. *Social qualities:* how well the individual conducts himself with other people, how well he knows the rules of etiquette that govern society, and whether or not he adheres to the prevailing customs and conventions

This classification of personality, however, should not lead you to assume that behavior can be divided into exact pieces. Behavior is primarily social in character. When judging a person's emotional make-up, the evaluation of his traits is made in terms of some kind of social setting. A man who has spent most of his life in solitary confinement would have little social experience, and evaluation of his personality by the usual standards would be impossible.

Personality has been divided into the convenient classifications mentioned above so that it will be easier for you to analyze and study yourself, to find out what makes a well-developed personality, and to improve your own personality so that you will be more effective in human relations.

24

# TO PROMOTE UNDERSTANDING OF THIS CHAPTER

1. Demonstrate your knowledge of each of the following terms by giving a definition, by using it in a sentence, or by giving an example.

   | | | |
   |---|---|---|
   | personality | ideal self | superego |
   | popularity | personal self | introvert |
   | psychophysical systems | ego | extrovert |
   | social self | id | mesomorph |

2. Make a personality inventory and indicate ways of self-improvement.

3. What factors are prominent in personality development and personality change?

4. What kind of behavior might be exhibited by a very short man? Whose theory would explain this?

5. What are the important factors in the child's environment that shape his personality?

6. Give an example of how the self concept might function as a determiner of action.

7. Why is it necessary for an individual to play an appropriate role to fit each situation?


## SUPPLEMENTARY READING

ADLER, ALFRED, *Understanding Human Nature,* trans. by W. B. Wolfe. Garden City Publishing Co., New York, 1928.

ALLPORT, GORDON, *The Individual and His Religion; A Psychological Interpretation.* The Macmillan Company, New York, 1950.

ENGLE, T. L., *Psychology.* Harcourt, Brace & World, Inc., New York, 1964.

FROMM, ERICH, *Man for Himself.* Holt, Rinehart & Winston, Inc., New York, 1947.

JUNG, CARL G., *Psychological Types; Or the Psychology of Individuation.* Harcourt, Brace & World, Inc., New York, 1923.

LEHNER, G. and KUBE, E., *The Dynamics of Personal Adjustment.* Prentice-Hall, Inc., Englewood Cliffs, N.J., 1955.

LEVINE, L. S., *Personal and Social Development.* Holt, Rinehart & Winston, Inc., New York, 1963.

MASLOW, A. H., *Motivation and Personality*. Harper and Row, Publishers, New York, 1954.

SMITH, K. and SMITH, W., *The Behavior of Man*. Holt, Rinehart & Winston, Inc., New York, 1958.

TUSSING, LYLE, *Psychology for Better Living*. John Wiley & Sons, Inc., New York, 1959.

YARBROUGH, R., *Triumphant Personality*. Macmillan and Company, Ltd., New York, 1949.

Donald G. Westlake

# 3

# Character Development

**Dr.** Basic Research may be trained in the crystallographic structure of zirconium, real variables, and how to measure the rate of hydrogen absorption in titanium, but his childhood environment is evident as he considers the date. His basic internal demands for knowledge of the World Series cause him to transform his fourteen thousand dollar tensile tester into a T.V. set.

## DEFINITION OF CHARACTER

Character is what one is. Character can also be defined as the habitual manner of bringing into harmony one's own demands and the demands of the outside world. Character is the tendency of an individual's behavior to be consistent with a set of values to which he is committed (see Chapter 11). It includes both the persisting habits of the individual and his tendency to make choices in line with his values. It includes the capacity to work toward long-range goals and to avoid being diverted either by obstacles or by the attraction of more immediate goals of lesser worth. Character is a part of personality.

## PATTERNS OF CHARACTER

The major patterns of character seem to be formed in the first years of life. However, values are learned and changed throughout life. The young child gets his character values from his parents. The parents' "yes" or "no," smile or frown, pat or slap carry the message of "good" or "bad" to the child. The child's reaction to this message determines whether values will be learned and accepted. A mistrustful child may either defy or simulate compliance. However, if the child trusts his parents, he will probably *introject* the value. *Introjection* is the process by which a person takes a

*"I'd like you to make me look humble."*

Herbert Goldberg, The Saturday Review

value "inside" himself. Through reward and punishment, a child learns first to comply with a value in the presence of his parents. Later, when his behavior away from the presence of his parents conforms with the value, he is said to have *introjected* the value.

The formation of character in childhood is not always a conscious process. Many values are learned in early childhood through conditioning. If the parents respond in a consistent, positive manner to a particular behavior of the child, he may behave more frequently in this way. He may come to feel implicitly that this is a "right" way to behave because it "feels good" when he behaves this way. This can be described as the learning of a value which is then thought of as part of the person's character structure. Neither the parents nor the child need have been conscious of the learning that took place. The same kind of unconscious learning can take place with negative values.

At first culture influences the child exclusively through his parents. However, as the child moves out of the family into increasing contact with neighborhood, school, and religious groups, his character is directly influenced by a variety of social factors such as class values, ethnic values, and later on the values of a business organization or of his profession.

This discussion of the development of character has been included to help you realize that your character—what you are—has been accomplished by forces both internal and external and conscious and unconscious.

## STAGES OF CHARACTER DEVELOPMENT

In order to understand the development of character, a set of five character types has been defined by Robert Havighurst and Robert Peck.[1]

These types are representative of a successive stage in the psychosocial (psychological and social) development of the individual:

| AGE | DEVELOPMENTAL STAGE | CHARACTER TYPE |
|---|---|---|
| 0–2 | Infancy | Amoral |
| 2–7 | Early Childhood | Expedient |
| 7–14 | Later Childhood | Conforming<br>Irrational-Conscientious |
| 14–on | Adolescent and Adult | Irrational-Conscientious |
| 21–on | Adult | Rational-Altruistic |

[1] Robert J. Havighurst and Robert F. Peck, *The Psychology of Character Development* (New York, John Wiley and Sons, Inc., 1960), p. 3.

Another system for classifying character structure is the Freudian or psychoanalytic system. It is the one most widely used by professional practitioners in the field of mental health. Developmental stages and character types in this method of classification are listed below.[2]

| DEVELOPMENTAL STAGE | CHARACTER TYPE |
| --- | --- |
| 1. Oral stage | Narcissistic character |
| 2. Anal stage | Obsessive—compulsive character |
| 3. Oedipal stage | |
| A. Phallic phase—hysterical character | |
| B. Genital phase—genital character | |

To help you understand each of these stages of character growth, these types will be defined and explained with a case study. Let us begin with the five character types as defined by Havighurst and Peck.

*Amoral* is an adjective that means without a sense of moral responsibility. The amoral character type, characteristic of infancy, wants what he wants when he wants it. The infant is not concerned that it is 2:00 A.M. and that his parents are tired. He is hungry and he wants to eat, so he cries until food is given to him and his hunger need is satisfied. The infant cannot be reasoned with. He must have his basic needs fulfilled immediately. He reacts on impulse according to physical or psychological needs. When one is in infancy we expect amoral behavior.

The word *expedient* means that which is immediately advantageous without regard for ethics or concern with consistent principles. The expedient character type develops in early childhood. The child finds that his needs are better satisfied if he learns to react with others. For example, the toddler may try to take a toy from another toddler. The child refuses to give up the toy, however, and so a tug-a-war begins. The first child may learn that if he trades his old truck for the toy airplane, which he wants, the other child may give up the plane without a struggle. Parents of very young children often use this stage of development to advantage. For example, when a young child insists upon trying to touch an expensive vase, the parent may distract him by offering a suitable toy, praising its merits and thus causing the child to leave the vase alone. This resolves the actions of the child for the moment. (*Expedient* describes an act that is apt and suitable to the end in view.)

[2] From *The Encyclopedia of Mental Health,* Vol. 1, p. 281. Copyright 1963 by Franklin Watts, Inc.

The *conforming* stage develops in later childhood when the child wants to be like everyone else. Visit a fifth grade classroom and notice the dress of the students. If it is a school where boys wear blue jeans and plaid shirts, all boys wear this outfit as if it were a uniform. Pity the new boy whose mother sends him to school in corduroy trousers, white shirt and tie. He is teased and soon wants to wear a plaid shirt and blue jeans. Youngsters in this age group need the security of the conforming activity. They are beginning to be independent and are able to go to scout meetings, baseball practice, and other events alone, without their parents. To take this new step toward independence they need the security of the group. Thus they thrive on conformity (state or quality of being in agreement or harmony) in dress, activity, and habits. Adults often object to this stage particularly if they feel that their child is conforming to the standards of friends whom they consider to be intellectually or socially inferior. At this stage of development, the environment or the neighborhood in which a child lives is very influential. The child will probably use the same speech, dress, values, and habit patterns of his peer group (people of the same age and position).

From the conforming period, the character grows into the *irrationally-conscientious* stage. In this stage of development, conformity to the group code is not the issue. Rather, it is conformity to a code the individual child has internalized and believes in. For example, a child who has been brought up to attend church every Sunday may make this idea a personal belief. He may believe that all people are good who attend church every Sunday and that those who do not attend church are bad. Thus he judges whole groups of people on one act which he has evaluated according to his own standard of right and wrong.

The *irrational* (not being endowed with reason or understanding) component (part) is visible in the individual's customary rigidity in applying a preconceived principle. An act is "good" or "bad" to him because he labels it as such, not necessarily because it has positive or negative effects on others.

The final stage, the *rational-altruistic* type describes the highest level of moral maturity. A person of this type thinks of assuring the welfare of others as well as assuring his own. The rational-altruistic (having reason or understanding and devotion and regard for the interests of others) person has a reasonable regard for others. To personify this character type, one might picture a high-school senior who is attending a basketball tournament. He wants his high-school team to win very much because winning the championship will mean that his school has the best team in the district. However, although he cheers his team wholeheartedly, he does not boo the referees when they make a judgment against his team and says or does nothing against the members of the opposing team. He does not abuse the members of the opposing team in deed or word because he has no need or desire to do so. In other words, a rational-altruistic person reacts with emotion appropriate to the occasion. This does not mean that he is un-emotional, for he is enthusiastic about promoting what is good and is, on the other hand, aroused to prevent what is bad. This high-school boy knows himself and faces his own reactions honestly. He does what is morally right because he wants to, not because it is "the thing to do."

This boy is as friendly and respectful to the custodian of the building as he is to his friends and to his teachers. He tries to be honest and kind to all and to respect the integrity of every human being. Further, he accepts responsibility for his own acts and accepts blame when it is deserved. He judges other people's individual actions without making blanket approval or condemnation of people as a whole.

Fortunately for him, his public and private values are just about identical. He sees himself as he is, works for deeper perception and understanding, and respects his own capacities as he does those of other men. He feels no unreasonable anxiety or guilt. If he errs, he feels guilty; but his response is to take steps to correct the error. When he succeeds, he no longer feels guilty.

At this time in his life his moral horizon embraces all mankind, as his behavior demonstrates. It is probable that as an adult he will assume an appropriate share of responsibility in his role as member of a family, community, nation, and the human race.

This picture of the rational-altruistic person represents an ideal goal, to be sought, perhaps to be approached as one moves toward adulthood, but probably never to be perfectly achieved and maintained. Maturity is on a continuum; that is to say, maturity is a process which goes on indefinitely and for which no distinction of content can be affirmed except by reference to something else.

## CHARACTER TRAITS IN RELATION TO DEVELOPMENTAL STAGE

If all conditions for character growth were ideal, one would go through the normal stages of development from amoral through expedient behavior, conformity, and irrational-conscientious to rational-altruistic behavior. All adults would then be in the rational-altruistic stage of development. If this were true all adolescents and adults would be characterized by the following descriptive words and phrases: honest, kind, willing to assume responsibility for himself and others, unselfish, capable of self sacrifice, constructively working in some area and producing results useful to everyone. Wouldn't it be a wonderful world if this were true?

Unfortunately, character growth does not always proceed through each stage, but may become blocked, stuck, or stymied at a particular stage for the rest of a person's life. For example, we all know adolescents and adults who act according to the amoral stage of development.

Let's look at two examples of amoral character development. The first is Harry W., a boy of 18, whom we like very much. He's charming but irresponsible. Although he is bright, he was not able to concentrate on studying and was distracted constantly by short-term pleasures. Rather than planning his assignments carefully in advance, he preferred not to start writing his papers until the night before they were due. Even though Harry can write well, his reports were not good enough to deserve passing grades due to the hastiness and carelessness with which they were written. Although he wanted to go to college after graduation, he wasn't able to pass the necessary exams.

In his social relationships Harry didn't do much better. One day, for example, he was invited to go on a picnic. On the day of the outing, everyone but Harry met at the appointed place. After the group had waited for over 25 minutes, a call was made to his house. Harry's mother, embarrassed, said that Harry had decided to go swimming instead. Thus he had kept everyone waiting while he followed an impulse to go to the lake.

Another kind of amoral boy is Karl, whom few persons like because he's always hostile and belligerent. Tales are told about his behavior behind the steering wheel of his car. He swerves out to pass all cars in his way without regard for other drivers. He toots his horn and swears at others who don't spin their wheels as soon as the stoplight turns green. When his driver's license was revoked, Karl was simply crushed.

The amoral person follows his whims and impulses without regard for the effect these may have on other people. He considers himself the center of the universe and sees other people or objects only as means to self-gratification. If he has a positive, pleasant view of others, he is more apt to be known as "charming but irresponsible." He may form temporary alliances with people, but will abandon them the minute he sees a better source of gratification. If, however, his basic emotional attitudes are mainly hostile, he is apt to be found committing delinquent or criminal acts.

In a way, this is a picture of an infant in its first year. Adults who have such a pattern are spoken of clinically as fixated (arrested in an immature stage of development) at an infantile level.

Here is an example of a certain college girl who shows characteristics of expedience. We'll call her Judy. She has seldom completed a lab experiment herself and copies the reports from her roommate and her friends. She also cheats on exams by all sorts of ingenious methods. Her social behavior is also expedient. She is particularly friendly with girls who have

33

good-looking brothers and does not hesitate to break a date if a more interesting person comes along.

Judy is a very restless and very lonely girl. Since she hates to stay in her room alone, she is always going in to someone else's room looking for company. She goes not only to copy notes but also to be with someone. In order to attract attention she knows just the thing to do and does it when she thinks people will notice.

The expedient person tends to get what he wants with a minimum of giving in return. He behaves in ways that society defines as moral only so long as it suits his purpose. For instance, he may act in "honest" ways to keep an advantageous reputation. If he can gain more by being dishonest, particularly if he can avoid detection and censure, he does so. He is not particularly concerned with other people's welfare, except wherein he may show concern in order to obtain approval.

Hence the motivation-behavior pattern of the expedient person is characteristic of many very young children who have learned to respect the reward-punishment power of adults and who therefore behave correctly whenever an adult is around. In the absence of such controls they immediately lapse into doing what they please, even if this involves shoving other people around, taking what they want, or otherwise gratifying their self-centered desires.

The adolescent or adult who stays in the conforming stage of development is the kind of person who has one general, internalized principle: to do what others do and what they say one "should" do. His only anxiety is for possible disapproval.

Irene is an example of a person who has a need to conform. Irene used to help in a Girl Scout troop as a program aide. She checked what the troop members had done to meet requirements for badges until it was noticed how severe she was in her checking. Every rule had to be followed to the very last letter. For instance, if there was something that made it impossible for a youngster to tie a muzzle on a dog, she wouldn't allow the child to tie the muzzle on a cat; it had to be on a dog. When the troop went camping, instead of letting everyone have fun and work in a way that was agreeable to all, Irene would insist that the right person do the right job in exactly the right way.

A rather easy way to distinguish the conforming type may be to ask whether the person feels bad because of shame (fear of disapproval by others) or guilt when he breaks a rule. Thus, a person who acts morally because he would be ashamed if others found him violating the moral rules is controlling himself according to external sanctions; a violation is not wrong in itself, nor because of its effects, but because other people say it is wrong and their approval is at stake.

34

We can also view conforming adults when we drive through the suburbs. As the men get off the train, they may be uniformly dressed in grey flannel suits, white shirts, and dark, sedate ties. The neighborhoods are similar, the automobiles are in the same price bracket, and the people tend to belong to the same social groups. A degree of this conformity is necessary in our world. A man needs to dress in a businesslike manner, but his character hasn't developed if this conformity of dress and appearance carries over into thought, deeds, and actions. If one must read the same books, drink the same drinks, and laugh at the same jokes because one is afraid to think for himself, then one's character growth is arrested at the conforming stage. The one redeeming fact is that this group is in the third stage rather than being in the first (amoral) or the second (expedient) stage.

The irrationally-conscientious stage of character growth is shown by the following example. John has a very strong conscience and holds firmly to a set of moral values. He believes that his religious faith is the only acceptable faith and insists that his set of firm, well-integrated moral rules are the only rules to be followed by all people.

When John meets a person of another faith, he tries to encourage him to follow his beliefs. He privately, if not publicly, discredits the particular values, beliefs or ideas that differentiate another person from himself.

The irrationally-conscientious character type is toward the top in level of maturity. Irrationally-conscientious character types have altered the course of history. This alteration has many times been in a positive direction, but it can also be negative.

More than by any other consideration, the irrational-conscientious type is ruled by the dictates of his conscience which acts from a firm, well-integrated body of moral rules. These rules, which are followed so faithfully, are much stronger than the person's ability to appraise present reality and figure out logical ways to behave morally. In fact, this person's weak-to-moderate ego strength (see Chapter 2) is not enough to enable him to test or question the rules he has internalized without question or critical thought.

Thus, these persons automatically behave in responsible, "loyal," "honest," "kind" ways. But it is more from force of habit than from personal intent. They demand as much of others as of themselves in the way of conventional morality. Nevertheless, their lack of any strong, positive concern for others as individuals, not to mention their repressed but definite hostility, makes them far too literal-minded and rigid in their righteousness to be very easy to live with. In fact, they do not begin to approach the spontaneous, sincerely considerate behavior which marks the highest level of maturity. They are likely to be "pillars of the church and the community" and often seem just about as warmly human as so many stone pillars.

The irrationally-conscientious person usually does not really like people, and usually does not have any very positive or warm self-acceptance. He is unable to make discriminating judgments about the purpose of the moral rules which weigh on him so heavily, nor is he able to let circumstances alter cases, in order to preserve the spirit of moral law. People may respect him, but not necessarily like him.

On the other hand, the rational-altruistic persons have firm, internalized moral principles which they frequently subject to critical inquiry and test to see if they work in practice. They act on rational moral principles rather than on "absolute" rules because they have a high regard for people and for themselves.

Margaret is a rational-altruistic person. Everybody likes her—young people, children, teachers, her family, elderly persons. She's tall and skinny and far from beautiful but she was made prom queen because of her vivacious personality. She was also valedictorian, although she was not the brightest student in the class. Although these honors pleased her very much, she had the extra pleasure of knowing that everybody was sincerely happy for her.

Margaret is well-liked because of the beliefs she really holds and the subsequent qualities she displays to people. When she talks to a friend, she truly thinks about the person and his ideas, problems, and joys. At a party for boys and girls she circulated and talked to everyone there, even though her best boy friend was with her. When one of her classes went to a mental hospital to give a party for the ill people there, she did her best to make the party a success. This included thinking about the people and helping to decide what would be best for them. Margaret was concerned that the persons to be entertained would have a pleasant time. Although some of her classmates were afraid or uneasy about the trip, Margaret was so busy thinking about the people at the institution and planning their party that she didn't think about herself and so she was not afraid.

Margaret has not achieved perfection. However, although she is not entirely grown-up, she has the rare quality of being open to indefinite growth. She is already as mature, emotionally and socially, as a person of her years could be. Since it is in her make-up to look at life, to know it, and to live by principles that will bring the greatest good to herself and to those whom she loves, she can scarcely help continuing to develop in wisdom, consideration, and knowledge of self and others.

## FAMILY INFLUENCE ON CHARACTER DEVELOPMENT

What are the kinds of family environments that produce children who can develop their individual characters to their greatest potential? This was one of the concerns of Havighurst and Peck's[3] study of character development. In summary, the following characteristics were found. The most striking feature of the parents of amoral children is that, without exception, they are markedly inconsistent. They are highly mistrustful and disapproving of their children. Havighurst and Peck found that these boys and girls grow up knowing very little love, little emotional security, and little, if any, consistent discipline. The typical amoral subject is a rejected child. His parents disapprove of him generally. The feelings of success that he can find through them are very few. At the same time parental control is extremely inconsistent, though it may or may not be severe. In his family environment, the child can never get a clear idea, or pattern, of moral principles. Not only do his parents show inconsistency in moral principles, but they also give abundant reason to make the child feel that he cannot please them no matter how he tries.

The typical background of the child with predominantly expedient character might be summed up as a laissez-faire home. That is, this is a home where the parents give the child indiscriminate freedom to make his own decisions. They approve of him and are very lenient in their discipline, but are also inconsistent in the moral and social pattern which they set for him.

The typical conforming person comes from a family which is regular in its rules and its way of life. *It is authoritarian and all-severe to extremely severe.* Authoritarian is used here to mean that the child must obey the rules and wishes of his parents. Such strictness provides them with stable moral patterns, but ones to be adopted without thinking. To put it another way, it trains these children to "do as others do" without asking questions. This pattern is followed as long as others are conventionally respectable people like their parents.

The families of irrational-conscientious children are usually all severe to extremely severe in their discipline. They, however, show mild mutual trust, approval, and confidence.

In view of the importance of the most mature kind of moral character as an ideal to aim for, it seems worthwhile to examine the families of the rational-altruistic children in greater detail. The parents of these families trust their children. The home is a democratic one in which leniency prevails over severity. The child is able to develop his emotional and social self in an atmosphere of acceptance. As he becomes increasingly able to reason, he confides openly to his parents, discusses problems with them and shares in family decisions. Since there is no harsh enforcement of rules in

[3] Havighurst and Peck, *The Psychology of Character Development* (New York, John Wiley and Sons, Inc., 1960), pp. 176–182.

the home, the child's morality (moral code) has the possibility of becoming flexible and appropriate to the occasion in a rational way.

Thus the rational-altruistic child goes out into the world with the experience of social success in the family behind him. He can participate with other people without a great deal of personal anxiety. This child's parents approve of his moving out into the world. Because his internalized morality is one that society approves and rewards, he receives even more success. Accordingly, positive concern for people, in general, becomes a realistic possibility.

## THE PSYCHOANALYTIC SYSTEM OF CHARACTER CLASSIFICATION

According to Freud's theory of psychosexual development, every person passes through a set sequence of stages. Each person's character tends to evolve around a conflict confronted in one of these developmental stages.

The *oral stage* is the period after birth when the infant is most dependent upon his mother for the satisfaction of his needs. The manner in which he is nurtured determines the amount of trust he becomes capable of feeling toward others. At first the infant, like Narcissus, loves only himself. To the extent that he learns to trust, he extends that love outward to others. Narcissistic character is found in a person who has developed only a minimal capacity to love and trust others, and who needs an excessive amount of attention from others. Such a person is incapable of intimate relationships with anyone, but instead may value and strive for the implicit or explicit applause of a crowd.

The *anal stage* is the period during which the child first learns to gain major control over his own body. In toilet training and in developing the use of his arms, his hands, and his eyes, he learns how to hang on and how to let go. He is confronted with his parents' values as to when he should hold tightly and when he should let go. He may vacillate between self-confidence and pride on the one hand and shame and doubt on the other. He may also waver between trusting acceptance and angry defiance in reaction to his parents. The *obsessive-compulsive* character is found in persons who protect themselves from shame, doubt, uncertainty, and anger by exaggerating the values of their parents. They become exceedingly conscientious and particularly meticulous with respect to details. Their lives become oriented toward doing their duty. Their emotionality is inhibited so that they experience very little in the way of feelings. They are typically hardworking but they have little capacity to relax.

The *oedipal stage,* in contrast to the oral and the anal, is characterized by the tendency of the child to reach out for sexual relationships with other people. The first persons toward whom the child reaches (usually in fantasy) are his parents. As he resolves the conflict involved in his first outreach, his desire shifts toward members of the opposite sex other than his parent. The first phase (called phallic) of this reaching beyond the family is marked by intrusion in which the individual is out to make conquests. An adult male with such an exploitative pattern is called a Don Juan character. Women may be equally active sexually although they may express it differently through teasing, provoking, or making themselves excessively attractive. In the *hysterical* character, which is found predominantly among women, guilt is associated with sexual expression, and sexual thoughts tend to be repressed. Such a woman may remain quite provocative sexually although she is unaware of this and tends to be tense and apprehensive about it. Her emotions are easily aroused and she tends to be both excitable and suggestible. While the obsessive-compulsive character places a high value on facts, the hysterical character is easily swayed by feelings, so that the boundary between fact and fantasy is a vague one.

The individual with a *genital character* is the one who is capable of achieving mutuality in interpersonal relationships. He has a strong sense of identity, and he is committed to a consistent set of values. Like the narcissistic character, he is able to receive from others but he is also able to give. Like the obsessive-compulsive character, he is able to work but he is also able to play. Like the hysterical character, he is capable of having strong feelings but without guilt reactions.[4]

This chapter has discussed the two main theories on character typing and some of the environmental factors that influence character. Character growth is uneven. Not all people progress through all stages; some stop growing at a very early stage while others develop a character type that helps them achieve good relationships with themselves and others.

## TO PROMOTE UNDERSTANDING OF THIS CHAPTER

1. Define the following terms:

   | character | anal | peer group | conformity |
   | amoral | expedient | introjection | altruistic |

2. When and how is character developed?

3. Is the formation of character always a conscious process? Explain your answer.

---

[4] From *The Encyclopedia of Mental Health*, Vol. 1, pp. 276–286. Copyright 1963 by Franklin Watts, Inc.

4. How does family environment affect character development?

5. What is the psychoanalytic system for classifying character?

6. What are the developmental stages in the psychoanalytic system?

7. What are the character types associated with each stage in the psychoanalytic system?

8. What are the developmental stages in the psychosocial system and what are the character types associated with each?

9. How does an obsessive-compulsive character develop out of the anal stage?

## SUPPLEMENTARY READING

CANDLAND, DOUGLAS K., and CAMPBELL, JAMES F., *Exploring Behavior*. Basic Books, Inc., New York, 1961.

DUVALL, SYLVANUS M., *The Art and Skill of Getting Along With People*. Prentice-Hall, Inc., Englewood Cliffs, N.J., 1961.

*Encyclopedia of Mental Health,* Albert Deutsch, ed., Franklin Watts, Inc., New York, 1963, Volumes 1, 3, 4, 5.

FLUGEL, J. C., *Man, Morals and Society*. Viking Press, New York, 1961.

FROMM, ERICH, *Man for Himself*. Holt, Rinehart & Winston, Inc., New York, 1947.

FROMME, ALLAN, *The Ability to Love*. Farrar, Straus and Company, New York, 1965.

National Forum Foundation, *Toward Adult Living*. National Forum Foundation, Chicago, Illinois, 1961.

PECK, ROBERT F., and HAVIGHURST, ROBERT J., *The Psychology of Character Development*. John Wiley & Sons, Inc., New York, 1960.

THIGPEN, CORBETT HILSMAN, and H. M. CLECKLEY, *Three Faces of Eve*. McGraw-Hill, Inc., New York, 1957.

*"It's probably just a phase."*

# 4
# Growth Toward Maturity

In circa 42 B.C., Publilius Syrys said, "It takes a long time to bring excellence to maturity."[1] Wordsworth stated that the child is the father of the man.[2] Milton said, "The childhood shows the man as morning shows the day."[3]

The absurdly incongruous dress of the parents and the child produces the humor of Busino's cartoon. Without subtracting from the enjoyment of the cartoon, let's look at the serious questions about maturity that it suggests.

[1] The translation (Maxim 780) is by Darius Lyman.
[2] Wordsworth in "My Heart Leaps Up When I Behold."
[3] Milton in *Paradise Regained,* Book III, Line 220.

Is one's maturity displayed in his manner of dress? Can one be mature in one way and not in another? In order to grow toward maturity, do we need direction and guidance from others? Mother and Dad Beatnik may be very mature in their philosophical and social views. They may, however, find it difficult to face their chronological maturity and the responsibilities of middle age. The child may be mature beyond his years or he may just be imitating the dress of a mature friend, whom he idealizes. How much importance do the attitudes and values of the child have upon him as a man? Wordsworth and Milton felt that one could make a direct correlation. This chapter will try to suggest some of the ingredients of maturity. With these ingredients, perhaps you can give direction to your growth toward maturity.

## DEFINITION OF MATURITY

Maturity is the ability to face your assets and your liabilities and to handle them intelligently. When you are judging your degree of maturity, you think not only of your abstract ideas, ideals, or even specific goals, but also of those levels of achievement that indicate whether or not you are ready for adult experiences, privileges, and responsibilities. This becomes apparent as one grows and develops. Have you ever smiled upon an action of the past in light of your present maturity?

There is, however, no need to be too critical for there are stages of maturity. Mature behavior for one age and stage of development is immature behavior at another age. There is no time in life at which one can say, "Now I am completely mature; I have experienced all possible things and I know that I will respond with intelligent judgment." Maturity is a growing process that is lifelong; each age brings new situations and new processes with which one must cope.

By definition, maturity is revealed whenever an individual uses all the resources he has to move in the direction of his full potential. In other words, the individual who is best adjusted has reached the highest level of maturity within his capacity.

The following examples are not meant to indicate a norm, but to further explain the discussion above:

Dawn is a six-month-old baby girl. She responds to her name with a smile. She manipulates her toys with her hands and plays alone for 30 to 45 minutes at a time. When she sees her food being prepared, she is patient for a short period of time. She recognizes her parents' voices and their image. When she is tired of a position, hungry, or lonesome, she cries. Although she likes to try to sit alone she frequently falls over. This frightens her and she cries to be consoled and reassured. For her age and stage of development and for her available resources, she is mature. However, if she still performed in the same way at eighteen months, she would be immature.

Ronald Gum is seventeen years old. The Gum family lives on a farm. Mr. Gum is a firm but gentle man, warmly human, and respectful of the rights of his wife and children as human beings. He has, at the same time, considerable self-assurance and is the head of the family. The mother says, "The kids know that when Dad says something he really means it. He doesn't scold them or give them a lot of direction, but whenever he does talk they listen."

In the course of Ronald's life he and his father have spent a great deal of time working together. Mr. Gum says, "Ronald's an A-1 worker. He can do just about anything, and anything he does, he does well. We all think a lot of him. He knows what is right. We have always been proud of the way he's done in school and the way he gets along. We're proud of him." Ronald says, "Oh, sure, lots of times I have to work when I don't want to but Dad always tries to fit the work into my schedule so I have plenty of time to do other things too. We usually talk it over and plan ahead. It's pretty interesting working with Dad. He's like a magician with plants."

Ronald once said of his mother, "If Santa Claus were a woman, Mom would be a good Santa Claus." It is difficult to improve on this description of Mrs. Gum. She is a jolly person. She is also generous and thoughtful of others.

In spite of the essentially accepting attitude that characterizes Mrs. Gum, she puts considerable emphasis on her values. She says, "I'm a stickler for keeping promises you make. I think it's not fair to yourself or others to go back on promises." Like her husband, she has genuine respect for other people as individuals and has a sincere interest in them. She, too, has fundamental self-assurance.

Mrs. Gum respects Ronald's judgment. For example, Ronald had been going out often and staying up late several nights during the week. She had been somewhat concerned and asked Ronald if he did not think his school work might suffer. When Ronald said, "No, Mom, I won't drop behind," she didn't say any more because she felt that Ronald knew what he was doing. Mrs. Gum tries not to tie Ronald down or censure him for his activities. Rather she has encouraged his participation in activities outside the family. Ronald reports, "My folks very seldom tell me when I should be in. I can usually judge for myself."

From the beginning, Ronald Gum has known what his parents expect of him. He has learned that meeting their expectations brings him rewards, abundant approval, and considerable freedom to express himself within the broad limits that have been established and are consistently maintained.

Now let's look at the case of Diane K. who has not used all her resources to move in the direction of her full potential. Diane K. is 18 years old. She looks and acts more like 14. She has superior intelligence and vocabulary, good work habits, and above average grades. Yet *her attitude is submissive.* As soon as she begins to talk, she gives the impression of being younger than she is. *She finds it very difficult to differ with anyone of authority.*

Her present behavior follows an orderly development. She comes from a family of lower-middle economic class. Her mother died before she started school and she was shifted from relative to relative as she developed. The relatives would keep her until another child was born in their family. As she grew older, she was asked to come to the homes of those who needed extra help. Her father was a laborer. He attributed all events in his life to luck. It was either a time of good luck or poor luck. The whole attitude of the family is one of submission to authority. Diane has the ability to do college work but has never considered college a possibility. She was greatly surprised to learn from her counselor that many students of her economic class had of their own initiative gone to college and earned their way.

When Diane thinks of the future she has a fear of mistakes, tension, insomnia, and a general lack of confidence in herself. She wants to assume responsibility, yet her *background causes her to fear every new venture that is not supported by authority.*

Dr. Strecker defines maturity as "the ability to stick to a job, the capacity to give more on any job than is asked for, reliability, persistence to carry out a plan regardless of the difficulties, the ability to work with other people under organization and authority, the ability to make decisions, a will to live, flexibility, independence, and tolerance."[1] It is quite clear that Strecker here describes the maturity of adult development—an adult who has used all the resources he has to move in the direction of his full potential.

We do not grow up evenly and consistently all at once. We have many ages and stages. There are many maturities to consider in any growing individual.

The most common types of maturity are shown in the following list:[2]

1. Chronological (how many birthdays you have had)
2. Physical (how mature your body is)

---

[1] E. A. Strecker, *Their Mothers' Sons* (Philadelphia, J. B. Lippincott Company), p. 211.

[2] Reprinted with permission of the Macmillan Company from *Family Living* by Evelyn Millis Duvall. Copyright 1955 by the Macmillan Company.

44

3. Intellectual (how grown-up your thinking is)

4. Emotional (how mature your feelings and the ways in which you express your feelings are)

5. Social (how mature your relationships with other people are)

6. Philosophical (how grown-up your beliefs, ideals, purposes, morals and values are)

## CHRONOLOGICAL MATURITY

Chronological maturity is definite. We know how many years old we are. This maturity is used to judge the legal age for a driver's license, a marriage license, a work permit or a permit to enter school, and the right to vote. Chronological age is only accurate for legal purposes. However, it may not be an accurate indication of individual readiness for these privileges, but it is a definite measure. Chronological growth is unalterable. There is nothing you can do to change your chronological age from what it really is.

## PHYSICAL MATURITY

Physical maturity is not easy to determine. It can be measured to some degree by looking into a mirror, or by measuring your height and weight. Physical maturity takes place over a good many years. Physical growth is orderly and sequential. However, it is irregular in pace. During the first year of life, one grows very rapidly. Then there is a slower pace until the big spurt toward physical maturity which comes between childhood and adulthood. This time of change is called puberty. Puberty is the period at which sexual maturity is reached. Pubic hair appears above the genitals and under the arms of boys as well as girls. It is at this time of puberty that the first ejaculation for boys and the first menstruation and breast development for girls takes place.

There are great differences in the rate of growth toward physical maturity among individuals. Puberty is usually reached between the ages of nine and twenty. Girls tend to mature at an earlier age than boys do. It is difficult for a boy or girl to be the first in his group to reach puberty or to be the last. One should remember that there are great differences in the rates at which individuals mature physically. Physical growth depends upon individual and inherited growth patterns unless it is altered by malnutrition or medicine.

## INTELLECTUAL MATURITY

Intellectual maturity is highly alterable and intellectual growth can continue as long as you live. Intellectual growth is dependent upon mental ambition and native intellectual ability.

A person is intellectually mature:

1. To the extent to which he can understand meanings

2. To the extent to which he can make up his own mind

3. To the extent to which he can look at himself and his problems from outside of himself

4. To the extent to which he can take responsibility for his own behavior and its consequences

5. To the extent to which he is able to postpone judgments

6. To the extent to which he can take a problem-solving approach to life[3]

Our intellectual growth is irregular because it is so dependent upon our environment. When we are in an environment that stimulates us to think and to tackle real problems, we grow intellectually. When our environment is not stimulating, we mark time. We also frequently mark time when the environment demands too much of us. When we are asked to perform much above our intellectual growth, we tend to become discouraged and stop trying to learn and grow. Intellectual growth is most rapid when we are challenged and gain some degree of success from that challenge.

## EMOTIONAL MATURITY

The emotionally mature person has a proper regard for himself, but his interests also move out to include the activities and well-being of others. Emotional maturity helps one make and keep friends. It contributes more than anything else to happiness in marriage. It is essential to our social well-being. Most of our social problems are caused by emotionally ill and infantile people. As more of us develop emotionally mature personalities, our communities, our country, and our world will benefit. The following diagram depicts the characteristics of the emotionally immature and the characteristics of the emotionally mature person.

[3] *Ibid.*, pp. 10–11.

# THE EMOTIONALLY IMMATURE

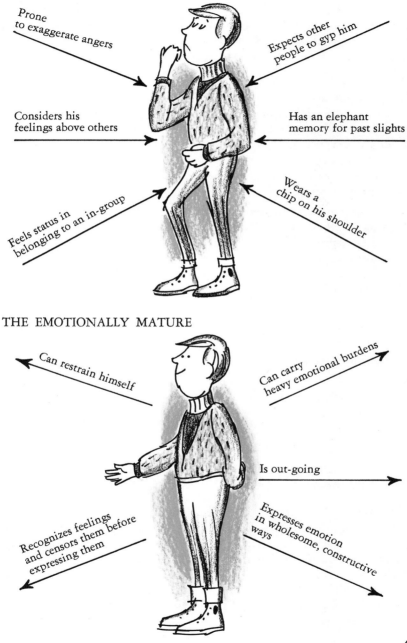

Prone to exaggerate angers

Expects other people to gyp him

Considers his feelings above others

Has an elephant memory for past slights

Feels status in belonging to an in-group

Wears a chip on his shoulder

# THE EMOTIONALLY MATURE

Can restrain himself

Can carry heavy emotional burdens

Is out-going

Recognizes feelings and censors them before expressing them

Expresses emotion in wholesome, constructive ways

47

## SOCIAL MATURITY

Social maturity, which is largely learned, involves so many skills and attitudes that it is difficult to measure it accurately. Your social age is measured by your ability to get along with people. Here are some of the characteristics of a socially mature person:

1. He accepts other people for what they are.

2. He avoids labeling other people. To call people names is very childlike and gives a false impression. If you label a group of people or a person, you blind yourself because you tend to stop thinking about them and accept, instead, a gross oversimplification. If you avoid labels, you leave the way open to meet, to know, and to enjoy a host of people. It is easy to put a false label on a group and to stop thinking about them. It is easy, but it retards social growth.

3. He has emancipated himself from childhood dependencies upon his parents. He makes his own decisions and takes the responsibility for the consequences of those decisions. He asks advice of his parents, but realizes that the final decision must be his own. He establishes an interdependency on a mature level with his parents. He doesn't blame his parents for his mistakes or expect them to rescue him financially.

4. He can meet strangers easily. He has mastered his social graces so that he enjoys meeting new people and is at home with both sexes of all ages in any number of situations.

5. He enjoys planning *with* others.

6. He can accept and adjust to the rules and laws of the group of which he is a part. If the rules make sense, he obeys them. If the rules need changing, he sets about changing them; but he does so in orderly ways, according to the rules for changing rules.

7. He makes a constructive contribution to the world around him.

## PHILOSOPHICAL MATURITY

Philosophical maturity is the most difficult to achieve. It takes time, thought, and a love of wisdom. To be philosophically mature, you must understand yourself, your values, and your goals. Your philosophy embodies your practical and moral wisdom. It is also an indication of your ethics.

A group of young people were asked to characterize a man who has a good philosophy of life. These young people mentioned the items listed on the opposite page.

1.  He has few inner conflicts.

2.  He has a sense of knowing where he is going; he has conscious goals towards which he is striving.

3.  He lives primarily for long-term values rather than taking what he wants at the moment.

4.  He does not show fear or worry regarding non-essentials.

5.  He has a grown-up conscience instead of a childhood conscience.

6.  He shows social-mindedness and concern for the welfare of others.

7.  He cannot be perfect in any one of these things, but he shows growth in all of them from year to year.

There are six kinds of maturity. One might say that each individual has six ages or scores. We might have a boy, Jack, who is nineteen years old chronologically. His physical age may be fifteen as evidenced by his unreliable voice and whiskerless chin. He may score 21 on an emotional maturity test. His social maturity score may be that of a twenty-five year old. He may be capable of doing college math and understanding meanings in the superior range of intelligence. He may be just beginning to formulate a philosophy of life. Thus, Jack's age is a composite of the six ages, or scores. The chronological age has been arbitrarily chosen for legal purposes because it is the one most easily measured. However, this is the age, or score, that contributes the least to Jack's behavior. When we think about our own maturity or the maturity of others, we will further our understanding of behavior if we recognize that we react differently to environmental and internal influences because of our many stages and ages of development.

## CHARACTERISTICS OF THE MATURE INDIVIDUAL

Maturity has many facets. Although one's growth toward maturity is never completed, we can measure maturity by looking at the general characteristics of the mature individual. This will be explored in terms of how the individual meets his basic needs as described in Chapter 1.

An individual is mature if he can support his own household. The mature individual makes contributions to the vocational world and can arrive at his own decisions and conclusions regarding the importance of those contributions.

The mature individual values life. He values people. He values himself. In this attitude of caring, he esteems himself and his associates as persons of worth, and he feels that each individual has a reason for living and a life goal to achieve.

49

The mature individual is constantly striving to understand himself and his associates, so that a mutuality of response to the needs of each will promote pleasant and satisfying relationships.

The behavior of a mature person is directed by inner controls. He does not behave in a certain manner because he fears authority or punishment, but because he believes his way of life is right. His moral code is one in which he accepts responsibility for his behavior.

The mature person shows controlled and directed emotionality. He is calm, deliberate, reflective, and capable of delaying his responses when necessary.

The mature person is heterosexual. He regards his own sex as a means of companionship and the opposite sex as a source of companionship and love.

A person is sexually mature if he is informed and has an understanding of sexual anatomy, physiology, and reproduction. The sexually mature individual uses this knowledge in a wholesome way and feels that experiences related to sex and reproduction are dignified life experiences.

Maturity is on such a continuum that all of the above is not enough to describe the mature individual. As psychologist Fred McKinney states:

> Not all persons who are heterosexual, sociable, and independent represent a high level of maturity in our complex civilization. This independence should go further. The best example of the mature person is one who not only supports himself but also controls to some extent his environment. Instead of being completely subjected to the forces of the outside world, he takes part in molding these forces. He recognizes his talents, and he sees his place in the world; he sees future goals and moves toward them.
>
> Maturity brings with it a point of view of life. If this is adequately verbalized, it deserves the title of a philosophy of life. It includes the individual's conviction on matters such as ethics, morals, politics, and the nature of the world and man.[4]

## TO PROMOTE UNDERSTANDING OF THIS CHAPTER

1. Draw up a list of both mature and immature acts or attitudes that you have noticed in others or in yourself recently.

2. Write a sketch about the most mature person you know.

[4] Fred McKinney, *Psychology of Personal Adjustment* (New York, John Wiley and Sons, Inc., 1961), p. 468.

3. Our growth develops from dependence through independence and on to interdependence. Describe briefly two or three experiences to illustrate these three stages in your own growth towards maturity.

4. How do the following help or hinder your progress towards maturity?
   a. The ask-as-you-go or dole system for getting money for your needs from your family.
   b. The appeal to "do this for mother's sake."
   c. Required courses and electives in your school program.
   d. The plan to lower the legal minimum voting age to eighteen.

5. How do you rate your growth toward maturity? Write a sketch describing your stage and ages of maturity.

6. Is Ronald mature for his age and stage of development? Why?

7. Do Ronald's parents contribute to his maturity? If so, how? If not, how do they hinder him?

8. Is Ronald using all of his resources to move in the direction of his full potential? Explain your answer.

## SUPPLEMENTARY READING

ABRAHAMSEN, DAVID, *The Road to Emotional Maturity.* Prentice-Hall, Inc., Englewood Cliffs, N.J., 1958.

DUVALL, EVELYN M., *Family Living.* The Macmillan Company, New York, 1955.

DUVALL, SYLVANUS M., *The Art and Skill of Getting along With People.* Prentice-Hall, Inc., Englewood Cliffs, N.J., 1961.

*Encyclopedia of Mental Health,* Albert Deutsch, Editor-in-Chief, A Division of Franklin Watts, Inc., New York, 1963, Vol. 1, pp. 37, 51–52, 109, 116, 135, 300; Vol. 2, pp. 387, 533, 545, 629; Vol. 3, pp. 953, 963, 969, 977, 1037.

FROMM, ERICH, *The Sane Society.* Holt, Rinehart & Winston, Inc., New York, 1960.

McKINNEY, FRED, *Psychology of Personal Adjustment.* John Wiley & Sons, Inc., New York, 1961.

MUSSEN, PAUL H., *The Psychological Development of the Child.* Prentice-Hall, Inc., Englewood Cliffs, N.J., 1963.

OVERSTREET, H. A., *The Mature Mind.* W. W. Norton and Co., Inc., New York, 1949.

PIERCE, W. G., *Youth Comes of Age*. McGraw-Hill, Inc., New York, 1948.

PLANT, JAMES S., *Personality and the Cultural Pattern*. The Commonwealth Fund, New York, 1937.

STONE, L. J., and J. CHURCH, *Childhood and Adolescence*. Random House, Inc., New York, 1957.

STRANG, RUTH, *The Adolescent Views Himself*. McGraw-Hill, Inc., New York, 1957.

STRECKER, E. A., *Their Mothers' Sons*, rev. ed. J. B. Lippincott Company, Philadelphia, 1951.

*"And when did you first start thinking of yourself as a common housefly, Mr. Tyson?"*

# 5
# Mental Health — Mental Illness

There are many cartoons and humorous stories about psychiatrists, mental institutions, and mental illnesses. The serious and tragic problem of mental illness is not humorous of course. We may use it as a source of humor in our society because it is too painful to contemplate seriously. Perhaps this is what James Thurber had in mind when he wrote, "Humor is emotional chaos remembered in tranquillity." Mental disorders are responsible for much unhappiness and heartbreak.

The previous chapters in this unit on Understanding Ourselves should help develop an understanding of the healthy self. To the question, "What is a healthy self?" three major ideas have been proposed.

First, a person is called mentally healthy when he understands himself and his own motivation, his drives, wishes, and desires. This self-knowledge is regarded as healthy when it leads a person to accept himself while recognizing his liabilities and assets, and his past as well as his present behavior. Although most persons think they know themselves, many actually do not. This is why it has been stipulated that a healthy self-image must also be a correct one even though it is not easy to decide whether a self-image is correct or false. It may be idealized or debased, and it may also be in conflict with what intimate associates of a person think about him. Many psychological conflicts in family life, for example, arise because a member of the family sees himself as being different from the way other members of the family see him.

The second major idea proposed about a healthy self views the person not at any one moment but from a perspective embracing his entire life span to the date of measurement. This kind of analysis examines the person's previous growth and the result of this progress; it is often described as self-realization, self-actualization, growth, or becoming. The idea appeals to many people because it recognizes that psychological development consists of a process of increasing differentiation in becoming what one potentially is. That is to say, the person has made a progressive development in each age and stage of his life. He has acquired a distinct character and has developed differential characteristics.

The third idea relevant to the healthy self is concerned with a process called integration of a personality. Integration is a term which presupposes that there are several structural units in a personality. In psychoanalytic terms, for example, the ego, id, and superego (see Chapter 2, pages 18–19) can, but need not, achieve a certain balance. The term integration is also used to indicate whether a person's conscious outlook on life is unified or contains contradictory elements. In either sense, the balance between the various units is regarded as flexible, not rigid. What is meant by a flexible balance is, perhaps, best illustrated by thinking of a person under some considerable stress. Where the balance is rigid (i.e., unhealthy), such a person will appear not to respond at all to the stress; however, after a certain degree of stress, he may well go to pieces completely. Where the balance is flexible (i.e., healthy), response to stress will appear sooner, hopefully at a point where readjustments are still possible. The most frequent response to stress is some degree of anxiety which serves as a warning signal to mobilize internal or external defenses. Thus, in contrast to much popular belief, anxiety of some kind is not a sign of ill health but a sign of health. For example, Jane Hall is a young, attractive librarian in a large suburban high school. To keep order in the library so that students can study, she often has to ask other students, who come to the library to disturb and to disrupt, to leave. Some of these students have threatened her when she asks them to leave or when she sends them to the Dean of Students for disciplinary action. Jane's apartment is six blocks from the school and she must walk because she doesn't own a car. There is a vacant lot by the newsstand, where these disruptive students usually congregate. Jane has to walk by this vacant lot on her way home and is always a little frightened as she walks in this area at night. Sometimes when there is a vociferous gang congregated, she stops at the newsstand and calls a taxi. Jane's anxiety and her precautions are a sign of good sense, not a sign of ill health. However, it is, of course, true that many forms of mental disease are characterized by states of intense anxiety with which the person cannot cope.

## THE MENTALLY HEALTHY PERSON

The following characteristics of the mentally healthy person are similar to the characteristics of the mature individual, the well-integrated personality, and the developing character. This similarity is natural because mental health is achieved by all the factors that contribute to self-understanding. They are presented here as a reinforcement of the previous chapters in this unit. The mentally healthy person:

1. enjoys life.

2. realizes that any unhappiness he experiences has understandable causes.

3. is generally self-confident.

4. is able to maintain close and satisfying relationships with a few people.

5. is able to meet problems without becoming more disturbed by them than their degree of seriousness would warrant.

6. is sensibly concerned about his health and is neither overly interested in his body functions nor repelled by them.

7. is able to express justifiable anger in a socially acceptable way.

8. is not afraid of people, things, or situations except where there is reasonable cause to be afraid.

9. has a conscience that helps him keep his behavior acceptable for himself and others.

*"—and just how long have you been an auto mechanic, Mr. McLean?"*

## MENTAL HEALTH AND HUMOR

Because a sense of humor implies certain desirable abilities and attitudes, it is an index of good mental health. Essentially, a sense of humor suggests that the individual is able to assume a light, playful attitude toward the world at certain times. He can detach himself from the seriousness and the cares of reality and joke about it or deal with it in a lighthearted way. This attitude means that the individual is not frightened by the situation, but is master of it. This is a fact that Freud so frequently emphasized. It means that the individual is able to relax his defenses against threat, for he has an inner strength; he can tolerate anxiety and frustration for the moment.

A sense of humor implies also that an individual is able to laugh at himself and not take himself too seriously; that he can take a benevolent and friendly attitude toward his impulses, wishes, and infirmities. The extreme moralist, ascetic, puritan, or prude, on the other hand, is incapable of taking a friendly look at himself. This kind of person judges himself by a stern, unbending rule. An individual with a good sense of humor is able to enjoy the pleasure of self-indulgence. Since he can laugh with others, he can relate to them in a friendly, intimate fashion. He can share his feelings with those around him. This is what it means to be free to laugh.

Laughter itself is a phenomenon since it is a universal expression of emotion. All people of all ages know laughter. Charlie Chaplin, for example, was able to make the most primitive and remote people laugh hilariously by his comic antics without saying a word. Laughter itself transcends culture, era, and civilization.

People laugh for many reasons. Besides the laughter at the comic, there is laughter that is expressed to hide other feelings. People laugh to mask unhappiness or distress and to cover up social discomfort. They laugh when they want to deny the seriousness of a situation or when they want to hide the fact that they are angry. People laugh when they are suddenly relieved from fear or when they are pleasantly surprised. Children laugh in play just from happy spirits. Even infants smile and laugh; these expressions become increasingly social responses and ways of communicating emotionally with another person.

According to Sigmund Freud, *humor* provides two different sources of pleasure: (1) so-called play pleasure (that is, the pleasure of playing, thinking, and acting like a child) and (2) release pleasure (the release of inhibition of unacceptable wishes, particularly the wish to injure or to hurt).

With respect to the first source of pleasure, humor enables man to regress to a childish level as a relief from the serious business of living in a real world. By means of a variety of techniques like a play on words or punning, humor is able to cause laughter as an expression of this sudden pleasure. In a sense then, humor means being foolish, or being able to think in a nonsensical way. To be humorous is to be playfully absurd. Everybody recognizes how much humor depends both upon childish ways of thinking and upon feelings. One can, in humor, suspend the rules of logic, reality, and reasonableness. Rules of language can be violated in the name of humor. This function of humor allows us to return to a time when thinking and acting involved a minimum of trouble and conflict, and when rules and regulations frequently did not hold.

Humor also serves as an outlet for the expression of a variety of feelings that are inhibited and cannot be expressed openly and directly. By means of such techniques as satire and wit, man often can express his hostile feelings with impunity (exemption or freedom from punishment). The laughter that humor brings is the reassurance that the true feelings expressed in the humor are recognized but accepted playfully. Thus, when one is angry with another person it is much easier and sometimes more effective to make a witty remark than to attack the person directly. For example, a teacher was taking a class of fifth graders on a field trip. One pupil began to yawn . . . then another followed and still another. Rather than reprimand them, the teacher asked, "Do you have a yawning permit?" The pupils laughed.

The yawning ceased and for the rest of the trip, they listened to the lecture and viewed the sights as they were explained.

*Off-color humor* serves several purposes. First, it serves as an outlet for interest in sexual matters. By sharing the laughter at off-color jokes, some persons are able to enjoy vicariously and momentarily the pleasures of sex. Off-color jokes provide some persons with the opportunity to laugh at the sexual inadequacies of others and thereby to reassure themselves of their own sexual potency.

Off-color jokes also provide individuals with the opportunity to belittle the actions and feelings of those who violate the sexual taboos—the homosexual, the sex pervert, the adulterer—because very often people fear these feelings within themselves. By laughing at and ridiculing sex offenders, the individual is able to feel that he is superior to them and not afraid of them. Again, the sharing of laughter becomes a form of self-reassurance.

However, when an individual becomes preoccupied with this form of humor, he is obviously manifesting some symptoms of disturbance. Sex is likely to be a problem for such an individual. By seeking this form of outlet, it is possible that the individual is not able to resolve his sexual problems in more direct and appropriate ways. For example, a man who is particularly frightened by women or is hostile toward them without being able to express it directly, may tell numerous off-color jokes at the expense of women. In this way he tries to reassure himself of his own adequacy. Thus, an individual who is unable to fulfill or gratify his sexual desires may substitute talking about sex or joking about it.

Generally, *sick humor* refers to the kind of humor that not only pokes fun at the most sacred institutions and revered persons, but does so with a violence that may be shocking. For example, many sick jokes are addressed to the murder and dismemberment of people in authority, members of opposing groups, and siblings. (Siblings refer to children in the same family; that is, brothers and/or sisters.) The reaction to this form of humor may be one of shock, and the laughter that it may produce includes discomfort and embarrassment. Sick humor often demonstrates the so-called double-edged sword of humor in the sense that there is a very fine line between its pleasure-giving qualities and its ability to arouse discomfort.

Sick humor seems to be most appreciated by adolescents, who often are in a state of rebellion against tradition. For the adolescent, the sick joke is another way of attacking authority and breaking with parental control. Many of these adolescents debunk family relationships and affection, and the institution of the home is often attacked as sentimental, old-fashioned, and useless. In our present turbulent times, where many of our values are in the process of major change, sick humor reflects the violence with which adolescents react to the old traditional ways.

58

In a sense, sick humor is a sign of the times, and each era has its own forms of sick humor. For example, throughout many periods of history much laughter has been directed at the disabled, the maimed, and the defective. Today we regard this as inappropriate.

## MAINTAINING MENTAL HEALTH

Because of the startling fact that over half our hospital beds are filled with people who are mentally ill, it is important that we should think more about maintaining mental health. An individual can be helped to maintain mental health if he:

1. develops a pattern of living that reinforces his basic psychological needs: love, a sense of security, respect for others, a philosophy of life, and satisfying relationships with others. As he makes a conscious effort to move from self to others, he satisfies these needs and thus, he moves from discomfort toward comfort, from being ignored to being admired, from being disliked toward being loved, from failing toward succeeding, from monotony toward new experiences, from danger toward tranquility. Satisfaction may be obtained by conscious effort to bring about such movement.

2. lives to meet his own goals, values, and standards without trying to compete or compare himself with others.

3. usually thinks kindly of others.

4. tries to make others happy when he is around.

5. achieves within his own range of abilities. This requires him to carefully evaluate himself and to know where he may be expected to find successful experiences.

6. believes that his problems and peculiarities are similar to those of other people.

7. recognizes reality as the state of affairs with which one must deal. Reality may be altered but not ignored.

8. develops the ability to face the world alone and with confidence. A desire to make the best of whatever happens is basic. Self-reliance is built up by being independent of any particular person or type of person, and by handling specific situations over a period of time.

9. ignores the common compulsion to save face, to prove that he has always been right, or to try to make another person admit fault or error first.

59

10. maintains a sound body. Proper diet, rest, exercise, play, and regular physical examinations make it easier to develop constructive emotional responses.

11. participates in activities which the whole self (the physical, emotional, social, and intellectual self) can enter without scruples or conflicts.

12. creates new experiences each day and limits the practice of reliving past glories and achievements.


## THE SERIOUS MALADJUSTMENTS

In order to understand mental health, one must have some idea of the serious mental maladjustments. Thus, a brief sketch of the major classifications of mental illnesses will be presented. The study of mental illness is a vast field and of prime importance. This brief resumé is presented only as an introduction to the student who may want to study the field of mental health in college or graduate school. We must realize that all psychiatrists do not agree with these classifications since most mentally ill people have a variety of problems and concerns. However, these classifications are given to help you with the nomenclature (technical terms) of the field.

The majority of mental disorders can be classified into four groups: (1) personality or character disorders, (2) psychophysiologic disorders, (3) psychoneuroses, and (4) psychoses.

The personality or character disorders are: drug addiction, alcoholism, sexual deviations, stealing, and other criminal acts. These are the personality disorders that we read about in the newspaper accounts.

Psychophysiological disorders (physical conditions that are psychologically caused) include such difficulties as: high blood pressure, constipation, hiccoughs, exzema, sharp seizures of abnormally rapid heart beat, asthma, and backache. When the cause is *psychological* rather than *physical,* it is a psychosomatic disorder. In this case, the individual focuses his attention on some organ in his body. When he is under severe emotional tension with which he cannot cope, the tension is exemplified by an illness in that particular organ.

Psychoneuroses or neuroses are emotional maladaptations due to unresolved, unconscious conflicts. A person who is psychoneurotic has maladjustments which trouble him greatly and make life very difficult, but he is still often able to carry on his daily activities in a fairly normal way. Types of neuroses and psychoses are usually classified according to the particular symptoms which predominate. These classifications form a foundation on which further knowledge can be built or developed, since it is a human trait to differentiate and put into classes things we observe. It helps the novice in the area of psychology to place nomenclature and phenomena in a more knowledgeable form. As our thinking develops, and we become acquainted with and start naming the things or phenomena around us, we start classifying them. As our experience and knowledge increase, the differentiation of observed things into classes becomes more sophisticated and involves dividing the same things according to various conceived qualities or criteria. A classification depends on how much we

## KINDS OF PSYCHOSES[1]

### Organic

| NAME | CAUSE | CHARACTERISTICS |
|---|---|---|
| General paresis | Syphilis | The symptoms are many and varied, depending on just how the brain is impaired. There is more and more deterioration of personality and intelligence. |
| Senile psychosis<br><br>Psychosis with cerebral arteriosclerosis | Brain changes due to aging<br><br>Hardening of arteries of brain | The symptoms are many and varied. Intelligence and judgment slowly deteriorate. There may be emotional instability, impairment of memory, confusion, delusions, depression, and so on. |
| Delirium tremens | Excessive use of alcohol over long period of time | Hallucinations. Tremors (shaking or shivering). Disorientation as to time and place. Strong fear. Great suggestibility. |

### Functional

| NAME | CHARACTERISTICS |
|---|---|
| Manic depressive reactions | Prolonged elation, overtalkativeness, excessive motor activity, seemingly without reasonable cause; prolonged depression, seemingly without reasonable cause; or alternation of the two. |
| Schizophrenic reactions | Retreat from reality, with personality disturbances of various kinds: delusions, silly behavior, stupor, excitement, or others. |
| Paranoid state | Persistent delusions. |

[1] "Kinds of Psychoses" reprinted by permission from *Psychology for Living,* second revised edition, by Herbert Sorenson and Marguerite Malm. Copyright © 1964 by McGraw-Hill, Inc.

know of the phenomena we classify and reflects the ideas or concepts that we derive from this knowledge. The classifications below are included to give you some structure that can be employed to make the terms dealing with mental disorders that you encounter in daily reading and conversation meaningful.

Common types of neuroses are the following:

1. *Anxiety Neurosis,* characterized by uncontrollable anxiety. The fear, uneasiness, or apprehension is out of proportion to any apparent external cause.

2. *Dissociative Reaction,* characterized by such behavior as amnesia, sleepwalking, and dream states.

3. *Obsessive-Compulsive,* characterized by behavior patterns that are associated either with repetitive and unwanted ideas or with repetitive, unwelcome impulses to perform certain acts. The afflicted person may feel compelled to carry out rituals such as repeated handwashing, touching, or counting.

4. *Conversion Hysteria,* characterized by conversion reactions such as blindness, deafness, or paralysis without physical cause.

5. *Psychosis,* characterized by a departure from normal patterns of thinking, feeling, and acting. This severe emotional illness is commonly characterized by loss of contact with reality, distortion of perception, regressive behavior and attitudes, diminished control of elementary impulses and desires, and abnormal mental content including delusions and hallucinations.

Dealing with mental disorders involves judgments of many observed and deduced phenomena in the past, current, and future life of an individual whose mental reactions are studied. The many factors that influence him and the multiple variations in the details of his behavior make a classification of people with mental disorder difficult but especially necessary for a common understanding of these phenomena. A useful classification not only establishes an ordering of these factors according to their relative importance but also provides a basis for a common rational understanding of their relationship to each other.

## TO PROMOTE UNDERSTANDING OF THIS CHAPTER

1. What is basic to good mental health?
2. How does the humor one uses define his personality?

3. Why do some adolescents like sick humor?

4. What needs are expressed by one who constantly employs off-color humor?

5. Is humor universal? Explain.

6. What are the common threads that tie together the mature person and the mentally healthy person?

7. Write a description of a mentally healthy person.

8. What are the four major categories of maladjustment?

9. Which of the mental maladjustments is most serious? Why?

10. What might have happened in the training of a child who grows up to be neurotic?

11. What might you do to help a friend maintain good mental health?

## SUPPLEMENTARY READING

CERF, BENNETT, *An Encyclopedia of Modern American Humor.* Doubleday and Co., Inc., New York, 1954.

*Encyclopedia of Mental Health,* Vol. 2, 3, 4. A Division of Franklin Watts, Inc., New York, 1963.

MENNINGER, KARL, *The Vital Balance.* The Viking Press, Inc., New York, 1963.

TUSSING, LYLE, *Psychology for Better Living.* John Wiley & Sons, Inc., New York, 1962.

SORENSON, HERBERT, and MALM, MAGUERITE, *Psychology for Living.* McGraw-Hill Book Co., Inc., New York, 1964.

© 1953 The Curtis Publishing Company

*"Does that help any?"*

# 6

# Adjustments to Frustrations

A person is said to be frustrated whenever any of his goal-directed activities are slowed up, rendered difficult, or made impossible. Our goal-directed activities are developed from our basic physical and psychological needs. A need, once aroused, causes activity until the need is satisfied. The tension accompanying the need makes us anxious and distraught, keeps us busy seeking ways to satisfy the need, and forces us to learn and to adjust. If we have established adequate patterns of behavior for satisfying our needs, we lessen our adjustment problems. But if we are thwarted or frustrated in our attempts to satisfy our needs, problems and conflicts arise.

64

*"Well, thank goodness we all remembered the mustard this time. Now, who's got the sandwiches?"*

## FRUSTRATION FACTORS

There are many factors which can lead to frustration. Some of these are the following:

1. Obstacles in the physical environment. We may be flying to keep an appointment and fog prevents our plane from landing at the appointed time. The child in his high chair who wants to get down and the man in jail who wants to be free both find the physical environment restrictive and frustrating.

2. Biological limitations. A promising pianist may suffer a crippling injury to his hand that forces him to the sideline. A girl may not meet the physical requirements to be a stewardess in the airline of her choice.

3. Complexities of psychological make-up.

   a. Frustration may occur because we have to choose between two goals, both of them attractive, but one near at hand, the other remote. Choosing the near one does not necessarily mean giving up the remote one, but may lead to considerable delay in reaching it. For example: Don and Helen are dating each other and know that some day they want to marry. They also want to obtain college degrees and know that they will have to pay their own educational expenses. They could marry immediately, give up scholarships, and work part-time and go to school part-time. Thus, reaching the one goal, marriage, immediately and slowly working on the remote educational goal is one possibility. They could also concentrate on the educational goal and achieve it before marriage. Don and Helen chose to take full scholarships, work to support themselves and thus attain their educational goal before marriage. Another couple might have decided differently.

b. Frustration may occur because we are faced with two demands, both negative. The small child who doesn't want to go to bed but who will be spanked if he doesn't go is one example. He can choose either going to bed or being spanked. Neither goal is a positive choice to him. As adults, we often are faced with a choice between two goals that have negative aspects and yet we have to choose between two unpleasant situations.

c. Frustration may also occur if to reach a desirable goal we have to accomplish negative tasks; i.e., tasks that are of no interest to us.

4. Social environment. Although social factors are present in the other three sources, we refer here specifically to the conflicting mores and taboos, the opposing regulations and laws of society that sometimes thwart us. We Americans place great stress on getting ahead, on beating the other fellow, on advancing relentlessly. But we also stress love and cooperation with our fellowman. Thus a conflict emerges between competition and cooperation.

Social regulations and conditions add to frustration in many ways. You would like to take an active part in your city, state, or national government, but the law says you are not old enough to vote. You would like to travel extensively and have many new experiences, but parents, schools, and financial problems keep you at home doing the usual things.

## THE FRUSTRATION CONFLICT

Sometimes frustration results not so much from being prevented from doing something but from having to choose between alternatives. Conflict is often very frustrating.

Young persons of late high school and early college age are often faced with many conflicts; to go on with formal schooling or not to go on; to leave home and get a job or to remain at home; to go along with the crowd using alcoholic beverages or not to go along; to smoke or not to smoke; to marry or not to marry. The list continues on to infinity.

Psychologists often speak of four kinds of conflicting situations: approach-approach, avoidance-avoidance, approach-avoidance, double approach-avoidance.

In the simplest *approach-approach* conflict situation, an individual may choose between two equally desirable alternatives. The two attractive choices are mutually exclusive. You would like to do both, but you can't. You may go to a party with your friends or to the theater with another friend, but the invitations are for the same evening.

The diagram below depicts what has been termed by Kurt Lewin as the *life space*. The life space is the psychological situation as it is perceived and experienced. The arrows represent the strength of the respective forces that are converging upon the person. In this case, both alternatives are positive, and the decision depends upon the relative attractiveness of the alternatives; the closer the alternatives approach each other in attractiveness, the greater the conflict.

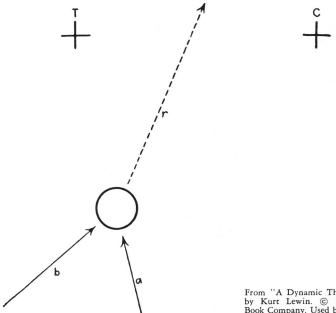

From "A Dynamic Theory of Personality" by Kurt Lewin. © 1945 McGraw Hill Book Company. Used by permission.

Imagine you are faced with two alternatives that are equally unattractive; you are, to use an old saying, "between the devil and the deep blue sea." The *avoidance-avoidance* conflict situation contains greater potential for precipitating frustration than does *approach-approach* conflict, since both choices are contrary to the person's desires. For example, Tom Baker had been enjoying college life and the freedom it afforded him. At the end of the first semester he failed one major subject and barely managed to pass his other courses. Upon receiving the transcript of Tom's grades, Mr. Baker wrote his son a letter that read, "It is up to you to choose what you want to do. You can either apply yourself to your school work next semester or return home and go to work. I will not pay your college expenses next year unless your grades improve." Tom knew that his father meant exactly what his letter had said, and neither of the alternatives presented appealed to him.

Sometimes you are attracted by a certain situation, yet at the same time you are repelled by it. You would like to approach a particular goal, but at the same time you would like to avoid it. You are faced with an *approach-avoidance*. It has both positive and negative value for you. Psychologists apply the word ambivalence to this tendency to be pulled in opposite directions, to like and dislike at the same time. For example, you are at the lake and to try water skiing with your friends seems most attractive. You put on the skis and then imagine yourself falling. The water seems very cold.

*There is room enough in life to crowd almost every art and science into it. The more we do, the busier we are, the more leisure we have.*

Major Morris

68

To water ski suddenly seems like something to avoid rather than something to approach. You run back to the beach. Your friends encourage you. You approach the skis again but you don't feel any braver and the water hasn't warmed up. You decide not to try it and your friends tease you about a lack of courage.

Perhaps you are trying to decide whether or not to apply for admission to college. You have heard a great deal about the pleasures and advantages of college life, and you would like to approach it. However, you have heard of long hours of study, of difficult examinations, and the heavy expense involved. You would like to avoid these unpleasant features.

Some conflict situations are perceived by the person as involving two alternatives, each of which has positive and negative features. In this complex situation the individual is both attracted and repelled by different aspects of each alternative.

The student who considers attending the homecoming football game instead of going to work on Saturday confronts a *double approach-avoidance* conflict situation. To attend the game would be enjoyable, but he would have to go to considerable trouble to make the necessary arrangements. By going to work, he would earn money to attend some of the evening homecoming festivities, but by doing so he is confined indoors all day and unable to take advantage of the pleasant weather and his need for association with his friends.

*There is no road to success but through a clear, strong purpose —nothing can take its place.*

Major Morris

69

## DEALING WITH CONFLICT

Reactions to conflicts are highly varied. The situation that creates a serious conflict for one person might not be considered as even conflictual by another person. You may even have experienced this thought as you read the examples used to explain the various kind of conflictual situations.

This means that the major focus in a study of conflict must be on the factors that determine the *individual's perception* of his situation. Each of the four types of conflict have been described in terms of situations as they were perceived by particular individuals.

Conflict situations which bring about some uneasiness and which present the individual involved with clearly defined and recognizable alternatives are encountered by everyone. They are helpful because they force us to make decisions and to move in some direction. First, however, we must learn to handle them.

In some instances the resolution of the conflict may be facilitated by taking the following steps:

1. Carefully defining the goals and alternatives

2. Obtaining all available essential information pertaining to the goals and alternatives

3. Listing the respective advantages and disadvantages under each goal

4. Eliminating from the list certain advantages or disadvantages that seem insignificant

5. Further clarifying the situation by discussion with a respected advisor

6. Adhering to a time limit or deadline for reaching a decision

7. Accepting the decision reached as the best possible one in light of the situation and the presently available information

## FRUSTRATION TOLERANCE

Frustration tolerance is a term used by psychologists to indicate the ability of a person to withstand frustration without becoming maladjusted or unduly emotionally upset. When a turtle meets a situation with which it cannot cope, it withdraws into its shell. When a person encounters a frustrating situation, he may withdraw into his "shell"; that is, he may not be able to tolerate the frustration. On the other hand, the person who is in good mental health accepts frustration as one of the realities of life. He may have to readjust his goals and his plans for achieving these goals, but he does not feel that everything is hopeless. He may find it helpful to begin tolerating little frustrations without becoming upset—for example, learning to accept an accident such as spilling a quart of milk over the kitchen floor when he is in a hurry. Frustrating situations do not seem to be so frustrating when one realizes that they are quite normal and that everyone experiences them.

A considerable amount of learning must occur in the development of frustration tolerance. For example, a person learns that immediate gratifications can be delayed and that long-term goals are sometimes best served not only by delaying immediate satisfaction but also by avoiding an outward expression of his frustration. Since internal deficiencies and external obstacles make it inevitable that every person must forego some of his goals and objectives, development of a capacity to tolerate frustration is a necessary part of the attainment of personal and social effectiveness. The ability to tolerate frustration does not mean that one pushes out of his conscious awareness all thoughts associated with unconscious impulses. It involves, instead, the conscious recognition of the desired objectives and the reasons for their being desired, and an evaluation of how they might be achieved, replaced by substitutes, held in abeyance, or even abandoned.

## POSITIVE VALUE OF CONFLICT AND FRUSTRATION

Frustrating experiences may disturb us, but they also may have value. In many cases frustration is a prerequisite for learning and for psychological growth; it also has a role in invigorating, enforcing, and increasing individuals' actions which uphold the values and goals of our Judeo-Christian culture. The struggles of the characters in John F. Kennedy's *Profiles in Courage* depict the positive value of conflict and frustration. Each story is an illustration of personal heroism, where the individual was faced with conflicting alternatives, and the resulting frustration. In some cases a senator voted for a bill that was spiritually and morally right, but his vote meant that his constituents would not re-elect him. In other instances it meant no hope for a more prominent office or loss of face in the eyes of his peers. However, the particular individual had the courage of his convictions and the strength of character to stand for those convictions.

In meeting frustrations and in developing techniques and skills to overcome obstacles, we learn, our personalities develop, and we adjust to our problems. The important point to consider is whether the child—or adult —possesses enough resources to handle frustration without becoming unduly upset. If a person becomes too distraught, he may begin to rationalize his shortcomings or he may withdraw completely instead of trying to find ways to handle his problems. The next chapter will deal further with some of the mechanisms employed to deal with frustrations and conflicts.

## TO PROMOTE UNDERSTANDING OF THIS CHAPTER

1. Define the following terms:

   life space    frustration tolerance    conflict    frustration    perception

2. Give examples of conflictual experiences and label them as to whether they are approach-approach, avoidance-avoidance, approach-avoidance, or double approach-avoidance.

3. Which type of conflictual experience is the most difficult for you to solve? Why?

4. Below are some statements that indicate frustration. Indicate the correct frustration factor in each.
   a. Physical Environment
   b. Biological Limitation
   c. Psychological Limitation
   d. Social Limitation
      (1) "The women of the Smith family do not study to be dentists," said Jean Smith's father.
      (2) "Of course he won't play professional basketball; he won't inherit the build for it."
      (3) Because John Brown was reared in a small town without a swimming pool, he did not learn to swim.
      (4) It is bad luck for the groom to see the bride on the wedding day before the ceremony.
      (5) To do graduate work at Harvard successfully, a research study found that students needed to have an I.Q. score of 120 or over.

## SUPPLEMENTARY READING

FENICHEL, O., *The Psychoanalytic Theory of Neurosis*. W. W. Norton & Co., New York, 1945.

LEVINE, LOUIS S., *Personal and Social Development*. Holt, Rinehart & Winston, Inc., New York, 1963.

LEWIN, KURT, *A Dynamic Theory of Personality*. McGraw-Hill, Inc., New York, 1945.

MASLOW, A. H., *Motivation and Personality*. Harper & Row, New York, 1954.

MILLER, D. R., and SWANSON, E., *Inner Conflict and Defense*. Holt, Rinehart & Winston, Inc., New York, 1960.

Norman Rockwell © 1953 The Curtis Publishing Company

# 7
# Defense Mechanisms

There is a constant conflict between the personality and environment. Sometimes the conflict is very slight and sometimes very severe. The conflicts occur because of inadequately satisfied needs. Inadequately satisfied needs give birth to additional or secondary needs called face-saving needs. The individual who has failed to satisfy a need, or who feels that such failure is imminent, suddenly finds it necessary to produce some sort of an ex-

73

planation for—or defense against—that failure. He feels a need to justify his failure in his own eyes as well as in the eyes of his associates. This chapter is about the defense mechanisms that we all employ. They are helpful if used sparingly, hampering if abused, and self-deceiving if overused.

## DEFINITION AND APPROACH OF DEFENSE MECHANISMS

Defense mechanisms are the face-saving devices that we use to satisfy the conflict between our personality and environment; attempts to satisfy the original need are abandoned in favor of attempts to avoid the discomforts of failure.

There are three ways that one can approach this struggle between personality and environment: attack or fight, reinterpretation or compromise, flight. The student pictured by Norman Rockwell at the beginning of this chapter evidently chose a fight reaction. Perhaps the Dean of Students will try to change her approach to one of compromise. The smile on her face indicates that her present approach was satisfactory to her.

### ADJUSTMENT APPROACHES OF DEFENSE MECHANISMS[1]

| ADJUSTMENT APPROACH | DEFENSE MECHANISM |
|---|---|
| Attack or Fight | Increased Effort |
| | Compensation |
| Reinterpretation or Compromise | Rationalization |
| | Attention getting |
| | Identification |
| | Projection |
| | Regression |
| | Repression |
| | Fantasy |
| Flight | Withdrawal |

## THE ATTACK OR FIGHT APPROACH

One of the most primitive reactions to thwarted behavior is aggression or hostility. The attack or fight approach is direct and natural. This approach often alters the situation in a negative manner, very often damages the

[1] George F. J. Lehner and Ella Kube, *The Dynamics of Personal Adjustment* © 1955. By permission of Prentice-Hall, Inc., Englewood Cliffs, N.J.

74

relationship, and sometimes even ruins it. For example, Eric is very fond of Jane. Jane has dated Eric, but recently accepted a date from John. Eric was hurt and felt embarrassed because he considered Jane his girl. He waited for Jane and John in a local hangout, where dating couples usually stop to eat. When he saw them, he challenged John to a fight. John was reluctant and so Eric attacked him, calling him names and blacking his eye. Jane really thought she liked Eric, but after this unprovoked attack on John—as she interpreted it—she never spoke to him again.

A milder form of the fight approach is argument. Refusal to cooperate and determined stubbornness are others. When one is angry at others, he can fight them by constantly nagging and annoying them. Or he can defy them and refuse to do what they ask.

The fight reaction becomes serious if a person uses it too often or at the wrong times. The social non-conformists who are constantly fighting society use the fight reaction consistently by refusing to live the way the world does. This is particularly an unhealthy approach when, after a reform is won, they still go on fighting.

## REINTERPRETATION OR COMPROMISE APPROACH

The compromise approach involves the adjustment to both the demands in yourself and in the environment. In constructive compromise your personality weighs the results of doing just as you wish against what you probably should do. Then you make a decision which seems best for all concerned. However, it does take mature people to adjust and settle differences by mutual concessions. For example, your wish may be expressed by an X; the other person's wish, by a Y. The outcome may be xY, or Xy, or xy, or after much discussion and reinterpretation the final decision may be Z. The small case x would mean a small part of your wish attached to his wish was unaltered. Xy would indicate the situation in reverse. The small case xy indicates an altering of both wishes, but keeping the original intent. The Z decision indicates a new approach that pleases both people.

Successful living depends on how intelligently one can make compromises with himself and others. Giving up something now for future gains, assuming responsibilities for tasks that aren't always pleasant, changing your wishes and actions after considering the welfare of others—these kinds of compromises pay big dividends.

## THE FLIGHT APPROACH

Have you ever suddenly had a very bad headache when you were to speak before the Student Council? Did you even succeed in convincing a classmate that he ought to speak in your place? As you look back on it now, it was probably just the thought of speaking before your peer (own-age) group that made your head ache. You were doing then what lots of people do to dodge or escape their problems. You were taking *flight*.

Other kinds of flight reactions are expressed by tiredness, boredom and lack of attention. Sometimes when a class is particularly difficult for students either in subject matter or in a sense of security, the students will use a flight reaction by day dreaming, sleeping, or making believe the situation is different.

Make-believe can be a worthwhile form of flight for small children. This approach helps the small child shove aside the unpleasant fact that he really doesn't have much power over his environment. In make-believe, the little girl can scold her dolls and release the frustration she feels and the small boy can become a brave fireman or famous doctor. In fact, through play and stories, children learn to fit make-believe and reality together.

Only when this type of make-believe becomes a main adult activity is it unhealthy. Adults who can't accept their environment as it really is often spend as much effort in trying to escape or dodge it in one way or another as it would take to constructively change the situation. The constant dodg-

ing of responsibilities or duties that are unpleasant is called "gold-bricking."

The flight reaction can be used too often and in too extreme form. Some people turn to alcohol to get drunk when they are worried or upset. Others run away entirely from the situation by losing their memory. A few even commit suicide.

## DEFINITIONS OF DEFENSE MECHANISMS

The three approaches, fight, compromise, and flight, have been discussed. These are overt (open to view, apparent) behavior patterns. We use the same approach but execute it with subtleness as we employ the *escape mechanisms*.

## COMPENSATION

This is a mechanism that lets you make up for some real or imaginary inadequacy by doing well in another activity. Toulouse-Lautrec was a crippled and unsightly person, but he compensated for his real physical inadequacy when he was able to become a great artist whose friendship was valued by many.

The process of turning a handicap into an asset is called overcompensation. As a child, Glenn Cunningham, who suffered serious burns on his legs, was told that he would never walk again; yet he later starred as one of the greatest mile runners of all time. He had refused to compensate until he fought the inadequacy directly and he won. Actors often overcompensate by using physical defects such as a large nose or big mouth, skinny or overly fat physique, or prominent eyes as marks of distinction.

A deficiency may lead to direct or indirect compensation. The individual may achieve success in some realm other than the one in which he is handicapped, such as the borderline student who becomes an outstanding extracurricular leader, athlete, or successful manipulator of business deals. Arrogance, loud talk or clothes, weird gadgets on cars, as well as superior accomplishments in music, art, or scholarship may represent compensation for an earlier feeling of inferiority.

Parents who wish to satisfy their own ambitions through their children are seeking indirect compensation. A father whose youthful dreams of a medical career were frustrated by lack of money may try to satisfy his ambition by urging his son to become a physician. A mother whose marriage was unhappy may try to compensate by arranging a brilliant marriage for her daughter. Although such compensation sometimes brings satisfaction to the parents, it may seriously frustrate the children.

77

Compensation helps greatly to solve problems when the path seems blocked in the direction that one wants to go. It makes many people strive and achieve much more than they would otherwise. It is a helpful or a harmful mechanism depending entirely on how it is used.

## RATIONALIZATION

A method of unconsciously justifying ideas and behavior in a way that seems reasonable to yourself is called rationalization. The person who rationalizes gives plausible, socially acceptable, or "good" reasons for his actions or beliefs in order to avoid acknowledging the "real" reasons which he regards as unworthy or improper—or which may not even be apparent to him.

There are many forms of rationalization. Perhaps the best known is the "sour grapes" reaction, derived from Aesop's fable about the fox who wanted the grapes but couldn't reach them. After several tries, the fox declared, "I don't really want them because they are probably sour." This same attitude was manifested by Barbara when she missed out on a part in the play that she had tried very hard to get. Instead of acknowledging her failure, she began to belittle the play. She said that she really didn't want a part, that the director wasn't well trained, that it required too much work and too much time.

The "sweet lemon" form of rationalization is rationalizing in reverse. Instead of trying to convince ourselves and others that we did not actually want the thing we were after, we talk ourselves into believing that our present situation really is best for us, that we are completely satisfied, and wish for nothing more. The *status quo* (the existing state), no matter how undesirable, assumes new value when changing it involves more talent or courage than we possess or means that we lose cherished status by the change. This might be illustrated by the girl who says "I don't have a date for the winter ball. It is just as well. Now my family can save the money that it would have cost for my formal dress and apply it on the clothing budget for the rest of the family," or by the boy who says, "I wasn't chosen to be a member of the varsity basketball team. This will enable me to spend more time on my physics course."

Rationalization is important psychologically because it helps us to maintain our self-respect and self-confidence. In everyday affairs we have neither the time nor the inclination to track down and explain all our motives. Rationalizations provide protection against anxiety and failure.

But rationalizations may be harmful if carried to an extreme. First, if we refuse to accept responsibility for our failures we shall never be able to overcome them. Second, rationalizations may in time shade into delusions.

If we consistently blame others for whatever goes wrong in our lives, we may become completely dissociated from reality and develop delusions of persecution or of grandeur.

## IDENTIFICATION

This is a device whereby you automatically imitate the behavior and mannerisms of someone else and put yourself in his shoes.

R. R. Sears, who represents one point of view, claims that identification by a child results from learning without anyone deliberately attempting to teach the child and without a conscious effort to learn on the child's part. In this type of learning, termed *role practice,* the child acts or pretends to act as if he were filling another person's role. Role practice occurs in fantasy, in daydreams, or in play behavior, and could be initiated by a desire to reproduce pleasant experiences. Sears notes also that the role-practice behavior can represent an attempt by the child to reassure himself that he has his parents' affection and love. By assuming the parental role in fantasy or daydream, he can give himself indirectly the affection he desires.

Identification is often used by individuals who have been unable to achieve their own goals so that they derive satisfaction and enhance their self-esteem by identifying themselves with the achievements of others. This form of identification is called hero-worship. An example of hero-worship can be seen in the case of an adolescent boy who avidly follows the exploits of his football idol and basks in the reflected glory of his accomplishments on the gridiron. His hero may live next door, or may be somebody he has never met personally, or even a fictional character.

Not only adolescents but also adults often identify themselves with recognized prestige groups, especially when approaching a new situation. The girl who transfers to another college mentions her membership in a well-known sorority; a man making new business contacts points out casually but intentionally that he is an active member in a service club.

The individual identifies not only with specific persons, but also with certain groups. He joins a club and it becomes his club. He speaks of his school, his state, and his country. The achievements of his group become his achievements, and he becomes upset when any slurring remark or attack is made against the group.

Whether or not identification plays a constructive role in the development of an individual depends on three factors: (1) in his adjustment to society it will make a great difference whether a person models himself after a gangster or a saint, after a doctor or a mechanic, (2) the example set by his hero or model may give direction and impetus to a person's own activities, or (3) in extreme cases of identification, an individual loses all sense of distinction between himself and the person with whom he identifies and actually believes himself to be the president, actor, or a great inventor. Paranoia is the chronic mental disorder characterized by delusions of persecution and of one's own greatness.

## PROJECTION

A device for attributing to others wishes or faults that you will not claim as your own is projection. This "misery loves company" process takes many forms. Pointing to guilt in others is so satisfying when one is troubled with impulses that lead to feelings of guilt in oneself. The many excuses for being late and for making errors fall in this category. "The majority of the class is flunking the course, too," the socially busy sophomore tells his dad. "She had a bad reputation before I ever saw her, so she better not talk about me," argues the fellow who feels guilt for his behavior toward a girl whom he dated. He tries in this manner to attribute the initiation of the undesirable behavior to her.

The same process operates with respect to prejudice against other groups, and the often contradictory nature of accusations against others becomes understandable when we realize that in the process of projection many different qualities that the individual finds disturbing in himself can be attributed to others.

One further consequence of the process of projection is that after a person has transferred his unacceptable or undesirable emotions or attitudes to another person or group, he is free to launch an attack, to direct suspicion toward the other person or group through innuendo (a remote and derogatory reference), gossip, or slander. He feels amply justified in withholding certain privileges from individuals or from members of a group, denying them equal opportunity, segregating or ostracizing them because of their alleged characteristics.

Thus the projective mechanism gives an individual the satisfaction of defending virtue by attacking evil or weakness in others. He places himself in a position of righteousness and moral vigilance, which helps to allay any additional doubts he may have about himself.

Projection characterizes some extreme forms of personality disorganization. The delusions of persecution in paranoia, for example, stem from one's tendency to project onto other persons his own dangerous tendencies.

## REGRESSION

Regression occurs when a person reverts to previous levels of behavior. A flight mechanism is often observable when a new baby is born into a family which has a toddler. The older child often reverts to bed wetting or thumb sucking or drinking from a bottle even though he has long since learned to use the toilet and to drink from a glass.

Homesickness and other forms of regressive behavior are likely to occur especially in overprotected and overindulged persons. Another factor contributing to regressive behavior is that we usually recall pleasant experiences, making the past appear much more attractive than it actually was.

A more general meaning of the term regression, and the one adopted here, refers to using primitive or earlier behavior in response to frustration. In such instances, relative to his general capabilities, the person displays behavior that is unorganized, gross, and ineffective. Regression in this sense does not imply the return to a specific behavior characteristic of an earlier period but rather implies a return to earlier and often less complex stages of behavioral organization. Regressive behaviors of this type are not enduring. A person may be petulant, childish, tearful, or ineffectual for a period, but with attainment of his objective (or its substitute), a decrease in the need for the objective, or diversion of his attention, he again exhibits the purposeful, organized activity of which he is capable. "Primitive behavior" refers to actions previously learned that are less refined, less differentiated, and less effective than those learned later.

## REPRESSION

In repression, wishes, thoughts, and feelings associated with pain and unpleasantness are excluded subconsciously from awareness. Consider all the unpleasant aspects of life that you do not dwell upon, the embarrassing moments, the times when you have felt that you acted the fool, or showed unusual ignorance, the times you have taken advantage of another, the terrible sights of an accident or of cruelty.

This flight reaction greatly complicates our adjustment to our problems. On the other hand, it would be a dubious advantage if we did remember everything that happened to us, the relevant as well as the irrelevant, the wrong solutions or answers along with the correct ones. Forgetting is a dynamic process; that is, we forget or remember experiences in accordance with our needs. The act of dismissing unpleasant memories from consciousness (repression) protects us against experiences that threaten or disturb our self-concept.

## SUPPRESSION

Suppression, on the other hand, is a conscious and deliberate act. Suppression is a willful tendency to dismiss a thought or an unpleasant experi-

81

ence or something that is socially taboo. We are continually suppressing things.

The art of being tactful is largely a matter of suppression. The person who ignores mature tact for the sake of cruel "truth" is being unkind to the feelings of others and is not likely to have many friends. It is certainly not advisable for married persons to dwell upon the negative aspects of each other's personalities. Of course, frankness also has a place in society.

## FANTASY AND DAYDREAMING

The word fantasy is used to describe imaginative and usually pleasant thinking in which one finds relief from his frustrations by living in a visionary world of his own. The young person may daydream of marrying a beautiful actress or handsome actor of movie or television fame, ignoring the fact that in the theatrical arts there are just not enough such unattached persons to go around.

Whether a daydream is psychologically desirable or undesirable can be determined only by a study of the daydream and the conditions under which it occurs. If the fantasy or daydream becomes an end in itself so that the individual ceases to try to succeed in the world of reality, we must question the desirability of his thinking. On the other hand, the daydream may be little more than an inexpensive form of entertainment and no more undesirable than temporarily losing oneself in a movie or television program. Daydreaming that leads to positive action can be highly desirable.

Daydreams and fantasies, then, depending on the extent to which we use them and the importance they assume for us, may operate in many different ways, affecting our adjustment. All of us have spent time daydreaming. Perhaps the success of such plays as "Harvey," which introduced an imaginary rabbit who made life more interesting for Ellwood P. Dowd and his associates, can be traced to the fact that many of us have at times felt the world of daydreams and fantasy more satisfying than everyday existence.

Many inventions, social reforms, and plays have been born out of daydreams. Daydreams are often first steps in the minds of people who create new things and develop new insights in old institutions or ideas. The daydream that materializes into reality has touched all our lives. Edison's idea of the incandescent light was certainly thought of as fantasy. Air flight was a huge daydream before the Wright brothers transformed it into reality.

## WITHDRAWAL

A frequently used defense mechanism to which many individuals resort when they begin to feel thwarted is known as withdrawal. A person who withdraws retreats from the situation in which he is experiencing adjustive difficulties.

Withdrawal may take various forms. The person who is reserved and formal in his dealings with others may be showing symptoms of withdrawing. His cloak of aloofness may be a screen to conceal deep-seated feelings of inferiority. He may keep others at a distance for fear that they may come to share his own low opinion of himself. His acquaintances, therefore, can never feel that they really know him. Such a person has no confidence in himself or in others.

Some people avoid the problems and conflicts of everyday life by withdrawing into illness. They may not deliberately make themselves ill, but they do become especially sensitized to certain physical disturbances that other people would scarcely notice.

Apathy and lack of interest also may be symptoms of withdrawal. Some people, in order to justify their withdrawing, profess a lack of interest in others.

What we popularly describe as narrow-mindedness is also a form of withdrawal. The narrow-minded individual is unwilling to expose himself to ideas contrary to his own. He dismisses as "propaganda" anything that opposes his own prejudices. He avoids opinions that threaten his own and withdraws from contacts with people who disagree with him. To some extent this is true of all of us. We are all selective in what we listen to and read. But when this selectivity becomes so pronounced as to blur our conception of reality, then it is maladjustive.

## DISPLACEMENT

In displacement, one transfers the emotion connected with one person or thing to a related person or object. The displacement process has been illustrated by Norman Rockwell in a cartoon where the boss bawls out the husband, the husband yells at his wife, the wife spanks the child, the child pulls the cat's tail and the cat eats a mouse, thus ending the displacement sequence. (Of course, one can imagine that the mouse caused the cat to experience indigestion.) The implication of the sequence is that since each is unable to express hostility toward the source, he redirects his pent-up feelings toward his subordinate. Since a clerk can't get angry at the cantankerous customer, displacement may be the answer for him.

Hate, annoyance, and irritation are not the only things you displace. You can displace love. It is a healthy kind of displacement when you feel secure because you believe that people love you. You then can pass on some of that love to people who you know don't love you. Some displacement of love is unhealthy. For instance, there are people who give all of their love to a dog when there are people around them who need love more. Although some people overuse displacement, others use it only occasionally.

## GENERAL PRINCIPLES

In summary, these five general principles concerning the nature and function of defense mechanisms should be considered. First of all, the escape mechanisms are learned forms of behavior. This learning may be formal or informal, conscious or unconscious. However, it is learned by the individual to help him establish an emotional equilibrium. The defense mechanism helps him establish a state of balance, or even adjustment, between opposing influences, interests and needs. These escape mechanisms protect the individual from threats to his security. The defense mechanisms are adjustive or maladjustive, depending upon the extent to which the individual utilizes them. They are adjustive if they provide flexibility in problem solving. They are also adjustive to the extent that they enable the person to face reality and to cope with it satisfactorily. They are maladjustive when the defense mechanisms prevent an individual from making an objective analysis of himself in relation to his problem. They are also maladjustive when the person is blinded to the possibility of alternative courses of action.

## TO PROMOTE UNDERSTANDING OF THIS CHAPTER

1. Define the following terms:

   | | | |
   |---|---|---|
   | compensation | repression | withdrawal |
   | rationalization | regression | displacement |
   | identification | fantasy | maladjustive |
   | projection | | |

2. Give contrasting examples to show when the adjustment approaches of fight, flight, and constructive compromise would be helpful and when they would be harmful.

3. Joan Brown is a girl who is withdrawn. Give some examples of how she might act in a club meeting.

4. What are the advantages of daydreaming?

5. When Jerry, who is four years old, found he had a new baby sister, he began to suck his thumb. Jerry is experiencing the flight mechanism of _____.

6. At age ten Betty was bitten by a strange dog; this experience frightened her and left both a physical and emotional scar. When Betty is asked about the scar on her hand, she says that she doesn't remember how she got it. Betty may be using the mechanism of _____.

7. Write the number of the mechanism opposite the example that explains it. (1) rationalization (sweet lemon), (2) compensation, (3) identification, (4) projection, (5) displacement, and (6) rationalization (sour grapes).

   a. "We haven't a very warm home and no running water, but it is good for the children to learn to do without these things. They'll appreciate them more later on."

   b. "My wife, Joyce, wanted me to have this deer rifle to even up the cost of the garbage disposal that she added to our kitchen."

   c. "Every time Mickey embarrasses himself by talking too loud at a party, he feels that he must buy his wife, Dora, a gift."

   d. "Don loves to joke about his big nose."

   e. Cecilia has recently had a back operation. When her sister realized her discomfort, she had such a sympathetic backache that the nurse had to get a straight chair for her to sit on.

   f. Lucy's mother works every day. While Lucy stays with her sitter, she likes to walk around the house in her mother's high heeled slippers.

   g. "Her son was picked up by the police for speeding long before my son ever rode with him."

   h. "I would have been on time this morning if my mother had made me get up."

   i. When asked why he was crying, four-year-old Billy said that it was because his bike wouldn't stand up.


## SUPPLEMENTARY READING

BERNARD, H., *Toward Better Personal Adjustment*. McGraw-Hill, Inc., New York, 1951.

COLE, L., *Attaining Maturity*. Farrar, New York, 1944.

DOLLARD, JOHN, and MILLER, N. E., *Personality and Psychotherapy*. McGraw-Hill, Inc., New York, 1950.

ENGLE, T. L., *Psychology*. Harcourt, Brace & World, Inc., New York, 1964.

HALL, C. S., and LINDZEY, G., *Theories of Personality*. John Wiley & Sons, Inc., New York, 1957.

HILGARD, E., *Introduction to Psychology*. Harcourt, Brace & World, Inc., New York, 1953.

LEHNER, G. F. J., and KUBE, E., *The Dynamics of Personal Adjustment*. Prentice-Hall, Inc., Englewood Cliffs, N.J., 1955.

LEVINE, LOUIS S., *Personal and Social Development*. Holt, Rinehart & Winston, Inc., New York, 1963.

MCKINNEY, FRED, *Psychology of Personal Adjustment*. John Wiley & Sons, Inc., New York, 1960.

SCHNEIDERS, ALEXANDER, *Personal Dynamics and Mental Health*. Holt, Rinehart & Winston, Inc., New York, 1965.

SEARS, R. R., MACCOBY, E. E., and LEVIN, H., *Patterns of Child Rearing*. Harper and Row, New York, 1957.

# 8
# Attitude Analysis

The influence which attitudes have upon behavior is attested in both scriptural and classical literature. "As he thinketh in his heart, so is he." Disraeli wrote, "We make our fortunes and we call them fate." In a lighter vein, the cartoon asks the question, "Do a man's ideas make the man?"

An *attitude* is an emotionally-toned idea or group of ideas. As such, attitudes usually have a direct bearing on behavior. Therefore, an attitude may also be defined as a readiness to respond favorably or unfavorably to a person, object, situation, or event. When a person expresses an opinion, he is revealing an attitude by verbalizing it (putting it into words). An attitude can be revealed in ways other than through verbalizing an opinion. For example, the way a person treats the members of another group reveals his attitude toward them. People have attitudes toward everything from their clothes to world problems. However, the primary concern to us in this chapter is to analyze our own attitudes and gain some insight into how these attitudes may have been formed.

## MECHANISMS FORMING ATTITUDES

The child's personal standards and values grow out of a variety of experiences with his parents, other adults, and his playmates. In this way he learns what types of behavior bring approval or disapproval by others. As he grows older, however, the judgments of others gradually become less significant than the approval or disapproval he directs towards himself. Nevertheless, his interpretation of the attitudes of others provides the basis from which he derives his own concepts of right and wrong (his "conscience"). From his process comes the feeling of shame experienced by the person who responds to an impulse or wish and then feels guilty for having gone beyond the limits he has set for himself.

## INTROJECTION

Introjection is the process by which a person unconsciously absorbs ideas, emotional attitudes, standards, and ideals from the people around him. Even as a very small child you absorb attitudes and ideas. This is one of the ways in which your conscience was formed; even though you do not remember the time when you didn't have one. Your ideals and your present standards of behavior did not originate with you. The beliefs of your parents regarding morals, education, or working conditions automatically became your beliefs. Although these beliefs may have changed somewhat as you had more education and experience, even these changes were absorbed mainly from people around you.

Everyone gets most of his ideas from someone else. You are a Republican—or a Democrat—probably because your Dad is. The following situation illustrates this point. A high school class was observing a nursery class in order to better understand children of four years of age. It was during a presidential election and, with the mechanism of introjection in mind, the high school students asked the children if they were Republicans or Democrats. The children replied with very definite responses, Democrat, Republican, and so forth, when suddenly a little boy said "Methodist."

The four-year-olds were allied to the big word they had heard most often. The little boy who replied "Methodist" had heard that word more often than either Democrat or Republican, so he replied accordingly. How often have you argued a point about which you feel very strongly? Then, when you are told to validate the source of your information, you realize that your older brother at the age of nine told you that when you were only six. You automatically absorbed it and never questioned its validity.

Sometimes, however, resentment toward parents causes children to take the opposite stand on various subjects. A great many young people have periods when they defy their parents and hold different points of view taken over from persons of their own age. This can be a very painful period because the young people are rebelling not only against their parents but also against a part of themselves.

You introject in many different ways. You absorb the spirit of a party— if it's a good party, you have a good time. If you are with someone you like, you usually accept his ideas. If you live in an environment in which there is prejudice against people of a different color or religion, you are likely to be prejudiced in the same way as the other persons around you. Because the process of introjection is automatic, you may not recognize it.

© 1966 The Curtis Publishing Company

## IDENTIFICATION

A device whereby you automatically imitate people whom you admire is identification. Little girls imitate their own mothers in the treatment of their dolls as children. The little boy imitates his dad. It is natural to imitate those around you for it is from these persons that you learn how to do many things. It is not just that a boy is his father's son that he walks or acts like his father. He is automatically imitating his father's mannerisms and behavior as well as absorbing his father's attitudes and ideals.

Identification goes on throughout life. When you fall in love with somebody you find yourself behaving and believing as he or she does. When you join a group you want to be like the other people in that group—whether it is the Y.M.C.A., an art club or a square dancing group.

## SUBLIMATION

Sublimation is a method by which your primitive energy is directed into socially approved activities. Every one of us has two high pressure psychological drives which continually seek expression in one way or another. One drive is toward loving. It expresses itself in thoughts and acts that are creative, constructive, healthful, and generous. The other drive is toward hating. It expresses itself in thoughts and acts that are mean, destructive, and hostile. To live in accordance with the laws, customs, and morals of the people around you, you must "sublimate" many of the impulses connected with your drives. In other words, things that you would like to do and attitudes that are socially or personally disapproved of must be changed into attitudes and activities which are acceptable.

If you stop to think of it, you can find illustrations of sublimation at work every day. If you are feeding a ten-month-old baby and spill applesauce on the high chair tray, he will immediately play in it; if you set the dish of food down in front of him, he will smear it all over the tray and himself. As he grows older, however, he is taught to sublimate this desire. He is allowed to sublimate this desire by mixing up pie dough and making a pie since this is an acceptable activity. He therefore has the opportunity to play in the shortening, flour, and water mixture while forming the dough to be rolled out.

Other sublimations of this desire to smear are painting, clay modeling, stirring up a batch of cookies, or mixing concrete. In this way, the same energy is put to work in a socially useful or acceptable way. Hence, subsitituting adult interests for infantile desires is sublimation.

Most of your everyday activities involve sublimation. Instead of saying your natural first remark on a subject, you consider the position of the other person, his feelings, and his associations. You say what you mean but with tact and consideration. Instead of buying worthless trinkets as you did in childhood, you may collect coins, stamps, or records which are of more interest and usually have real value.

## ATTITUDES AND YOUR WAY OF LIFE

Your philosophy of life is your deliberate effort to make your beliefs, morals, and behavior patterns sensible and to unify them so that you may have a basis for action when you are confronted with problems. Your *personal philosophy* can be defined as the conscious statement of your credo (set of professed opinions) and the attitudes that are formed and reformed in an attempt to unify your thinking into a total pattern.

However, *your way of life* is formed by the attitudes that you have gained from the mechanisms previously discussed. Many people reach maturity without having raised or answered very many questions concerning behavior, and yet they consistently act in definite directions. Attitudes and habits, although not clearly formulated and rarely stated by these persons or their acquaintances, guide their actions. Their behavior toward their fellow man, their sincerity, and their dependability suggest certain attitudes. These attitudes, traits, and daily habits account for these persons' consistency and stability as individuals. These attitudes and traits may or may not be socially oriented. For example, a criminal may justify and rationalize his behavior as he relates to others in his antisocial environment.

Attitudes can be developed from education, society, propaganda, prejudice and superstition, moods or emotion and from generalizing from facts. Differences in attitudes are not only important as they determine social behavior but also as they affect individual emotional adjustment. The person who always thinks he is getting "a raw deal" is usually being treated as everyone else is. It is his attitude which creates the "raw deals." Our attitudes color our world in ways that profoundly affect our general outlook and happiness.

## ATTITUDE ANALYSIS

There are opinion polls and standardized tests which measure attitudes. These are valuable and very worthwhile when one is trying to measure other people's attitudes. Also, they are important when the attitudes of groups of people need to be measured. However, we are going to ask you to measure your own attitudes without the aid of a standardized test.

The objective in writing an attitude analysis is to further your understanding of yourself. It is not written for another reader. It should repre-

91

sent a critical analysis of the factors and experiences which have formed the attitude and feelings you have about the topic you have chosen. It is assumed that if you are able to analyze adequately your feelings and attitudes in one area, you will be able to apply that skill to other areas. Then you should be more able to understand your own behavior.

Before you start to write your analysis, you should make an important decision. You should decide to be as objective and as honest as possible; otherwise the value of the analysis is lost. The goal is to examine what your attitudes and feelings about a topic really are, and then to try and discover how and why you came to feel as you do. Therefore, do not approach this task with an attempt to write what you think your attitudes should be, or what you think others think they should be. Look at your attitudes as they really are.

An adequate and thorough analysis will call for a lot of thinking—deep thinking. First of all, it is suggested that you try to record and examine what your attitudes and feelings are. Then trace your past experiences which relate to these feelings and attitudes as far back as you can remember. Since it is highly unlikely that you can recall every detail in chronological order, it is better not to start with the expectation of writing your analysis from beginning to end. There is another method that will aid you. As you try to recall your earlier experiences, one thing will lead to another, but not necessarily in chronological order. Therefore, use small note paper. As various items are recalled, write each one on a sheet of paper. At the top of each sheet put the approximate date, age, or whatever is needed to identify and classify the item. When you are certain that you have recalled all that you can, sort the sheets either as to association of items or as to chronological order. Then on the basis of these sheets, write the complete analysis.

Undoubtedly, some things will be remembered more easily than others. But from what we know of the functioning of the mind, we are relatively sure that many experiences which are not available to immediate recall, may be remembered if we work hard enough at it. If you seem to have no recollection of some particular period of your life, or if there are some things that do not seem quite clear, don't give up until you have exerted considerable effort to recall the experiences or circumstances that may reveal the answer for which you are looking.

You may choose any area for an analysis. For example, attitudes concerning education, children, parenthood, love, friendship, pets, honesty, religion, and so forth. There is no limit to the possibilities which can be analyzed. Choose an area that has intrinsic appeal to you as well as possible answers. Work on your attitude analysis with dedication to self understanding. As you work, your attitude might be strengthened by considering this statement attributed to Socrates, "The unexamined life is not worth living."

## TO PROMOTE UNDERSTANDING OF THIS CHAPTER

1. Define the following terms:

   attitude    introjection    identification    sublimation    way of life

2. What is the value of knowing how your attitudes are developed?
3. Write an example that reinforces or discredits the quote from Disraeli, "We make our fortunes and we call them fate."
4. If John Jones has never analyzed his attitudes, how is it possible for his attitudes to cause him to act in definite directions?
5. How can an attitude be changed?
6. Mary Berry says that she has no attitude toward snakes because she never thinks about them. Is she correct? Why?
7. What is the difference between an attitude and a personal philosophy?
8. Let's look at two college roommates and their attitudes toward study. Libby and Helen are enrolled in the same English class. An announcement is made that a written paper is due the next day. The girls have no other required assignments.

   Helen realizes that she can best enjoy the remainder of the day and assure herself of a good grade by going to her room immediately, making an outline of the theme, determining what references must be cited, estimating the time required, then planning and writing the theme. She finds it exciting to write. At supper time her work is completed. She goes to supper with the satisfaction of having completed her task and now has time to relax in any manner she desires. She may turn either to a new job, using the zest that results from a completed one, or she may go to a show, engage in a game, or read for pleasure.

   Libby says, "I have all night to do this. I'm tired after a day's work. I ought to go get a soda." She meets some friends and spends the time until supper in light conversation. She eats a hearty meal, lounges on her bed while reading a magazine, and then decides to take a nap. She sleeps an hour, wakes up too befuddled to work, and decides to set the alarm clock so she can awake for an early morning session. She awakens at four, goes to her desk, spends a half hour trying to recall the specific requirements of the paper, becomes panicky as daylight broadens, and writes as well as she can under the strain. Finally, she finishes the theme and dashes to class without breakfast.

What attitudes toward work or study are depicted by the two cases? How could Libby's efficiency be improved? Which girl do you think is getting the most out of college? Explain your answers.

## SUPPLEMENTARY READING

ALLPORT, G. W., *The Individual and His Religion.* Macmillan and Co., Ltd., London, 1950.

CANDLAND, D. K., and CAMPBELL, J. F., *Exploring Behavior.* Basic Books, Inc., New York, 1961.

LEVINE, LOUIS S., *Personal and Social Development.* Holt, Rinehart & Winston, Inc., New York, 1963.

MCKINNEY, FRED, *Psychology of Personal Adjustment.* John Wiley & Sons, Inc., New York, 1960.

MENNINGER, KARL, *The Vital Balance.* The Viking Press, Inc., New York, 1963.

TIFFIN, J., and KNIGHT, F. B., *The Psychology of Normal People.* D. C. Heath and Co., Boston, 1940.

Mischa Richter, *The Saturday Review*

*"Live and let live, I always say."*

# 9
# Religion

In order to understand ourselves, we need to understand our religious beliefs and our religious commitments or our lack of commitment and belief. The part of religious doctrine that you "buy" is very important to your development. However, the part that you don't buy is equally important. As we mature and gain insight to ourselves and our fellow man, we learn that trust must be earned and is not given blindly out of respect for the individual's position or for a particular institution because he or it should merit respect and trust. With maturity, we begin to recognize that living up to high ideals is easier in thought than deed. We also begin to recognize that words and actions, as in Richter's cartoon, are often in strict opposition to each other.

## IS RELIGION BASIC?

When the basic needs of man were discussed, it was seen that one of them was the need for man to have a religion and/or a philosophy of life. For some of us, our religion is our philosophy of life. We live our religious convictions to the extent that they form our life pattern. For others of us, our philosophy of life, which has evolved from introspective thought, reinforces our life choices, and thus we do not need a religion. Others of us

Herbert Goldberg, *The Saturday Review*

*"I'll buy that."*

have developed a combination of religion and philosophy and thus have a basis upon which to act. Which is best—a religion, a philosophy, or a philosophy and a religion? This question can only be answered individually.

## DEFINITION OF RELIGION

The people who value religion define it as the outward quest for truth and the inward struggle for integrity. Religious beliefs are seen as enriching man's search for the meaning and the purpose of his life. Religion might also be defined as that activity by which man attempts to find his place in the universe and develop valid goals for himself and his fellow man within the framework of the forces which control his destiny. This definition implies that religion is man's attempt to give cognition to the process of life, especially his own life, and death. People who value religion consider it a way to give meaningfulness to life in the face of the more immediate frustration of cherished goals. They also believe it is necessary to help one face the absolutely certain death of one's only body. In brief, religion may be betting one's life that God exists and is good.

The people who do not value religion describe it as the opiate of people. They feel that religion leads to abject dependency on a set of false, meaningless rituals and beliefs, and they consider religion a device concocted to rule people by exploiting their fears, especially their fear of the unknown. To the opponents of religion, religion is a malady which makes man hate and oppress his natural tendencies.

## SOCIAL CHANGE AND RELIGION

Our society is currently questioning some of the traditions and rituals of religion as well as religious practices *per se*. Theorists proclaim that God is dead. Drug advocates declare that religious experiences can be produced or at least heightened by the use of LSD and other drugs. New scientific feats such as the development of life by man, the transplanting of living organs, and space exploration appear to contradict fundamental beliefs. The controversial world crises have increased the number of young men who use conscientious objection on religious grounds as a basis for non-participation in the armed services.

What does all of this signify? Is it an indication of a mature objection to a previous childlike acceptance of God as a personal God who answered our prayers and watched over us? Is it an indication of a drastic change from belief in God to a godless society—a society in which it is no longer possible to accept a belief in a divine power, a supernatural being, or a comforter for all things unknown?

97

The changes in religion and our acceptance or non-acceptance of these changes is influenced by our stage of development. The acknowledgement of life's dichotomies, the recognition that white is not always white and black is not always black but much of both is gray, should reinforce in our mind the emphasis of the stages of character and personality growth. To recognize that religion changes with growth is a facet of maturity. Children, because of their position in the life cycle, are considerably religious, at first holding fairy tale beliefs, later accepting the standard ideas of their group. Intellectual doubts start at a mental age of 12, followed by emotional stress; these conflicts are often resolved at about the age of 16, either by conversion to religion or by a decision to abandon the religion of childhood. During the years from 18 to 35, there is a sharp decline in all

Drawing by Alain; © 1950
*The New Yorker* Magazine, Inc.

*"What gets me is that having to love
everybody whether you like them or not."*

aspects of religious activity except for those who felt a religious calling earlier. Then there is a steady increase from about 35 until old age, which is marked by a widespread belief in God and the afterlife.

Yet, this twentieth century, which has produced atomic weapons capable of killing every living organism on earth, drugs which simulate or stimulate religious experience, and surgery techniques which hint at a future immortality for man, has also aroused adolescents, in particular, to question their religious beliefs and, indeed, the religious beliefs of society as a whole.

Evidence is growing that significant numbers of adolescents are experiencing serious doubts of religious faith. Although this matter is very complex, there seem to be three main reasons for this situation: (1) the religion of their parents fits too comfortably into that total world which adolescents consider phony and a menace to their freedom, (2) adolescents today are increasingly intellectual and literate and are discovering each day that the faith-world of their childhood is regarded by the creators of contemporary life as mythological, irrelevant, and meaningless for the future of mankind, and (3) organized churches have failed to put their extensive resources behind the humanitarian movements.

Thus, adolescents are taught to love their fellow man, yet they see "religious" people and/or the church ignoring the plight of minority groups; adolescents are told to strive for peace and brotherhood between all men, and yet they see "religious" men from "God-fearing" countries killing and bombing each other; adolescents are taught that God exists and is good, yet they see "religious" people supposedly acting in God's image by contributing to violence and prejudice and ignoring the poverty of others less fortunate than themselves. It is no wonder that young people are confused about their own relationship with God and critical of other people's relationship with God and their church.

## SOME INDIVIDUAL THOUGHTS

The basic psychological need for a religion and/or philosophy of life is met differently by each person. The six sketches below may help you recognize and appreciate the many ways people try to meet this need.

MRS. WILSON: I believe that one should go to church every Sunday. It is important to be a part of the church organization, to work for the church causes, and to support the church with time, energy, and money. I believe in life after death and believe that I will meet my loved ones who have gone beyond for an eternity together in heaven. In order to accomplish this, I must follow the doctrines of my church in my actions, thoughts, and deeds. I worry about members of my family and my friends who do not closely follow church doctrine. I feel that people who do not regularly attend church are not really preparing themselves for life after death or giving their best to their family and their community. I am 63 years old, have been in the choir for forty years, and have held most of the church offices. I am a deaconness and am on the ministerial board.

MRS. WEBER: I am a widow, twenty-eight years old, with three sons. I believe that God is love. I attend church every Sunday and see to it that my sons also attend. I don't believe that church attendance makes me any better, but it gives me support. When you lose your husband suddenly and have the added responsibility of being both mother and father, it is helpful to feel that there are people and an organization for support. I really don't believe in a hereafter or that going to church makes me any better than anyone else. I do, however, think that it may give my sons a focus upon which to make decisions and a stronger foundation by which to judge experiences.

TOM (college sophomore): I really don't have any guidelines. I feel what I do is really up to me, not anyone else. For the first twelve or thirteen years of my life I more or less just accepted what I had heard and learned as being the right and truthful way of thinking. Anyone who didn't agree with what I had learned was just wrong. Then, suddenly, I began to question what parents and authorities said. I began to want to know why a thing or a situation was this way or that way. The questions weren't answered for me and it really disturbs me a lot. I'm searching now, so I can't say what guidelines I'll use or what ethics or morals I'll follow. I'm just confused.

DOUG (high school senior): I try to be kind, honest, and considerate of people at all times and hope to do something useful in my lifetime. When I am faced with a hard decision or get myself into a tight spot, I think about my beliefs about people and my belief that God is with me. Then I feel that if I try to do what's right, everything will come out right in the end. When I question my beliefs I feel strengthened and convinced that I should follow them more closely. I think over bad decisions and troubles that I have experienced, and each time I find that if I had been completely honest with someone or done as I thought God would have wanted me to do, these bad decisions would have righted themselves more quickly or been avoided entirely. As I get older, these beliefs seem to triumph more often. I believe that with these beliefs I will make a worthwhile contribution to our society.

NANCY (high school junior): As far as I'm concerned, my main judgment of right and wrong comes from the Ten Commandments. I believe in following their teachings as closely as possible. Even though the Bible has many debatable points, I believe that the Ten Commandments are very valuable. I cannot accept many of the stories in the Bible, but I do not think that this weakens me in any way as I think its authors meant well in trying to get a general point across—the goodness of God. In making my personal decisions on debatable moral or ethical questions, I rely on rather impulsive actions, stemming from parental or family influence, peer group influence, and what I think is acceptable to me at the particular time. My religion only enters into my decisions on strong questions, such as stealing.

KENT (high school sophomore): I don't believe in a strong religious belief. I don't believe that man was made all of a sudden. I believe in evolution. I believe that all religions are right; men can believe as they wish. As for me, I follow all laws and rules (but try to change them when I believe they are wrong) and try to do right to all people regardless of race, creed, age, religion, or position. I like people, all people, and enjoy making them happy. I try to be extra kind to little children because they particularly need love. My decisions are based on what is right for others and on how I want others to treat me. Of course, I haven't met a strong challenge, so perhaps my beliefs aren't any good.

## THE CHURCH AND CHANGE

The essential character of religion is not only being examined and attacked by young people; clergymen and layman alike are seeking new and more meaningful doctrines to cope with the twentieth century. For example, ancient doctrines are being criticized as never before and significant changes are occurring in church dogma. Denominational lines are lessening as Catholics, Protestants, and Jews hold inter-religious conferences and teach in each other's colleges and seminaries. Churchmen are beginning to redefine their roles as problems of war, discrimination, as urban unrest disturb this country.

As Ardis Whitman says, "The church will change because it has to. The morning service, with its rites, rituals, dress, hymns, and traditional readings, is without meaning and significance to people who want to relate to the present. It represents a cultural museum where one can look and see what was once meaningful and important."[1] Yet, now that the church is

[1] Ardis Whitman, "The View from the Pulpit." *McCall's,* Vol. 95, No. 5 (February, 1968), p. 145.

starting to change, what direction will it seek? What impact will the changes make in the lives of the people and in the effectiveness of the church as a social institution? Will the service be in native tongue rather than Latin or Hebrew? Will the organ be replaced by an electronic instrument? Will hymns be sung in jazz or folk-song style? Will the clergyman sling his guitar into place and sing the message of the sermon? And, if these changes did take place, would they make a lasting impact?

Although it is commonly agreed that the church will change, and change radically because of the unique and pressing problems of this century which require a commitment in one direction or another, there are many people in all denominations who are not sure of the best direction the church can take. Even members of the same congregation may differ as to intensity of change and direction. Even so, two main directional changes seem possible.

Some people think that religious institutions might change in the position they take in the community. Thus, religious groups would live their teachings by actively denouncing war and working for peace. They would act as leaders and supporters of poverty programs, urban renewal, and slum clearance. In this way, churches would become the conscience of movements for social improvement, the main concern. The clergymen, as individuals, would step out of the limits of the church and mingle with the laymen, whether they are in the concert hall or pool hall. Thus, the church would see God as the basis of being, the force of life, the principle of love, ultimate reality. God, then, would be the love we encounter when we turn to help others. Prayer would be essentially a dialogue of love. Salvation would be being loved in a community characterized by love. Thus, the theology change would involve love, community, and social action.

Other people believe that religious institutions should be more concerned with spirituality and mission. Thus, the churches could take the direction of inwardness, of personal experience for a new search for identity. In this case, the church and its leaders would advocate more of a withdrawal from society as a whole and more of an introspective awakening of the purely spiritual mind. In this way, a new and more ultimate relationship with God might be achieved.

Margaret Mead, the noted anthropologist, has aptly described this century's religious confusion and need for a new religious commitment in these words:

> It is the way of those who follow the Judeo-Christian path to be troubled, to search in the sky and in their own hearts for signs and portents that all is not well. Such exercises of furious and exacting imagination are then often followed by long periods that some call stagnation

and apathy and others call betrayal—when the flame of religious witness burns very low, the young men who should be seeing visions go elsewhere and the life of the Church gives little light to the world.

We are just emerging from such a period, when it has seemed that the churches were powerless to wrestle with the new forces of worldwide revolution, with forms of warfare that threaten the whole of mankind and with powers from science that seem to give man incalculable capacities either to destroy the world or to make it new. With these earth-shaking changes, a new sense of helplessness, of being strangers in a world too large to love, has fallen upon many of the churches.

Today, above all else the task of the Church is to understand what is happening, to use with wisdom and dedication all that is known, and to demand that what is needed for the safety and well-being of man be pursued until it is known.

In particular, we need the support of the churches for the application of all existing knowledge to the cause of world order, international law and world-wide institutions; the establishment of food banks around the world to guard against famine; application of known methods and continued research on new methods of conception control to bring the population of the earth into balance; interim measures to bridge the gap between the richest and the poorest countries; the equalization of opportunity for racially and socially deprived peoples within all nations; the purposeful, controlled planning of our growing cities; opportunities for youth to participate responsibly in the modern world.

Only with such support from the churches can we hope to build a world in which the people of each nation are the keepers of the people of each other nation. With knowledge and no faith, we may well see a world destroyed. With faith and no knowledge, we may still see a world destroyed. With faith and knowledge bound together, we can hope to cherish and protect the lives of men and the life of the world.[2]

## TO PROMOTE UNDERSTANDING OF THIS CHAPTER

1. What part does religion play in your life today?
2. Should your church change? If so, why? If not, why not?
3. Should other churches change? Why? Why not?
4. Why is religion considered a part of human relations?

[2] Margaret Mead, "Is the Church Powerless in a Scientific World?" *Redbook*, Vol. 129, No. 44 (July, 1967), pp. 44, 47. Reprinted by permission of the author.

5. Is religion basic? If so, why? If not, why not?

6. Your understanding of religion would be advanced if you would write a paper of any of the following:

   a. The Orthodox Eastern Church

   b. The Lutherans

   c. The Presbyterians

   d. The Congregationalists

   e. The Episcopalians

   f. The Baptists

   g. The Mormons or Latter-Day Saints

   h. The Methodist Religion

   i. The Jewish Religion

   j. Ethical Culturists

   k. The Church of Christ, Scientist

   l. The Universalists or Unitarians

   m. The Friends

   n. Jehovah's Witnesses

   o. Adventists and Neo-Fundamentalists

   p. The Protestant Religion

   q. The Roman Catholic Church

   r. Any church or religion of your choice

## SUPPLEMENTARY READING

BACH, MARCUS, *Adventures in Faith*. T. S. Denison and Company, Inc., Minneapolis, 1959.

—— *Had You Been Born in Another Faith*. Prentice-Hall, Inc., Englewood Cliffs, N.J., 1961.

—— *Let Life Be Like This!* Prentice-Hall, Inc., Englewood Cliffs, N.J., 1963.

—— *Major Religions of the World*. The Abingdon Press, Nashville, Tenn., 1959.

BLAKE, EUGENE, *Church in the Next Decade*. The Macmillan Company, New York, 1966.

BOSTROM, CHRISTOPHER, *Philosophy of Religion.* Yale University Press, New Haven, Conn., 1962.

BRANTL, GEORGE, *Catholicism.* George Braziller, New York, 1962.

CHIARI, JOSEPH, *Religion and Modern Society.* Hillary, New York, 1964.

COLLINS, JAMES D., *Emergence of a Philosophy of Religion.* Yale University Press, New Haven, Conn., 1967.

DUNSTAN, J. LESLIE, *Protestantism.* George Braziller, New York, 1962.

GAEUR, JOSEPH, *The Wisdom of the Living Religions.* Dodd, Mead, and Company, New York, 1956.

GARD, RICHARD A., *Buddhism.* George Braziller, New York, 1962.

HERTZBERG, ARTHUR, *Judaism.* George Braziller, New York, 1962.

HICK, JOHN, *Philosophy of Religion.* Prentice-Hall, Inc., Englewood Cliffs, N.J., 1967.

HOWE, REUEL L., *Herein Is Love.* The Judson Press, Chicago, 1961.

KIRSCHENMANN, FRED, "The Credibility Gap in Theology." *The Christian Century*, Vol. 84, No. 19 (April 19, 1967), pp. 498–500.

LUCKMANN, THOMAS, *The Invisible Religion.* The Macmillan Company, New York, 1967.

MAGEE, JOHN, *Religion and Modern Man.* Harper and Row, New York, 1967.

NORTHBOURNE, WALTER, *Religion in the Modern World.* Hillary, New York, 1963.

POTTER, CHARLES FRANCIS, *The Faiths Men Live By.* Prentice-Hall, Inc., Englewood Cliffs, N.J., 1954.

RENOW, LOUIS, *Hinduism.* George Braziller, New York, 1962.

SOMMERFELD, RICHARD, *Church in the 21st Century.* Concordia Publishing Company, St. Louis, Mo., 1965.

STRENG, FREDERICK J., *Emptiness—A Study in Religious Meaning.* Abingdon Press, Nashville, Tenn., 1967.

"Teens Talk About Religion." *Seventeen,* Vol. 26, No. 4 (April, 1967), pp. 146+.

THURMAN, HOWARD, *Disciplines of the Spirit.* Harper and Row, New York, 1963.

WHITMAN, ARDIS, "The View from the Pulpit." *McCalls,* Vol. 95, No. 5 (February, 1968), pp. 83+.

Peter Paul Porges, *The Saturday Review*

*"Describe your dream fully."*

# 10
# Philosophy

Man's philosophy may be like the symbol of the dream . . . a collection of shapes, concepts, and designs in a conglomerate that is very difficult to define or understand. Our philosophical age is probably the last to mature, for it takes years of reflective thinking, study, and living to untangle what we really think about a particular subject.

One may be at different levels in his philosophical development. One may have a philosophy which deals with some one area of experience and not with another. Thus, one may have developed a philosophy toward education but not toward knowledge; one may have a philosophy about honesty but not integrity. In other words, our philosophies are often fragments.

However, all men, unless spoiled by a faulty education or by some intellectual vice, possess a natural understanding of some of the great truths. Those whose understanding has never been cultivated are not able to give any account, or at least any satisfactory account, of their convictions. That is to say, they cannot explain why they possess certain beliefs. They may feel a certain way about a particular subject after much thought, and then years later with study find that their thought is similar to that of someone who wrote centuries ago.

The philosophical thoughts of an individual direct his life. They determine his actions, activities, and his basic behavioral patterns. Thus, it

Herbert Goldberg, *The Saturday Review*

*"You just have to accept the fact that people may agree with your unorthodox opinions."*

is important to begin to consider some of the philosophical questions, recognizing that only time, effort, and the insight of maturity will give more satisfactory answers.

## PHILOSOPHY AND THE INDIVIDUAL

Ordinary knowledge consists for the most part of mere opinions or beliefs, more or less well founded. But it also implies a solid kernel of genuine certainties in which the philosopher recognizes (1) data of the senses (for example, bodies possess length, breadth, and height), (2) self-evident axioms (for example, the whole is greater than the part; every event has a cause), and (3) consequences immediately deducible from these axioms (proximate conclusions). These certainties which arise spontaneously in the mind when we first come to the use of reason are thus the work of nature in us, and may therefore be called an endowment of nature proceeding from the natural perception, consent, instinct, or natural sense of the intellect. Since the source of these certainties is human nature itself, they will be found in all men alike. They may, therefore, be said to belong to the common perception, consent, instinct, or the "common sense" of mankind. The great truths without which man's moral life is impossible belong in this area of common sense.

In order to sharpen this domain, let us briefly mention some of the things philosophy may do for us. Such a discussion may show why a person needs a philosophy for living.

1. Life forces us to decide questions of right and wrong, truth and falsity, ugliness and beauty. Each person must make decisions and act. In order to decide well and to act consistently, we need a philosophy of life. Our decisions must be made. in light of our goals, beliefs, and understanding of the world around us. Thus, philosophy may furnish a basis for social action as well as for personal conduct.

2. Our conduct is our own and we are really free only when we rely upon inner controls or self-chosen ends. If a man does what he does merely because of tradition, culture, or law, he is not genuinely free. When Aristotle was asked the value of philosophy, he answered that it allowed him to do willingly what other men did merely because of fear of the law.

3. Philosophy may help us cultivate a wide range of appreciations and sympathies. A broad range of interests and appreciations is a condition for ultimate intellectual and emotional living. We need to reach out to the great masters who have lived and thought deeply

and who can open up for us new vistas of thought. We also need to reach out to people who are less fortunate and who need understanding. We should develop a sufficient depth of inner life and a wide enough range of appreciations and sympathies in art, literature, nature, and great ideas to have life bring us zest and happiness.

4. We live in an age of uncertainty and change, when many of the older beliefs and ways of doing things are inadequate. Under such conditions, we need a scale of values and a sense of direction. Just as we feel a physical discomfort when we are confronted with cruelty and injustice, so there is a mental discomfort when we are in the presence of fragmentary and confused views of the world. To achieve unity in a world in turmoil, we must gain an inner integration to know what to approve and what to disapprove and in order to gain a sense of the meaning of human existence.

## WHAT IS PHILOSOPHY?

Philosophy is approached and defined from different points of view. These points of view are supplementary rather than contradictory.

1. Philosophy is an attitude toward life and the universe. The mature philosophical attitude is the searching and critical attitude; it is also the open-minded, tolerant attitude, or the willingness to look at all sides of an issue.

2. Philosophy is a method—the method of reflective thinking and reasoned inquiry.

3. Philosophy is a group of problems. There are certain problems which perplex mankind and for which philosophers seek answers. A philosopher's question is not, "Did John tell Mary a lie in the student council meeting?" but rather, "What is truth or the distinction between right and wrong?"

4. Philosophy is a group of theories or systems of thought. Some people think of philosophy as certain world views and certain terms like idealism, realism, pragmatism, humanism, pessimism, optimism, and materialism. To others, philosophy means the various philosophical theories or systems of thought which have appeared in the history of philosophy and which are attached to the names of the great philosophers. They think of men like Plato, Socrates, Aristotle, Augustine, Thomas Aquinas, Descartes, Spinoza, Kant, and James, to name a few.

## DEFINITIONS OF PHILOSOPHY

There are many and varied definitions of philosophy. Will Durant has defined philosophy as total perspective, as mind overspreading life and forging chaos into unity. He also says that philosophy is harmonized knowledge making a harmonious life; it is the self discipline which lifts man to serenity and freedom.[1] Another current writer, Jacques Maritain, calls philosophy human wisdom. He says that philosophy alone among the branches of human knowledge has for its object everything which is. Philosophy is the science which by the natural light of reason studies the first causes or highest principles of all things. In other words, it is the science of things in their first causes, in so far as these belong to the natural order.[2]

Most definitions of philosophy seem to describe it as embracing a world view, or reasoned conception of the whole cosmos, and a life view, or doctrine of values and purposes of human life. Thus, philosophy is the attempt to give a reasoned conception of the universe and man's place in it.

Most of the definitions of philosophy emphasize the use of reflective thinking. They state or imply that the aim of philosophy is to gain unity and to see life in its totality. Consequently, we may say that philosophy is a study of nature, both in its inorganic and organic aspects, and the social and spiritual orders. Philosophy seeks to unify the results of the special sciences with the principles of morality and religion.

## PHILOSOPHY AND CHANGE

Philosophy, unlike religion, is not directly affected by change. There is such a variety to the various philosophies and philosophers that philosophical truths, rather than being altered by social change, merely move in and out of vogue. The philosophies that are in favor during a certain period in time tend to describe that particular portion of history. For example, Stoicism and Epicureanism flourished when the Greek city-states were disintegrating, about the 4th century B.C. The Stoics believed that man should accept his fate without complaint and, indeed, should suppress any and all emotions and live the unbending life of duty and reason. Thus, the Stoics believed it was essential to be indiffer-

---

[1] Will Durant, *The Pleasures of Philosophy* (New York, Simon and Schuster, 1953), p. xii.

[2] Jacques Maritain, *An Introduction to Philosophy* (New York, Sheed and Ward, 1962), p. 76.

ent to pleasure or pain, joy or grief. The Epicureans, on the other hand, believed that pleasure was the only good in life. However, the basis of this belief was that genuine pleasure is derived from a life of prudence, honor, and justice. As scientists, the Epicureans believed that reality is a grouping of material atoms in random movement; thus, they maintained that the world is governed entirely by chance and not design.

The rise of nationalism in the nineteenth century in Europe brought a resurgence of interest in national language, background, poetry, traditions, and culture. This century was characterized by a cultural nationalism, romanticism in literature and the arts, and an interest in history. During this period, however, there was also a recognition of value in the individual. The philosophies of the time reflect conflicting interests. Nationalism, which advocates a national unity, independence, uniqueness, and subjection of the individual's interests to those of the nation, is quite the opposite from individualism, which assumes the individual and not society or the nation is the paramount consideration or end.

The present era has been described as a time for philosophical pragmatism. This American philosophical movement, founded by C. S. Pierce and William James, has as its characteristic doctrines that the meaning of conceptions is to be sought in their practical bearings, that the function of thought is as a guide to action, and that truth is preeminently to be tested by the practical consequences of belief. The twentieth century has also been described as a time for materialism, the ethical doctrine that consideration of material well-being, especially of the individual himself, should rule in the determination of conduct.

Philosophical trends in the future are seen as hedonistic or idealistic, depending upon the pessimism or optimism of the viewer. In hedonism and idealism we have primary philosophical convictions, while pessimism and its opposite, optimism, are only secondarily philosophical theories or convictions.

Hedonism can be described as the doctrine that pleasure is the sole or chief good in life and that moral duty is fulfilled in the gratification of pleasure-seeking instincts and dispositions. Today's change in moral codes, dress, and leisure-time activities is seen by some to be the harbinger of a world of hedonists. As such, our time is likened to the Roman Empire with dire predictions of a repetition of history.

Idealism is a theory which states that all that exists is a form or object of experience. Idealism regards reality as essentially spiritual or the embodiment of mind or reason. The idealist identifies reality with perceptibility. He denies the possibility of knowing anything except the mental life—the life of thought, ideas, and ideals. On the other hand, materialism denotes an absorption in more concrete, or material, ends. The

112

materialist identifies reality with what he can feel, taste, touch, and smell. He tends to give greatest importance to material interests and possessions. In popular usage, the terms "idealism" and "materialism" often imply moral attitudes. In this context, idealism suggests a devotion to high ideals or an optimism about the ultimate goodness of mankind, whereas materialism suggests a devotion in grosser and more material ends. The terms as used in philosophy, however, denote opposing views of the nature of reality.

This brief section on philosophy and change has been included to help you understand the dynamics of philosophy and change. From this discussion, you can see that contradictory philosophies can and do exist at the same time. Although certain philosophies may be in the foreground during particular periods of time, other philosophies which are sometimes contradictory are also present. The dominant philosophies may give historical focus to a particular century, but one must remember that the others were also in existence. Thus, in our own time, we may be described as a civilization given over to hedonism, idealism, materialism, and/or pragmatism. As you consider yourself and what is most meaningful to you, however, you may find that you are a stoic, an epicurean, or an interesting, new philosophical conglomerate.

Chapter 9 discussed the basic need of man for a religion and/or philosophy and in this context explored the nature of religion. This chapter considered the concept of philosophy and surveyed some of the philosophical attitudes which were (and are) popular. The next chapter will help you think about your own philosophy of life.

## TO PROMOTE UNDERSTANDING OF THIS CHAPTER

1.  Define philosophy from your point of view.

2.  Re-read the statements that describe some of the things that philosophy does to aid individuals. List some examples from your own life that reinforce these aids.

3.  What direction would you like to see the philosophy of the twenty-first century take? Why?

4.  Write a paper on a philosopher or a philosophy of your choice. For example:

| | | |
|---|---|---|
| Socratic philosophy | Cartesianism | Pluralism |
| Platonic philosophy | Spinozism | Mysticism |
| Stoicism | Neo-Hegelianism | Transcendentalism |
| Aristotelianism | Pragmatism | Dualism |

5. Santayana said, "It is a great advantage for a system of philosophy to be substantially true." What ideas does this statement bring to your mind?

6. Discuss Montaigne's statement, "Admiration is the foundation of all philosophy; investigation the progress; and ignorance the end."

## SUPPLEMENTARY READING

COMMINS, SAXE, and LINSCOTT, ROBERT N., eds., *The World's Great Thinkers*. Random House, New York, 1947.

DURANT, WILL, *The Pleasures of Philosophy*. Simon and Schuster, New York, 1953.

MARITAIN, JACQUES, *An Introduction to Philosophy*. Sheed and Ward, New York, 1962.

THOMAS, HENRY, *Understanding the Great Philosophers*. Doubleday and Company, Inc., Garden City, N.Y., 1962.

© 1965 The Curtis Publishing Company

*"Of course people can't think—They just repeat what they hear."*

# 11
# A Personal Philosophy of Life

In order to develop a personal philosophy of life, we have to disprove the statement of the two crows in the cartoon. We must recognize our own personal goals and values since these goals and values are the threads that weave the fabric of our philosophy. The previous chapters were written to give us a bird's eye view of some philosophical concepts and reasons for religion. In this chapter, we'll try to consider this material in terms of our own personal *values* and goals.

## VALUES

Values are many things. They are our objectives and our goals. In this sense they are real, tangible, and attainable. Yet values are more. Values are the ideals toward which we live and those things that we hold most dear. Our ideals are motivational forces toward the goodness in our lives and the humanity in the human spirit. Values are also the importance or worth we give to ideas, goals, and attitudes. This makes it possible to put ideas, goals, and so forth in an order of hierarchy which, in turn, encourages decision-making and consistent behavior. For the group, values are the accepted rules which direct behavior toward the very best we know from the experiences of mankind. For the person, values are the rules, the goals, the ideals and the judgments which integrate the personality and thus make it predictable, consistent, and whole.

Drawing by Steinberg; © 1966
*The New Yorker* Magazine, Inc.

Our values are our yardsticks with which we measure our own behavior. They are the controls; the direction of our action. By them we judge our everyday actions as they relate to ourselves and our fellow men. Even more, we use our values to judge our behavior as it relates to our future. Values serve as brakes on desire for immediate gratification and satisfaction. They are the holding qualities which keep us steadily on our way toward that which we believe is of ultimate worth, and for which we must wait and strive. William James, an American Philosopher (1842–1910), showed his values in the following excerpt:

> We have little to fear, declares James, so long as we sustain our affections, so long as we have a home to play in, and a family to play with. This is the meaning of Pragmatism—the philosophy of the practical life —as applied to our family relationships. The family satisfies our universal hunger for "the dear togetherness." In mutual service, every member of the ideal family arrives at its fullest spiritual growth. He finds that it pays to make our home cheerful with the brightness of love.
>
> In the development of his pragmatic idea about family relationships, James widened the boundaries of the home to those of the world —here again we have the philosophy of a united mankind. The world, he observed, is our common home, and all its inhabitants are the members of our single family. The most profitable business of life, therefore, is the friendly exchange of affection and good will among all men.[1]

By our faith in these values, we move closer to them as ideals.

Our moral values are our group experiences at their very best, our group aspirations which protect our sacred institutions of freedom of man, democracy in our republican form of government, homes with free and easy interaction and love between generations, schools, and free economy built around the profit motive. We respond to our moral and religious values with respect, as obligations and as objects of reverence, because they are, in truth, the best from mankind for mankind. Because of our religious and spiritual values, because of our moral values, we *become* persons of dignity, of worth, of integrity, as we live by and toward them.

Values for society as a whole are the general principles which guide our group behavior. When a nation or a society loses its values, that is, its understanding of them and their reality, then the nation itself deteriorates. If a nation lets its values degenerate, and proclaims them but does not live them, then disintegration of the culture is inevitable.

[1] Henry Thomas, *Understanding the Great Philosophers* (New York, Doubleday and Co., Inc., 1962), pp. 330–331. Reprinted by permission of the publisher.

Values and the personality have important inter-relationships. Personality has been defined as our usual ways of behaving with other people. If you would like to know your own values, consider how you behave with others. Behavior always has within it conformity to the larger moral, spiritual, religious, and social values of the group. Without conforming with one another in light of the best we know, there would be no order in personal or group life. Chaos and anarchy would result were there not healthy, creative conformity by free men. Individuality and creativity can never arise either out of chaos or rigidity in persons. The inner self, the core of personality, is composed of those values that the person regards as the more important, drawn from his experiences with other people. These are those which carry him toward his goals and gain for him basic satisfaction in his life within himself and with others.

Each is a person in his own right, but he is, also, always a person among persons. William Menninger has said that our personalities are all that we

"I'm afraid I have no opinion at the moment. All my journals of opinion have been late this week."

Drawing by Donald Reilly; © 1967
*The New Yorker* Magazine, Inc.

have been, all that we are, and all that we will be. Our personalities are not static because our ways of behavior change to meet new situations even as our values which we use as guide posts change. The integrating principles of personalities are values from past experiences which we build into the future. Giving consistency to our outlook and predictability in our behavior, these values continue through growth toward our ultimate objectives.

## DEVELOPING A PERSONAL PHILOSOPHY

Values and their organization into a personal philosophy grow, like other human products in a random manner. Their growth is through trial and error as we try to solve problems that confront us, and their development is the result of the consistent example of those whom we respect, the teaching of dedicated teachers and of our own personal study. If the solution is of a physical nature, so that we do not think in terms of ideas and do not verbalize our solution, it probably does not become a part of our philosophy of life. Much of this philosophy may be taken from a writer, from the Bible, the Torah, the Talmud, or from proverbs of an unknown source. If these ideas are to function as ideas in life, we must experience real satisfaction as we see their roles in our behavior. They must have the vividness of insights or discoveries. The admonition, "Do unto others as you would that they would do unto you," means little until the individual has found through experience the meaning and value of it. Rarely does a personal philosophy come from a single experience. Single books, courses, or essays may sum up one's attitude and the reaction tendencies that have grown from numerous previous personal experiences. One does not build a philosophy of life during one weekend in which he writes a term paper, but he can bring to consciousness attitudes that have had a long previous existence.

An individual's personal philosophy, like all such complex patterns of experience, is influenced in growth by the many other aspects of his personality. His intelligence, temperament, physique, physiological urges, emotional experiences, contacts with other people, books, plays, sermons, and lectures, his friends, his enemies, and his teachers—all play a part. The compatibility of his philosophy and behavior is dependent upon the extent to which his philosophy has taken into account his basic constitution and important past experiences.

## VALUE OF A PERSONAL PHILOSOPHY

A philosophy of life should guide behavior. It should allow one to act on the basis of rational principles, rather than through fear, selfishness, and external force, such as parental or social pressure. It, however, cannot ignore inner tendencies such as anxiety or outer forces such as social standards. These should be realized in developing one's philosophy. If the philosophy helps self-understanding and involves a certain amount of acceptance of oneself as one is, it can be a real source of direction for the future. A personal philosophy brings relative serenity to most people. It provides perspective and allows one to see oneself in retrospect and to project ambitions realistically into the future. It can organize or integrate our derived values so that they will form a "united front" and strength of conviction when a conflict arises and a decision must be made. History shows that those men who have received the gratitude of society because they espoused a worthy movement, spent their lives developing it, and so merged their own personalities in the movement that they and the movement became indistinguishable.

## FORMATION OF VALUES

Values are the end product of human experiences which have become recognized generally as being for human well-being and as offering possibility for the full development of the human personality. Values are convictions which we have arrived at out of the richness of human living and out of knowledge of what it takes to make life good and worthwhile.

Every human being can participate in the formation of his own values. Participation in the formation of values is not a matter of age or maturity. Every age, according to the maturity of that age, can participate in the creation of values by living, exploring, and experiencing them, by discarding those that are unworthy, and by strengthening those which are of deep worth. The process of the creation of values is also shared with those who are older and wiser in experience. Value formation, then, is as dynamic as life itself because out of living, out of creativity, out of change, and out of progress, grow values which men have created and do create to meet their ever changing needs.

## VALUE STABILITY

Values that change and grow in strength are those which are related to new and to different situations. Values that hold steady are those which hold us steady. They are time proven. They are our religious, spiritual, and moral values. Our religious and our spiritual values are our eternities, the ideals toward which we grow. For us in the United States, out of our Judeo-Christian faiths were derived two major values. We believe in the dignity and worth of each man, regardless of race, creed, color, or abilities

120

because of our belief that man was created in the image of God. We believe as well in the brotherhood of all men under God. These are eternal values toward which we strive, work, and live.

In short, a realistic personal philosophy can assist those who are in difficulties, give perspective to one's self and to the world, foster personal integration, growth, and adjustment, and increase creativeness.

## SOME THOUGHTS FROM PHILOSOPHERS

Philosophers have written on various values. Each philosopher writes about those ideas that seem to be of greatest value to him in his life and in his field of vision. The following quotes are included with the hope that you may find a kindred value to your own value system and thus read more in the writings of the particular philosophy that has the most appeal and challenge.

"In the long run, declared Gandhi, all men have an equal destiny. All are born in order that they may study how to serve God's plan. Every one of our lives is a special task assigned for our education in cooperative living. And our greatest duty is to teach and to befriend our less fortunate brothers. . . . The purpose of man's life is to lighten the sufferings of his fellow man."[2]

Santayana declared, "It is war that wastes a nation's wealth, kills its flower, narrows its sympathies, condemns it to be governed by adventurers, and leaves the puny, deformed, and unmanly to breed the next generation . . . (Therefore) instead of being descended from heroes, modern nations are descended from slaves."[3]

Friendship, to Emerson, is the most sublime thing in the world. The essence of friendship, writes Emerson, is "entireness," the fusion of different personalities into one essence. This fusion enables men to rejoice in one another's triumphs. "I feel pride in my friend's accomplishments as if they were mine."[4] Emerson believed that cultivating the art of friendship enabled one to come close to the heart of reality; that true friendship brought one in touch with the divine meaning of life.

Kant stated that morality, like mathematics, prompts us to live in accordance with the harmonious process of life. "Act as if the maxim of your conduct were to become by your will the maxim of all the world's activity."[5]

Croce said that Christianity, like Judaism, Buddhism, and Mohammedanism, "lives on in spite of its defects because it has a vital function

[2] *Ibid.*, p. 357.　　[3] *Ibid.*, p. 343.　　[4] *Ibid.*, p. 322.　　[5] *Ibid.*, p. 257.

and satisfies a universal need."[6] The important thing in life, Croce maintains, is not only to conceive the right image, but to perform the right act.

## FORMULATING A PHILOSOPHY

Your philosophy of life is your deliberate effort to make your beliefs, morals, and behavior sensible. It is your deliberate effort to unify them so that you may have a basis for action when confronted with problems.

We should not confuse our *philosophy of life* with our *way of life.* Our way of life is composed of attitudes, traits, habits, and directive motives that we use but that we have not defined. They may be a part of our philosophy at a later date. The term *personal philosophy* is reserved for our conscious statement of our credo. That which is composed of our real beliefs after we have thought through our attitudes, values, goals, and experiences is our personal philosophy of life.

## TO PROMOTE UNDERSTANDING OF THIS CHAPTER

1. Define the following terms:

   values        interaction      realism
   eternities     admonition      creativeness

2. Write your personal philosophy of life. There is no experience that can give you more personal insight. You may use whatever method you wish to write your philosophy. But if you want a suggestion you might work through these steps:

   a. List ten values that you hold most dear.

   b. Rank the ten values in the order of most important to least importance. This is very difficult. As you do this take note of your thoughts. These thoughts will help you formulate your philosophy.

   c. Now list the goals that you hope to accomplish this year, in the next five years, next ten.

   d. Now compare your goals with your values. Are they compatible?

   e. Think of the people in your life that you respect. What do you respect about them?

   f. Think of the maxims, creeds, and so forth which you hold dear. Do you believe them in your heart or do you think that you should believe them?

[6] *Ibid.,* pp. 308–309.

3. Now with this evidence about your own thoughts, write the philosophy that seems to represent *YOU*.

4. Here is an autobiography written by a young man after college graduation. What are his values? What philosophy does he portray from this autobiographical sketch?

At the age of six I started to school and quite fortunately I found the teacher, the kids, and the school work very much to my liking. From the first day, I knew that some day I would go to college.

I was always a runt. I can remember one of our neighbors saying, "It's no wonder you stay thin, you run everywhere you go." I was very headstrong and liked to see things done my way. Therefore, from the ages of eight to twelve I found myself in a fight on the average of about four times a week. (I never lost a fight.) Eventually, I learned, however, that I could solve my problems much more satisfactorily in a peaceful manner and since that time I cannot remember having a serious argument with anyone. (Even my wife.)

I have always been extremely interested in athletics and despite my miniature size I played on the grade school varsity basketball team every year after third grade. My favorite sport was basketball although I played them all.

I graduated at the head of my class scholastically and went into high school standing an even five feet tall and weighing an even one hundred pounds. Again, despite my stature, I was fortunate enough to play quite a bit of varsity basketball in my freshman year.

During my sophomore year, I started to grow up. I also started to look for the "right" girl. And I didn't have to look very long for during my junior year I began going with a very cute blonde who turned out to be the one.

During my high school years I was president of the freshman class, student council representative four years, president of the student council two years, captain of the basketball team two years, and first place winner in oratory in the conference speech contest. During my senior year, I set a high jump record in the conference track meet and played the lead role in the class play. I graduated valedictorian of the class.

I entered state college where I put myself through school without financial assistance by working in the school cafeteria during the school term and as a carpenter each summer. I majored in chemistry and minored in mathematics. My campus activities included the following: President of Alpha Phi Omega fraternity; President of Sigma Zeta honorary science society; secretary of Men's Union; vice-president of the senior class; vice-president of Cavaliers, honorary organization of twelve senior men, an active member of Tau Beta Rho, Math Club, Varsity Club, and the President's Council. I played varsity basketball three years and was graduated from college with high scholastic honors.

The afore-mentioned blonde and I went to college together and found each other's company very pleasing. We took the vows of marriage in October a year after college graduation and now find happiness in living in an apartment in the town where we both teach.

5. The following comments are those of a forty-year-old scientist. What factors in his youth may have led to the development of his values and philosophy?

I value my relationships within my own family above all. While my wife and I were very happy before we had children, our family provides an even richer fulfillment. I feel our greatest challenge is to provide a home so that our children arrive at adulthood healthy in mind, body, and spirit. I have no specific goals for our children, but I would hope to instill in them a desire to do well in whatever their capabilities allow them to undertake.

At each stage of my adult life, my decisions with respect to my profession have been influenced by what seems to be an inherent desire to make a contribution to mankind as meaningful as possible with the limited capability and time allotted to me. I feel little ambition for public acclaim, but sense gratification in successful completion of a task which represents my best efforts.

Moderation governs most of my actions—eating, drinking, exercising, emoting, spending, and so on. My wardrobe is small and we live in a house more modest than my income would allow. While we have travelled in Europe, Canada, Mexico, the Caribbean, and all of the United States except Alaska, each trip has been planned with economy in mind. The friendships, experiences, knowledge, photographs, and memories acquired in our travels are among my most valued possessions.

My interests are varied enough so that I have never become *totally* involved in any one pursuit, hobby, or even in my work. I consider diversion extremely important to one's health, and lively fun as essential to happiness. We are regulars at the theatre, concerts, and movies. I thoroughly enjoy all sports both as a spectator and participant. I play guitar, banjo, and ukelele, sing folk songs, and am even known among my friends as a joke teller.

I do not participate in an organized religion, but could never be described as an atheist. I am constantly awed by the order of our universe which I cannot dissociate from a concept of God. I firmly believe that man could live happily and peacefully if he could learn and practice the rudiments of Judeo-Christian moral teachings.

## SUPPLEMENTARY READING

GILLESPIE, J. M., and ALLPORT, G. W., *Youth's Outlook on the Future.* Doubleday and Co., Inc., New York, 1955.

HARTSHORNE, H., and others, *Studies in the Nature of Character.* The Macmillan Company, New York, 1930.

JACOBS, P. E., *Changing Values in College.* Harper and Row, New York, 1957.

THOMAS, HENRY, *Understanding the Great Philosophers.* Doubleday and Co., Inc., New York, 1962.

Unit 2

Understanding Ourselves in
Relation to Others

*"It was a daring gown till mother got her hands on it."*

# 12
# Parent-Sibling Relations in Late Adolescence

Although the young woman in the cartoon wants to dress in a provocative manner, her mother feels that something more modest would be more fitting for her little girl. Upon graduation, the son is shocked by his Dad's declaration of his adult status. The cartoons aptly depict the contradictions of adolescence. Adolescence is indeed a time of strong ambivalence (attraction toward and repulsion from an object, person, or thing) both for the

128

*"Well, don't just stand there; start supporting yourself!"*

adolescent and for his parents. The adolescent is torn between an unwillingness to give up the indulgences of childhood and a willingness to accept the privileges and responsibilities of adulthood. The adult is torn between the desire to see his child launched as a responsible, contributing adult and the inability to trust the judgment of the adolescent as he makes the decisions inherent to independence.

## DEFINITION OF ADOLESCENCE

The term "adolescence" is derived from a Latin verb meaning "to grow up." It is defined in the dictionary as the period of life from puberty to maturity. For the biologist, adolescence is the period of rapid growth. It begins with an accelerated phase that continues until the attainment of sexual maturity, merges into a decelerating phase, and terminates when skeletal growth has ended. But adolescence is also a social phenomenon.

129

Its duration is determined not only by biological factors but also by the way the particular society defines childhood and adulthood. Thus, the sociologist may describe adolescence as a period when society has ceased to regard the young individual as a child but has not yet accorded him full adult status.

Two conflicting themes can be detected in these definitions. In one view, adolescence is a period of positive attainment, of growth, and of maturation; in the other, it is a period between, a stage of transition. This prepares us for the issues with which we shall have to deal in trying to understand adolescence.

## DEVELOPMENTAL GOALS OF ADOLESCENTS

In order for the adolescent to move from the dependence of childhood to the independence and interdependence of adulthood he must accomplish certain goals. The adolescent may be working on a number of these goals simultaneously. Success in one facilitates progress in another; failure in one may interfere with his accomplishments in other areas of his life. In the accomplishment of these goals, he is trying to define the place he will occupy in adult society. The older the adolescent the more he is confronted by the problem of where he stands with respect to the entire adult world of independence, marriage, jobs, and politics. He must find an identity as himself rather than as a member of either his family or his gang. In the attainment of these developmental goals, the young adolescent is concerned with who he is and what he is; the older adolescent is preoccupied with what to do about it.

There are many possible ways to list the goals of the adolescent period. The ten goals listed below go from goals for early adolescence to those for later adolescence:

1.  Achieving physical competency—accepting and making the most of one's physical capacities

2.  Getting along with one's family—gaining emotional independence from parents and other adults without hurting their feelings too much

3.  Getting along with age-mates of both sexes—making friends, learning to work with others for a common purpose

4.  Achieving scholastic success—including choice of courses, relationships with teachers, and development of communication skills— speaking, reading, writing, listening

5.  Making sound educational plans—choosing, preparing for, and entering a vocation for which one has the necessary ability and interest

130

6. Developing a workable set of values, moral standards, and religious beliefs—evolving a functional philosophy of life which takes into account one's place in the world

7. Developing socially responsible behavior

8. Achieving identity—discovering and developing one's most acceptable self

9. Preparing for marriage and family life

10. Being economically independent—including not only the ability eventually to make a living, but also the ability to earn enough money, while going to school, to satisfy one's needs and desires

These developmental goals are accomplished over a long stretch of years. All of us are always working on them in one way or another. By accomplishing them, the adolescent is able to bridge the gap between what he was as a child and what he is to become as an adult. These goals constitute a unit: if a person has done well with them up to a certain age, he is likely to complete them successfully.

## TASKS OF PARENTS OF ADOLESCENTS

Parents of adolescents have many tasks to perform. This section is written to help the adolescent appreciate the role of his parents during this complex time. Just as children grow and develop from one stage to another, parents must grow and develop in relation to them. Some parents can meet dependent needs easily but are unable to give up being the central figures in their child's life. This is particularly true when they have devoted all their time, energy, and money to their child. When their child has been the main or only focus for their existence, they see puberty as the beginning of a change that will lead the child out of the home and into his own life. They fear loneliness and abandonment because they are unable to develop a more mature relationship with their child. They are made anxious by the prospect that he will make his own decisions and they feel unable to cope as equals with him.

For parents whose relationship with their child has a strong sexual charge to it, the emergence of overt sexual characteristics in adolescence may be threatening because it brings these unwelcome and unaccepted parental feelings more clearly to the fore. There are several reasons for the strong sexual charge between child and parent. The parent may envy the physical beauty or physical prowess of his child of the same sex or of the opposite sex. For example, an insecure mother may see her beautiful young daughter as a threat to her relationship with her husband or as a challenge

131

in the mother-daughter comparisons usually made by friends and family. The father, who may have always been physically undersized, insecure, or clumsy and whose head is becoming bald, may feel threatened by his tall, handsome athletic son. In addition, because young girls try out their feminine wiles on the least threatening male (hopefully their fathers) and young boys try out their manners and "line" on the least threatening female (hopefully their mothers), the insecure parent may feel that he is being replaced in the affection of his spouse.

The parent who does not understand this stage of development may not recognize these sexually charged advances as a tryout of young adult wings. Without this kind of recognition, the parent may be either repulsed or attracted. Either reaction would be detrimental to the relationship, for repulsion would create insecurity in the adolescent, and attraction on the part of the parent would only lead to a feeling of abandonment when the young adult moved on to the more mature stage of a relationship with the opposite sex in his own peer group.

Thus, the emergence of sexuality in the child is frightening to parents who have never worked out a mature solution for their own sexual feelings. They may fear that the adolescent will display forbidden impulses and wishes which they harbor themselves, and they may react by projecting their own inner concerns onto the child. Unjust accusations of sexual misbehavior are often the result. Sometimes this action on the part of the parent develops in the adolescent either a paralyzing sense of guilt or a reaction of doing just what his parents fear since he is already being falsely accused.

Parents have to learn how to let go and how not to let go. Prior to late adolescence, however, the child has needed the assurance that his parents were not letting go for good. Adolescence, by contrast, is an exercise in letting go for good and a preparation for a new kind of relationship between parent and child, based on mutual respect between older and younger adults. Parents must give up their child and, remembering the adolescent's own perplexity and ambivalence, they must likewise help him give them up.

Parents must be at least as committed to the adolescent's need for independence from them as he is. This, however, does not mean that they abruptly throw him on his own resources. Adolescence is a preparation for independence, not a time when it is imposed all at once. The adolescent's demands for self-determination are in part a demand for reassurance that he is capable of it and that his parents will stand by him while he tries his wings. If his parents literally give him everything that he claims he wants, they may frighten him because he needs them as a sounding board for his ideas and his decisions. The adolescent, in his ambivalence, will

132

often fight the most vociferously for something he is afraid to have. But parents must be aware of their own ambivalence as well as of the adolescent's. They must be basically and firmly on the side of the adolescent's freedom. If they are, they can set forth consistent, clear, and sincere growing standards for the adolescent to meet.

Parents must also resist taking literally the adolescent's rages, defiance, and belittlings of them. These statements spring less from a sweeping rejection of his parents than from his need to assert himself as somebody different and independent. In the language of adolescent ambivalence, "I hate you" sometimes means, "I'm afraid I love you too much."

The adolescent who has no conflicts at all with his parents may have evolved elaborate techniques for lulling his parents' concern, while outside the home he does exactly what suits him. Or, more usually, he may have been cowed or manipulated into inert acceptance. This inert acceptance can curtail his growth toward maturity. He may remain his parents' good child who stays home, voices their ideas and attitudes, and fears to dissent. He becomes his parents' companion and nurse in their old age, and he becomes lonely and alone when he himself becomes old.

Adolescents who can think and act for themselves should try out and oppose the ideas and doctrines with which they disagree. Usually, it is only when one doubts the worth of his own convictions that he is unwilling to risk their survival in the marketplace of ideas.

While in general some disagreements during the development of interdependency arise between the adolescent and his parents, this time should not be one of constant storm. Stress and hostility carried to extreme may be a sign that the parents are pressing too hard or that the adolescent has a false idea of his role. More often, however, it means that earlier, unresolved developmental issues have been reactivated by the adolescent crises. When this happens, outside intervention may be necessary: by a psychiatrist, a psychologist, a family counselor, or perhaps simply by a neutral party who can help both sides see the issues more clearly. Adolescence is peculiarly a time when stresses from earlier stages of development are laid bare (and it may also bring out latent conflicts between parents). When a youngster becomes overly suspicious of other people's attitudes and intentions, when he becomes unduly guarded, or negativistic, or excessively violent, there is reason to suspect that his difficulties date back before adolescence. Circumstances may have flawed his basic trust, he may have failed to develop an adequate degree of autonomy, he may have developed excessive guilt about his body and its functions, he may have met social rejection, he may have become embroiled in parental discord. However, the experience that a child had at two or five or ten are a part of him at fourteen, seventeen, or twenty. It is not helpful to continually blame the past for his present behavior. He must instead deal constructively with the person that he has become.

Parents, as you can see, have many tasks to perform during the adolescent period. A teen-ager needs to recognize the impact of late adolescence on the status of the parent to understand the interrelationships at this period of family development. As an adolescent, you need to forgive and forget past mistakes made by your parents just as you wish them to forgive and forget your errors.

## SEXUALITY IN ADOLESCENCE

The sexual awakening that comes with biological maturation is one of the main concerns for parents and adolescents. In Freudian terms, pubescence spells the end of latency with the beginning of adult genitality (see Chapter 3, page 39). The concern of this age is to learn to deal with his sexuality (i.e., to inhibit, control, and direct) in the service of mature love and to transform surplus sexual energies—that is, to sublimate them, into productive work. Thus, this section on adolescent sexuality will discuss how sexuality appears to the adolescent; our society's often ambivalent ideas about it; what the facts seem to be; and, finally, the job that the adolescent has of reconciling his feelings with his own values, imposed restraints, the evidence of widespread violation of these restraints, and the secondary feelings of guilt, anxiety, and tension that are likely to be accompanying sex in our society.

The sexual capacities that come with puberty are not the same for boys and girls. The sensation accompanying sexual desire, in boys, is centered in the genitals. It can be aroused by a variety of external stimuli—pictures, words, jokes, or by random thoughts, or it may be deliberately sought. Among girls, there are wide normal differences. Some girls experience desire in much the way that boys do. Others may not experience direct sexual urges until later in life. Most adolescent girls, however, experience sexual desires that are diffuse and not as clearly differentiated from other feelings. These feelings may be evidenced by romantic yearnings, maternal cravings, enthusiasm, pity, malaise, sensual pleasures, such as having one's hair combed, or one's hand held, or even such emotions as anger and fear. Ordinarily, in girls, deep sexual arousal must be brought about by direct stimulation of the body, particularly of the erogenous zones.

For boys, sexual cravings are not necessarily associated with notions of love. Such arousals are a natural part of his physiology and require no overt action to cause their cessation. Some boys, however, may seek release through masturbation (self-manipulation or friction) or homosexual activity (activity with one of the same sex). Later they seek female sex part-

134

ners for this release. Thus if a girl invites a boy's favors, even though she yield herself only within sharply defined limits, the boy may very well be easily aroused whether he feels an affection for the girl or not. Even if there is affection, it is certainly different from the emotion he feels in later years as a husband and father. The qualities that he sees in the girl might be a projection of his own needs onto a convenient object, and may have little to do with her actual characteristics.

For girls, love usually takes priority over sexuality. Young girls strive mightily to fall in love, partly because it is the thing to do and partly because it seems the answer to some inner need. In the adolescent girl, love is often expressed in a desire to surrender to someone stronger. This may mean, both to the girl and her partner, sexual surrender, but its more basic origin may be a need to merge her identity with a stronger one. True sexuality and mature affection, including such elements as respect, understanding, appreciation, and tenderness, can emerge only after the girl has found security in belonging to (which in practice may mean possessing) someone else. For the adolescent girl, relations with the opposite sex seem to be directed quite consciously toward finding love. Although boys are not always aware of it, she is usually seeking a husband—or practicing finding one. Going out with boys may also have a meaning in the competition with other females, as a kind of self-validation and as evidence of desirability. Some boys, too, are seeking a wife or practicing finding one. But, in surveys of a large number of boys, marriage ranks behind sexual stimulation and gratification, companionship, and love as the motive for dating.

Intellectual curiosity about sex is greatly intensified in adolescence. The curiosity goes beyond simple anatomical and physiological information. One of the difficulties comes from the idea that there must be something more that one does not know about. Many adolescent discussions of sex, and much reading of erotic literature, have as their unspoken theme the search for the "something else" that lies beyond the immediate human experience. This craving for knowledge is not merely a desire to find out what sex does or should feel like to them, but equally what it is like to the opposite sex. In folklore, in literature, in scientific publications, there is an ignorance of female sexuality. Boys often project their own sexuality onto girls or see girls as indifferent or hostile to sex. Girls have a better idea of what boys are seeking, but are not particularly understanding or sympathetic with such different goals.

The ambiguity of standards for boys and girls is most confusing to them and to their parents. While boys are expected manfully to restrain their baser urgings and while they are threatened with various unpleasant consequences of sexual indulgence, it is nevertheless often taken for granted that they will "sow some wild oats." As a result some boys are ashamed of their virginity, while others cling to it. For girls, the formal standards, although beginning to change, still remain, reinforced by fears of unmarried pregnancy, the desirability of being a virgin at marriage, and the lesser acuteness of sex drives. Ambivalence does enter, however, in two ways. According to Stone and Church,

> First, there is the matter of maintaining popularity with the peer group, and more particularly with the boys who are potential husbands, which may require promiscuity or near-promiscuity. Second, there is the effect of the moral revolution, which has produced a psychiatrically backed mythology attributing to girls a sexuality identical with that of boys. Particularly in the educated classes, this has had the result of making many girls feel that to be normal they must want sexual experience, that they should attain a sexual climax readily, that they should engage freely in sex. It is probable that this view has left a fair number of girls and young women feeling guilty and inadequate because their own feelings fail to correspond to what they have been told about them. It is also likely that some girls have become actively promiscuous in search of what they are told to believe is normal experience, and have ended up feeling cheated, blaming either their own 'frigidity' or the inadequacies of their partners. In short, works such as Kinsey's have been treated not only as descriptions of what does go on but have also been taken as prescriptions for what should go on.[1]

Now that we have talked about how sexual capacities differ between male and female and some of the natural tendencies and cultural ambiguities of sex, it is important to consider some possible attitudes. New kinds of understandings and feelings must be assimilated by us so that we can make positive progress in this business of becoming a man or becoming a woman. We must realize that our own sexuality is an important part of our whole personality. Sex can not be singled out just on its own because it is part of the whole life of a person. Sex is a life force that has many purposes. It is not only the foundation stone of the marriage relationship, but it is also a great power that gives life, color, creativity, and meaning to all of our human relationships. If we limit our concept of sex purely to the physical act, then we limit our whole lives, for this single physical act is not enough by itself to carry us for our adult lives.

Understanding the profound differences in male and female sexual make-up should enable each sex to help the other in the management and

[1] Joseph L. Stone and Joseph Church, *Childhood and Adolescence, A Psychology of the Growing Person* (New York, Random House, 1957), p. 314.

136

appreciation of their own sexuality so that it becomes an integral part of a mature individual personality that is really ready for a mature and loving marriage. One must realize that sex is an important part of marriage, of course, but the real part of marriage, the strong part, is based on the trust and companionship that the woman and the man create in their relationship. This is what will help them as they face the changes in society and in their life together.

Our relationships are the most important structures of our lives. Whether it's parent to child, friend to friend, brother to sister, boy to girl, or man to wife—the moralities, the ethics are the same. *Sexual morality is no different from any other morality—it has to do with the honesty of our relationship to each other, the trust and confidence we have in ourselves, the trust and confidence we have in each other, the conviction we have that the other person's welfare is much more important than our own.*

In matters of sexual morality as well as in any morality, one must look beyond the present moment and realize the future consequences. People use sex to prove certain things—their femininity or masculinity, or that they are independent of their parents. People also use sex to get something they want—they use it as a bribe or as a punishment or for revenge or as a reward. Now when sex is used in any of these ways it becomes a thing used for gain, and that means that the people themselves are using each other as things. This is exploitation. It may possibly work at the moment, but in the long run people feel cheated.

## ADOLESCENT-ADULT

The adolescent can more easily enter the adult world if he is a part of it, not alienated from it. Some adults feel that the problems of the world come soon enough; let youth enjoy his childhood. However, one of the worst aspects of any alienation of young people from the adult world is that they are cut off from discussions of adult problems. To live through these vicariously is an essential preliminary to making responsible decisions when they are actually faced. To isolate adolescents from money worries; business troubles; domestic issues; and the topic of sex, birth, marriage, and death, including the personal tragedies involved in illegitimacy, marriages based on expediency, and delinquency—to isolate them from adult concern about all of this is to do them a great disservice. Young people must not be protected from the troublesome aspects of civilized living. Adolescents are ready to respond to any overture which welcomes them into the adult community and which demonstrates a genuine desire to acknowledge their opinion. The adult community, in turn, needs the idealism of adolescents.

137

## TO PROMOTE UNDERSTANDING OF THIS CHAPTER

1.  Define the following terms:

    | | | |
    |---|---|---|
    | adolescence | sexuality | masturbation |
    | ambivalence | negativism | homosexuality |

2.  How might the Peace Corps help an adolescent achieve his developmental goals?

3.  List the characteristics of parents which would be most helpful to an adolescent as he strives for adulthood.

4.  What factors complicate the struggle of many adolescents for emancipation from the family?

5.  How might a group of adolescents be encouraged to raise their standards with respect to boy-girl relations?

6.  The search for sincerity is the theme of two fine novels about adolescents, Mark Twain's *The Adventures of Huckleberry Finn* and J. D. Salinger's *The Catcher in the Rye*. Read or reread one of the novels and write a discussion of Huck Finn's or Holden Caulfield's search for sincerity, idealism, and goals.

## SUPPLEMENTARY READING

HILGARD, ERNEST R., *Introduction to Psychology*. Harcourt, Brace & World, Inc., New York, 1953.

OSBORNE, ERNEST G., *How to Deal with Parents and Other Problems*. Grosset and Dunlap, Inc., New York, 1962.

STONE, L. JOSEPH and CHURCH, JOSEPH, *Childhood and Adolescence*. Random House, Inc., New York, 1957.

STRANG, RUTH, *The Adolescent Views Himself*. McGraw-Hill, Inc., New York, 1957.

Courtesy *Better Homes and Gardens* © 1962

*"See what I mean? He needs a brother."*

# 13
# Sibling Relationships in the Family

If Junior had other siblings (brothers or sisters) in his family, he would not need the educational toy being demonstrated by the salesman. This chapter poses questions about sibling relationships: sibling rivalry and competition, sibling position in the family and personality, the adolescent and siblings, sibling associations and role, and sibling relationships outside the family. With these items in mind, we shall try to understand ourselves in regard to our sibling relationships.

# BROTHERS AND SISTERS

No two siblings have the same family. This is true for all families. The above statement is startling until one stops to consider its implications. The firstborn comes into a family of father and mother. He is the only child and his parents may be a little concerned about their ability to handle him. They may also be worried about money, their own relationships, and their status in the community and in their profession. The second child is born to a family composed of three, instead of two. His parents feel more competent in their ability to handle a baby. Perhaps by now, father is more settled in his career and mother is more aware of the demands of motherhood and homemaking. The third sibling comes to a family of four, one that has established itself as a family. Perhaps a grandmother has been added to the circle. Whether the family changes are positive or negative is not important here. The emphasis is on change. The family changes as it grows; thus, no two siblings have the same family.

## RIVALRY

The child's first experience with competition usually occurs within the home. Sibling rivalry, jealousy between brothers and sisters in the family, is almost a universal phenomenon. This can be observed among American families, where expression of aggression by children is more tolerated than in many other societies. Rivalry tends to be greatest when the children are more than eighteen months but less than thirty-six months apart in age. However, spacing to avoid this critical period is not likely to make any practical difference. The jealousy of the older child is focused around being dispossessed from his privileged place in his parents' affections. It is the older child whose reaction is likely to be most intense. Baldwin's study showed that this reaction may be caused by the changes that he himself observed in the behavior of mothers toward an older child before and during pregnancy, as well as after the birth of the baby. The changes were dramatic. Over a period of a few months, the mothers showed a marked drop in affectionateness, approval, and just plain attention with a corresponding rise in restrictiveness and severity in discipline.

This finding points to a major principle for dealing with sibling rivalry, or more realistically, for restricting it. It is important that the transition in the psychological status of the older child be neither too sudden nor too severe. At the same time, it is not only futile but foolhardy to try to eliminate such a change altogether, for it is a natural part of growing up.

One of the ways in which a young child tries to get over the pain of having a younger rival is to act as if he himself were no longer a child, competing on the same basis as the baby, but as if he were a third parent. Usually the left-out feeling is more apt to be experienced by the first child when the second baby arrives, because he has been used to the spotlight and has had no practice in sharing his parents' love with others. A middle child doesn't have to decide between being a parent and being a baby when a new infant arrives. He can see that he is still just one of the children.

When a condition of intense rivalry exists, it is sometimes openly displayed, sometimes not. It shows directly when a youngster tries to harm a baby brother or sister. It may appear indirectly when a child tries to mutilate a baby doll. Sometimes, however, children suppress feelings toward a sibling rival and even convince themselves that no rivalry exists. There are adults who will say, for example, that they had no inkling of the intensity of their bitter feelings toward a brother or sister until they reached adult years. An adult who has acknowledged only a mild rivalry situation in his childhood may, in discussing early experiences, come forth with an outburst of rage and a flood of tears.

Parental attitudes toward children's rivalries will be influenced by their own experiences. A parent's childhood rivalries may persist in his life as a parent and cause him to treat his children as potential rivals. An adult who has not resolved his own feelings of sibling rivalry may introject those feelings into the competitive struggles of his own children. This makes the competition among his own children more dramatic than it would normally be without his interpretation.

If parents (or other adults) are obviously unfair or openly favor and admire one child more than another it is quite understandable that the unfavored child might feel hurt. However, sibling rivalry illustrates the fact that we cannot understand what will actually happen in a social situation simply by studying the separate characteristics of each individual involved in the situation. Nor can rivalry be averted simply by a process of manipulating the environment.

Rivalry becomes an especially acute problem if one or all the siblings in the family happen to have a strong streak of possessiveness, or if the children are especially demanding. Some youngsters seem much more inclined than others to want to establish a monopoly to have everything for themselves—all the attention, all the care, all the favors. Others, even at an early age, seem to find it easier to share.

## JEALOUSY

Sometimes parents unwittingly discriminate against one child by showing greater admiration for another child in the family. It is only human for adults to prefer some traits and characteristics to others, and in the process one child may get the notion that he does not rank as high in his parents' estimation as does his brother or sister. Where there are children differing in age, sex, interests, and abilities it is impossible for parents always to treat the youngsters in a way that seems fair to all. *It is therefore likely that all siblings near each other in age will exhibit symptoms of jealousy at some time or another.*

The link between jealousy in early childhood and a jealous disposition in later years has not been traced adequately in scientific studies. Children normally lose their more obvious symptoms of jealousy as they grow older and become more absorbed in interests outside their own family. However, there are times when they may exhibit even more jealousy toward their associates in daily life.

Among adults, the degree of jealousy a person exhibits frequently bears little relationship to his relative status or power as compared with others. The person who has "arrived" and has achieved the outward semblance of success will sometimes begrudge the recognition bestowed upon an underling, much as a big hound bristles when his master pets another dog. A person who was intensely jealous of a younger sibling may, as far as he can see, have outgrown this jealousy, but traces of these early bitter experiences may remain, even though jealousy is no longer shown toward the brother. An attitude of jealousy persists in an adult, for example, if he feels hurt when another gets recognition or wins good fortune. His feelings may also express themselves in the way he takes sides against some people in his environment who represent, psychologically, objects of jealousy similar to what his brother represented when he was younger.

## SIBLING POSITION AND PERSONALITY

A person's behavior is likely to be affected in various ways by the social position he holds vis-a-vis the positions of other significant persons in his life. His relationship to others is one such important variable in his development, and of all others his brothers and sisters are likely to exert the greatest influence on him.

The following results have emerged from a study of the personality patterns of five- and six-year-old children in relation to ordinal position (first born or second born), sex, and age spacing (one or two years). These results can be attributed to a sibling's direct effect upon the behavior of the child. For siblings far apart in age, the effect is likely to be indirect, manifesting itself through differences in parental behavior.

The studies indicated that firstborns tend to be more self-confident and to have fewer nervous habits (nail-biting, thumb-sucking) than second children. Firstborns, close in age to their siblings, do not recover from upsets as readily as the second children. Second children are less hesitant to express anger.

Particularly at the two to four-year sibling-age-difference level, the child whose sibling is of a different sex is more self-confident, cheerful, active, healthy, less vacillating, and more inclined to recover poise easily. These differences have been interpreted as suggesting a greater degree of stimulation between members of pairs whose sibling is different in sex than between members of pairs of siblings of the same sex. In other words, in families of two children there is more stimulation if the family is composed of a boy and a girl rather than being composed of two boys or two girls.

Differences in personality related to differences in age spacing are greater for boys than for girls. The two-to-four year spacing, especially for first-borns, seems to be more stressful than shorter or longer age spacing. First-born boys of the two-to-four-year age spacing are more confident, emotionally intense, excitable, moody, angry, and decisive, and more given to alibiing, projecting of blame, and indirection than those boys whose siblings are closer or more distant in age.

From 1900 to the 1940's, there were many studies on sibling position and its resultant personality effects. Bohannon,[1] Adler,[2] and Toman[3] suggested that sibling position is the prime determinant of personality and that personality structure can be predicted from this position. Another group of researchers, Goodenough and Leaky,[4] and Koch,[5] contends that sibling position is a determinant of personality but not necessarily a prime or primary one.

More important than position in family *per se,* they believe, are other factors such as relative intelligence, differences in age, appearance and personality, and the parents' attitudes, emotional needs, and personal preferences.

The relationship between sibling position and personality of the child is still a matter of some controversy. One can find research to support any position from one of a positive effect to one of a negative effect with all gradations in between.

---

[1] E. W. Bohannon, "The Only Child in the Family," *Pedagogical Summary,* Vol. 5 (1898), p. 494.

[2] Alfred Adler, *Understanding Human Nature* (Garden City, New York, Garden City Publishing Co., 1927), p. 152.

[3] Walter Toman, *Family Constellation* (New York, Springer Publishing Co., 1961), p. 6.

[4] Florence Goodenough and Alice Leaky, "The Effect of Certain Family Relationships upon the Development of Personality," *Journal of Genetic Psychology,* Vol. 4 (1927), pp. 45–71.

[5] Helen Koch, "The Relation of Certain Family Constellation Characteristics and the Attitude of Children Toward Adults," *Child Development,* Vol. 26 (1955), p. 37.

## SIBLINGS AND THE ADOLESCENT

The adolescent may respond to the birth of a new child by developing parental feelings that will lead to caring for the baby like a young mother or a young father. However, it is also possible that he may instead feel acutely jealous and see the baby as a rival for his parents' affection. If his understanding of the roles of sex in procreation is poor, the birth of a sibling may be distressing because of his preoccupation with the parental sexual activity that it implies. He may therefore displace his aversion to sex onto the new child whom he then shuns. It should, however, be stressed that the birth of a sibling need not lead to conflict; if it does, it indicates that earlier issues have not been resolved in a healthy fashion.

With the advent of adolescence, some changes may occur in sibling relationships. Conflicts about dominance and submission are more likely to become more acute in the adolescent in relation to his siblings. He will demand more privileges and more recognition than the younger children. He will challenge the dominance of older siblings established in an earlier period. As he becomes more aware of body changes and sensual feelings, he may become uncomfortable with siblings of the opposite sex and avoid closeness.

The situation becomes more serious when parents prefer one child to another. Parental favoritism toward another child may decrease the adolescent's self-esteem and generate hostility. The presence of more brilliant and successful siblings may prevent him from perceiving himself as a competent person.

## SIBLING ASSOCIATIONS AND ROLE

Some recent research has shown that sex-role learning is in part a function of the sex of the sibling and the ordinal position; for example, a boy with an older sister has more feminine traits than a boy with an older brother or a boy with a younger sibling, male or female.

The social learning in a family of two or three boys close together in age leads to high sex-role masculinity and high interest in conventional economic activities. The first-born boy is differentiated from the second-born male by his interest in a strategic success style, and the latter is differentiated by his interest in a power success style.

A strategic success style is best described as a position of behavior that is directive and projective. The individual is capable of commanding and directing others in an indirect manner or through the use of strategy. For example, the first-born male in our society must play the role of the older protective brother. He must not use his greater physical strength to

144

make his little brother perform in the way he wishes; thus, he learns to use psychological means or a strategic success style to manipulate the younger sibling. The younger brother, however, can respond with his fists, since there is no stigma against hitting a bigger, older boy. Hence, for the second-born male, a power success style is fostered.

The family made up of girls has a high feminity role and an interest in routine occupations. However, the success styles are reversed from those of the all male family. The first-born girl is distinguished by an interest in a power success style and the second-born female is distinguished by an interest in a strategic success style.

The social learning in the opposite sex sibling family (boy-girl or girl-boy) contributes to an interest in expressive creativity. The older brother and the younger sister relationship often comprises the most creative combination.

## SIBLING RELATIONSHIP OUTSIDE THE FAMILY

If siblings are fairly close in age, and are all within the age span of the school years, their contacts at home are likely to be marked by taunting, bickering, battling, and bedlam, interspersed with some joint activities, some comparing of notes on people and school, and some more or less harmonious sharing in whole-family enterprises and chores. However, outside the home, siblings close ranks in family solidarity. The terms "kid sister" and "big brother" may be used in disgust, but they also carry considerable affection. Also, as in the case of sibling solidarity, the same children who criticize their parents freely will not tolerate the slightest slur on them from outside the family.

In conclusion, studies point out that the sibling does not want his parent to be a pal. He has plenty of his own age group outside of the family to serve as pals. The child at all ages needs his parents as parents—which means as adults and not as pseudo-children. He needs them as refuges when he finds himself cut off from the gang in one of its periodic realignments, when he is sick or at other vulnerable moments, and simply at times when he wants to be a member of his family, trading news and jokes and confidences, asking for information, advice, and help.

## TO PROMOTE UNDERSTANDING OF THIS CHAPTER

1. Define the following terms:

| | | |
|---|---|---|
| sibling | strategic success style | jealousy |
| rivalry | power success style | |

2. What are the most important factors concerning sibling relationships and personality?

3. Jane is two years older than her sister Jean. They are the only children in the family. What characteristics might you expect them to manifest?

4. Give an example of family solidarity shown between siblings outside the home.

5. What are the major causes of sibling rivalry?

6. How does rivalry precipitate jealousy?

7. Interview some of your friends who have younger siblings. What are their main areas of concern?

## SUPPLEMENTARY READING

ADLER, A., *Understanding Human Nature,* trans. by W. B. Wolfe. Garden City Publishing Co., Garden City, N.Y., 1928.

BALDWIN, A. L., "Changes in Parent Behavior During Pregnancy." *Child Development,* Vol. 18 (1947), pp. 29–39.

BECKER, S. W., and CARROLL, S., "Ordinal Position and Conformity." *Journal of Abnormal Social Psychology,* Vol. 65 (1962), pp. 129–31.

BOHANNON, E. W., "The Only Child in the Family." *Pedagogical Summary,* Vol. 5 (1898), p. 494.

BOSSARD, J. H. S, "Personality Roles in the Large Family," *Child Development,* Vol. 26 (1955), pp. 71–8.

GETZELS, J. W., and JACKSON, P. W., *Creativity and Intelligence.* John Wiley & Sons, Inc., New York, 1962.

GOODENOUGH, F., and LEAKY, A., "The Effect of Certain Family Relationships Upon the Development of Personality." *Journal of Genetic Psychology,* Vol. 4 (1927), pp. 45–71.

KOCH, H., "The Relation of Certain Family Constellation Characteristics and Attitude of Children Toward Adults." *Child Development,* Vol. 26 (1955), p. 37.

LASKO, J. K, "Parental Behavior Toward First and Second Children." *Genetic Psychology Monographs,* Vol. 49 (1954), pp. 97–137.

McCANDLESS, B. R., *Children and Adolescents: Behavior and Development.* Holt, Rinehart & Winston, Inc., New York, 1961.

MCCLELLAND, D. C., *The Achieving Society*. D. Van Nostrand Company, Inc., New York, 1961.

SCHAUTER, STANLEY, *The Psychology of Affiliation*. Stanford University Press, Palo Alto, California, 1959.

SUTTON-SMITH, BRIAN, JOHN M. ROBERTS, and B. G. ROSENBERG, "Sibling Association and Role Involvement." *Merrill-Palmer Quarterly,* Vol. 10, No. 1 (Jan., 1964), pp. 25–38.

TOMAN, WALTER, *Family Constellation*. Springer Publishing Co., New York, 1961.

Drawing by Stan Hunt; © 1967
*The New Yorker* Magazine, Inc.

*"I was supposed to contact you, but I'm not sure I have."*

# 14
# Relationships Outside the Family

In Western industrialized society, a man's job is not only a means of earning a living but is also a way of establishing himself as an adult. In evolving his basic social role through his work, a man also has some way of judging his own adequacy, worth, and contribution as an adult. The idea of establishing oneself early in an occupational role is so important that we give heavy emphasis to vocational guidance in secondary schools, and we even go so far as to ask many preschool children what they are going to do when they grow up.

In addition to the importance of a man's job for his identity as an adult and for the experience of being needed, work is important simply because so much of one's life is devoted to it. Man spends more than a third of his

Peter Paul Porges, *The Saturday Review*

waking hours at his work (often many more) over the course of a working lifetime. His work frequently precedes his marriage and usually continues long after his children have become adults. Within this time span, a person establishes relationships with other people from which he derives status, prestige, affection, social membership, and support in personal emergencies. He takes part in a social system apart from, but often influencing his family relationships.

A job is an avenue for evolving comfortable relationships with other people. Some people prefer to work very closely with others and can seek jobs which provide that closeness. Others, to be comfortable, seek out more isolated jobs. When a man is forced into situations in which the distance is not comfortable for him, he is often unhappy in his work.

Balanced distance from other people has a counterpart in balanced distance from other aspects of life. In going to work, many people are able to separate themselves temporarily from personal and family problems. When they return from their work, having put these problems aside for the day, they are more psychologically refreshed and better able to cope with their personal problems. This is particularly true for many women who go to work primarily for respite from home and family pressures.

149

An important consideration is a person's relationship to the organization in which he works. A business organization and the social structure surrounding it have increasingly come to take the supportive place of the fast-disappearing small community. When ours was primarily an agricultural society, people depended on their neighbors for help in emergencies, and their roles in their communities were their avenues for achieving adult identity. Now a business organization often meets these needs for many people, particularly for those in larger organizations in metropolitan areas. This is evident in fringe benefits, especially in post-retirement interest in and help for the retired employee. It is also evident when the role or status of a person is referred to, for the person is identified not alone as "Jack Brown," but usually as "Jack Brown, Vice-President of I. V. M." or "Jay Smith, foreman at Alpha Electric."

## EMPLOYER-EMPLOYEE RELATIONSHIPS

Achievement, recognition, the work itself, responsibility, and advancement are the factors most closely related to increasing work satisfaction. Note the close relationship of these to our basic psychological needs. Leadership (or non-leadership), company policies, administration, supervision, and working conditions are the major factors which cause job satisfaction or dissatisfaction.

Despite many studies, there is no common agreement on the qualities of leadership. What makes a good leader seems to vary with the kind of group to be led, the task of the group, and the conditions under which it operates. This becomes very evident in Golding's *The Lord of the Flies,* when one compares the leadership qualities of Ralph and Jack.

However, from the cartoonist's point of view, Mr. Folsom might be more successful if he looked for a new employer who might be a more sensitive leader. Paramount to good employer-employee (leader-follower) relationships is mutual respect. A good executive, whether he leads people in a work situation, social club, or educational organization, is a guide, a director, a counselor, and a protector. He must be able to permit his subordinates to be dependent on him but at the same time he must be able to depend on them too. He must give them consistent support and respect to foster psychological growth and the assumption of adult responsibilities. The employer must also keep a constant focus on the task to be done and create a structure within which people can do it. Psychologically, a good leader is like a good father. Mr. Folsom's boss has failed all the criteria for good leadership.

Unfortunately, Mr. Folsom is not the only employee to encounter this type of leadership. His problem is similar to many that exist in employer-

150

Joseph Mirachi, *The Saturday Review*

*"Dammit, Folsom! Can't you see you're wasting your time trying to speak to me on the level of one human being to another?"*

employee relationships. These problems all seem to assemble themselves into three general areas which are the same for both small and large firms.

The first is the difference in perception between the expectations of the employee and those of the company. There is often considerable difference between what a man thinks he is to do on his job and what his supervisors expect him to do. These great differences in perceptions and expectations result in built-in conflict and frustration.

A second major problem is the implicit assumption on the part of management, and usually on the part of union leadership as well, that man is a rational and machine-like animal, motivated solely by money. Despite considerable research and much lip service to the idea that man does not live by bread alone, most incentive programs and efforts to motivate people are based on individual monetary rewards. Furthermore, most businesses are organized in such a way as to ensure a maximum of control over the individual on the assumption that he cannot be otherwise motivated or guided. From our previous study of human needs, personality, and character development, one can see that these concepts of management are psychologically obsolete and result in irresponsibility, apathy, and hostility.

An example that shows motivation precipitated for the public good rather than for personal monetary gain follows. After an ice storm had disrupted its facilities, a public utility company made a survey and found that

151

there had been no accidents in emergency work done under great pressure and dangerous conditions. The men were so motivated by the feeling that the community was depending upon them to restore service that they rendered almost superhuman service.

A third important problem, and one that is gaining in importance, is the feeling expressed in the phrase, "I don't know where I stand." This usually does not mean that the person does not know how his superiors judge his work, but rather that personal contact with superiors is so limited that he feels nobody really cares about him. The fact that a man is useful to his organization for only very limited skills does not make him feel useful as an individual human being. While no organization can use all the skills and talents available to it, very few people seldom use more than a small fraction of their capacities in their work. Furthermore, many people live uncomfortably with the knowledge that they can quite easily be replaced by machines at any time.

In general, these dissatisfactions can be alleviated if the administration will recognize the employee as a responsible adult. In our society, when a person is twenty-one he is credited with having sufficient intelligence to help elect the President and the Congress and in that way to contribute to the policies of the government. In business and industry, however, rarely is he asked to share in a responsible way in decisions relating to his work. The widespread use of suggestion boxes indicates how little face-to-face conversation goes on in business organizations about the job itself. Many company studies indicate that there are significant increases in productivity and decreases in the expression of various forms of hostility when people have a responsible share in planning the work they are going to do. Participation indicates also that management cares sufficiently about employees to listen to them and to permit them to express their feelings.

## WORK SATISFACTION AND FEELINGS OF INDIVIDUAL WORTH

An individual's feelings about his work can affect his feelings about his home, his family, and his future. Years ago there was a *Saturday Evening Post* cover that showed a man being criticized by his boss, who in turn had an argument with his wife. She spanked the child, the child kicked the dog, the dog chased the cat, then the cat ate the mouse. This sequence was used to illustrate the escape mechanism of displacement in Chapter 7; that is, displacement of feelings from a situation in which they cannot be expressed to another situation in which they can. A person's feelings about his work are frequently displaced onto the home situation. Anger and frustration on the job may well result in hostility or irritability at home.

152

On the other hand, people who take pride in their work and whose occupational identity is important to them quite often extend that pride to include the appearance of their homes. Many home appliance and automobile companies reinforce this by making their products available to their employees at cost. For example, a man will say that he must keep his lawn neat and his house painted because people identify him with his company. His pride in his company enhances his pride in himself, his family, and his home.

At the same time, the positive feelings about his work are usually correlated with a positive, optimistic outlook on life. A person can be comfortable about the future when he trusts it.

When work experience holds no promise of further growth or achievement, a man will invest the major part of his energies elsewhere. This often happens at middle age when some men recognize they will remain essentially in the same relative positions for the rest of their working lives. If their salaries are adequate to meet their needs and if they can earn their salaries by meeting the minimum requirements of the job, they will do only that which is required of them. Some men in executive positions jokingly refer to this as the "male menopause" and complain of the loss of initiative on the part of their subordinates. Sometimes there is a subsequent greater investment in home and family which will often be to the advantage of both the man and his family, provided the man does not go to work with a feeling of inadequacy or of failure.

The employee, young or older, who does not meet the standards set by his employer, is subject to a rude shock. In a psychological way, hiring and firing on a job is comparable to the early childhood experience of being given or being denied love and affection. When a person is employed, he is told in effect that he is desired and that he is looked upon as worthy of working with others. When he is discharged, he is told that he is no longer wanted. The importance to a person of being wanted and needed, whether in the family or outside of it, has long been recognized.

## CONFORMITY AND THE CORPORATION

The recent Broadway play, *The Absence of a Cello,* by Ira Wallach, is a comedy based on the demands of large corporations and the effect of these demands on the life and the wife of a possible future executive. The college professor in Wallach's play resented his prospective company's interest in his personal life, which he regarded as an unwarranted intrusion into his privacy. The professor is asked to join the corporation as a consultant and also to do research on their business techniques. He is offered a salary of fifty thousand dollars, which is considerably more than a college professor earns. However, before the position is finalized, the professor and his wife are told that they must be visited in their home by the personnel executive of the company. The professor's hobby is playing the cello and his wife's hobby is writing. Thus, you can imagine the amount of music and unfinished manuscript that clutters their home (and the stage). They also collect and study ancient ceramics, either whole or broken specimens. The comedy begins when the doorbell rings to announce the company visitors. The cello is absent and the desk is transformed into a television table with the manuscript stored in the sound chamber. The visit goes well, but the professor decides that he and his family are not the people the executives in the company think they are accepting. Thus he does not accept the position on the company's terms.

Others, however, recognize that in high executive positions it is difficult to separate personal life from business life. In many instances, for all practical purposes, husbands and wives are employed as a team. Wives are expected to play social roles in their communities to help with their husbands' positions.

Corporate concern with the personal lives of executives is destructive if it is paternalistic, i.e., if the corporation treats its executive and his family as if they were children. This generates resentment. In some cases, however, the corporation is not concerned enough with the problems of personal life, and particularly with the corporation's impact on personal life. This can result in the executive often having to spend far too much of his time away from his family. The company often demands that the executive not only devote extended hours to the company's business, but also that he undertake considerable community participation. Many wives and children are chronically angry, sometimes not consciously, at being deserted in this way.

From time immemorial man has, in various ways, been conforming to the demands of his fellows in order to survive among them. To some extent we must all conform to remain in any community or work situation. The corporation does not create the conforming man; however, it may help to increase his numbers. Just as it is true that certain kinds of people are attracted to certain communities, so people are attracted to certain companies. For example, people who value job security above rapid promotion will tend to choose banks or public utilities, and these institutions, in turn, because they deal in public service, will seek to employ people who can get along well with the public. Thus, in a vague, general way, businesses tend to develop corporate personality types.

In any hierarchical structure, people move up because they gain the approval of their superiors and to that extent they conform to superiors' wishes and expectations. Many people are quite comfortable with such

154

arrangements because the controls imposed by the organization enhance their personal controls, because the structure of the organization meets their psychological needs. In some cases, however, they risk loss of their own purposes and goals and substitute those of their superiors. This results in subsequent discontent with themselves. Many people who wish to do so cannot leave large corporations because they would lose their vested rights in pension and other benefit funds. These people often remain with the corporation but are frequently angry and apathetic. Also, a number of recent novels about the business world have been written by men who left in anger, and then attacked it, primarily because these individuals felt that they demeaned themselves when they conformed to the demands and expectations of the business world which were foreign to their own desires.

## PECKING ORDER

In Chapter 8 of his book, *The Art and Skill of Getting Along With People,* Dr. Sylvanus M. Duvall, discusses the importance of position in a

Drawing by Kraus; © 1967
*The New Yorker* Magazine, Inc.

group. He says that the "unofficial positions of status, rank, and power include not only those at the top and bottom, but everybody in between. Your relative position—your unofficial position—in any group is something referred to as your position in the 'pecking order.' This is a term that comes from a study of rank among flocks of chickens."[1]

In the study, it was observed that usually every chicken not only had a definite rank in the flock, but also that every other chicken knew what that rank was and scrupulously observed it. That is, each chicken knew which other chicken it could peck and which chickens could peck it.

When we think about it, we can visualize our place in such an order at school, at home, in a club, in church, and perhaps even at work. There are people who defer to you, and people to whom you defer.

In organizations to which you have belonged for a long while, you probably have come to sense who "rates" and who does not, and how much. Groups without formal organization also observe the pecking order. For example, at a class meeting about the annual dinner-dance, Miss Talk-All-The-Time springs to her feet and gives her ideas on all facets of the party. The class lets her talk, but nobody listens. Mr. Able Accomplishment then quietly makes a few proposals to which everyone listens. After discussion, Mr. A. makes a final suggestion that is accepted. Of interest, however, is the fact that a person's place in the pecking order will vary in different groups. In the class meeting Mr. Accomplishment may be top-notch and the one to whom everyone listens with deference and respect. However, in his church group or his work group, he may be only one of the "guys" whom everyone likes but whose words hold little significance for anyone.

It is difficult to decide why a person's rank is such-and-such in the pecking order. Here are some factors that Dr. Duvall identified:

1.  Official Position. (It always helps!) Although, under Mussolini, the King was powerless to affect national policy, he did enjoy a status, and even a limited authority which he would not otherwise have had. The mayor who is a puppet of a political boss certainly has more power than he would have as an ordinary citizen.

2.  The Favor of Those in Power. Many people enjoy high prestige because they have the ear of the boss. Lysenko was a scientist who was able to talk scientific nonsense in the Soviet Union as long as he had the endorsement of Stalin. Being the fairhaired boy of someone in an important position can put you right up there. All of us try to help our

---

[1] Sylvanus M. Duvall, *The Art and Skill of Getting Along with People* (Prentice-Hall, Englewood Cliffs, N.J., 1961), p. 111.

friends. Those in positions of influence are not different. One interesting phase of this came out in a study of a thousand advertising executives who carried briefcases home with them at night. Investigation revealed that two thirds of them never opened their briefcases or did any extra work at home. Their bosses usually knew this. Yet they thought that taking the briefcase home showed the proper spirit. As a result those who brought their briefcases home had conspicuously better chances of promotion than those who did not; another instance of the importance of the favor of those in power.

3. **The Disfavor of Those in Power.** Some people are deposed from higher positions, or fail to get promotions, because of antagonisms of those at the top. In this respect not only the higher-ups, but the subordinates may play a part. A group of children take a dislike to a teacher. They are so disorderly and cause so much trouble that officials believe the teacher to be incompetent. Or the group in an office want to get back at the office manager. They sabotage him on every occasion, and the manager is dismissed. Sometimes such opposition is justified. Sometimes it results because the individual is too honest, too conscientious, and thereby arouses the antagonism of his subordinates.

4. **Some People Inherit It.** Careful studies have shown that you don't buy your way into the top crust of American society. You must either be born there or marry into it. Business positions are more open. The son of the boss does not always succeed his father. Yet there is no doubt that he has the first chance and the inside track. He is given the earliest and best opportunities for learning the business. He has the best contacts. If he has the ability it takes (and sometimes when he doesn't), he will get the top post if he wants it.

5. **Some People Are Lucky.** Luck is far less important than most failures believe, but it does sometimes play a real part—particularly in the matter of timing. A Hollywood scout drops in on a play to see a well-known star. The star is ill and her place is taken by an unknown understudy who does a superb job. Undoubtedly her talents would have come out sometime, but had the star been ill one day earlier or one day later, the movie career of the understudy would have been delayed, possibly for years. Some people have risen to the top because there happened to be a vacancy at the particular time when they were available and others, who might have done as well or better, were not.

A word of caution. Don't be too quick in labeling someone else's success as luck. Sometimes, though it appears to be, it isn't. . . . Sometimes the "lucky" person is one who has prepared himself, watches for breaks, and grabs them when they come.[2]

From this discussion of leadership, especially in employer-employee relationships, you can see that there is a hidden power structure in any group. This is particularly true in the world of work. As the pecking order points out, titular power is not always the effective power. The real boss may be someone with no title at all. Regardless of title, and sometimes in sharp variance with it, each person in any group in the family or outside of it has his place in the "pecking order."

## TO PROMOTE UNDERSTANDING OF THIS CHAPTER

1. Upon what does good leadership seem to depend?

2. As an executive of a large firm, you are concerned with maintaining good employer-employee relationships. What would be the theme of your instructions to your subordinates at a board meeting?

3. How would you help an employee develop the same perception of the expectations of the job that you, as his employer, have?

4. How does the importance of a job affect one of your associates, your parents, or yourself? Are some of the effects mentioned in the chapter exemplified by your experience?

5. How do the work "satisfiers" reinforce our basic psychological needs?

6. How can a large business corporation cause one to conform?

7. Now that you are aware of a "pecking order," what are some of your observations about its function in your life?

8. What qualities seem to you to be the most important in a job?

## SUPPLEMENTARY READING

ADORNO, THEODORE W., and others, *The Authoritarian Personality*. Harper and Row, New York, 1950.

ALBEE, GEORGE W., *Mental Health Manpower Trends*. Basic Books, Inc., New York, 1959.

ALLEN, W. C., *The Social Life of Animals*. W. W. Norton and Co., Inc., New York, 1938.

[2] *Ibid.,* pp. 113–115.

DUVALL, SYLVANUS, M., *The Art and Skill of Getting Along With People*. Prentice-Hall, Inc., Englewood Cliffs, N.J., 1961.

GOLDING, WILLIAM, *Lord of the Flies*. Faber and Faber, Ltd., London, 1954.

HERZBERG, F., MAUSNER, B., and SNYDERMAN, B., *The Motivation to Work*. John Wiley & Sons, Inc., New York, 1959.

LASSWELL, HAROLD D., *Power and Personality*. The Viking Press, Inc., New York, 1962.

WALLACH, IRA, *The Absence of a Cello*. Samuel French, Inc., New York, 1965.

YOUNG, PAUL T., *Motivation and Emotion*. John Wiley & Sons, Inc., New York, 1961.

*"When is she coming and how long is she staying?"*

## 15
# Relationships Between
# Attitudes in Youth and Old Age

**Senescense** (aging or growing old) is made difficult in our culture because, as the cartoons suggest, the aging relatives do not have an honored place in our modern family system. The visit from the aging relative is more of a chore than a joy. The real threat of the aged to the young may be brought about by our preoccupation with youth. It is important in our culture to look and act young, and it is a compliment to be called young. Thus the problems of the aged are increased because individuals fail to recognize that aging is part of the continuous process of growth.

Shakespeare, in *As You Like It,* wrote poignantly about the aging process in Jacques' famous soliloquy on the seven ages of man.

> All the world's a stage,
> And all the men and women merely players.
> They have their exits and their entrances;
> And one man in his time plays many parts,
> His acts being seven ages. At first the infant,
> Mewling and puking in the nurse's arms.
> And then the whining school-boy, with his satchel
> And shining morning face, creeping like a snail
> Unwillingly to school. And then the lover,
> Sighing like furnace, with a woeful ballad
> Made to his mistress' eyebrow. Then a soldier,
> Full of strange oaths, and bearded like the bard;
> Jealous in honour, sudden and quick in quarrel,
> Seeking the bubble reputation
> Even in the cannon's mouth. And then the justice,
> In fair round belly with good capon lined
> With eyes severe and beard of formal cut,
> Full of wise saws and modern instances;
> And so he plays his part. The sixth age shifts
> Into the lean and slipper'd pantaloon,
> With spectacles on nose and pouch on side!
> His youthful hose, well saved, a world too wide
> For his shrunk shank; and his big manly voice,
> Turning again toward childish treble, pipes
> And whistles in his sound. Last scene of all,
> That ends this strange eventful history,
> Is second childishness, and mere oblivion,
> Sans teeth, sans eyes, sans taste, sans everything.

"Aging," as the term implies, is a process. It begins even before birth and continues until death. As such, aging is synonymous with human development. Customarily, however, the term "aging" is taken to mean the later stage or stages of the process. The chronological age arbitrarily selected at which aging is legally said to begin is sixty-five.

161

Glenn Bernhardt, *The Town Journal*

*"I tell you my wife's relatives are an organized charity!"*

## FAMILY STRUCTURE

History illustrates that there has been a transition from the extended family to the nuclear family. The extended family was a family unit that was composed of mother, father, the children, and then extended to include grandmother, grandfather, aunts, uncles, and cousins. The nuclear family, however, consists of just the immediate family unit—mother, father, and children. The autonomous nuclear family seems destined to be the family of the future. However, in the past the patriarchal extended family and the matriarchal extended family were well intrenched. To understand better the differences among the various family types, we will discuss the patriarchal extended family on the farm and in the towns, the matriarchal extended family in urban industrial neighborhoods, and the autonomous nuclear family of urban residential districts.

*"How do you expect me to remember your birthday when you never look any older?"*

## THE EXTENDED FAMILY

The extended family was once the prevalent form in all human societies. Among peoples of ancient civilizations, and still today in Oriental countries, it took the form of the large patriarchal family with authority and decision-making in the hands of its head, usually the oldest male member. The patriarchal form of the extended family was an economic unit of production both in farming in the country and in carrying on trades in towns. The patriarchal extended family has almost disappeared; it has been threatened by industrialization, the growth of cities, and the rise of individualism. However, it sometimes develops where the owner of a family business employs his sons and perhaps sons-in-law and especially if all the component nuclear families live near or occupy apartments in the building belonging to the patriarch.

The matriarchal extended family is characterized by these outstanding features: (1) the nucleus of the matriarchal extended family is constituted by the grandmother, her daughters, and granddaughters, (2) the men visit relatives but less frequently than do the women, (3) husbands and wives enjoy much of their recreation and social life independently, (4) a system of mutual help in time of need is carried on by grandmother, daughters, sisters, and granddaughters, and (5) there is a strict separation of the conjugal roles of husband and wife. In this system, the husband controls the money and does not tell the wife what he earns. He gives her the housekeeping allowance customary in the neighborhood. Those participating in the matriarchal extended family believe that a good conjugal relation is one with harmonious division of labor rather than with joint activities and shared interests.

The matriarchal extended family appears to be still well intrenched in homogeneous working-class neighborhoods where the residents are employed by local industry. It is most stable where at least three or four generations have been born and reared in the same locality. Geographic separation of family members is a serious impairment to the functioning of the matriarchal extended family. The departure of couples to residential suburbs loosens their membership in this type of extended family and breaks any strong ties which may have been formed.

## THE AUTONOMOUS NUCLEAR FAMILY

Prominent characteristics of the autonomous nuclear family are as follows: (1) equal authority is shared by husband and wife, (2) division of labor between husband and wife is flexible and roles are easily reversed, (3) compatibility of personality and complementary differences are regarded as desirable by the couple for a happy marriage, (4) nearly all friends are joint friends of husband and wife, (5) there is a minimum of social control by friends and neighbors, and (6) leisure-time activities are largely together, with emphasis upon entertaining and being entertained by friends.

The autonomous nuclear family has the characteristics which seem adapted to the urban way of life. Husband and wife no longer seek their chief companionship outside the home—the husband with friends and the wife with relatives—as in the matriarchal extended family. They find it with each other. They select friends not on the basis of those who live in the same neighborhood but rather on the basis of corresponding tastes, interests, and similar backgrounds. These friends are likely to reside in other neighborhoods, and thus the couple is freed from the control and the responsibility of kin and neighbors.

164

## CHANGES IN THE RELATIONS OF AGING PARENTS AND THEIR ADULT OFFSPRING

The autonomous nuclear family is a product of the effects of the economic and social trends of the times. As mentioned, friendships and associations are based on common tastes, interests, and backgrounds. With our social mobility, the adult offspring probably have a higher educational level, different tastes, and more sophisticated interests than their aging parents. The aging parent in the nuclear family threatens the status of his adult children both psychologically and economically. With our fetish for youth and its charms, the adult offspring is threatened by the mannerisms of his aging parent. He recognizes that these symptoms may too soon be his characteristics. It is easier to ignore the advancing years when one isn't reminded by the presence of an aging relative. Also, the adult offspring with his changing status strives toward economic mobility hand-in-hand with social mobility. Thus the acquisition of automobiles, better housing, and prominent club memberships places economic stress on him and the care of the aged might be an additional strain.

A minority of aging parents still live with their adult children. It is, however, important to distinguish cases where the grownup offspring live with parents and those where the parents live with their adult offspring.

Where the children who are now adult live with their parents, the older generation takes the dominant role. The aging mother, if physically able, is in charge of the housekeeping. This arrangement proves more satisfactory to the older generation than to the married younger couple. In general, it works better if the daughter and her husband live with her parents than when the couple live with the husband's parents.

If the aging individual or couple live with a married son or married daughter, the arrangement is generally difficult on both sides. It is likely to be especially frustrating to the older couple who frequently feels in the way and useless.

## ALONENESS OR ALIENATION

With tremendous advances in industrialization, urbanization, communication, technology, and science, the pace and complexity of social life have multiplied rapidly. Paradoxically, the same forces that conquered the ignorance, disease, and deprivation of earlier times have created new stress in the modern era.

For individuals or for societies, periods of rapid change tax older modes of behavior that no longer properly fit new challenges. Thus, for example, movement of population necessitated by industrialization and urbanization

165

*No alienation here. "I'm Grandpa's sweetheart."*

strains the traditional family organization and roles. The grandparents are cut off from the emotional and economic support of their children (meanwhile being kept alive longer by medical advances). The offspring lose the skills and knowledge of their parents, while having to deal afresh with the problems of their own children, who in turn lack the emotional acceptance and guidance of the extended family and instead have to seek status and achievement in their peer groups.

With the above thoughts in mind, one could say that each group is alone and distinct. However, there is "loneliness" or "aloneness" that is privacy, and there is alienation. Many in the older generation and many in the younger generation are growing up alienated, unable to attach to other people. Such people are lonely and alone, not because they enjoy their own aloneness, but because they are incapable of enjoying relations with others or incapable of making relationships with others. When this incapability exists, old age is not seen as a part of life, the way death, birth, and puberty are seen as a part of life.

There is an often-stated presumption held by much of our society, that older people "want to be needed"—an interesting reflection upon the state of real affairs, because if they were, in fact, needed, they would not need to wish it to be so. Older people, while they want to receive recognition for *having been* useful, find that it is *present* activity that is rewarding and not prior activities.

166

*"This Dr. Steinkraus we've got working on the biochemical key to immortality has reached mandatory-retirement age. Do we keep him on or give him the heave-ho?"*

**The** problems of aging are compounded by the inability of our society to create for older persons satisfying places and worthwhile roles. The old family system had a place for the older person, but modern society has no room for him. This, however, is not a matter of aging alone, but is a reflection of the larger social changes which have taken place. In a society such as ours, in which high values are placed upon economic and social success, family solidarity is all too often incompatible with occupational and social mobility. One often must make a choice which can work to the detriment of the older persons within the family circle.

Thus, many of the stresses of modern social life are by-products of social change. It is futile to wonder if life would be better if the "good old days" could be restored, for society can no more retrace its history than an individual can regain the pleasures of childhood without losing the achievements of adulthood. More important is the question of whether new values and institutions can evolve that will permit not only greater freedom from stress but also greater opportunity for harmonious and creative living.

## INTERACTION BETWEEN INDIVIDUALS

Older people are part of our ongoing society, and their characteristics, like those of all others, are developed in large part through social inter-

167

course. The interaction between people, the process of socialization, operates in such a manner as to develop a series of stages in the continuing processes of social change. There is an old saying which states that what one is at fifteen is what he was given; what one is at sixty is what he has made of himself. People who have a satisfying old age are people who are doing things that interest them. They are involved with life. They are involved with people. Such persons will be sought by people of different ages; they will not be put aside; they are people who are alive. They are alive because they grew that way. They are people who have resources and are engaged in life now. They grew up engaged in life, not protecting themselves from work, not protecting themselves from exertion, not too lazy to go out and really get involved with people. They are the old people that young people like to talk to, the people they like to visit.

Old age is a developmental stage in the continuing process of socialization which we call aging. The aged of today are yesterday's children; the aged of tomorrow are the youth of today. The problems of the youth foreshadow the problems of the aged. The behavioral patterns erected for us today, and the adjustments that we make to the situations in which we find ourselves, all reflect the kinds of persons we shall be in the future. To illustrate this, let's think about two girls in the senior high. Jean and Polly are both seventeen; both reasonably attractive and intelligent. Jean baby-sits for extra money, tutors some children of the inner city in reading, reads stories to some of the older ladies in a rest home, has taught herself to play a guitar, and has a vast number of friends of all ages and in all stations. Polly is restless if she doesn't have a weekend party or date. She complains that her parents are not generous in her allowance and that she never has anything to wear. Polly is bored and can't wait until graduation.

The actions, attitudes, and adjustments of these seniors at seventeen predict the kind of people they may be at seventy. Those who learn to interact, to become involved, who cultivate the art of social intercourse will not be alienated at any age.

## PLANNED COMMUNITIES

For people of various ages and stages of development to learn to interact with each other, they must know each other. Our planned communities with their homogeneous groupings have developed alienation between different ages. These communities have grown up with highly compacted age populations. The people who live in one kind of planned community are people in their late 20's through the early 40's and their children. There are almost no older people and relatively few teen-agers. This development of a society with an age structure that is totally abnormal creates problems

168

for our youth. Older persons have always provided us with role models; that is, understandings of what it means to grow old and how to change and adapt to the later years. If there are no older persons around, young people have no models after which to pattern themselves as they themselves grow older. There is also a reverse process in these communities. If the planned community is composed of "old agers," "golden agers," or "people in their bonus years," they do not have a chance to know and observe the young people. Thus, their only knowledge of the youth and their activities is that of the 8 to 10 percent who make newspaper headlines.

In the planned communities occupied by the young, people don't die. What happens then is that young people have no way of adapting to bereavement; they don't learn to accept death as a part of life. The people who can die gracefully are those who have lived a rich life. The people who are afraid to die are those whose lives are empty, who always hope somehow or other that they will catch up with something real in life. When our vital old people die, we are the ones that suffer because of the loss. It is not a tragedy for them, it is part of the life process.

To further discuss the importance of the need for the different ages to know each other, Dr. Dorothy Lee, an anthropologist, tells this story:

> I recall that one of the teachers in a Hopi school reported that the Hopi children had been given a party in the school, but did not turn out. When they were asked why they said, "What would we do all alone? We would be just children. There weren't going to be any parents to watch us, no grandparents to tell us stories, and no babies to hold or watch, just children our age." They did not enjoy themselves just being alone, because they felt that a rich party included even babies.

When we can have gatherings where all ages participate and mingle, we won't have the deep misunderstandings about the various stages of development.

## PREPARATION FOR OLD AGE

As stated previously, one starts to prepare for old age at birth. However, it is not until people approach middle age that they really begin to concern themselves with questions of security, health, and death. The past experience of the person, at this mature stage of development, plays an important, even determining role in his growth toward greater maturity. All age groups are much under the influence of their early years and experience.

The great challenge of middle age lies in the necessity to adjust downward from the previous period of activity and responsibility. Skill and self-

169

understanding are required to negotiate a proper accommodation to a slower pace, a less crowded day, or to lighter responsibilities. There is a need to relinquish control and to accept the shift in attention from oneself to others. Above all, one must find satisfaction and stimulus in younger people, despite differences in values between generations. The world does not fall to pieces because familiar ways change or take on new forms, or because one is less needed in a family or a job.

Acceptance, flexibility, and independence are the cues. A certain degree of vicarious living through one's children's lives is natural and even healthy, but a person should not depend upon his family to supply the energy and motivation for his own life at any age, perhaps least of all in middle age. Free from restricting and confining family ties, many people find in middle age their first opportunity to be truly independent. Adult offspring should be viewed as friends, peers, and colleagues, rather than as indebted persons obligated to support parents or to accept parental authority and guidance.

## TO PROMOTE UNDERSTANDING OF THIS CHAPTER

1. Define the following terms:

   | | |
   |---|---|
   | senescence | the nuclear family |
   | aging | the patriarchal extended family |
   | matriarchal extended family | the autonomous nuclear family |

2. What social changes affect the relationship between aging parents and their adult offspring?

3. The Swedish people have a saying, "Heaven in this world is to be alone when I want it; Hell is to be alone when I don't want it." What is the relationship between this saying and the role of the grandparents in our society?

4. Which characteristics of the autonomous nuclear family meet basic psychological needs?

5. How might the characteristics of the autonomous nuclear family conflict with the role expectations of the older generation?

6. What causes adult offspring to feel threatened by their aging parents?

7. What is the difference between alienation and aloneness?

8. How does our society compound the problems of the aged?

9. If death is part of the life process, how can one best accept it?

170

10. What are the characteristics of an older person who has "grown old gracefully?"

11. Discuss this statement: "A community without its senior citizens is as artificial and wrong as a retirement community without any young people."

## SUPPLEMENTARY READING

*Aging in Western Societies,* ERNEST BURGESS, ed. The University of Chicago Press, Chicago, 1960.

CUMMING, ELAINE, and HENRY, WILLIAM E., *Growing Old.* Basic Books, Inc., New York, 1961.

HAVIGHURST, R. J., and ALBRECT, RUTH, *Older People.* Longmans, Green and Co., Ltd., London, 1953.

JHABVALA, R. PRAWER, *The Nature of Passion.* W. W. Norton and Co., Inc., New York, 1956.

SIMMONS, LEO W., ed., *Sun Chief.* Published for the Institute of Human Relations by the Yale University Press, New Haven, Conn., 1942.

ZBOROWSKI, MARK, and HERZOG, ELIZABETH, *Life is with People.* International Universities Press, New York, 1952.

# 16
# Love-Infatuation Relationships

Within each individual there is an urge to grow toward his fullest potential. The most lasting, worthwhile, growth-producing love relationships are those that allow each member involved in the relationship to develop to his fullest capacity. Love should grow as in the first example. It should not start out full grown and then dwindle. Some of the saddest words are, "I used to love her, we thought we loved each other, he said he loved me." The love relationship that grows and matures doesn't have these phrases in its refrain. For example, Mr. and Mrs. Jones are celebrating their tenth wedding anniversary at a dinner for two in an elegant dining room. They

begin to reminisce about their days together in college before their marriage, their first apartment . . . suddenly Mary Jones laughs and says, "How could I have thought that I loved you enough to marry you? Because in comparison to my love for you now, the love I felt then was small indeed. I wonder if on our twenty-fifth anniversary our love will have grown even larger—if I'll consider our love now as small in comparison."

"I hope so," said Mr. Jones. "I hope so!"

## DEFINITION OF LOVE

Today we examine love critically, even clinically, for we realize that love, *the ability to form meaningful and satisfying relationships with other human beings,* is essential to successful lives. Just as we play many roles, we have many loves in our lifetime. Past and present love relationships help us build toward future love relationships. Sometimes, if our past and

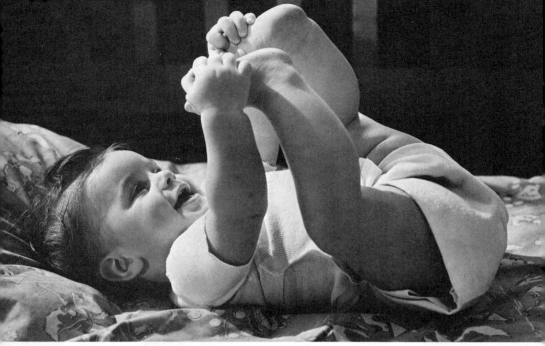

*The self-love of baby as he plays with his fingers and toes.*

present love experiences are not satisfying, it is more difficult to build valuable future relationships.

One of Alice's strange experiences in Wonderland involves a Cheshire cat which sits smiling in a tree. While she is chatting with him, all at once the cat begins to disappear, tail first, until little by little the whole cat has vanished and only his smile remains. Alice objects; she has seen cats without smiles but never a smile without a cat.

We, like Alice, can find a person without love, but not love without its being embodied in another being. Love becomes personified through the thoughts and deeds of man in his relationships. We learn to love as we learn other abilities. Love can be given only if it has been received. The ability to love can be likened to a solar cell. The solar cell cannot work until it is charged. It needs to absorb energy before it in turn can generate energy. Human beings are like the solar cell in their generation of love. They need to receive a great deal of love for a long period of time before they are able to return love to others.

## STAGES OF LOVE DEVELOPMENT

Love development is a step-by-step process that progresses from the cradle to the grave. Love starts with birth and goes through several stages.

174

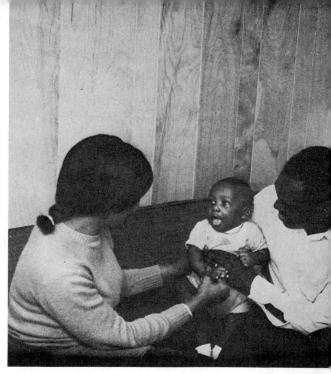

*Here is solace, satisfaction, and security.*

Robert Forget

Little babies are capable of loving no one else at first. They have not had enough experience even to be aware that there are other persons to love. So they love their fingers and toes and enjoy their bodies in a vigorous, lusty way as they kick, jabber, and laugh. This is called *self-love.*

It is quite possible that from time to time one still feels and acts as he did in that first stage. Haven't you seen yourself and others in front of a mirror admiring that new hair style, a new haircut, a dimple, or a clean shave?

This stage is so apt to recur all through life that we have a name for it: narcissism, love of self. The word comes from the old Greek story of Narcissus who fell in love with his own image in a quiet pool of water. He so adored his reflection that he pined away and died, whereupon the flower that bears his name sprang up to mark his resting place. Today when a person loves and admires himself, we call him narcissistic.

A baby forms his first attachment or love for the human being who satisfies his needs. In our society this is usually his mother. We have seen how the infant, taking his food from his mother, becomes attached to the hand that feeds him, the arms that hold him, the mother figure herself, or himself, depending upon who is meeting the baby's needs. As his awareness of reality grows, the baby comes to realize how very little he can do for himself. His mother, who does everything for him, represents solace, satisfaction, security. This type of love is called mother and/or father love.

*Love is an alliance of friendship, discovery, and enthusiasm.*

*Nature's loving proxy, the watchful mother.*

176

The next significant period of love comes between the ages of six and twelve. The child has stepped out into a larger world and the world encourages him to form social attachments. These social attachments are usually with youngsters of the same sex.

These new relationships or loves are for the most part asexual; boys play with boys, girls play with girls. A boy who shows an interest in girls is considered a sissy and a girl who wants to play with boys is a tomboy. It is a period when children are encouraged to develop and accept their sexual role in life by pursuing all the interests characteristic of their masculinity or femininity, with one exception: an interest in the opposite sex.

This is the age when a girl asks, What is it like to be a woman? What kind of woman do I want to be? To help her make this identification, she watches older women and has movie stars or outstanding women athletes as her idols. She tries to be close to an older sister, to her mother, or to any favorite adult to see how they act in the hope of answering her questions.

Boys in this age group form attachments to male heroes. They too, are trying to answer the same questions: What kind of man do I want to be? What is it like to be a man?

It is important that boys and girls of this age are in close contact with adults with whom they can identify—adults who recognize the reasons behind these attachments and do not rebuff or ridicule them for their struggling efforts to please. The typical experience of the youngster falling in love with his coach or teacher should be a happy one, guided and under-

*Adults are patterns for children.*

Robert Forget

177

stood by the adults involved. It is a further step in the direction of the mature, heterosexual love which unites people in marriage.

"Love for love's sake" and "in love with love" are phrases that describe the stage of love development which encompasses love for all members of the opposite sex. An adolescent girl is in love with boys. She wants to be where boys are, she wants to see how they will react to her, she is interested in all boys. Boys and girls at this stage of development need the hangout, ice cream shop, or youth center where they can come into contact with each other. They need the gang or crowd. Even though an individual has this great interest in the opposite sex, he isn't sure enough of himself alone and needs the security of the crowd and the noise of the records to cover up his own verbal inadequacies. He needs the chance to observe and to talk to many girls so that he can begin to narrow down his ideas to the kind of girls he really likes.

When the individual passes this stage, the field has been narrowed. The young woman says she likes a boy who has certain characteristics that seem important to her. She has developed standards for her dates. She knows the kind of boy from whom she will accept a date and she can say no to in-

*Adolescents need to be with others to observe and learn.*

John van-Schalkwyk

vitations from boys who do not meet her ideals. She has matured in her attachments; she is no longer in love with boys but interested in certain boys.

The young man also has developed a list of characteristics he is looking for in the girls he dates. He has an idea of the kind of woman he wants for his wife. He has given some thought to the type of home that he would like to originate and foster. The early rush for many dates and many types of dates has now been altered. He also dates with more definite ideas and ideals in mind.

Finally the love attachments settle on *the one*. The focus is on this person because he or she seems to be one's ideal and complements one's personality and because one would rather be with this person than with anyone else.

## MATURE LOVE FOR OTHERS

The individual who has successfully come up the ladder of love development eventually reaches a kind of love that affects not only his own dear ones with whom he is in closest contact, but in addition many people whom he has never met. He is concerned with his responsibility to mankind. Such an attitude is considered mature love for others. He does things to promote human welfare and feels warmly toward the men and women and children whom he meets. He has faith in the power of parental, fraternal, and romantic love. The development of mature love enables a person to promote the brotherhood of man by helping to provide an opportunity for all individuals to develop their best potentials and by giving them the gift of loving support to enrich their positive efforts. While it inevitably leads one into hard work and some difficult trials, this kind of love builds character. Its strength comes from an inner peace that enables one to bear the hardships of life. It can be attained not in a single step but only through the mastery of the other stages of love development that lead to it.

## LOVE AND INFATUATION

To love a person, one must know him. What usually happens in "love at first sight" is that the two people are strongly attracted to each other, perhaps even infatuated, from the very beginning. Then this strong attraction develops into love without any break in the process. It only seems as if it were love at first sight.

Love at first sight may also be compulsive in nature. The individual has a strong urge to love someone and this urge becomes focused on a particular person. What should be expressed as "This is the individual I must love" is expressed by the persons concerned as "This is the individual I do love."[1]

Such an urge to love is not uncommon in adolescence, when new emotions, with which the young person has not yet learned to live and which are largely the result of his own physiological and psychological development rather than his experience, begin to well up within him. Such "love" may also be an outgrowth of an individual's feeling of inferiority or his fear that because of personal unattractiveness or inability to meet members of the opposite sex he may never marry.

Love grows out of an appraisal of all the known characteristics of the other person. Infatuation may arise from an acquaintance with only one of these characteristics.

When an individual is genuinely in love, he is in love with the other person as a total personality; his feelings grow primarily out of his relationship with that other person and his estimate of him. An infatuated individual may be "in love with love."

Love is other-person centered. It is outgoing. It results in sharing. Infatuation is in contrast, self-centered. The other person is a means of self-gratification.

An individual in love works for the other person or for their mutual benefit. He may study to make the other person proud of him. His ambition thus spurred, he may plan and save for the future. He may day-dream, but his dreams are reasonably attainable. An infatuated person may lose his ambition, his appetite, and his interest in everyday affairs. He often day-dreams, but his dreams are sometimes not limited to the attainable and are given free rein.

Love leads to idealization but, because the ideal is partly an outgrowth of an understanding and of an appreciation for the other person, it may be checked against reality without loss. In infatuation there tends to be idealization accompanied by a disregard of reality.

Two people in love face problems frankly and attempt to solve them. In infatuation, problems tend to be disregarded or glossed over.

Physical attraction is a relatively smaller part of their total relationship when a couple is in love, but it is a relatively greater part when the two are infatuated. Let us imagine, for example, that physical attraction is represented by a three-inch square. In infatuation, this square is part of a four-inch square; in love, however, it is part of a twelve-inch square because there are so many other considerations.

[1] Willard Waller, *The Family; A Dynamic Interpretation* (New York, The Cordon Company, Inc., 1938), p. 284.

With mature people in love, an expression of affection tends to come relatively late in the couple's relationship. In infatuation it may come earlier, sometimes from the very beginning.

When a couple is in love, the physical contact that they have tends to have meaning as well as to be a pleasurable experience, but physical love is not usually considered an end in itself. It tends to express what the couple feels toward each other. In infatuation, physical contact tends to be an end in itself. For most people it represents only pleasurable experience, devoid of ultimate meaning.

Love tends to endure. Infatuation may change suddenly, unexpectedly, unpredictably. When love changes, the reasons tend to be more or less apparent. Infatuation may change for no apparent reason.

Two people in love are not indifferent to the effects of postponing their wedding and do not prolong the period of postponement unduly, but they can usually wait a reasonable time; most do not feel an almost irresistible urge toward haste. They tend to think of the period of postponement as one of further preparation. An infatuated couple tends to feel an urge toward immediate marriage. Postponement is intolerable to them and they interpret it as deprivation rather than preparation.

## COMPLEXITIES OF LOVE

The word love tends to be bandied around without due consideration to its intended meaning. One may love to participate in certain activities or love to collect items and cherish his collection. One may love to eat certain foods or listen to a particular composer or a favorite musician. Thus one may say that he loves cats, loves oranges, or loves sports. Yet the word love as used in these examples is on a much lower plane than the word love which is told to a parent or husband or wife.

The facets of love that make this emotion generally sparkle are the relationships that produce a reciprocal affection. To love and to be loved by a person or an animal is the brightest facet of all. The faithful animal who greets you upon your return home, who welcomes your touch, no matter what struggles the day has brought, is a comfort.

A marriage based on a deep reciprocal love can comprise the very best facets of love. When two people love each other with romantic love, intellectual love, and physical or sexual love, they have the three ingredients for a mature and lasting love relationship. Romantic love is often described as the love of the courtship and honeymoon. Romantic love is the smile across a room, the kiss on the nape of the neck while peeling potatoes into the garbage disposal, the bouquet of roses, the thoughtful note, and the hand that pats a tired shoulder.

Intellectual love is the respect for the other person's intelligence, his integrity, and his opinion, and the willingness to try to understand his point of view. This love is probably the most important of all three. The respect for the intellect of another person is the basic foundation of conversation and communication. Without a sharing of ideas, ideals, opinions, and thoughts as well as humor, a couple cannot build companionship. Intellectual love is a basis of all relationships and it is an integral part of a lasting marriage relationship.

Sexual love is the joy of the other person's embrace, the warmth of physical closeness and the desire to be the reciprocal parent of a child that may be created from this love.

Love, however, is often identified and confused with sex. Sexual love is certainly a part of marriage. But only a part because to have the love grow the other components, romantic love and intellectual love, must be present. The amount of each of these loves will vary, because two people love each other as a result of mutual attraction based on a complexity of factors and facets.

For a lasting love relationship, each type of love—romantic, intellectual, and sexual—must be put into proper perspective and balance by the couple itself.

## TO PROMOTE UNDERSTANDING OF THIS CHAPTER

1. What is the difference between love and infatuation?
2. We learn to love just as we learn to eat, walk, and read. Discuss the life experiences that are important in developing the ability to love.
3. How is love diffused to others?
4. What factors are involved when love dwindles?
5. What is narcissism?
6. Love involves empathy with the loved one. Explain.
7. What are the three kinds of love that enhance a mature relationship? Explain each.

## SUPPLEMENTARY READING

BOWMAN, HENRY A., *Marriage for Moderns*. McGraw-Hill, Inc., New York, 1948.

DUVALL, EVELYN M., *Family Development*. J. B. Lippincott Co., Philadelphia, Penn., 1957.

———— *Love and the Facts of Life*. Association Press, New York, 1963.

FROMME, ALLAN, *The Ability to Love*. Farrar, Straus & Giroux, Inc., New York, 1965.

WALLER, WILLARD, *The Family; A Dynamic Interpretation*. The Cordon Company, Inc., New York, 1938.

———— and HILL, REUBEN, *Family*. Dryden Press, New York, 1951.

# 17
# Relationship Between
# Attraction and Dating

Mr. Sports Car hasn't attracted Dad in a favorable way by honking his musical horns. How this action affects his date will be related to the relationship that she has with her father. If she has great respect and regard for her father and wants a boy friend with some of the same values and ideals, then her father's reactions will be very important to her. Thus, Mr. Sports Car just made an error if this is the girl he hopes to continue to date. However, if the young miss is hoping to establish a very different kind of relationship and if she rejects the opinions and attitudes of her father, she may be more attracted to Mr. Sports Car because Dad is upset.

184

*"You're always welcome around here, Hector. I want my daughter to get good and sick of you!"*

In Cartwright's cartoon, the father is quite confident that Hector is not the man for his daughter. He feels that his daughter will recognize this fact if she sees enough of Hector. This wise parent may feel that if he forbids his daughter to see Hector this would make him more attractive to her.

We have all at times wondered why we like some people at first glance, why we have to know some people for a long time before we begin to like them, and why we immediately dislike some people. Our likes and dislikes are not planned by us, but they have a basis in our individual makeup and our past and present experiences.

### PRINCIPLES OF ATTRACTION

According to Duvall and Hill, some of the unconscious tendencies that determine our preferences for people are these:

1. We tend to like the people and the things that remind us of pleasant and comfortable experiences in our past, many of which go way back

185

into our early childhood and are forgotten except for the powerful, unconscious role they continue to play in our choices. "I loved him the minute I set eyes upon him."

2. We tend to be repulsed by the people and the things that are associated with uncomfortable and unpleasant experiences in our past. The original, painful experience may no longer be remembered, but its influence continues to deflect us from anything and anybody that resembles some aspect of that unhappy situation. "Don't ask me why, I just don't like her."

3. We tend to be attracted to those people who reassure us, do not make us feel less worthy or less able or attractive than we like to think we are. "She's much too smart to suit me," or "I can't stand him, he's always so superior," and "She makes me feel as though I am somebody."

4. We tend to seek the people who are considered attractive by those around us and to leave the unsought alone. "I want the kind of girl the other fellow will whistle at."

5. We tend to like those who satisfy some particularly hungry spot in our makeup. The boy who has not had as much mother love as he wanted may be strongly attracted to a mother type of girl.

6. We tend both to reproduce and to repudiate the relationships in which we grew up. A boy may be attracted to anyone who reminds him of his mother and who can reproduce the feeling of the old parent-child relationships. A girl may be unable to tolerate anyone who even remotely reminds her of her father, a repudiation of the former parent-child relationships. "I want a girl just like the girl who married dear old dad," or "I can't stand her. Who does she think she is, my mother?"[1]

In dating, it is very important to be aware of these principles of attraction, particularly if we are attracted to the people who are considered attractive by our friends and peers and if we are repelled by the people who are considered unattractive by our friends and peers. Often when we go with the crowd, we betray ourselves. We should remember that we have individual needs. Conforming to the crowd's standards for a date may not allow us to meet or to date the person whom we can, in the long run, respect and love.

We should also consider our stage of maturity when we reject the date that our parents recommend. We should ask ourselves if we really reject

[1] Evelyn Duvall and Reuben Hill, *When You Marry* (Boston, D. C. Heath Company, 1962), p. 34.

the individual or if we are just negative to parental suggestions because we are trying to establish our independence.

The person who has grown up in a home that met his needs and who wants to reproduce that home has an easier task in dating. He knows the relationships that he wants to create and maintain. He has a pattern to follow. Whereas, the one who rejects his past home relationships looks for something opposite. However, he is always confronted with the questions pertaining to the nature of being "opposite" or "different." He doesn't know what he is looking for because he has no pattern.

This lack of home pattern makes it necessary for one to be more cautious in his search for a mate. Coming from an unhappy or broken home, however, does not mean that one cannot create a happy home. It just means that he needs additional experiences in living before he can establish the kind of home that he seeks.

When men or women are old enough to think of marriage, they may unconsciously seek out mates who resemble their parent of the opposite sex as they remember that parent from childhood days. They also may tend to see their role in the newly-created home as played by the parent of the same sex. Thus, if one is unable to identify with his parents, he must make new identities which makes the task more difficult, but not impossible.

## THE RELATIONSHIP BETWEEN INFATUATION, PHYSICAL ATTRACTION, AND MATURING LOVE

As described in Chapter 16, infatuation may occur when one meets a person who seems to fit the idealized image of the person one hopes to marry. Or it may be that young people are normally so unsure of themselves as they begin to try to act adult that they over-respond to anyone who treats them like an adult. Since girls mature earlier than boys and have fewer obstacles to marriage, an infatuation usually begins with a girl deciding she likes a boy and letting him know it. This makes him feel wonderful, so he thinks she's wonderful. Also, being desired as a partner gives both of them status with their peer groups. Acting as they have seen adults act (mostly on movie and television screens) makes them feel very adult and very good about themselves and each other. Trouble occurs when one or the other, because of preoccupation with his own emotional needs, lacks consideration for the other. The ego is hurt and the growth cycle turns into a vicious cycle unless one or both are mature enough and care enough to say, "I'm sorry"—two of the most important words in our language.

Physical attraction has played a larger role in mate selection—and in divorce—since the automobile and the scuttling of chaperones gave young people the privacy for necking and petting. In her need to assure herself that she is attractive and lovable, the adolescent girl often permits, and even encourages, affectionate exchanges. The continuation of the intimacy tends to stimulate both boy and girl sexually. The male is more easily aroused, but if necking progresses to petting, the girl also may experience sexual desire. This confusion of love-sex feelings leads some young people into premarital intercourse. Others, whose idealism prevents this, are often hurried into marriage. Young people must understand these differences in sexual emotional responses so that they neither drift into sexual intimacy nor rush into marriage. Learning to limit physical demonstration of affection gives love a chance to mature and prevents much heartbreak and ego damage during adolescence.

Maturing love implies an increased capacity to care about the happiness and well-being of another person. Young people who take time to "grow to love" each other usually have more successful marriages than those who "fall in love" as a result of infatuation or physical attraction, although there are elements of both in all love relationships.

Growing to love implies taking time to really learn to know another person, that is, his background, his beliefs, and his attitudes. Getting to know his family, and seeing him interact with them, helps greatly in understanding him. The boy who has a good relationship with his mother, and the girl who is fond of and respects her father tend to relate more comfortably to someone like them. On the other hand, if there is a poor relationship with the parent of the opposite sex, the person may unconsciously be attracted to someone of the opposite personality. For example, a girl who resents a dominating father may choose an indecisive man who lets her dominate the relationship, and then she may resent his inability to make decisions.

Growing to love implies increasingly realistic acceptance of the other as he is, sensing that one is strong where the other is weak, and weak where the other is strong. Each will then need the other and a mutually satisfying, largely nonsexual companionship will develop, to which the sexual intimacies of marriage can be added.

## REASONS FOR DATING

Dating gives the individual a chance to learn the ways of others without committing himself to any permanent involvement. Since he is so largely a product of his own experiences and family environment, each person's ideas of people are conditioned by the characteristics of his parents and close associates. Adequate evaluation of a possible mate means, most often, that individuals outside the family need to be known intimately, and the ways in which they think, act, and plan need to be understood. Only as

188

acquaintance is broadened to include a variety of personalities does the individual free himself from the limitations of choice and action that are unconsciously imposed upon him by his home environment.

Dating also affords the individual an opportunity to improve adequate methods of communication and social maturity with members of the opposite sex. It takes time and experience to develop maturity in the heterosexual stage of psychosexual development. Dating gives the individual a natural experience in which to develop these necessary social graces and competencies.

In addition, dating affords opportunities for the young people to share these adjustments to the responsibilities of adulthood. For example, they become responsible for their conduct together without the watchful eyes of parents or friends. They adjust to the possibilities for entertainment on a date and the limitations imposed by financial funds, transportation problems, and age requirements. They learn to respect differences in choices and decisions and attempt to solve these differences in a mature manner. In short, they are learning to see to the welfare and well-being of the dating partner.

These adjustments may originate in the relationship of the youth to his family, teachers, or peers. They may stem from the adjustments he is required to make in his values or behavior patterns or from his personal feelings about himself. Dating allows an opportunity to interact with others with similar tensions, share his frustrations with them, and be "understood" by those who think as he does.

In other words, the young adult needs to date to share his thoughts, concerns, wishes, ideas, and ideals with a peer member of the opposite sex. This enables him to prepare for an adult relationship. The "bull sessions" around a party table or a camp fire enable dating couples to develop as adults and to share their concerns about the responsibilities of adulthood.

## DATING—PATTERNS AND PROBLEMS

Dating patterns are essentially socially controlled opportunities for young people to learn about potential partners of the opposite sex. Healthy individual development requires a fairly wide exposure to a variety of different patterns so that a wise choice of marriage partner may ultimately be made.

The stages of involvement from least to greatest commitment can be identified as not dating, casual dating with different persons, frequent dates with one person, going steady (for convenience or security), going steady with marriage as a possibility, informal engagement, formal engagement, and marriage.

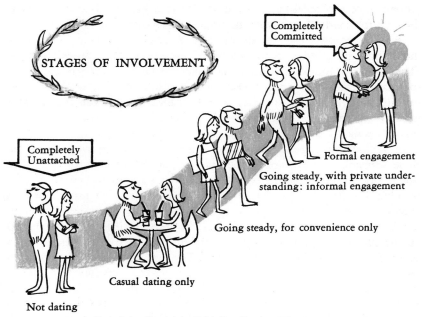

Although dating can be an exciting social experience, it has certain problems inherent in it. Dating, especially in high school, may well be termed pseudo-courtship (*pseudo* means unreal or deceptive), but it is impossible to generalize as to the form this pseudo-courtship takes. Dating varies from community to community and even from one adolescent group to another within the community. In some cases, "going steady" is the peer-prescribed way of dating; in others, going steady is frowned upon.

There are as many reasons for going steady as there are couples who choose to do so. Going steady has advantages in that it gives the individuals concerned an opportunity to get to know each other more fully than is possible in ordinary dating situations. On another level, there is a certain security in knowing that one is guaranteed a partner for all heterosexual social functions.

However, steady dating also has some disadvantages. Young couples going steady may deprive themselves of the right to find the most suitable marriage partner. They may become so deeply involved with their first dating partners that they are psychologically unable to make a change, even if time indicates that theirs is not a relationship that promotes mutual growth and development. While going steady, a girl is typed as being out of circulation and it is not easy for her to get to know other men. Even after the couple "breaks up," it is difficult for the girl to erase the image of being known as her ex-steady's girlfriend and off limits.

Another concern in going steady and, in fact, in all dating, involves the holding of sex to its proper place and proportion in the total relationship. The Judeo-Christian tradition upon which our culture is based emphasizes premarital chastity; the result, very often, is for the individual to experience a conflict between the sex drive, which has come to the fore at puberty or shortly thereafter, and his emotional conditioning about sex. The question may then be raised as to "how far one goes" before marriage in any of the stages of courtship. Sexual drives are cumulative. Once having been given some opportunity for expression, they build progressively toward fulfillment through sexual intercourse. If not given complete fulfillment, the residuum is discontent, frustration, and inner conflict. It is this unresolved residuum that makes heavy petting an unsatisfying and unhappy experience. To suggest that the casual kiss or even the kissing and fondling commonly known as necking is detrimental to a later love relationship is to approach the ridiculous. Whether heavy petting is physically detrimental is open to question, but its harmful psychological effects can very often be identified, especially where a sense of guilt is involved.

Petting is an unsatisfactory means of satisfying the sex drive in courtship for still other reasons. The sexual stimulation that results from such activity, at least where extreme, may well lead the individuals to forget or abandon their original intent to abstain from sexual relations. In such cases, guilt feelings may assume significant proportions. Yet, if petting becomes an end in itself, it tends to limit the values expected to accrue from courtship. Thus the problems related to sexual activity in courtship can be solved only by seeing the situation in its totality rather than in its immediate aspects.

By progressing through the successive stages of dating, young people will gradually discover the person who would be the best potential marriage partner. Time is the key factor in this relationship; young couples should give themselves the advantage of time to know one another. Couples in Hollywood movies have only two hours to progress through the stages of a relationship; couples in real life have lifetimes.

## TO PROMOTE UNDERSTANDING OF THIS CHAPTER

1. Give an example of an experience that you have had that reinforces one of the principles of attraction.

2. How may dating a person considered attractive by the peer group be an advantage? A disadvantage?

3. How might your present home affect your choice of a dating partner?

4. Why does physical attraction play a larger role in mate selection in a country that does not require chaperones?

5. How does learning to limit physical manifestation of affection give love a chance to mature?

6. What is the value of time as a function of dating?

7. What are the disadvantages of going steady?

8. What are the advantages of steady dating?

9. Why is it easier for one who has made a positive identification with his home and parents to establish his own home than for one who refutes his home and parents?

10. What are dating patterns?

11. How can the dating patterns of a community or an adolescent group influence one's life?

12. What are the dating patterns of your group?

## SUPPLEMENTARY READING

DUVALL, EVELYN M., and HILL, REUBEN L., *Being Married*. D. C. Heath & Co., Boston, 1960.

———— *When You Marry*. Association Press, New York, 1962.

GINZBERG, ELI, *Values and Ideals of American Youth*. Columbia University Press, New York, 1961.

GOTTLIEB, BERNHARDT, *What A Boy Should Know About Sex*. The Bobbs-Merrill Co., Inc., Indianapolis, Ind., 1960.

KOOS, EARL LEMON, *Marriage*. Holt, Rinehart & Winston, Inc., New York, 1957.

LERRIGO, MARION O., and SOUTHARD, HELEN, *Learning About Love*. E. P. Dutton & Co., Inc., New York, 1956.

Amos Sewell © 1955 The Curtis Publishing Company

# 18
# Relationship Between
# Sex Codes and Morality

The gentleman with the scythe indicates that there are several possible directions that one might take to reach the sought destination. This is analagous to the many directions and the conflicting values given to youth about sex ethics, sex codes, and subsequent moral behavior. Youth is faced with problems their forebears had no concept of, and certainly did not have to face. On every side society is bombarded with examples of public and private immorality, as though expediency and opportunism were the basis of ethics for most everyone.

Moral choices are not so easy anymore. No longer does society have standard, clear-cut, ready-at-hand answers. Sex has come to play a role in every facet of life. Sex is used to sell everything from refrigerators to automobiles. A provocative appearance is sought by both sexes. Studies and surveys indicate the rise in sexual promiscuity. Newspapers and magazines carry on discussions of the various contraceptive devices; their advantages and disadvantages.

The Judeo-Christian code is taught by adults as the most meaningful code to follow. However, the adult world does not provide enough models who live this code. Adults often live by one standard but talk another—as is evident in the adult world's frustrated and juvenile obsession with sex. This obsession saturates the adolescent world with inescapable and distorted images. Yet the political speech-making and educational sermonizing stress such phrases as "moral and spiritual values" in a way that makes them appear to be a commodity to be bought and delivered—quite apart from the realities of life.

It is quite conceivable that one could get the impression that there are too many detours for a person to develop a set of sex ethics that would lead to what he believes is moral behavior for him. It seems on the surface that such a project would be of no importance if achieved.

## MORAL CODES IN TRANSITION

We must realize that there have always been people who deviated from society's moral codes with regard to sex. We have always had unwed mothers, illegitimate babies, venereal disease, and a variety of sexual practices that lead to sad and serious consequences for their practitioners. Theories on promiscuous behavior are probably as numerous as sexually promiscuous people. The fact that statistics show that this type of behavior is increasing is a problem of grave and great concern.

Premarital sex has a variety of meanings for people. It can symbolize a struggle for independence, a superficial reach toward maturity, a desire to keep up with the crowd. It can be a means of expressing rejection of parents, teachers, or church leaders. It can be an expression of loneliness and a wish for affection, or it can be used as a commodity. It may also occur as an aspect of the commitment of a couple soon to be married.

Today, studies indicate that approximately one-half of all first marriages occur between people in their teens; half of the high-school marriages are occurring because pregnancy happened first, often in exploitative sexual

194

relationships. An estimated 1300 or more adolescents catch venereal disease —syphillis or gonorrhea—every day, comprising 56 per cent of the total number of new daily infections. These young people range in age from 15 to 20 years. Many of these adolescents come from very fine homes where they are given "everything they need," including the cars in which many become infected. Venereal disease is ascending the social scale, while descending the age scale.

The situation today is different because of the rising numbers of people engaging in premarital intercourse. However, it is also different because of the changing social attitude. In the past, those who engaged in premarital intercourse and those who did not were walking parallel paths. They tolerated each other. Today some of those who do not engage in premarital intercourse may even feel selfconscious because they don't; they are not sure that to abstain from sex relations before marriage makes any sense at all, and sometimes they are told so by their age-mates. Also our current empirical thrust in learning gives high priority to experimentation in all areas.

The present-day trends summarized above are validated by research studies. The fact that this is a current trend does not imply that this behavior is positive. The trends are researched so that professional people in the fields that deal with human behavior can understand the trends and find ways to counteract them when it seems necessary. The studies are only first steps to a systematic theory of human sexual behavior. The data confirms the need for further understanding and study.

With a recognition of the widespread confusion on the subject, one either needs to adopt traditional sex ethics and sex codes or develop a code which is personal and which leads to moral behavior. The widespread disregard of traditional codes of sex behavior and the increasing willingness to bring into the open relationships which have previously been considered wrong make it necessary for a person to choose his own course of action. A person's choice will be most satisfactory if he understands the development of the individual and then in turn understands himself in relation to his own developmental stage. Some say that the break from the traditional do's and don't's gives the individual freedom. *Real freedom is being willing to take responsibility for one's actions.*

The responsibility for the adoption of an ethical code of sexual behavior is left up to you. Its success or failure will depend upon your self-understanding, your ability to implement the code in your life, and your capacity to make wise decisions and to assume responsibility for the decisions that you make. You have the freedom of making choices. You, however, must be responsible for your decisions. A consideration of the value of moral codes or ethics should help.

# MORAL CODES AND ETHICS

A moral code is concerned primarily with regulating human behavior in the interest of establishing and maintaining a social order. In this situation, the individual person is significant primarily, if not exclusively, because of his acceptance of the social order, and ultimately, because of his capacity to maintain it.

*Moral codes* imply or state explicitly those modes of behavior that are acceptable and those that are forbidden. A code may also prescribe rewards and penalties. The individual person who is looking for some sort of guidelines by which he may conduct himself has the formally stated rules for what he must and must not do.

If we reflect upon morality, we will realize that, like legal codes, moral codes are rules which have been proclaimed by some authority, usually a leader or prophet. Moral codes become social instruments which impose regulations and restrictions upon the individual members of a group so that in all their activities they will support and carry on the institutions and social practices of that social order.

Moral codes are formulated with the expectation of preventing injury or damage to others—forbidding those actions which long experience has shown to be potentially detrimental to others and the way of living of the group for which the codes are formulated. Moral codes have prevented injustice and injury to others whose property or person would have been exposed to injury or damage by the actions which the moral or legal code forbade (e.g., adultery).

*Ethics* is the science of moral values and duties, the study of the ideal human character. When we and our peer groups talk about our major concerns, hopes, and aspirations and when we reveal our evaluations of current moral codes, we indicate that we are seeking some guides, some *ethics*. One of the major steps in sex orientation is to try to provide some form of self-awareness of your traditional beliefs and personal feeling in regard to sex and your own individual life experience. We are at the mercy of our forgotten childhood only as long as it is forgotten. When we can recall and recognize the source of our beliefs and feelings, we can self-consciously examine them and replace them with others when they defeat their own purpose. But this is more difficult than it seems since our early sex orientation takes place before we can remember and continues to operate strongly in the present as it has in the past.

No one can formulate a sex ethic that will be fully responsive to the aspirations and needs of young people today. Many who would seek such a sex ethic would find it inadequate because it does not provide definite rules or the sanctions to which they have been accustomed in our traditional

196

moral codes. Still others may recoil from the responsibility that an ethic imposes upon them—the responsibility of being aware of and concerned for oneself and other individuals which, as we know, is probably the most difficult task man has attempted.

The crux of a sex ethic is that each individual recognize what he or she may do to another person by any attempted or proposed sex relation. Also a sex ethic emphasizes what a sex relation does to the individual personalities of the people involved.

While we are searching for an ethical orientation for sex, we may invoke enduring religious values as offering the best available criteria for trying to develop this orientation. Insofar as we sincerely believe in the worth of the individual personality and recognize his or her uniqueness and his or her worth as a personality, not as an object or an instrument, we have one dependable criterion for ethical orientation in sex behavior. Moreover, insofar as we genuinely and effectively believe in the dignity of another person whose integrity may not be violated but must be protected and maintained in all human relations, we also have another dependable guide to ethical sex conduct.

## A CASE STUDY

This incident in the lives of two young adults may precipitate discussion that may help you make some personal decisions about your own ethical code.

This is the story of a girl we shall call Linda Ryder. She is 19, and when interviewed she was expecting a baby. She is a blonde girl with violet eyes and a habit of plucking at the long hair which keeps drifting over the right side of her face. She was wearing a simple skirt and white blouse. In spite of her pregnancy there was about her the coltish awkwardness of youth. She was a resident of the Florence Crittenden Home in Washington, D.C.

"They say it's the good girls who get caught," Linda said. "I was always a good girl, except with Joey. It isn't that I didn't know what we were doing. I guess it just never seems like it could happen to me."

Linda lived in a pleasant suburb of Philadelphia. Her father owns a small business in town; her mother is a partner in an interior decorating firm. Linda has a 14 year old brother.

Linda herself was always a pretty, popular girl. She brought friends home and never went with a wild crowd. At the end of her first college term she met Joey. "He was awfully goodlooking and a wonderful dancer, but that wasn't it. It sounds silly, but there was something in

197

his eyes. He'd been hurt a lot, and his home hadn't been happy, and he didn't have any money at all. He was so sad and lonely.

"We just began going together. We read and studied together, and we talked about how much better this was than going out all the time with lots of different people. We used to talk about how this was the good kind of love, not like you get from your parents. I think they love you sometimes as if—well, almost the way a child loves a teddy bear. With us it wasn't like that. We were comfortable, and it really was good —then anyway.

"The rest just happened. We didn't use any—well take any precautions. It wasn't that we didn't know the facts of life. It just didn't seem right to be so businesslike about it."

Last April Linda and Joey made a mistake in timing. Linda had a feeling she was pregnant even before the biological signs. When the signs were unmistakable, her fear exploded into panic: "I cut a lot of classes. I began to go to the movies, why I don't know. I couldn't face telling Mother. And I couldn't bear what knowing about me would have done to Daddy."

Having to confide in someone, she told a more experienced girl friend. "I went to visit her for a weekend," said Linda, "and we tried everything from hot baths to hot gin. For three days I was the cleanest, drunkest pregnant girl in Eastern Pennsylvania. Nothing worked."

Linda lived alone with her knowledge for three weeks. "It seemed more like months," she recalled. "I didn't want to tell Joey, but finally I couldn't stand it anymore. I told him after class one day. He was drinking an orange soda. It's silly to remember that now, but he changed right from that minute. I know it took weeks, but slowly but surely he began to disintegrate right in front of my eyes. Right then all he said was 'Oh, God, no,' and then we walked back to his apartment. We didn't say anything for a long time. I felt I just couldn't reach him any more. Finally I made him tell me what he was thinking, and he said, 'I'm sitting here being ashamed of you. God help me, I'm ashamed of you.'"

During the next awful week Linda and Joey drove to another town, where, under an assumed name, Linda got medical confirmation of her pregnancy. On the ride back they talked about an abortion, but neither of them had the money. "I never really wanted one anyway—not really," said Linda.

"I didn't mention marriage. I was waiting for him to. I didn't even mean it would have to be right then, but all he ever said was that it would be a disaster. Maybe he was scared. You know, it's awful when you know you aren't going to marry someone ever, ever, ever. You start questioning how much you really did love each other.

"From then things just got worse. A couple of times he got really drunk, and once he even asked me how he could be sure the baby was his. I saw him only once after that.

"After we broke up I couldn't study any more at all. Then I had to tell Mother. When I finally got it out she just looked at me and then walked out of the room. When she came back the first thing she said was, 'We can't tell your father. He couldn't stand it.' "

Mrs. Ryder moved promptly on the practical arrangements. Through a family agency in Philadelphia she got maternity-home reservations. Through a friend she got Linda a job to keep her busy. Two months later Mrs. Ryder told Linda it was time to go away—before her father found out or the family's reputation was compromised. "It was sort of an ultimatum," Linda said. They told her father that Linda was going to visit a girl friend who had moved to Kansas. "We said it was because of the courses I'd flunked that I wasn't going back to school for a year," she said. And just about the time she would have been reentering college, Linda, alone again, got on the train for Washington and the Florence Crittenden Home. "There are people here I can talk to, and that helps," Linda said. "It's easier for some people to forgive than for others." Her mother has not been able to get down to see her.

So she waited. The baby would be adopted, Linda said, "because I don't think any unmarried girl has the right to keep her baby, I don't think it's fair to the child.

"It's funny, though, a lot of the girls don't feel it, and I know I don't have the right. But I'm starting to feel like a mother and that this is also a child who will need a mother."

Linda hopes to be able to return to school, perhaps living with an aunt in Philadelphia and working part-time to help pay the bills. Beyond that, she doesn't know. "I want a home. I want to be married. I want children I can keep and love. Maybe that's why I'm here. Maybe I just need someone to love. I've been so lonely. . . ."[1]

## BASIS FOR DECISION

What value standards should one use in his sex behavior? The decision would be so much easier if the man with the scythe had given us just one direction. However, we can point out some of the attitudes, decisions, and actions which seem to be most beneficial to the individuals concerned.

[1] Jonathan Rinehart, "Mothers Without Joy," *Saturday Evening Post,* Vol. 236, No. 11 (March 23, 1963), p. 30. Reprinted by permission of the author.

# TO BALANCE OUR LIVES WE NEED
# TRUST and AN IDENTITY

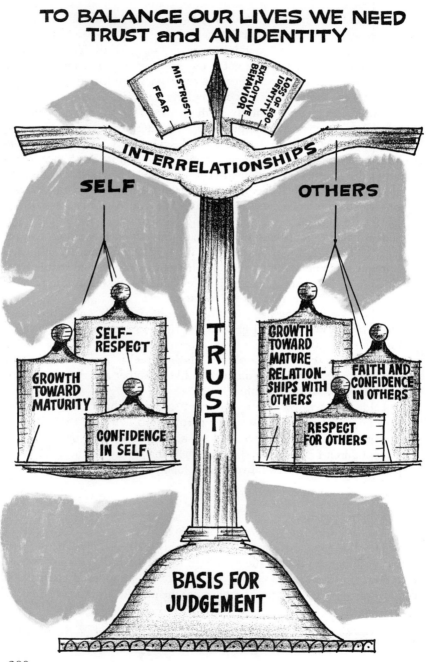

200

If one acts so that he develops (1) increased capacity to trust people, (2) greater integrity in relationships, (3) cooperative attitudes, (4) enhanced self-respect, (5) general attitudes of faith and confidence in people, and (6) fulfillment of individual potentialities and a zest for living, he has acted in the best interest for himself and others. If, instead, his actions produce (1) increased distrust of people, (2) deceit and duplicity in relationships, (3) barriers between persons and groups, (4) resistant, uncooperative attitudes, (5) diminished self-respect, (6) exploitive behavior toward others, and (7) thwarted and dwarfed individual capacities and disillusionment, he is being detrimental to himself and his relationships with other people.

Perhaps another scale or balance that would help in making a decision would be for us to look at the requisites for the maintenance of love. As this author sees it, the requisites for the maintenance of love are these:

1. Involvement in the welfare of the other

2. Loyalty and trust

3. Acceptance of the other with all his faults as well as his virtues

4. Taking delight in him, not for what he ought to be, but for what he is

5. Willingness to put oneself in the other's place and, in addition, a desire to improve and make that place as happy as possible

If an individual acts in accordance with the ideas expressed on these two pages, his relationships with himself and others will be more fulfilling and satisfying. If more people thought about their actions in these terms, perhaps it would then be possible to avoid unfair or hasty judgments concerning moral or immoral behavior.


## TO PROMOTE UNDERSTANDING OF THIS CHAPTER

1. Define moral codes.

2. Define ethics.

3. What is the difference between moral codes and ethics? Which requires the greatest personal involvement?

4. What are the difficulties encountered in formulating sex ethics?

5. What are the guides for ethical sex conduct?

6. What is the main basis for decisions in our sexual behavior?

7. What is the value of research?

8. What advice would you give Joey?

9. Do you think that Mr. and Mrs. Ryder have a companionable relationship?

10. What advice would you give Linda?

11. What decisions do you think Linda should make for her future?

12. How do you account for Joey's attitude toward Linda? Linda's attitude toward Joey?

13. Would Linda have a problem if she had not become pregnant?

14. What problems will Linda face in a future marriage?

15. Will future marriage produce any problems for Joey?

16. Does Joey need help in self-understanding? Why? Why not?

17. If no pregnancy had occurred, would Joey's opinion of Linda been altered?

18. Does freedom carry responsibility? Explain.

## SUPPLEMENTARY READING

ANDERSON, WAYNE J., *How to Understand Sex.* T. S. Denison and Co., Inc., Minneapolis, Minn., 1966.

BLOOD, ROBERT O., *New Roles for Men and Women.* Association Press, New York, 1963.

DUVALL, EVELYN MILLIS, *Love and the Facts of Life.* Association Press, New York, 1963.

———— *Why Wait Till Marriage.* Association Press, New York, 1965.

———— and HILL, REUBEN L., *Being Married.* D. C. Heath and Company, Boston, 1960.

FREEMAN, LUCY, *Why People Act That Way.* Thomas Y. Crowell Company, New York, 1965.

GENNE, ELIZABETH and WILLIAM, *Christians and the Crisis in Sex Morality.* Association Press, New York, 1962.

LORAND, RHODA L., *Love, Sex and the Teenager.* The Macmillan Co., New York, 1965.

RHYMES, DOUGLAS, *No New Morality—Christian Personal Values and Sexual Morality.* The Bobbs-Merrill Co., Inc., Indianapolis, Ind., 1964.

RINEHART, JONATHAN, "Mothers Without Joy." *Saturday Evening Post,* Vol. 236, No. 11 (March 23, 1963), p. 30.

ROSENBERG, MORRIS, *Society and the Adolescent Self-Image.* Princeton University Press, Princeton, New Jersey, 1965.

SUSSMAN, MARVIN B., *Sourcebook in Marriage and the Family.* Houghton Mifflin Company, Boston, 1963.

TRIMBOS, C. J., *Healthy Attitudes Toward Love and Sex.* P. J. Kennedy and Sons, New York, 1964.

*"I'm singing against my daddy!*
*I'm singing against my mom!*
*I'd like to blow them both up*
*with a nuclear-fission bomb!*
*Oh, boom! Tiddy oh boom!*
*Boom; boom, blast!*
*I'd like to blow them both up*
*and be done with them at last!"*

# 19
# The Deviate

Deviancy may be defined as departure from typical, average or model behavior, appearance or attitude. The attitude expressed by the lyrics of the
solitary singer are deviate in their extreme. We shall hope that the young
man dispels his hostile feeling in song rather than in aggressive hostile be-

204

havior. Hostile aggressive behavior, which may be directed against other persons or public and private property, is the most frequent and annoying form of juvenile delinquency.

## KINDS OF DEVIANCY

There are desirable and undesirable forms of deviancy. The desirable forms generally consist of behavior or appearance that contributes to the welfare of society and to the feeling of well-being in people who observe them. Some of these are as follows:

1. Highly developed skill in any of a variety of socially approved areas, such as athletics, drama, dancing, clothing construction and design, conversing, bridge, chess playing, and so forth

2. Creative behavior in the arts

3. Highly intelligent behavior in school

4. Physical beauty or attractiveness

Some of the undesirable forms of deviancy are as follows:

1. Stealing

2. Excessive apathetic behavior such as a person who behaves with general shyness, seclusiveness and self-doubt

3. Psychotic behavior

4. Neurotic behavior

5. Extreme lack of responsibility in relationship to another human being; *e.g.*, illegitimate motherhood, appears in two major forms which are quite different in their personal significance. The teen-age illegitimate mother is deviant partly because of her youth, while the woman in her twenties or thirties is of an age when child bearing is expected. Both are deviant in having a child out of wedlock.

The unacceptable forms of social deviancy obviously should be minimized by society, and the acceptable forms should be maximized. There are, however, several other forms of deviancy whose qualities are at once both attractive and repulsive to many people.

There are four main types of deviancy about which people have mixed emotions or ambivalent opinions. They are:

1. Privatist behavior

2. Girls who have highly developed masculine skills and interests

3. Boys who have highly developed feminine skills and interests

4. Skeptical and critical social attitudes

*Privatist* behavior is part of our current youth culture. Youth communicates with each other in a special language adults may not understand. The culture has roles, values, and ways of behaving all its own; it emphasizes sexual attractiveness, daring, immediate pleasure, disengagement from adult values, and comradeship in a way that is true neither of childhood nor of adulthood. This group then tends to alienate itself from the adult world. This retreat to a world of private and personal satisfactions brings forth an attitude of privatism.

According to Kenneth Keniston, such a person, when he becomes older declines to become involved with political and social problems and prefers to spend his time with art and music. He feels powerless to affect society and turns to things closer to home that he feels able to control. He may value family closeness above meaningful work because he can control things within his family, but not in his occupation. Leisure activities may be more important to him than work because he can control what he does in his free time. Keniston states:

> Many young people expect to find in leisure a measure of stability, enjoyment and control which they would otherwise lack. Hence, their emphasis on assuring leisure time, or spending their leisure to good advantage, or getting jobs with long vacations, and on living in areas where leisure can be well enjoyed. Indeed, some anticipate working at their leisure with a dedication that will be totally lacking in their work itself.[1]

An honor graduate from Mills College expressed a concern over this attitude of privatism. As spokesman for her 156 fellow graduates, she dwelt on an oft-noted paradox.

> In an age during which we have multiplied mechanical means of disseminating information, we are plagued with an inability to communicate and to understand. We have turned in upon ourselves too long and now we feel trapped by our own psyches. The world is too big and too fast for us to feel able to take our places as part of the whole. We have been sectioned off into splinter groups: the blacks and the whites, the

[1] Reprinted with permission of *Daedalus,* Journal of the American Academy of Arts and Sciences, Boston, Massachusetts. Winter 1962, "Youth: Change and Challenge," p. 158.

religious and the skeptics, the American and the rest of the world, the suburban and the rural, the Democrat and the Republican, the liberal and the conservative, the old and the young.[2]

*People who exhibit traits of the opposite sex* are often regarded with some misgivings. Girls who have highly developed masculine skills are generally accepted as tomboys. But after the age of twelve or thirteen, a girl who is a good ball-player or who plays boys' games with boys is often regarded with some doubt. There are other more acceptable athletic skills such as swimming, water skiing, tennis, and golf; but even in these sports, a girl who is regularly more outstanding than boys may be viewed with some skepticism.

Boys who have highly developed feminine skills and interests are regarded with amused tolerance as young children, but if they grow up to talk and act like girls this is generally seen as undesirable.[3]

[2] Norman Ross, "Voice of Youth Addresses the World of Adults," *Chicago Daily News* (June 25, 1966).

[3] Robert Havighurst, "Social Deviancy Among Youth: Types and Significance," in William Wattenburg, ed., *Social Deviancy Among Youth* (The University of Chicago Press, Chicago, 1966), pp. 61–62.

Drawing by Stevenson; © 1966 *The New Yorker* Magazine, Inc.

*"I don't disapprove of dissent, young man. I just
don't happen to know a heck of a lot about it."*

207

*Skeptical and critical attitudes* are regarded normal for young people. Adults want youth to be a time of independent thought and also a time of responsibility. However, draft card burnings, sit-ins and challenges to the authority of campus and government officials are behaviors that perplex society.

The following story can serve as a case study for this type of ambivalent situation.

## MY PROBLEM AND HOW I SOLVED IT—MY SON AND I.[4]

The worst jam Larry ever got into turned out to be a blessing. It showed us both we weren't as far apart as we thought.

One evening about six months ago I came home from work and found a picture of Larry, my 16-year-old son, parading with a group of youngsters in front of our high school. The caption over the picture read, "Students March for Civil Rights." You can imagine how I felt. Surprised, angry, upset—among other things. I couldn't believe that a great boy like Larry would do such a thing to a father like me.

Up to that point I'd never been able to understand why women put themselves through so much soul searching when they have problems. Whenever I'd looked at the articles in this series (my wife gets GH), I used to wonder why women made things so difficult for themselves. It has seemed to me that a businesslike approach—analyze the facts, make a reasonable decision and act on it—would make much more sense.

Well, I've changed my mind since Larry's picture turned up in the newspaper. Since then I've decided that business methods aren't necessarily any help at all when it comes to personal problems. Sometimes you accomplish more by trying to get at feelings than by collecting facts.

Like a lot of fathers and sons, Larry and I had not been especially close to each other. It was mostly my fault, I suppose. I'm in the real estate business, which means I have to work most weekends, when people are out looking for houses. And I'm also involved in several civic groups—the local real estate board, chamber of commerce, Kiwanis, things like that. Larry was busy, too. What with studying and dating and working on the school paper and being a member of the student council—it seemed he was hardly ever home. The upshot was that I hadn't much of a notion what he was up to from day to day. Also, I'd gotten used to letting his mother handle the boy and make decisions when needed. But that newspaper picture took her by surprise too. I

[4] Reprinted by permission from the July, 1966, issue of *Good Housekeeping Magazine*. Copyright 1966, by the Hearst Corporation.

208

guess neither of us knew how strongly he felt about civil rights. Taking the paper with me, I went up to Larry's room. "What's this all about?" I asked.

Larry looked at the photograph. "Hey, I didn't think they'd run that! he said excitedly. That's great publicity!"

"Never mind that, I want to know why you're mixed up in this. Don't you have better things to do with your time? You're a junior now. Shouldn't you be concentrating on more important things, like studying hard and making sure you get into college?"

"But there isn't anything more important," Larry said. "What good is it going to do me to be in college if the country's in a mess?"

That didn't make sense to me at all. In fact, it annoyed me more. "I don't agree that this country is in such a mess," I said. "And suppose it were? Who are you to solve it, with all the experience and wisdom of your 16 years?"

"Okay, so I'm 16," Larry said. "But people my age seem to be the only ones willing to do anything about anything."

"About what, specifically?"

"Why . . . all the things that're wrong," Larry said. "Civil rights . . . poverty . . . peace . . . honesty . . ."

I know youngsters are idealists, but that was a little too much for me. "And all those things are wrong in this town, eh?"

"You know what I mean, Dad," Larry said. "Somebody's got to stick his neck out, wherever injustice exists. We can't just play it safe and easy with our eyes shut to the rest of the country or world."

He was so earnest that for a moment I didn't know what to say. But I did know I didn't want my son to be a professional bleeding heart, so I decided to crack down right away.

"Now you listen to me," I said. "From now on, forget about all this nonsense and concentrate on what you're supposed to be doing. You've got plenty to keep you busy. Stop worrying about the world until you know more about it."

I hated to have to play the heavy that way, but the boy needed to be brought down to earth. Now, I figured, he'd straighten out. Well, as I suppose other parents might have warned me, it turned out I was mistaken. A week or so later a business acquaintance, a man I'll call Dave Jones, telephoned. With a rather nasty edge to his voice he said, "Phil, how about telling that boy of yours to lay off me?"

"What do you mean? What's he doing?"

"Making a lot of trouble for me, that's all," Jones said.

It turned out that Jones owned an empty store next door to his own sporting-goods center. A peace organization wanted to rent the empty space as a temporary headquarters. Jones was reluctant—not, he said, because he was against the group's aims, but because he felt they'd be undesirable tenants from a business viewpoint.

"You know as well as I do what would happen," he said. . . . "There'd be rallies, and pickets from anti-peace groups, and pickets picketing them—all kinds of rows right next door to my own store."

But now Jones was being picketed by the peace group. Among the demonstrators was a group of high school students led by Larry. Jones had explained his position, and finally offered to rent the store if the peace organization would make an additional security deposit to cover possible damage to the premises. But the group had rejected this as "discriminatory."

"All I'm trying to do," Jones said to me, "is protect my business and my property—which I have a perfect right to do. But agitators like your son have the nerve to attack me. . . . From the signs they're carrying you'd think I was ready to drop the bomb myself!"

"Listen, Dave," I said, "kids these days have all sorts of crazy ideas. I didn't know Larry was involved in anything like this. I'll talk to him."

"Well, you ought to for your own sake, if not mine," Jones said. "You carry a lot of weight among businessmen in this town, Phil. There's been talk about putting you up for the town council. It isn't going to do you any good for your boy to keep carrying on this way."

I had another talk with Larry that night that left us both shaken up. First I appealed to his common sense, trying to show him that his actions would only harm him in the long run. Then I asked if he'd known about Jones's offer to rent the store on the basis of the additional security deposit.

"No, I didn't know that," said Larry.

"Don't you think you ought to get the facts before you go off half-cocked?" I asked.

"Maybe you're right," Larry said defiantly, "but that particular fact doesn't change my mind. . . . It just proves that your friend Jones is more concerned with property rights than human rights!"

"For heaven's sake, stop talking in slogans," I said. "It doesn't prove anything of the sort. All it proves is that you have the judgment of a five-year-old."

Larry's face showed me I was getting nowhere. "Listen," I said, trying to be calmer, "there's something else to think about." I tried to put my arm around his shoulder, but he shook it off. "You're putting me in a difficult position with the people I work with in town. A lot of them can't understand why my son should be mixed up in all these causes. Frankly, Larry, there seems to be some talk about running me for

210

office. . . . The way you've been carrying on, people will change their minds."

"So you want me to chicken out on what I believe in so you can be elected . . . or just to make things easier for you and your friends?"

"I wouldn't put it that way," I said. "But I do want you to try to be practical . . . to think like a grown man."

Larry looked at me icily. "Like you?" he asked. Then he turned and walked out of the room.

For the next week or so Larry was as silent and sullen as only an outraged teenager can be—and you know what that's like. For my part, I was disturbed, not just by his behavior, but by my inability to reach him and show him how childish his attitude was. Then one day at a meeting I happened to sit next to Ted Mitchell, the editor of our local newspaper. Not long ago, *The Sentinel* had run a series on young people. I asked Mitchell if he had any good advice left over. He smiled, then sobered. "I guess it's not funny," he said. "I saw your boy's picture with those high school marchers."

"There's been more of the same ever since. I've talked to him, but it hasn't done any good."

"I went through pretty much the same thing with my boy a couple of years ago," Mitchell said. "I guess it's likely to happen to any parent with a bright son or daughter. These days, youngsters are terribly idealistic, and terribly impatient. They think our generation has messed up things—and, let's face it, we *have* messed up a lot. They want to make the world better—right away. You can't argue with their motives."

"Maybe not," I said. "But you certainly have to argue with what they do and how they do it."

"Sometimes you do," said Mitchell, "but you don't get anywhere trying to force your opinions on them. What you've got to do is show them *how*—not *what*—to think. I don't see anything wrong in a boy's standing up for what he believes in, provided he really knows what he's doing and isn't just following the herd."

That's about all Mitchell said, but it was enough to start me thinking along a new track. I found myself remembering a history teacher I'd had when I was about Larry's age—a man who probably had more influence on me than anyone else in my life at that time. I can still see him, pacing up and down in front of the blackboard, pounding away at what he believed in, prodding us to ask questions and dig out facts and to think for ourselves—really *think*—instead of being stampeded into either blind acceptance or blind rebellion.

Maybe that was why Larry and I were at sword's point; I'd been trying to stampede him into my way of looking at things and what I actually

211

was doing was making him more rebellious. Anyway, I knew I'd have to find some way to work things out with him. Otherwise, I'd be losing him.

Things came to a head sooner than I expected. Larry was managing editor of the school-paper. He and the rest of the staff, I learned later, had long been trying to convince the school authorities that their editorials should not have to be approved by the faculty adviser before they were printed. In student-council meetings, Larry had called this a "violation of freedom of the press." He had drawn up petitions demanding an end to "censorship."

Then one day when the paper was scheduled to go to press, both the chief student editor and the faculty adviser were out sick. That same day Larry happened to hear that a Negro science teacher who had been slated to join the all-white faculty was not, after all, going to be hired. What Larry did not know—and didn't even try to find out—was that the man had turned down the job because of a better offer elsewhere. Larry—as usual, long on indignation and short on facts—took advantage of his one day as top dog and wrote a violent frontpage editorial denouncing the school administration for being "reactionary" and "prejudiced."

Of course I wasn't aware of any of this until Larry came to me and asked if he could talk about "something important." Then he told me what had happened. "There's going to be a meeting in the principal's office tomorrow. He wants you to be there if you can."

I suppose my son expected me to chew him out right there and then, and maybe, if this had come up a couple of weeks earlier, that's just what I would have done. But now, though I was appalled at Larry's lack of judgment, I also felt that, bad as the situation was, perhaps he (and I, too) could learn something from it. So I just said of course I'd be at the meeting.

I'll say this for Larry—he's got a lot of guts. He stood there, pale and scared, in front of everybody, and took all the blame without flinching. But even while he admitted his mistake, his bad journalism, his bad judgment, his violation of the rules—he still defended his principles about "censorship." One part of me was furious at him, but another was proud. In the toughest spot he was standing up for what he believed was right. I couldn't let him down at a time like that.

"You realize how serious this is, Larry," the principal said. "You've libeled me, attacked the school administration, embarrassed the faculty as well as the man who turned down the position, and defied the rules of the paper. That's putting it mildly. You know I could expel you."

"Yes, sir," said Larry.

212

There was a silence. Suddenly the principal turned to me. "What do you think about all this?"

Larry glanced at me, then looked away. I knew what he expected me to say. And I did—up to a point. I agreed with everything the principal had said. I said Larry deserved to be punished for his disregard of the rules. I said he needed to be taught the hard way, to be more careful about facts before he pronounced judgments. I said he needed to learn respect for other people's opinions.

"But there are a couple of other points here," I went on. "Larry knows I disapprove of a lot of his ideas and of many things he's said and done recently. But maybe he doesn't know that, in spite of the way he's been going about things, I'm proud that he has ideals and is trying to think for himself. Regardless of what he may think I think, I don't want to slap him down for having an inquiring mind. And I don't want the school to, either. Seems to me that your job, sir, and mine, is to help boys like Larry learn *how* to inquire."

I don't know who was more surprised—Larry, the principal or I. In the silence the principal looked down at his desk, picked up a pencil, crossed his legs. Then he said, "Yes . . . that's true . . . I agree." Another pause, then to Larry, "I'm suspending you from the paper and from the student council for the rest of the term. If your behavior warrants it, I'll consider lifting your suspension next semester."

Out in the corridor a few minutes later, I said to Larry, "That's tough, being knocked off the paper and the council."

Larry swallowed hard and nodded. "But it was worth it. . . . No, I don't mean about the editorial," he added not looking at me. . . . "I mean . . . what you said, Dad. I really appreciate that."

Strange how a man can be embarrassed by the way he feels about his son. "Forget it," I said. Then I corrected myself. "I mean, remember it." I put my arm around Larry's shoulder. This time he didn't shake it off.

## SEXUAL DEVIATION

Sexual deviation is a form of deviancy that most people agree should be prevented if possible. Perhaps the greatest factors in preventing sexual deviation would be (1) an intelligent citizenry which is respectful of psychotherapy in its various forms and ready to urge patients toward help as early as possible and (2) a mobile educational system aware of emotional problems in children when they first appear.

To reduce sexual deviation in adolescence, young people need to develop a proper identification with normal, mentally healthy parents or parent substitutes, in schools, churches, and social organizations. An atmosphere that is neither too restrictive nor too permissive is essential for the healthy sexual development of a child. Among older persons, sexual deprivation (the denial of sexual needs) may be a factor in sexual deviancy, or a disharmonious marriage may occasion the rise of neurosis, which may result in "acted out" or overt behavior.

To help you become a more intelligent citizen, aware of the problems of the sexual deviate, we shall discuss the *types of sexual deviation*. The most prevalent and important type of sexual deviation is *homosexuality* which refers to sexual relations between two adults of the same sex. In a general way, homosexuality refers to a love relation between two males or two females. It may range from an intense love affair in which sexual relations are a significant aspect of the love relation to a temporary sexual contact without affection, endearment or tenderness. Homosexuals are sometimes referred to as "gay" (the term preferred by homosexuals themselves), "queers," "fairies," "fruits," and so on. Women homosexuals are referred to as "Lesbians" or "Lesbia."

*Child molesters* or *pedophiles* are the next most significant type of sexual deviate. These are males who obtain gratification by touching or sexually playing with minor female children, or having the children touch them.

*Peeping Toms* or *voyeurs* are classified as sexual deviates if their gratification is obtained through the act of watching a woman disrobing or by witnessing sexual activity of others. The voyeur wishes to observe sexual activity without being seen himself.

*Exhibitionism* consists of displaying the sexual organ to an unsuspecting member of the female sex. The chief purpose of the exhibitionist is to shock a woman or girl, usually at the time of an erection. The psychological reaction of the female toward whom the exhibition is being made is closely watched by the exhibitor. This is the source of much of the exhibitionist's pleasure and gratification.

*Sadists* (those who derive pleasure from inflicting physical and psychological pain in others) and *masochists* (those who derive pleasure from suffering the pain themselves) are also classified as deviates. They are more likely to come to attention as a result of criminal activity or in the process of treatment of neurotics. The enjoyment of sexual satisfaction through sadistic activity is seen among psychopaths, whereas masochistic satisfaction is more common among neurotics.

*Fetishism* is a type of deviation in which sexual gratification is derived by collecting clothing normally worn by a woman, such as shoes, underclothes and stockings. Occasionally fetishists employ symbols worn by males, as in a recent case where large numbers of cowboy boots were collected by a homosexual.

214

*Transvestism* (dressing up in clothes of the opposite sex) is considered a deviation, even though it may occur on festive occasions such as a homosexual "drag" or party.

*Frottage,* which consists of obtaining gratification from rubbing against clothed women, as in a subway crowd, is a type of deviation not seriously considered by law.

Sexual deviation is not an inborn characteristic. Homosexuality develops as a psychological defense against an enormous (unconscious) fear of the opposite sex with subsequent retreat to members of the same sex for sexual expression. In relation to other types of deviates, the mechanism of deviation serves to erase or to minimize the unconscious fear lurking beneath the surface. For example, the exhibitionist, by his display, strives to overcome his strong inferiority feelings either about his genitals or the meaning of his whole life; the fetishist develops a fixation on an article of female attire as a defense against fear of expressing his sexual desires directly. The intellectual levels of sexual deviates run entirely parallel to that of the general population.

## SEXUAL DEVIATION AND THE LAW

The laws governing homosexuality differ in various states. Often they cover all types of deviations without specific references to homosexuality as such. Furthermore, many state laws make no references to female homosexuality. Chiefly, offenses against public decency, offenses against minors, offenses associated with force, disorderly conduct, or open soliciting for homosexual acts are indictable and punishable crimes.

## UNDERSTANDING SEXUAL DEVIATIONS

This brief description of sexual deviation has been presented to help you understand the significance of the terms connected with deviant behavior.

The goal of most institutions or counselors dealing with the sexual deviate is to help him by reducing his anxieties, modifying his social patterns and hastening his emotional maturation. If an informed citizenry recognizes negative deviancy as a public and social problem and has sympathy for the offenders rather than relying on punitive judgment, progress will result. At the risk of oversimplification, it can be pointed out that social maladjustment, besides involving internal emotional reactions, also results from an individual's inability to cope with the here-and-now of his environment. There are realities of the environment as well as feelings of the individual which must be managed. We have an obligation to try to understand an individual's coping techniques. These coping techniques are

215

the inclinations he brings to bear on problems presented to him by his environment. Coping is a purposeful, problem-solving behavior. We need to ask if the individual's environment allows him an opportunity to develop a worthwhile coping technique for any form of deviancy that he exhibits, whether it is a constructive or a destructive deviancy.

In the development of one's coping ability, the affluence of one's home is not important. A child may live in a home that is favored with wealth and high social position and yet meet with a good deal of rejection. A child may be one of many children in a home judged inferior by sociologists; he may feel that everyone shares and shares alike.

When individuals enter into a relationship in which the usual symbols of status or prestige no longer count so much—when the trappings of wealth, home surroundings, family name, education, rank and the like are for the moment set aside—it can soon be discovered that the most important elements of human existence are not arranged according to the boundary lines of social class or economic status. Fear in the rich person is just as painful as fear in the life of the one who is poor. Rejection has as bitter a taste for the person who lives in a mansion as for the person who lives in a one-room cold-water flat. Anger and love, hope and despair, grief and joy, have the same poignancy in the house that is high on a hill as they have in a home that is deep in the slums.

## TO PROMOTE UNDERSTANDING OF THIS CHAPTER

1.  What is the most frequent form of juvenile delinquency?

2.  What is deviant for one social class or religious group may be normal for another group. For instance, going to college is normal for upper-middle-class youth but abnormal for lower, working-class youth. Can you give other examples?

3.  An educator has said that education for deviancy is as important as education for conformity. How would you explain this statement?

4.  Can you give an example of a person who has an undesirable form of deviancy and how he copes with it? The example may be from fiction if you wish.

5.  Why are people ambivalent about the deviancy of privatists?

6.  How can sexual deviation be reduced in adolescents?

7.  Define the following terms:

| deviate | sadist | transvestism | frottage | pedophiles |
|---------|--------|--------------|----------|------------|
| voyeurs | homosexual | masochists | lesbian | fetishism |

216

8. What are the causes of sexual deviation?

9. Why should young people study deviancy?

10. What are coping techniques?

11. What form of deviancy did the boy in the case study characterize?

12. Do you think his father coped well with the situation? Explain your answer.

13. What needs were important to the son? to his father?

## SUPPLEMENTARY READING

BLAINE, GRAHAM B., and MCARTHUR, CHARLES C., *The Emotional Problems of the Student.* Appleton-Century-Crofts, New York, 1961.

ELLIS, ALBERT, and ABARNEL, ALBERT, *The Encyclopedia of Sexual Behavior.* Hawthorn Books, New York, 1961.

GOTTLIEB, BERNHARDT, *What A Girl Should Know About Sex.* The Bobbs-Merrill Company, Inc., Indianapolis, Ind., 1961.

HAVIGHURST, ROBERT J., "Social Deviancy Among Youth: Types and Significance," in William W. Wattenberg, ed., *Social Deviancy Among Youth.* The University of Chicago Press, Chicago, 1966, pp. 59–76.

JERSILD, ARTHUR T., *The Psychology of Adolescence.* The Macmillan Company, New York, 1957.

KENISTON, KENNETH, "Social Change and Youth in America." *Daedalus,* Vol. 91 (Winter, 1962).

LANDERS, ANN, *Ann Landers Talks to Teen-agers About Sex.* Prentice-Hall, Inc., Englewood Cliffs, N.J., 1963.

ROSENBERG, MORRIS, *Society and the Adolescent Self-Image.* Princeton University Press, Princeton, N.J., 1965.

*Youth: Change and Challenge,* Erik Erikson, ed. Basic Books, Inc., New York, 1963.

# Unit 3

# Understanding Ourselves in the Interrelationship of Marriage

Edward Frascino, *The Saturday Review*

*"Let's get married now while we can still blame our mistakes on our youth."*

# 20
# The Age for Marriage

Unfortunately for many young couples their marriage ends in the divorce courts because of their youth. Too many couples wed without considering the numerous responsibilities of marriage. A happy love within marriage is in fact not easy to come by. It is so different from the love which most people bring to their marriage that it might as well be a completely different emotion. We are speaking, of course, of romantic love, the falling in love and being in love that usually ushers in a marriage.

Love before marriage is romantic love, part-time love, for which dates are arranged. The young couple not only arranges the date and what they will do together but they arrange their feelings and their behavior. They show each other only their nicest, most agreeable, and most interesting selves. Sometimes they show not themselves at all but some other kind of person, someone they would like to be or someone they think their boyfriend or girlfriend would like them to be.

According to Allan Fromme,

> Love, before marriage is a time of great intensity of feelings, and of great awareness of himself, of his joys and pains, his thoughts and feelings, his hopes and dreams. Love before marriage, despite all it claims to be, is largely narcissistic.
>
> Romantic love also exaggerates; it inflates not only the lover's feelings but the qualities he loves in his beloved. And these qualities, however delightful they are before marriage, are usually the kind that will have least importance once the lovers are married. For their courting time is spent in leisure-time pleasures, pleasures which are much enhanced if one's sweetheart is pretty or witty or a good dancer or skier. Obviously these talents will never be so important in their lives again.
>
> The lovers also exaggerate the qualities that first attracted them to each other. And if they discover other characteristics which perhaps they find not quite so attractive, the discovery gives them little pause— the intensity of their love will surely overcome their differences.
>
> In marriage, however, the lovers must not only delight in each other but also work with each other. They are called upon to fulfill all their promises of undying love, at the same time that each is confronted by the everyday reality of the other as a human being. From intense and exclusive self-awareness, each now is forced into daily awareness of the other. The change from pre-marital to marital love is thus to a large degree a conversion from self-love to love of another person. It is a conversion from the idea of love to the reality of love, from an attachment to the idea of marriage to marriage itself.[1]

## READINESS FOR MARRIAGE

Conversion from the idea of love to its reality and conversion from an attachment to the idea of marriage to marriage itself takes maturity in all

[1] Fromme, Allan, *The Ability to Love* (New York, Farrar, Straus & Giroux, Inc., 1963), pp. 274–276. Reprinted with permission of Farrar, Straus & Giroux. Copyright 1963, 1965 by Allan Fromme.

*"I've passed my identity crisis and am ready to fall in love."*

of its forms: emotional, intellectual, social, philosophical, and so on. The old folk belief that early marriages work out well because of the adjustability of youth only had substance in the fixed relations of agrarian societies. In our rapidly changing society, the person who has acquired a greater degree of maturity and a greater breadth of experience is more adjustable than the teen-ager with his limited horizon and circumscribed existence. The experiences of leaving home, preparing for a career, changing communities, meeting and working with strangers, and developing a personal philosophy of life seldom, if ever, come before the twenties. In our society, these experiences contribute to one's adjustability and toward a growth to maturity.

Every state has a certain minimum age at which individuals may marry. In forty-four states the minimum age for males to marry without parents' consent is twenty-one. In thirty-six states the minimum age for girls is eighteen. However, if the parents' consent can be secured, the minimum age for both sexes is somewhat lower. (See Table 1.)

222

# TABLE 1.  SOME LEGAL REQUIREMENTS FOR MARRIAGE IN THE UNITED STATES

Marriageable age, by states, for both males and females with and without consent of parents or guardians. But in most states, the court has authority, in an emergency, to marry so young couples below the ordinary age of consent, where due regard for their morals and welfare so requires.

| STATE | WITH CONSENT Men | WITH CONSENT Women | WITHOUT CONSENT Men | WITHOUT CONSENT Women | BLOOD TEST Required | BLOOD TEST Other State Accepted | Wait For License | Wait After License |
|---|---|---|---|---|---|---|---|---|
| Alabama (b) | 17 | 14 | 21 | 18 | Yes | Yes | None | None |
| Alaska | 18 | 16 | 21 | 18 | Yes | . . . . . | 3 days | None |
| Arizona | 18 | 16 | 21 | 18 | Yes | Yes | (g) | None |
| Arkansas | 18 | 16 | 21 | 18 | Yes | No | 3 days | None |
| California | 18 | 16 | 21 | 18 | Yes | . . . . . | None | None |
| Colorado | 16 | 16 | 21 | 18 | Yes | . . . . . | None | None |
| Connecticut | 16 | 16 | 21 | 21 | Yes | Yes | 4 days | None |
| Delaware | 18 | 16 | 21 | 18 | Yes | No | None | (c) |
| District of Columbia | 18 | 16 | 21 | 18 | None | None | 4 days | None |
| Florida | 18 | 16 | 21 | 21 | Yes | Yes | 3 days | None |
| Georgia | 17 | 14 | ** | 18 | Yes | Yes | None(b) | None |
| Hawaii | 18 | 16 | 20 | 20 | Yes | No | 3 days | None |
| Idaho | 15 | 15 | 18 | 18 | Yes | Yes | None | None |
| Illinois (a) | 18 | 16 | 21 | 18 | Yes | Yes | (g) | None |
| Indiana | 18 | 16 | 21 | 18 | Yes | No | 3 days | None |
| Iowa | 18 | 16 | 21 | 18 | Yes | No | 3 days | None |
| Kansas | 18 | 16 | 21 | 18 | Yes | . . . . . | 3 days | None |
| Kentucky | 18 | 16 | 21 | 21 | Yes | No | 3 days | None |
| Louisiana (a) | 18 | 16 | 21 | 21 | Yes | No | None | 72 hours |
| Maine | 16 | 16 | 21 | 18 | Yes | No | 5 days | None |
| Maryland | 18 | 16 | 21 | 18 | None | None | 48 hours | None |
| Massachusetts | 18 | 16 | 21 | 18 | Yes | Yes | 3 days | None |
| Michigan | 18 | 16 | 18 | 18 | Yes | No | 3 days | None |
| Minnesota | 18 | 16 | 21 | 18 | None | . . . . . | 5 days | None |
| Mississippi (b) | 17 | 15 | 21 | 21 | Yes | . . . . . | 3 days | None |
| Missouri | 15 | 15 | 21 | 18 | Yes | . . . . . | 3 days | None |
| Montana | 18 | 16 | 21 | 18 | Yes | Yes | 5 days | None |
| Nebraska | 18 | 16 | 21 | 21 | Yes | Yes | None | None |
| Nevada | 18 | 16 | 21 | 18 | None | None | None | None |
| New Hampshire (a) | 14(e) | 13(e) | 20 | 18 | Yes | . . . . . | 5 days | None |
| New Jersey (a) | 18 | 16 | 21 | 18 | Yes | Yes | 72 hours | None |
| New Mexico | 18 | 16 | 21 | 18 | Yes | No | None | None |
| New York | 16 | 14 | 21 | 18 | Yes | Yes | None | 24 hrs. (h) |
| North Carolina (a) | 16 | 16 | 18 | 18 | Yes | Yes | None | None |
| North Dakota (a) | 18 | 15 | 21 | 18 | Yes | No | None | None |
| Ohio (a) | 18 | 16 | 21 | 21 | Yes | Yes | 5 days | None |
| Oklahoma | 18 | 15 | 21 | 18 | Yes | No | None | ** |
| Oregon | 18 | 15 | 21 | 18 | Yes | No | 7 days | None |
| Pennsylvania | 16 | 16 | 21 | 21 | Yes | No | 3 days | None |
| Rhode Island (b) | 18 | 16 | 21 | 21 | Yes | No | None | None* |
| South Carolina (a) | 16 | 14 | 18 | 18 | None | None | 24 hrs. | None |
| South Dakota | 18 | 16 | 21 | 18 | Yes | No | None | None |
| Tennessee (b) | 16 | 16 | 21 | 21 | Yes | Yes | 3 days | None |
| Texas | 16 | 14 | 21 | 18 | Yes | Yes | (b) | None |
| Utah | 16 | 14 | 21 | 18 | Yes | Yes | None | None |
| Vermont (a) | 18 | 16 | 21 | 18 | Yes | . . . . . | None | 5 days |
| Virginia | 18 | 16 | 21 | 21 | Yes | Yes | None | None |
| Washington | 17 | 17 | 21 | 18 | (d) | None | 3 days | None |
| West Virginia | 18 | 16 | 21 | 21 | Yes | No | 3 days | None |
| Wisconsin | 18 | 16 | 21 | 18 | Yes | Yes | 5 days | None |
| Wyoming | 18 | 16 | 21 | 21 | Yes | Yes | None | None |
| Canal Zone | 17 | 14 | 21 | 18 | None | None | None | None |
| Guam | 18 | 16 | 21 | 18 | None | None | None | None |
| Puerto Rico | 18 | 16 | 21 | 21 | (f) | None | None | None |
| Virgin Islands | 16 | 14 | 21 | 18 | None | None | 8 days | None |

(a) Special laws applicable to non-residents. (b) Special laws applicable to those under 21 years; Alabama—bond required if male is under 21, female under 18. (c) 24 hours if one or both parties resident of state; 96 hours if both parties are non-residents. (d) None, but male must file affidavit. (e) Parental consent plus Court's consent required. (f) None, but a medical certificate is required. (g) Wait for license from time blood test is taken; Arizona, 48 hours; Illinois, 1 day. (h) Marriage may not be solemnized within 3 days of blood test.

The World Almanac, 1967, p. 686

There are three obvious reasons for such control. Each married couple represents a new family unit. If those who marry are too young to assume financial responsibilities for the new family unit, then their families or other groups must assume them. The establishment of a new family also means the shouldering of the emotional responsibilities involved. If those who marry are too young to have emotional maturity, there is an increased chance that these responsibilities cannot be met. Also, the establishing of a family very often results in an early pregnancy. Those who marry too young are often not able to fulfill their physical and psychological obligations to the child. For example, the incidence of maternal and infant deaths is higher among women who become mothers in their sixteenth year than for those who bear a first child in their twentieth year. Such deaths are due to two factors: (1) many births of babies of sixteen year-olds take place under unfavorable circumstances and (2) the very young mothers are often not biologically ready for the processes associated with pregnancy and natality. Thus society must try to regulate the age of marriage to be sure that family units can take care of their share of individual responsibility.

## CURRENT CONCERNS ABOUT AGE AND MARRIAGE

Statistics compiled from many sources indicate that American youth are marrying at earlier ages than ever before and that the United States has one of the highest marriage rates in the Western World. There is always a close relationship between marriage rates and affluence. As economic conditions improve, the number of marriages increases; as economic prosperity declines, so does the number of marriages.

Young married couples in the United States are younger and closer in age at first marriage than are those in any other urban industrialized country in the world. In 1960, the median age[2] was 22.8 for grooms and 20.3 for brides. More men married at 21 than at any other age, and more women at 18.

However, in our affluent society an individual's earning power is closely correlated with advanced education. The individuals who marry at an early age often curtail their earning power or at least make it more difficult to attain the educational level that will merit a higher income.

Hugh Carter of the Public Health Service: National Center for Health Statistics (formerly the National Office of Vital Statistics) and Paul C.

---

[2] Median age: that age which divides a group into two equal parts. In terms of marriage, this means that half the grooms were under 22.8 years and that half the brides were under 20.3 years.

Glick of the Bureau of the Census, in a study of the relationship between the age of marriage and education attainments made these statements:

> Within a given economic setting, not all groups have equal opportunities to marry or to obtain an education, and not all groups attach the same values to marriage and to educational achievement. Men in the middle and upper economic strata tend to have not only a high amount of education but also a high marriage rate, an above-average age at marriage, and a low divorce rate. These facts suggest that circumstances which encourage persons to continue successfully through high school or college and to postpone marriage past teen age also discourage them from dissolving their marriage by divorce.
>
> Persons who discontinue their education before they complete high school tend also to have low incomes and high rates of marriage dissolution by separation, divorce, or widowhood. In addition, they have more than the average number of children. Thus, persons in the lower educational strata face the cumulative effect of higher birth rates and lower incomes—plus such associated conditions as poorer health, need for larger living quarters, and smaller likelihood of assistance from the older generation. These conditions place a heavy strain on the family relations of that segment of the population which has the poorest educational background.[3]

## EARLY MARRIAGE

The trend toward early marriage seems to indicate some emotional problems. Because of the additional time needed in preparation for adulthood in a highly technical and sophisticated society, as discussed in Chapter 12, young people often marry with the hope of escaping from their feelings of boredom, jealousy, fear, and loneliness. The boredom comes from early steady dating and the trend that keeps the same couples seeing each other, in the same clique, doing the same things. To escape this boredom, marriage appears as an exciting adventure. The current emphasis on large weddings and the many social functions surrounding the wedding certainly make the young couple the center of an exciting adventure. Admittedly marriage is an exciting adventure, but hopefully it lasts a lifetime. In order to allow it to be an adventure filled with the richness and vastness of a

---

[3] Paul C. Glick and Hugh Carter, "Marriage Patterns and Educational Level," *American Sociological Review,* Vol. 23, No. 3 (June, 1958), p. 300. Reprinted with permission of the American Sociological Association.

growing human experience, one must be prepared. To use marriage as an escape from youthful boredom is not preparation for marriage. Unfortunately, the bored youth will probably make a boring husband or wife. The most striking characteristic of the people who find love and happiness is a sparkling, outgoing zest for life. They are not escapees from boredom.

Jealousy as an emotion that leads to teen-age marriage takes several forms. In some of our high schools, it becomes "the thing to do" to receive an engagement ring at the Junior Prom. Marriage after graduation is a natural consequence. Often the desire for marriage and the assumption of the responsibilities of a home are not the real reasons for the marriage. Instead the couple wish to be in the limelight as much as some other members of their peer group. Also, when an individual has not matured enough to accept and understand himself, he may feel that his present girl is the only girl he will ever be able to interest. Fear and jealousy may force a youthful marriage. He is jealous and fearful if his girl talks to other boys. To escape from these emotions, he sees marriage as a way to make her true to him.

Many young people "go steady" with somebody that they are not really in love with because they are afraid to go to parties or dances alone. The teen-age emphasis on couples also makes them stay together because in some instances if you haven't someone to go with, you're not included in the peer group activities. Fear of being an unwanted person, fear of being alone, fear of facing adult responsibilities alone, fear of meeting new people, and fear of growing sexual desires often are factors in early marriage. Marriage, however, doesn't destroy these fears. The fear instead destroys the marriage. This fear robs a young person of the experience, the gratification, and the thrill that comes from being an individual in his own right. Marriage takes two individuals who can stand on their own feet and build a solid foundation for their life together.

Loneliness is akin to boredom. Loneliness boils down to having "nothing to do." Many people are lonely because they haven't learned to use their talents; to relate with others. Two together can be as lonely as one. If both haven't learned to communicate, they have nothing to talk about or suggest as an activity, and the time drags. Translate this situation into two lonely people made even more lonely by rushing into marriage which they had hoped would give them something more.

Many studies have been conducted on the factors that have contributed to youthful marriages. Some of these factors are results of the emotional problems discussed above. Briefly these factors are the following:

1. An escape from an unhappy school, community or home situation. Some young people are asked to achieve in school beyond their ability or interest . . . they see marriage as an escape.

2. Marriage and the acceptance of family obligations are seen as providing immediate satisfaction in the pursuit of personal happiness.

Two quotes from married high school girls interviewed in Iowa by Lee Burchinal illustrate this view of marriage:

> "I've had no fun since I was married. I've missed several years of important living, the dating period, living with another girl, being away from home, working. I wouldn't get married so young again. I'd probably marry him when I was about 20. I was in love with him. He was so anxious to get married."
>
> "We've had a lot of trouble. We weren't ready for the responsibility. We shouldn't have married so young. We should have waited until after high school at least. We thought we were in love, we would get married and have good times. We had a very poor idea of what marriage was. We thought we could come and go, do as we please, do or not do the dishes, but it isn't that way."[4]

3. The romantic and glamorous image of marriage and unrealistic overevaluation of marriage gives encouragement to youth to marry young.

4. The bandwagon effect; one marriage contributes to another and soon "everybody is doing it."

5. The continuation of the draft fosters youthful marriage . . . through the fear of separation and loss.

6. The reduction of economic risk in marriage as a result of current affluence, parental contributions, occupational fringe benefits including health and hospitalization plans, and employment of wives.

7. Stimulation of sexual drives by sex appeals and the intense physical expression of love in our mass media lead to difficulties in handling sexual arousal. Increased "forced" marriages are the result of the inability or unwillingness to postpone sexual gratification until after marriage.

Unfortunately, the seven factors above and their accompanying emotional problems that lead to youthful marriage are all characteristics that are more likely to contribute to unsuccessful than to successful marriage. When a marriage is unsuccessful, many segments of society suffer. The two individuals involved suffer from emotional insecurity, a feeling of failure in an undertaking that they hoped would be idyllic. The professional world suffers from the loss of the intellectual development of the individuals.

---

[4] Lee G. Burchinal, "How Successful Are School-Age Marriages?" *Iowa Farm Science* (Ames, Iowa, Iowa State University, March 31, 1959), pp. 7–10.

Society suffers from the loss of a contributing family unit. The children of such a unit suffer the most because they lose their identity—the identity of belonging to a particular family unit that contributes to their basic physical and psychological needs. As we studied in Chapter 1, these are the foundation-stones for all of our individual growth and development.

Individuals and society, particularly in our culture, suffer severely from an unsuccessful marriage. Therefore, it is important that young people as individuals and as couples planning marriage have the knowledge of the factors that lead to happiness in marriage, the pitfalls that must be guarded against, and the relationships that must prevail.

Marriage is an important institution. As Louis Kaufman Anspacher said, "Marriage is that relation between man and woman in which the independence is equal, the dependence mutual, and the obligation reciprocal."[5]

## TO PROMOTE UNDERSTANDING OF THIS CHAPTER

1.  What is the difference between romantic love and marital love?
2.  What are the qualities that contribute to a successful date that do not contribute to a successful marriage?
3.  What are the qualities that contribute to a successful marriage?
4.  What contributes to a readiness for marriage?
5.  Why is there control on the legal age for marriage?
6.  What are the societal causes of youthful marriages?
7.  What are the emotional causes of youthful marriages?
8.  How do the societal and emotional causes of youthful marriage reinforce each other?
9.  What are the influences of an unsuccessful marriage?
10. One cannot really put an age on marriage because maturity is the quality most needed. However, age contributes to maturity. Thus age is arbitrarily used. How would you solve this problem?
11. Can you think of any advantages of youthful marriages?

## SUPPLEMENTARY READING

BURCHINAL, LEE G., "How Successful Are School-Age Marriages?" *Iowa Farm Science,* Iowa State University, Ames, Iowa (March 31, 1959), pp. 7–10.

[5] John Bartlett, *Familiar Quotations* (Boston, Little, Brown & Co., 1948), p. 879.

FROMME, ALLAN, *The Ability to Love.* Farrar, Straus and Giroux, New York, 1963.

GLICK, PAUL C. and CARTER, HUGH, "Marriage Patterns and Educational Level." *American Sociological Review,* Vol. 23, No. 3 (June, 1958), pp. 294–300.

LANDIS, JUDSON, and LANDIS, MARY, *Personal Adjustment, Marriage, and Family Living,* 4th ed. Prentice-Hall, Inc., Englewood Cliffs, N.J., 1966.

LEVINE, LOUIS S., *Personal and Social Development.* Holt, Rinehart, and Winston, Inc., New York, 1963.

OGBURN, W. F. and NIMKOFF, M. F., *Technology and the Changing Family.* Houghton Mifflin Co., Boston, 1955.

SAKOL, JEANNE, *What About Teen-Age Marriage?* Julian Messner, Inc., New York, 1961.

SUSSMAN, MARVIN B., *Sourcebook in Marriage and the Family.* Houghton Mifflin Co., Boston, 1963.

*"When you told me you wore a wig, I naturally assumed...."*

# 21
# Mate Selection and Marriage Plans

A bald-headed wife would no doubt be a shock to the groom, but there are other sources that can contribute to the disenchantment that many people experience after marriage. Two of these sources in particular require elaboration: the tendency to misperceive the "loved one" prior to marriage, and the expectations of the marital relationship. These misperceptions have several possible sources. First, the dating and courtship may have involved only fun. The couple may have known each other only under the most favorable circumstances; this provided only a limited basis for knowing the many aspects of individual make-up that are important in the marital relationship. Second, the person may be desperate in his search for a perfect relationship. This desperation is sometimes related to anxieties about remaining unmarried, which are common in our culture. Thus, this need to be loved by a perfect person may result in the distorted perception of the loved one as being that person. Third, the loved one may be regarded as possessing the actual or wished-for qualities of persons who have been loved in the past. Mr. Groom in the cartoon should cheer up because it is easier for his bride to put on a wig than to develop new characteristics.

## CHOICE OF MATE

The most successful marriages seem to develop between people who share the same basic social, religious, educational, and economic values. Opposites may attract at a party, but usually repel under the vicissitudes of daily living.

All marriages are "interfaith" marriages to some degree, for our real "faith" results from our life experiences, and no two people have the same experiences. People who grow up in the same religious group are likely to have more experiences and beliefs in common. Yet, difference in religious devotion by two people of the same faith can also be a serious problem. All marriages have difficulties. Interfaith, international, interracial, or interclass marriages have all the problems of the typical marriage, plus the special problems of their differences.

Educational similarity of husband and wife is also desirable. Statistically, women who marry men with considerably less education are among the most unhappily married women in our culture. Exceptionally bright girls have a hard time finding men who will respect rather than resent them. In part, this may be due to a school system that forces boys to compete with girls who are more mature than they are during the elementary and junior high school periods. When the boy starts dating, it is usually with a younger girl. The early developing girls and late developing boys have the hardest time feeling accepted.

Money problems are among the most common in marriage. There is never enough money to satisfy all desires, and unless the couple learns to cooperate in the spending of it, there is trouble. Each partner has grown up in a family that has chosen to spend its money to satisfy certain values, and each tends to feel that this is the proper use of money. Families with different incomes tend to value different things, as do certain ethnic and religious groups. If a person marries someone with values similar to his own, there is likely to be less conflict in the use of money.

231

*"May we interrupt this program for a brief word from you?"*

Couples naturally find it easier to adjust upward to freer spending than downward because the husband's earning power does not equal that of his or her father. If both husband and wife work, they may be able to maintain their high spending patterns. But if the wife becomes pregnant and they are cut to a single income at the very time that all basic expenditures are increased by the growing family, they may be in for real trouble, particularly if they are heavily in debt because of installment buying. If the child was unplanned, or is unwanted, the parents may unconsciously resent his coming and the drastic change it makes in their way of life. This may be part of the "first child problem" that is fairly common in our society.

## THE IDEAL VERSUS THE CHOSEN MATE

Anselm Strauss investigated to see if people are influenced in their choice of an actual mate by their image of an ideal mate.[1] The term "ideal mate" refers to the image or images which a person of a marriageable age may have of the kind of person he would like to marry.

Data were gathered from 373 engaged or recently married persons (200 women, 173 men), who filled out a detailed questionnaire concerning their

[1] Anselm Strauss, "The Ideal and the Chosen Mate," *Sourcebook in Marriage and the Family,* Marvin B. Sussman, ed. (Boston, Houghton Mifflin Co., 1963), pp. 120–124.

ideal and actual mates. Data were collected also from 50 engaged or recently married women. The group was composed of people who were in their twenties, of college level, white, and American. In addition, at least one person of each couple included in the study resided at one time in Chicago. Keeping in mind that the findings just given may have application only to this kind of population, here is a summary of how the ideal image affected mate selection:

1. An overwhelming proportion of individuals (59.2 percent) judged that their mates came very close to, or were identical with their physical ideal; an even larger proportion (73.7 percent) believed that their fiances were close to, or identical with, their ideal of personality.

2. For individuals who admired their parent of the opposite sex, the ideal was often patterned after that parent.

3. The ideal was also linked with the subject's own personality. The individual psychological necessities, such as a need for recognition, approval, gentle consideration, emotional support and the like, whether consciously or unwittingly sought, quite understandably entered into the individual's anticipations of married life and more or less determined his ideal.

You have no doubt already recognized that the findings of this study support the principles of attraction discussed in Chapter 17.

## THE FORMAL ENGAGEMENT

When two people announce their engagement, they are telling the world, their families, and their friends that a new relationship exists. The more personal problems can now be talked about and plans can be made. The engaged couple seems to need to become accustomed to the idea of "belonging together" before they have to live together twenty-four hours a day. Each has a new status as a family member in the other's family, and both of them need time to become members of the larger family of in-laws. Taking time to court the family and relatives probably reduces in-law problems later.

Another factor in the period of engagement is that mothers need time to plan the wedding. This is one of the rewards that make up for many of the problems of rearing a family. Taking the time to plan the wedding and trying to fit together everyone's dream for this day makes it possible for both mother and daughter to be treated royally and come through it as two adults who can enjoy each other in a mature way.

Statistically, the longer the engagement, the better, up to two years. But it is not really "how long" the engagement lasts that is important, but how well the young people get to know each other's ideas, ideals, and aspirations for their life together as a married couple. If they have known each other a long time, the engagement can safely be shorter. Few divorces occur when two people have gone steady for a year and then have been engaged a year before marriage.

However, for two people who see a good deal of each other, an engagement of more than a year can become increasingly frustrating. The longer they are together, the more intimate, affectionate, and passionate they tend to become. Those who of necessity face a long engagement must learn to limit their intimacy and keep their sights on their values.

## IMPORTANCE OF PRE-MARITAL COUNSELING AND EXAMINATIONS

The blood test is the only medical requirement demanded by law in most states. However, the pre-marital examination is recommended for both the man and the woman. A comprehensive pre-marital examination includes, besides the physical examination and a blood test, counseling with regard to attitudes that may interfere with marital adjustment and an inquiry into family background.

Pre-marital counseling by trained school persons, clergymen or other professionals, social workers, psychologists and related professionals is most advantageous. The pre-marital counseling is a personal course of instruction, adapted to prepare young people for marriage by giving special attention to the individual background and specific needs of the couple concerned. In general it includes: (1) personality and emotional stability tests and interviews to study the characteristics, temperament, disposition, and emotional inclinations and attitudes of the people involved, (2) a review of family and personal backgrounds to locate any important factors that may influence marriage and avert avoidable mismating, (3) an opportunity to ask questions about sex in order to clear up any misconceptions and fears, and (4) instruction in the healthiest approach to marriage, its problems and responsibilities as well as its possibilities for growth and development.

The detailed physical examination is desirable because it gives the couple information on their physical condition at the time of marriage. It may also lead to the correction of any physical ailments that they have as well as telling the couple what their chances are for having children and whether difficulties might be involved in child bearing.

The physical examination should occur far enough in advance of the wedding to make it possible to carry out the physician's recommendations without excess haste. It is wise for the couple to feel free to ask the physician anything they do not understand in connection with sexual adjustment and reproduction. In some cases this discussion will pertain to contraception. The doctor can then make recommendations when he knows their medical history and their aspirations as a couple.

The blood test required by law is to insure that each member of the couple is free from venereal infection. This requirement is necessary because of the serious effects venereal diseases have upon the individual and particularly the children born of such a union. Syphilis and gonorrhea are the two most serious venereal infections.

A corkscrewlike organism called a spirochete is the cause of syphilis. This germ is caught from the infected person at the point of contact. Since syphilis is usually contracted from a person with the disease through intercourse, it usually appears in the genital area. A few days after the infection a hard sore called a chancre (pronounced shanker) appears at the point of infection. The second stage of skin rash and patches on the mucous membrane follows. These symptoms, however, may go unnoticed or be disregarded by the infected person. After these pass, the disease may be latent for months or years, after which severe damage to the central nervous system (brain and spinal cord), the blood vessels and heart, or other vital organs may cause insanity, paralysis, and death. A baby born of a syphilitic mother may contract congenital syphilis. Syphilis is diagnosed by the Wassermann or Kahn blood test.

Gonorrhea in men is the most frequent cause of male sterility, since it produces closure of the tubes of the epididymis. Gonorrhea in women has its start as an infection of the urethra and cervix. The early symptoms of gonorrhea are painful and frequent urination, and a lemon-yellow discharge from the site of the infection. The gonococci (germs of gonorrhea) can cause an infection and blindness in babies born of an infected mother.

The use of sulfa or penicillin has effectively treated gonorrhea infection. But for a speedy and complete recovery it must be treated early. Gonorrhea is diagnosed by the microscopic examination of a smear from the cervix and urethra.

Because of the serious effects of these diseases, the law in most states requires the examination of blood samples from both men and women before marriage for presence of venereal diseases. Since these are contracted through sexual intercourse with an infected person, persons who have not had such contact have no worry.


## THE HONEYMOON

The honeymoon is a time for the young couple to establish themselves as a new family unit. It is a time to develop the conjugal love that is made up of romantic love, companionship, interdependence, mutual respect, and trust.

The honeymoon should be free from financial worry. Thus the honeymoon should be of a cost in keeping with the couple's standard of living. If the honeymoon is too expensive and too elaborate in comparison with the life that the pair will lead upon their return, it may fail to fulfill its function of enabling them to make the easiest transition to married life and may result in a let-down feeling. Romantic as it may sound to have an elaborate and unusual honeymoon to look back upon, it is not conducive to marital happiness to have one's present and permanent situation compare too unfavorably with the first few days of marriage. The first year of marriage has enough expenses without the financial burden of a honeymoon that was taken with a "fly now—pay later" attitude.

## THE VALUE OF ADEQUATE PREPARATION FOR MARRIAGE

This chapter has discussed the conventions of engagement, marriage preparation, and the honeymoon. We have emphasized that an adequate courtship may enhance a more realistic choice. Some people have romantic ideas of an ideal husband or wife, a synthesis of twenty-four-hour beauty, brilliance, charm, perfect health, a never-sinking bank account, poise, versatility, and vivaciousness. Since there is probably no such living person, the one whom they marry, no matter who he or she may be is a disappointment. Likewise, married existence is real and lifelike; if faced and responded to, it challenges one's adaptability to life. If viewed, however, from a standpoint of false idealism it may be imperfect and ugly. There are meals to prepare, laundry to do, messy children, broken china, and tense moments contrasted to the more romantic episodes that are more apt to be the theme of daydreams.

Hasty marriages are inadvisable. Young married couples should go through a period of courtship long enough to learn if they are irritated or pleased by the behavior of their "loved one." They should see each other in many situations and compare each other with many others of the opposite sex. Happier marriages are based on longer periods of acquaintance and engagement as contrasted with an acquaintance of a few months. A marriage that is contracted too early or too impulsively does not allow a sufficient period for an ideal test of compatibility.

The popular singer and song writer, Oscar Brown, Jr., in his song "Time" expresses his idea of the value of time. Time is the one factor that allows us the opportunity of knowing ourselves. It is the only thing in which we are all equal. We don't have the same good or bad looks, abilities, or talents, but we all have a day composed of twenty-four hours, a year

236

of twelve months. In planning for our future and particularly in planning for our marriage, we need to give ourselves time; time to grow, time to learn, time to understand.

"TIME"

*By Oscar Brown, Jr.*

Once time was quantity untold
Just there to try my patience
But time has turned as I've growed old
And altered our relations
It started as my life long mate
Albeit quite a boor
Big lump on which I had to wait
And always there'd be more
Time, time, time, time.

'T'was time I figured for a fool
And time I used to curse
In knowing time is nature's tool
To school the universe
Time being a twinkle in my eye
Assured me I was cute
Then played the maiden fleeting by
With me in hot pursuit
Time, time time.

With time I grew more wise and strong
And as I hit my stride
Time brought experience along
To serve me as my guide
Experience it was in fact
That led me to the truth
By taking me behind time's back
To view my dying youth
Time, time.

Old time had taught my youth to flee
And with my youth had flown
But now my youth was left to die
As time flew on alone
I begged my youth, don't die like this
Remain with me awhile
Time turned and gave us both a kiss
And youth died with a smile
Time.

### Coda

You killed my youth I cried
A crime too frightful to be true
Yes, "Happy Birthday" shouted time
And "Happy New Year too."

## TO PROMOTE UNDERSTANDING OF THIS CHAPTER

1. What are two of the main sources of disenchantment that many people experience after marriage?

2. What are the important things that must be considered in the choice of a mate?

3. What is meant by the statement that all marriages are interfaith marriages?

4. How does the image of an ideal mate affect the actual mate selections?

5. What are the functions of a formal engagement?

6. What determines the length of the engagement?

7. Why does the law in most states require a blood test?

8. Write a list of questions that a young couple might ask a marriage counselor; a physician; a lawyer.

9. Why is a physical examination before marriage important?

238

10. What are the effects of syphilis? of gonorrhea?

11. Why is a honeymoon important?

12. What considerations should a couple make when planning a honeymoon?

## SUPPLEMENTARY READING

BOWMAN, HENRY A., *Marriage for Moderns,* 5th ed. McGraw-Hill, Inc., New York, 1965.

BUTTERFIELD, OLIVER, *Marriage and Sexual Harmony.* Emerson Books, New York, 1957.

CALL, ALICE L., *Forward Adulthood.* J. B. Lippincott Co., Philadelphia, 1964.

DUVALL, EVELYN MILLIS, *Facts of Life and Love for Teen-Agers.* Association Press, New York, 1956.

———— and HILL, REUBEN, *Being Married.* D. C. Heath and Co., Boston, 1960.

———— *When You Marry.* Association Press, New York, 1962.

HOEFLIN, RUTH, *Essentials of Family Living.* John Wiley and Sons, Inc., New York, 1964.

McKINNEY, FRED, *Psychology of Personal Adjustment.* John Wiley and Sons, Inc., New York, 1960.

*Sourcebook in Marriage and the Family,* SUSSMAN, MARVIN B., ed. Houghton Mifflin Company, Boston, 1963.

*"Oh, I don't mind. After all, she helps me make the beds."*

# 22
# Role Expectation in Marriage

Role expectation is a predictor of role satisfaction. If individuals bring to their marriage diverse ideas of their individual roles in the new relationship, they will experience conflict unless their role expectations reach a closer proximity. The cartoon characters may be both very satisfied or very unsatisfied if their activities are not related to their role-image in marriage.

240

Men and women and the roles of each are cultural products. A great deal of socialization is required to form the personality and role expectations of each sex. In most cultures, male and female subcultures are different, and an individual growing up in one subculture is never quite at home in the other, no matter what the biological sex category is. The boy becomes a man by participating in the male subculture and imitating males; the girl becomes a woman by living in the female subculture and imitating females.

One of the major functions of any society is to develop the personality and role-expectations of male and female in such a way that the majority of individuals will become identified in psychological orientation and social interests with the roles and expectations of their own sex. In the past, this was done so automatically that neither the society nor the individual was particularly aware of the conditioning process. Usually a person forgot by adulthood, the steps by which he or she was inducted into the sex roles of male or female.

## TRADITIONAL ROLES

The traditional roles played by male and female were distinguished by station and a division of labor. Physical strength, the biological sex differences, and social and cultural attitudes towards differences were all factors here. Men went out to hunt and conquer, explore, and organize. Women stayed near the fire, cared for the young children, and prepared the food. Theirs was the cherishing role, the care of the young and the sick. It was the woman who nursed and nurtured, who brought the children into the world at birth, and who prepared the dead for burial. It was the task of women to spin and weave, bake and cook, tend the garden, and clean the house. She was to sit at the sidelines or to be excluded entirely from important rituals. It was men's work to perform the rites, mark the passage of time in the society with social events, make and execute the laws, and plan the government. In order to be free to execute his duties, man's needs were served by women. It was in this cherished and traditional role that woman achieved her security, gratification, sense of adequacy, and worthiness; just as man satisfied these needs through his prowess in conquest, discovery, and leadership.

These traditional roles of men and women have been altered somewhat by technological advances, cultural change, significant sociological pattern changes, and psychological advances in the study of human nature. The increasing emphasis upon the democratic system, particularly in America, represents a constant challenge to older traditions in all areas because young people no longer follow traditional role expectations.

241

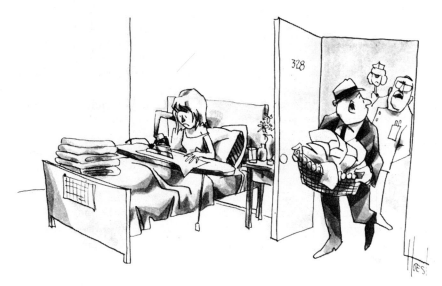

William Hoest, *Look*

*"May I have a word with you, Mr. Schneider?"*

## THE CHANGING MALE ROLE

There are many factors that have contributed to changing or domesticating the male. This change has positive and negative values. The judgment of which is positive and which is negative will be determined by your own personal values, standards, and attitudes. Some factors that have contributed are these:

1. To the extent that women have gained privileges, men have had to change attitudes and expectations or suffer considerable loss of self esteem. For example, the nineteenth amendment to the Constitution, which gave women the vote, altered the male prerogative of making and executing the laws and planning the government.

2. The training of the child is left up to the mother and the female school teacher because of the long daily absence of the father from the home and the disappearance of the male teacher from the grade school. Thus, the male child is left with only female models much of the time.

3. Human brawn and brute strength have been replaced by atomic power, electricity, machines and horsepower.

4. The amount of work a man has to do outside the home has diminished so he has time to share in the child care and other domestic tasks. This is especially true if he lives near his work and works regular hours.

*"O.K., dear—take five."*

5.  The disappearance of the servant class has made it necessary for both man and wife to work at home. The increase in the mechanical servants (dishwashers, garbage disposals, etc.) have made this more acceptable to male interests.

6.  The change in our value system toward occupations and interest that were previously considered effeminate for a man such as drama, beauty culture, sculpture, dress designing, interior decorating, and food preparation have made vast differences in career training and acquired skills.

7.  The entrance of women into numerous vocations has often reversed the roles of the male and female in the field of parenthood itself. In many families both parents work. One may work during the day while the other works at night. Thus, each parent plays the dual father-mother role during their portion of the day alone with the children.

## THE CHANGING FEMALE ROLE

Some of the factors that have contributed to changing the female role are as follows:

1.  To the extent that the man is away from the home, the wife must assume the role of a male as well as a female figure in the family.

243

2. Women are becoming increasingly better educated. They are capable of wage-earning outside the home and of assuming responsible community positions.

3. The change in our value system allows us to accept career women in medicine, business, law, politics, and other professions formally closed to women.

4. Until recent years, women were more or less second-class citizens. Higher education was not deemed important, women were economically dependent, and had few legal rights.

5. New technological advances have decreased the time needed for home maintenance.

The following case study shows role change. Karl and Freda met in college. Karl was majoring in industrial arts and Freda was a medical student. Karl taught industrial arts at a junior high school and Freda opened her medical office after graduation. Freda was a driving, ambitious doctor, who was well-liked and respected by her many patients. The tax referendum for the school system failed to pass, so in order to curtail educational expenses, the industrial arts program was cut from the curriculum. Karl was unemployed and by now the couple had two children. Because of her irregular hours, Freda had left the routine care of the children up to a baby-sitter and Karl. Freda's practice became more and more demanding. As the children grew, baby-sitters were less competent to handle their growing needs, Karl decided to stay home and take over the maternal role. Because he had been with the children more than Freda and also because he was more easygoing, more affectionate, and a willing listener, he was already the emotional center of the household. Today, Karl and Freda are a very happy couple, who have a delightful family. While these instances are rare and are perhaps not yet fully approved by the culture, they do represent the extreme to which the male role has been modified and can be modified in our day.

## MARITAL ROLES

When marriage and family relationships are based upon companionship rather than upon economic considerations and rigidly-patterned institutional rules, it has been found that the male seeks the company of his wife and children more than in the past. As the man finds his work less likely to bring him the fulfillment of his wishes, he may not only turn to family for increased opportunities for gratification, but also extend the range and depth of his interests. He may also acquire a more philosophic, less hurried attitude, and a greater awareness and appreciation of family and friends.

244

When a marriage partner exaggerates his masculine or her feminine role, there is likely to be difficulty unless he (or she) has a marriage partner who exaggerates his (or her) role too. For most modern partners, there is a list of feminine duties, a list of strictly masculine duties, and a large list of duties and responsibilities that are conjointly carried out, depending upon who has the time. Thus, if one partner in a marriage is overly strict about his duties, while the other disregards sex roles as such, difficulties might arise. Attitudes toward masculinity and feminity are said to be "exaggerated" when there is a rigid listing of the distinct roles of the sexes. The two sexes are viewed as total opposites and no overlapping of traits is allowed.

According to William Kenkel, "a man or woman scoring high in this dimension of traditionalism would support the beliefs that a wife should obey her husband, that it goes against nature to place women in positions of authority over men, and that it reflects on a husband's manhood if his wife works outside the home. The personal traits of the male stressed by those with an exaggerated concept of masculinity would include ruggedness, lack of emotion, ambition, determination, and assertiveness. Those who hold an extreme version of femininity believe that women are more emotional, more moral, and more visionary than men."[1]

[1] William F. Kenkel, "Observational Studies of Husband-Wife Interaction in Family Decision-Making," *Sourcebook in Marriage and The Family*, Marvin B. Sussman, ed. (Boston, Houghton Mifflin Company, 1963), p. 152.

245

The family life cycle, depicted in the following sketches, brings with it changes in roles, conflicting roles, and shifting role expectations.

FAMILY-FOUNDING — This is the establishing phase. The young couple faces conflicting loyalties between parents and spouse. Husband may feel guilty about neglecting his mother.

CHILD-BEARING — Young husband may feel guilty if his wife is very uncomfortable. He may also feel displaced by a new baby. Wife may be uncertain about her new role and her changing appearance.

CHILD-REARING — As children grow and develop minds of their own, they normally disobey. However, this may make the parents feel incompetent and anxious about the way they are playing their roles as father and mother. The father, engrossed in earning a living, may feel guilty not spending more time with his wife and children.

246

*CHILD-LAUNCHING*   In this phase children leave the family to establish their own lives away from the family. Mother may feel neglected and misunderstood. She may feel worthless since her child care duties are over.

*THE EMPTY NEST*   The husband and wife have to readjust to having just the two of them in the home. They now have time to have a social life that is geared to their wishes and needs rather than having to consider the children's wishes and needs. They can take more responsibility for life outside their family unit. They need to adjust to living at the retirement income level. They need to consider their role in taking care of themselves and each other physically. They have to prepare for the prospect of the death of either spouse and becoming widow or widower.

## THE CONFUSING FEMININE ROLE

During their changing status, women have lost many of their traditional roles. The American family goes to outsiders for most of the traditional services once performed by the housewife and mother. We buy our clothes and food ready-made and ready-mixed. Outsiders take care of our sick and our dead. Our aged and infirm are placed in homes. The traditional ministering role of the woman has virtually disappeared. Running a home today

247

is a managerial job, dependent on a knowledge of purchasing, organization, personnel management, and consumer economics. However, it also includes such subsidiary but important duties as being family chauffeur, dietitian, interior decorator, and such community responsibilites as PTA chairman, canvasser for the cancer fund, and block leader for the League of Women Voters.

The important role of the family as the rearing, nurturing, and socializing unit for the child has not changed. Role concepts and role expectations have an additional responsibility and dimension when a child or children complete the family circle.

In the highly complex and stratified structure of a large company, there may be special roles expected of wives. According to William Whyte, a sociologist, the good executive wife is a stabilizer who makes the home a place where the lonely and the overworked executive may relax. However, at the same time, she must be a gregarious, socially-aware person who can put everyone at ease in her presence. She applies several unwritten rules to her conduct. She (1) doesn't talk shop or gossip with the girls, (2) doesn't invite superiors in rank until after they have made the first bid, (3) isn't disagreeable to company people she meets, (4) is attractive, (5) keeps away from the office, (6) avoids getting chummy with wives of men her husband may pass in his rise in the company, (7) never drinks too much at a company party, and (8) doesn't have more status symbols than those in the company at the same level.[2]

The modern woman has a confused role. The feminist movement in the middle of the nineteenth century wiped out the outrageous disadvantages —political, legal, educational and occupational—to which women had been subjected. Today, she is challenged to take her place in the world because the world needs her. The world needs her brains, time, knowledge, courage, sensitivity, and dedication. Women must now recognize themselves as people—not just wives, not just mothers, not just "good as men" but individuals of social worth who can give intellectual leadership in an emerging society.

To complicate matters, however, a young girl is to be attractive, feminine in a traditional sense, and ready to play the role of wife and mother. Bruno Bettelheim has discussed this contradiction:

> Consider the contradictions which are thus thrust upon the growing girl. For fifteen years or more she is officially encouraged to compete with boys in the schoolroom, to develop her mind and her initiative, to be second to none. She may study the same physics and history as her

[2] William H. Whyte, Jr., "The Wives of Management," *Fortune,* Vol. 44 (October, 1951), p. 88.

boyfriends, work at jobs not too different from theirs, share many of the same political and social interests. And then our curious system insists she "fall in love" with a potential husband. She is, in fact, expected to love giving up what she may have loved until then, and suddenly find deep fulfillment in taking care of a child, a home, a mate. Her life is to be filled with what are, to her husband, afterhours occupations, and the training of her youth is seemingly intended to fall away like an after-birth. After years of apparent equality, it is made clear that males are more equal, and some females resent this. And they should. Our educational system has ostensibly prepared them for a kind of liberated marital and occupational life that in fact rarely exists in our society; at the same time it celebrates the values of an antiquated form of marriage inherited from a time when wives were prepared for little else.

If many girls seem to accept these hypocrisies calmly, perhaps it is because they have been made aware, quite early in the game, that their role in society will in fact be very different from that of the boys sitting next to them in the classroom. The boys have no doubt that their schooling is intended, at least, to help them make a success in their mature life, to enable them to accomplish something in the outside world. But the girl is made to feel that she must undergo precisely the same training only because she may need it if she is a failure—an unfortunate who cannot somehow gain admission to the haven of marriage and motherhood where she properly belongs. Surely this is absurd.

Actually, the gravest damage is done long before this. The little girl's first storybooks and primers, for example, hardly ever show a woman as working or active outside the home. It makes no difference that over five million American children under twelve have full-time working mothers. The little girl is expected to shape herself in the image of maternal housekeeping women in these stories, and never mind what certain unfortunate mothers may be obliged to do. And emphasizing society's ambivalence, this image of the stay-at-home woman is presented by her female teacher who may well be a working mother. In these early years, it is rare indeed for girls to hear the slightest suggestion that they might one day do the interesting work of this world quite as well as many men or even better.

It is little wonder then that, as adolescence approaches in the last year of grade school, many girls are already quite convinced that what really counts is not any commitment to their studies—although they may be conscientious—but their ability to carry on social, emotional, and sexual relations that will make them popular and ultimately attract the right boys. And here matters are made more difficult by the fact that young girls tend to mature faster physically and emotionally than boys, al-

249

though the boys may do better academically. The girls soon perceive that they are ahead of the boys in the maturity and sophistication of their desires. The boys seem more childish, less grown up, less certain about their ability to cope with the other sex. What is more, they often come from homes where mother knows best, and now they find themselves ruled by female teachers who day after day impress upon them their authority and competence. In this situation it is not easy for a boy to gain confidence in his maleness, to say the least. (Later on, of course, both sexes are exposed to male teachers in high school and college, but by then it is often too late to undo the damage.)

Thus the high school and college girl must face a frequently awful predicament. She—and her mother—feel she must be popular with boys. And to get the dates she wants, she must try to reassure the boys that they are really superior to her; but deep down she cannot believe in this pretense, and she may resent the necessity for it. Once she has gained the ultimate objective and is safely married, she will, as likely as not, drop the mask and begin to assert in her home what she is convinced is a superior maturity."[3]

The modern, professionally trained woman is unsuccessful if she doesn't find and excel in the position for which she was trained. She must perform as a chemist, if trained to be one, or as a nurse if so trained. However, in some of the same circles she may be labeled unsuccessful if she returns to her profession after the birth of a child.

Perhaps the chief problem is that though women differ as individuals, they are all expected to play the same role. Because they are women they are usually expected to make a home, *which requires practical ability* and a discerning heart.

Our archer may be more likely to hit the bull's eye if she learns to know herself well enough to choose a role. Not to perform a role from duty or habit while longing for a different role, but to prepare herself for a role that uses all her talents is her challenge as she aims at the target, life. However, if she is going to try for a dual role, then she needs to educate herself for the world of work and for the world of home. If she is going to be a chemist and a homemaker, her college electives should be taken in child care, home management, and family relationships. With training and an understanding husband, she can be highly successful in both roles.

## THE MARRIED WOMAN ROLE

Clifford Kirkpatrick has made a distinction between three roles provided in our society for the married woman. Each role implies certain privileges and certain obligations.

The *wife-and-mother role* is the traditional role of the married woman. It implies as privileges security, the right of support, alimony in case of divorce, respect as a wife and mother, a certain amount of domestic authority, loyalty of husband as the mother of his children, and sentimental gratitude from husband and children. Corresponding obligations include bearing and rearing children, making a home, rendering domestic service, subordinating herself loyally to the economic interests of the husband, accepting a dependent social and economic status, and tolerrating a limited range of activities.

The *companion role* is essentially one which fulfills joint psychological needs. The privileges pertaining to this role include pleasures shared with the husband, a more romantic emotional response, admiration, respect for the opinions and requirements of the other, shared leisure in social and educational activities, plus chivalrous attention. On the other hand, it implies as obligations the preservation of beauty, the rendering of ego and erotic satisfaction to each other, the cultivation of social contacts, the maintenance of intellectual alertness, and the responsibility for exorcising the demon of boredom.

251

Finally, the *partner role* corresponds to a new emergent definition of family relationships. This role encompasses acceptance as an equal, the privilege of economic independence, equal authority in regard to family finances, the exemption of one-sided personal domestic service to the husband, equal voice in determining the locality of residence, and equality in regard to social and moral freedom. On the other hand, obligations of this role include renouncing of alimony, except in the case of dependent children, contributing economically in proportion to earning ability, accepting equal responsibility for the support of children, sharing legal responsibilities of the family, dispensing with any appeal to chivalry, dismissing special privileges in regard to children, and sharing equal responsibility to maintain the family status by success in a career.[4]

The three roles are an attempt to make a definite distinction between the kinds of relationships studied. It would seem that a vital marriage might be a combination of some aspects from each of the roles.

## THE MASCULINE ROLE

The social role of the male, in our culture, is such that masculinity, and even virtue, are especially equated with success, notably professional or business success. Therefore, men are expected to give up passivity, dependency, and even sexuality in order to succeed. Yet, although aggressiveness may be expressed in intense competitiveness, excesses must be curbed.

Anthropologists, sociologists, and psychiatrists alike take note of the impact of cutthroat competition in the American culture. The psychiatrist is especially aware of how the exhausting striving for success comes sharply into conflict with unconscious wishes for relaxation, security, and love—the derivatives of dependency and parental love and protection. Men's goals, therefore, are hard, the risks great, and the failures numerous.

Typical adaptations required of young men between the ages of 21–40 include those of military service, economic independence, marriage, fatherhood, and vocational achievement. The ideal of masculinity in our culture requires that the adult male "act like a male" in all of these situations and crises. He is expected to be "stronger" and better controlled than women. Any real or apparent failure to live up to this masculine ideal—for example, inability to support a wife and children—invites loss of self-esteem, feelings of guilt or shame, and even depression. It is therefore harder for a man to be sick, injured, unemployed, or in any way "inadequate" than it is for a woman or child.

[4] Clifford Kirkpatrick, *The Family: As Process and Institution.* Second Edition, Copyright 1963, The Ronald Press Company, New York, pp. 168–169.

A major problem for most young men is how to be a good father. The "good father" is at cross-purposes in our culture. On the one hand, he must be successful, and this usually means being away from home during most of his children's waking hours, five or even six days a week. On the other hand, he must be a good example for his children, a good leader, a good disciplinarian, a good friend, and a good companion. For the sake of his children, he should be a good husband to his wife, because a happy wife is a better mother, other things being equal, than an unhappy one.

It is apparent that the tasks of balancing out the physical, social, and emotional needs of all members of a family is by no means an easy one.

## DECIDING ON ROLES

Increased concern over marital roles is normal and natural in a culture that increasingly emphasizes freedom for individuals. Pressures from society, however, often make today's mates feel guilty because of their personal rejection of the traditional patterns of behavior.

Many conditioning factors influence role expectations in marriage. These include early family experiences, cultural sex influences, environmental factors, and group factors such as ethnic and social-class background.

253

One major modern-role concern involves the family power structure. Originally, the male was supreme head of the family. His position has been supported by such influences as religion, law, a belief that man was superior to woman and that woman was naturally more submissive.

There are many frustrations for modern well-educated wives and their husbands who try to conform to traditional marital roles. Some of these stem from the fact that modern wives lack sufficient training or skills in homemaking, having sadly neglected this side of their education. A deeper appreciation for homemaking, family relations, and child development by both sexes is lacking. In some cases, the professional career of the husband appears to dictate the role of the wife. Often this role appears to be too low on the priority list to suit a modern, ambitious girl.

The time to consider these problems, however, is before marriage, not afterward. This challenges each of you to know your chosen mate well enough before marriage so that you have an idea of his or her role expectation as well as your own. This knowledge takes time, maturity, career preparation, and the ability to communicate with another person.

Modern couples cannot return to the traditional patterns of family living any more than they can return to an agrarian or agricultural-oriented society. Instead, they must prepare themselves socially, technically, and psychologically for today's life. Biological limitations will aways mean that the roles of the sexes will be different. However, when that difference is accepted by and acceptable to each sex through an appreciation of role expectation in today's society, stronger marriages will emerge.

## TO PROMOTE UNDERSTANDING OF THIS CHAPTER

1. How is one's role expectation a predictor of one's role satisfaction?

2. How were the traditional roles played by male and female distinguished?

3. How has the male role changed?

4. What has caused the role of the male to change?

5. What is your opinion of the male-female roles as played by Karl and Freda? Would you like to be Freda? Why? Why not? Would you like to be Karl? Why? Why not?

6. What are the different kinds of marital roles?

7. Write a case study for a family in one of the phases of the family life cycle.

8. What are the causes of the confusion in the modern female's role?

9. Which sex seems to be changed the most in terms of traditional roles? What do you think explains this situation?

10. Describe several areas in which the line of demarcation between male and female roles seems to be disappearing.

## SUPPLEMENTARY READING

BETTELHEIM, BRUNO, "Growing Up Female." *Harper's Magazine,* October, 1962, pp. 120–128.

CERVANTES, S. J., and LUCIUS, F., *And God Made Man and Woman.* Henry Reanery Co., Chicago, 1959.

DUVALL, EVELYN MILLIS, *Family Development.* J. B. Lippincott Co., Philadelphia, 1962.

FOOTE, NELSON N., "New Roles for Men and Women." *Marriage and Family Living,* Vol. 23, November, 1961.

FRIEDAN, BETTY, *The Feminine Mystique.* Dell Books Inc., New York, 1964.

KENKEL, WILLIAM F., "Observational Studies of Husband-Wife Interaction in Family Decision-Making." *Sourcebook in Marriage and the Family,* Marvin B. Sussman, ed. Houghton Mifflin Co., Boston, 1963.

KIRKPATRICK, CLIFFORD, *The Family,* 2d ed. The Ronald Press Co., New York, 1963.

LANDIS, PAUL H., *Making the Most of Marriage.* Appleton-Century-Crofts, Inc., New York, 1960.

LUMPKIN, KATHERINE DUPREE, *The Family.* University of North Carolina Press, Chapel Hill, N.C., 1933.

MEAD, MARGARET, *Male and Female.* The New American Library of World Literature, Inc., New York, 1955.

WHYTE, WILLIAM H., JR., "The Wives of Management." *Fortune,* Vol. 44, October, 1951, pp. 86–88+, and "Corporation and the Wife," *Fortune,* Vol. 44, November, 1951, pp. 109–111+.

WOMBLE, DALE L., *Foundations for Marriage and Family Relations.* The Macmillan Co., New York, 1966.

*"O.K. . . . O.K.! Call the baby sitter and I'll take you out to dinner!"*

# 23
# Career versus Marriage;
# Career and Marriage

### CAREER VERSUS MARRIAGE

In the past, when the traditional roles (discussed in Chapter 22) were in full flower, the woman who chose a career was destined to remain unmarried. If she chose to be a school teacher, this was her career and her contract to teach was not renewed if she married. The same was true for girls in other professions as well as for those in college. Their marriage meant the end of their schooling or their work in a chosen profession. Thus, there was a clear-cut choice; a career or marriage.

Today, however, women have a choice. Some women choose lifelong careers. Much of the world's work is done by these women and their choice is a very valid one for them and for the world.

Some women want careers because of their interest in the work or activity involved or because of their desire to maintain "freedom" and independence, to have an independent income, or to find an outlet for "self-expression." The finding of "self-expression" is a goal that men and women, married or unmarried, seek. If the woman can find adequate self-expression through a career rather than marriage, good.

Some women choose careers rather than marriage because they see these careers as rendering great service to some segment of mankind or to mankind as a whole. Others choose lifelong careers because they are wage earners for aging parents or dependent siblings. They may feel that this duty is theirs and is too great a burden to share with a marriage partner.

Some women do not choose lifelong career roles but drift into them. They may spend a great deal of time training for a particular profession to the neglect of seeking a husband. They may share an apartment with another professional woman. Time passes and they become engrossed in careers and career associates. Their housemate meets their need for companionship and their sex drives are sublimated into the career.

A girl raised in a traditional family setting may feel that if she has a career interest, she must choose between this interest and marriage. She may have been reared to believe that to combine them is to be a failure in both. However, there are both married and unmarried women in many careers.

## WORKING WOMEN

The American labor force is now 33½ percent women, 60 percent of whom are married. Most working women are in the white collar occupations. Women constitute more than two-thirds of the clerical force of the country. In 1960, there were 1½ million more women in professional work than in 1940.

Forty-five percent of all professional women are teachers and 27 percent are medical and other health workers—nurses, doctors, medical technologists, x-ray technicians, physical therapists, dietitians, pharmacists, and so on. Women made their greatest *numerical* gain between 1950–1960 in the fields of accounting and auditing. The number of women lawyers has also shown a small but consistent gain. Of particular interest is the relatively large increase in the number of women engineers. In addition, there were over twice as many women proprietors, officials, and managers in 1960 as in 1940. About half of these persons were salaried workers; the

257

*LABOR FORCE BY AGE AND SEX: 1945–1967*[1]

| Year or month | MALE | | | | | | FEMALE | | | | | |
|---|---|---|---|---|---|---|---|---|---|---|---|---|
| | Total | 14 to 19 Years | 20 to 24 Years | 25 to 44 Years | 45 to 64 Years | 65 Years and over | Total | 14 to 19 Years | 20 to 24 Years | 25 to 44 Years | 45 to 64 Years | 65 Years and over |
| 1945 | 46,020 | 4,530 | 5,760 | 19,900 | 13,370 | 2,460 | 19,280 | 2,720 | 3,300 | 8,350 | 4,420 | 490 |
| 1950 | 46,069 | 3,444 | 5,224 | 20,996 | 13,952 | 2,453 | 18,680 | 1,982 | 2,681 | 8,267 | 5,167 | 584 |
| 1955 | 48,054 | 3,378 | 4,851 | 22,297 | 15,002 | 2,526 | 20,842 | 1,987 | 2,458 | 9,069 | 6,546 | 780 |
| 1960 | 49,507 | 3,821 | 5,089 | 22,270 | 16,039 | 2,287 | 23,619 | 2,409 | 2,590 | 9,447 | 8,266 | 907 |
| 1964 | 51,118 | 4,307 | 5,704 | 22,195 | 16,788 | 2,123 | 25,854 | 2,732 | 3,220 | 9,805 | 9,129 | 966 |
| 1965 | 51,705 | 4,591 | 5,926 | 22,157 | 16,899 | 2,131 | 26,653 | 2,940 | 3,375 | 10,060 | 9,301 | 976 |
| 1966 | 52,350 | 4,913 | 6,139 | 22,156 | 17,054 | 2,089 | 27,814 | 3,361 | 3,601 | 10,277 | 9,612 | 963 |
| March 3 | 50,600 | 3,550 | 5,939 | 22,141 | 16,950 | 2,020 | 26,444 | 2,382 | 3,460 | 10,128 | 9,442 | 1,030 |
| 1967[2] | 51,368 | 3,717 | 6,303 | 22,230 | 17,130 | 1,990 | 27,581 | 2,559 | 3,852 | 10,573 | 9,626 | 973 |

*Statistical Abstract of the United States*, U.S. Bureau of the Census, Washington, D.C., 1967, p. 222.
[1] In thousands of persons, 14 years old and over, except as noted. Prior to 1960, excludes Alaska and Hawaii. Includes armed forces abroad.
[2] Persons 16 years old and over.

# MARITAL STATUS OF WOMEN IN THE CIVILIAN LABOR FORCE: 1940–1966[1]

| Year | Female Labor Force (1,000) | | Married | | Percent Distribution of Female Labor Force | | | Female Labor Force as Percent of Female Population, 14 and over | | Married | | |
| | Total | Single | Total | Hus-band present | Widowed or divorced | Single | Mar-ried | Widowed or divorced | Total | Single | Total | Hus-band present | Widowed or divorced |
|---|---|---|---|---|---|---|---|---|---|---|---|---|---|
| 1940— | 13,840 | 6,710 | 5,040 | ¹4,200 | 2,090 | 48.5 | 36.4 | 15.1 | 27.4 | 48.1 | 16.7 | 14.7 | 32.0 |
| 1944[2]— | 18,449 | 7,542 | 8,433 | 6,226 | 2,474 | 40.9 | 45.7 | 13.4 | 35.0 | 58.6 | 25.6 | 21.7 | 35.7 |
| 1947[2]— | 16,323 | 6,181 | 7,545 | 6,676 | 2,597 | 37.9 | 46.2 | 15.9 | 29.8 | 51.2 | 21.4 | 20.0 | 34.6 |
| 1950— | 17,795 | 5,621 | 9,273 | 8,550 | 2,901 | 31.6 | 52.1 | 16.3 | 31.4 | 50.5 | 24.8 | 23.8 | 36.0 |
| 1954[2]— | 19,726 | 5,412 | 11,209 | 9,923 | 3,105 | 27.4 | 56.8 | 15.7 | 33.1 | 49.0 | 28.1 | 26.6 | 36.0 |
| 1955[2]— | 20,154 | 5,087 | 11,839 | 10,423 | 3,227 | 25.2 | 58.7 | 16.0 | 33.5 | 46.4 | 29.4 | 27.7 | 36.0 |
| 1956— | 20,842 | 5,167 | 12,278 | 11,126 | 3,397 | 24.8 | 58.9 | 16.3 | 34.2 | 46.4 | 30.2 | 29.0 | 36.9 |
| 1957— | 21,524 | 5,378 | 12,696 | 11,529 | 3,450 | 25.0 | 59.0 | 16.0 | 34.8 | 46.8 | 30.8 | 29.6 | 37.6 |
| 1958— | 22,000 | 5,365 | 13,032 | 11,826 | 3,604 | 24.4 | 59.2 | 16.4 | 35.0 | 45.4 | 31.4 | 30.2 | 37.9 |
| 1959— | 22,376 | 5,162 | 13,586 | 12,205 | 3,628 | 23.1 | 60.7 | 16.2 | 35.2 | 43.4 | 32.3 | 30.9 | 38.0 |
| 1960— | 22,516 | 5,401 | 13,485 | 12,253 | 3,629 | 24.0 | 59.9 | 16.1 | 34.8 | 44.1 | 31.7 | 30.5 | 37.1 |
| 1961— | 24,199 | 5,663 | 14,612 | 13,266 | 3,924 | 23.4 | 60.4 | 16.2 | 36.8 | 44.4 | 34.0 | 32.7 | 39.0 |
| 1962— | 23,978 | 5,481 | 14,770 | 13,485 | 3,727 | 22.9 | 61.6 | 15.5 | 35.7 | 41.7 | 33.7 | 32.7 | 36.6 |
| 1963— | 24,675 | 5,614 | 15,362 | 14,061 | 3,699 | 22.8 | 62.3 | 15.0 | 36.1 | 41.0 | 34.6 | 33.7 | 35.8 |
| 1964— | 25,399 | 5,781 | 15,790 | 14,461 | 3,828 | 22.8 | 62.2 | 15.1 | 36.5 | 40.9 | 35.3 | 34.4 | 36.1 |
| 1965— | 25,952 | 5,912 | 16,154 | 14,708 | 3,886 | 22.8 | 62.2 | 15.0 | 36.7 | 40.5 | 35.7 | 34.7 | 35.7 |
| 1966— | 26,820 | 6,106 | 16,676 | 15,178 | 4,038 | 22.7 | 62.2 | 15.1 | 37.3 | 40.8 | 36.5 | 35.4 | 36.4 |

*Statistical Abstract of the United States*, U.S. Bureau of the Census, Washington, D.C., 1967, p. 229.

[1] Persons 14 years old and over. As of March, except as indicated. Prior to 1960, excludes Alaska and Hawaii.

[2] As of April.

other half were independent ones. Today, significant numbers of women are entering the fields of insurance, real estate, banking, and credit.

Nevertheless, it must be noted that the proportion of women is much smaller in the higher levels of an occupation than in the occupation as a whole—even in their traditional fields of work. In the library field, for example, women hold a large proportion of the staff positions but a small proportion of the administrative positions. In teaching, where women fill about one-half the teaching positions, only about 9 percent are principals in junior high schools and 5 percent in senior high schools. Only 3 percent of the nation's lawyers are women; only 6 percent are physicians.

Careers require education. There has been an explosive increase at the top of the employment pyramid—the area that represents professional and technical positions. However, the proportion of professional and technical workers who are women decreased from 45 percent in 1940 to 37 percent in 1965. The route to jobs and success clearly lies more and more through the portals of the nation's colleges, rather than through its factory gates or its offices.

However, many young girls are taking the advice of Sharon's mother. They are not marrying Guggenheims necessarily, but they are dropping

*"Sharon, darling, this is only a mother talking—but why don't you forget the fellowship and just marry a Guggenheim?"*

out of college to marry. This causes a problem if they do decide on a career and marriage, because for women who want to return to work after marriage and child-rearing or who want to combine marriage and a career, the path to good jobs lies along the educational route.

Robert Heilbroner discusses this problem in an article in *Saturday Review*. He says:

> Curiously, the boom at the top of the job market has largely by-passed one big college-going group. For the past two decades the proportion of women pushing on into graduate study has actually been below the ratio of the 1930's. Although the percentage of girls going to college is now at an all-time high, so is the percentage dropping out. More than half of all female college entrants fail to get their degrees, mainly because they get married along the way.
>
> But the changing world of work is affecting the women no less than the men. For what the young marrieds do not realize is that their working days are far from over. The average American girl who today marries at the age of eighteen and shortly thereafter begins to have a family will nevertheless return to the labor market within fifteen or twenty years and will spend twenty-five years of her life working. Half a million women made the transition from housewife to working wife in 1965, and as many are expected to enter the offices and shops and factories every year for at least the next ten.
>
> What are they going to do? "Most of them," says Jane Schwartz, Director of Placement at Barnard College, "are looking—at least to begin with—for part-time work. In fact, part-time work has become a whole new category of employment. Many women, especially in the middle and upper income groups, go back to work not alone for the money, although that is not unimportant, but to get out of the house, to have the stimulation of being part of the active world, to fulfill themselves."[1]

## MARRIAGE AND A CAREER

Women choose the dual roles of homemaker and employee for many reasons. Some of the reasons are the same as those for the unmarried professional woman. She, too, may seek self-expression, feel that she should add her talents and training to her chosen professional field, and believe that she can render a service to mankind.

---

[1] Robert L. Heilbroner, "No Room at the Bottom," *Saturday Review,* Vol. 49, No. 8 (February 19, 1966), p. 30.

However, she may also seek employment because she resembles the homemaker in the cartoon. She may feel like a prisoner of the home routine. She may seek employment to escape household duties, to escape boredom, to escape the care of children, to prevent stagnation, or to escape dissatisfaction with the marriage relationship.

On the other hand, some women may combine marriage and a career to buy more *things*. Today, there is a growing emphasis on acquiring goods and services. There is a tendency to classify and judge people on the basis of their relative success or lack of it in the acquisition of wealth and income, and the things money can buy.

Women may work more from force of habit than anything else. Some work before marriage and get so used to working outside the home that it simply never occurs to them to stay home afterward. This type of woman may get interested in community affairs. If so, she usually finds even more satisfaction in those activities than in salaried employment.

A few women work to gain a sense of independence; they dislike the feeling of being dependent, which may arise from the assumption of the traditional female role within marriage.

To some, work offers a sense of future financial security. They feel that if the husband should die or some other tragedy should occur, they will have some security. This, however, may be rationalization, for it would be just as logical for everyone to have two jobs.

It is probably safe to say that most women work today not for one particular reason, but for a number of reasons. We have listed some of the personal reasons above. However, there has also been a shift in popular attitude regarding the compatability of a career and marriage. World War II was probably the national crisis that started this shift in attitude. During that time, women workers were desperately needed to carry on the nation's work while the men were engaged in this worldwide conflict. Presently, there is such a need for professionally trained people and for brain power that few married women who also wish a career meet a negative attitude toward their dual roles.

The decision to work or not to work after marriage is dependent upon many factors. It depends primarily on the individual situation and the attitudes of the husband and wife concerned. Generally speaking, questions of overfatigue, pressure, and strain from attempting to fulfill two functions might be anticipated. Resentment toward necessity for employment might also occur. In a study of working wives,[2] it was found that the wife's

[2] Artie Gianopulos and Howard E. Mitchell, "Marital Disagreement in Working Wife Marriages as a Function of Husband's Attitude Toward Wife's Employment," *Marriage and Family Living,* Vol. 19, No. 4 (November, 1957), p. 378.

working became a problem only when the husband did not approve. When both husband and wife approved, the fact of the wife working in itself did not constitute a problem.

The first and most important factor, then, is the individual attitude of both husband and wife. If they both have a positive attitude toward the wife's employment, then they might consider the situation with these questions in mind.

1. Is the wife's health such that carrying two jobs will not overtax it?

2. Is the husband willing to share in the household tasks or willing to have the family spend additional money to have these tasks done by outside help?

3. Is the husband's profession the type that needs the full-time help of his wife? Wives of certain professional men, such as business executives, officials in government, members of the clergy, and so on, may be needed as helpers and hostesses for their husbands.

4. Does the wife have special talents or skills which she should use because of a shortage of trained professionals in her field?

5. Does the wife feel she must have employment outside of the home to keep herself emotionally stable?

6. Does the wife have the ability to manage a job and a home or does the management of the home alone tax her abilities to the utmost?

7. How will the two incomes be used? No one can dictate the best arrangement for the couple, but some plan agreeable to both of them must be worked out if friction is to be prevented.

8. Will there be a lack of common friends? There may be a tendency to form two separate groups of friends if husband and wife work in different places.

9. If there is a child or children, how will they be cared for? Is it possible to find a person who will adequately administer to their needs in their mother's absence?

It should be noted that many women are employed outside of the home but are unpaid. The professional club woman who is prominent in the various civic, social and community organizations and enterprises is not unemployed because she is not paid for her work.

## THE TRIAD—CAREER, MARRIAGE AND PARENTHOOD

For the working mother, the husband and wife relationship is of considerable psychological significance. Again, the circumstances that lead to the mother's employment, the personalities of husband and wife, and the immediate situational factors must be considered. Generally, as we have noted, the employment of the wife will necessitate changes in the traditional roles of husband and wife.

In addition to these role changes, a change in the more subtle aspects of familial relationships occurs when the mother is out of the house during the work periods. The father will probably have more direct contact with his children and more direct responsibility for their physical care. Such contact with the father may be beneficial or detrimental to the children and the father, depending upon both parents' capacity to adapt to the role changes.

Mothers who are on the scene all the time differ widely in how they care for their children. When they are away part of the time, whether the child is better off will depend upon the nature of the child's relationship with his mother and with the substitute. It is the quality of the relationship between mother and child that is significant, and not the amount of time they spend together. There is no linear relationship between spending a great deal of time with one's child and the amount of affection that will be afforded him.

For some women, outside employment is such a contrast to the constant strain of child care that, when the day's work is done, they are able to return home refreshed by the joy of seeing their children. They are ready to give ungrudgingly of their ingenuity and patience. Many such mothers contribute much more in the short time with their children than they could in a whole day before they started to work. Sometimes mothers who are working outside the home actually spend more time with their children than do those women who are home all day but send their children outside to play without supervision.

Whether the child is better off or not is a question that cannot be answered with an absolute yes or with an unqualified no. It depends upon the degree to which the substitute mother respects the mother's authority, the similarity between her values and those of the mother, and the setting in which the care is provided. All will influence the child's relationship with his mother. Most important is the feeling that the parents themselves have about the situation.

Dr. Lois Hoffman, reporting on the effects of mothers who work, discussed the findings of a study of 176 white, intact families. In this study, there were 88 working-mother families and 88 non-working-mother families matched on occupation of father, sex of child, and position of the sibling in the family. The overall patterns of the findings suggested that the working mother who likes working is relatively high on positive effect toward the child, uses mild discipline, and tends to avoid inconveniencing the child with household tasks because of her employment; the child is relatively non-aggressive. The working mother who dislikes working, on the other hand, seems less involved with the child altogether and obtains the child's help with many tasks; the child is relatively assertive and hostile.[3]

The effects of the mother's working on delinquent behavior of boys was studied by the Gluecks.[4] In this study, five hundred delinquent boys were compared to a group of non-delinquents. The two groups were similar with respect to intelligence, ethnic background, age, and economic status. The last factor is, of course, crucial when the effects of the mother's working are to be considered. It was found that both groups had about the same proportions of regularly working and non-working mothers; thus, regular work by the mother did not seem to influence the likelihood of delinquent behavior in the son.

Ruth Whitmarsh found in a pilot study that the adolescent daughters of employed mothers had fewer recognized problems than the daughters of full-time homemakers.[5] The middle-class adolescent girls in this study whose mothers were employed seemed to be particularly well adjusted in the area of home and family life if an absence of personal problems may be used as a criterion of personal adjustment.

Bruno Bettelheim has indicated that he feels that a woman who enjoys her work makes a better mother than one who rejects it.

Since work around the house is now less than interesting, children are the natural target for the young wife's energies. Here at least she feels considerably more sophisticated than her mother. After all she has had extensive schooling, and has perhaps worked briefly at a demanding job, and motherhood has been depicted to her as another tremendous and enlarging experience—the climax, somehow, to what has gone before. Yet in fact the care of an infant forces her to give up most of her old interests, and unless she is fascinated by the minute developments of the baby, she will seldom find that any new and different enrichment has entered her life to replace them.

This impoverishment is particularly acute when she has her first child. Later on, the concerns of her older children may enliven her days while she cares for a newcomer. However, I believe the current trend toward

[3] Lois Wladis Hoffman, "Effects of Maternal Employment on the Child," *Sourcebook in Marriage and the Family*, Marvin B. Sussman, ed. (Boston, Houghton Mifflin Co., 1963) pp. 241–247.

[4] S. and E. Glueck, "Working Mothers and Delinquency," *Mental Hygiene*, Vol. 41, (1957), pp. 327–352.

[5] Ruth Whitmarsh, "Adjustment Problems of Adolescent Daughters of Employed Mothers," *Journal of Home Economics*, Vol. 57, No. 3 (March, 1965), pp. 201–204.

larger middle-class families reflects not merely a greater prosperity but also the needs of the middle-class mother who finds existence empty without small children to care for. Reluctant to return to the outer world—or perhaps lacking confidence in her ability to do so, she must find something to occupy her which seems vital and demanding of her concentration.

But things change once her children are of school age—and even more so in their teens. They certainly need a mother, but they actually need far less of her than she may devote to them. Chauffeuring children around the suburbs, for example, takes time and requires someone who drives a car, but this person need not be a mother. The children themselves would prefer to be free of it and the tight scheduling it imposes. The same goes for arranging the children's social life, which again they would much prefer to do themselves.

Of course, the professed concern of many mothers is to watch over their children's educational life, and help them with their psychological problems. But in these things, too, the children would often rather be on their own, except for those occasional crises where the parents are needed for support. And sadly enough the modern mother is often in a poor position to give support when her child is doing badly in school or is not very popular and hence feels defeated. Having invested so much emotionally in her child's achievement, her pride suffers at his failure and as likely as not she administers a bawling out when understanding and compassion are needed. Thus she may fail as a mother because her inner needs make her work at it too hard. The children of women who are doing interesting work of their own during the day will often find more sensible and sympathetic mothers to help them with their studies and problems in the evening. On the other hand, the mother who urges her girl on toward intellectual achievement while staying at home herself poses a contradiction which probably is not lost on the girl.[6]

Lee Burchinal, a sociologist, conducted a study of both working and non-working mothers. This study found, in general, that children whose mothers had worked at various times in the children's lives were not different from children whose mothers had not worked. This conclusion was especially important in that it exposed the myth that working mothers categorically did damage to their preschool and early-school-age children. The argument that the psychological or social development of children is disturbed when their mothers work—especially when the children are quite young—simply was not supported in this study.[7]

This research and the attitudes of Dr. Bettelheim are presented as further evidence that maternal employment in and of itself should no longer be used as a "scapegoat" for marital or familial adjustment problems. However, it is not presented to indicate that the thousands upon thousands of mothers who stay at home should leave their chosen position. If the activities of the home, the community, and their children stimulate their minds and satisfactorily fill their days, then this is, of course, the best choice for them.

We also need to recognize that there are many volunteer groups which desperately need the time, talent, and energy of qualified citizens. The community needs library board members, women to conduct and instruct in the programs for youth such as the Girl Scouts, the 4-H Clubs, Boy Scouts, Y.W.C.A., and Campfire Girls and to work in other civic organizations. Most churches and hospitals would have much more unfinished work if it were not for the activities and contributions of their various women's organizations. Thus, the woman at home can certainly stimulate her mind as well as contribute to her home and her community.

There is no magic formula to follow when an individual attempts to make a decision concerning marriage and a career. As Dorothy Cotton states:

> Being an effective mother (working or not), rearing happy, healthy, responsible children, building a successful marriage—these have always been the most subtle and difficult of all human endeavors.
>
> Those mothers who devote themselves to the care of their families can chalk up as many difficulties with their youngsters as those who do not, and working mothers have their own built-in set of unique problems with their families. No two working mothers are alike. No two stay-at-home mothers are alike. There is simply no "always right" solution to be discovered in any one special prescription for parenthood. Just as staying home will not automatically make a mother 'good' neither will going to work automatically make her 'bad.' One thing is certain: no clear-cut pattern of what a mother should do, or be, exists to fit all mothers.[8]

[7] Lee Burchinal, "Working Mothers: What Effect on Children?" *Iowa Farm Science,* Vol. 17, No. 6 (1962), pp. 9–11.

[8] Dorothy W. Cotton, *The Case for the Working Mother* (New York, Stein and Day, 1965), p. 22. Copyright 1965 by Dorothy W. Cotton. Reprinted with permission of Stein and Day Publishers.

## TO PROMOTE UNDERSTANDING OF THIS CHAPTER

1. Why do some women choose a career rather than marriage?

2. Why are there less women in executive positions?

3. How important is a college education to the girl who hopes to combine marriage and a career?

4. Why do some women choose the dual role of wife and career-girl?

5. What is the most important factor when a wife considers employment outside the home?

6. Write a story of a couple whose situation is such that (a) the wife should work outside the home; (b) the wife should not work outside the home.

7. What factors should a mother consider when she elects to work outside the home?

8. What position does the research reported take in regard to working mothers?

9. How do the attitudes of Bruno Bettelheim agree or disagree with your own attitudes?

10. Boys: Write a paper titled (a) I want my wife to work because . . . or (b) I do not want my wife to work because. . . .

11. Girls: Write a paper titled (a) I want to work after marriage because . . . or (b) I do not want to work after marriage because. . . .

## SUPPLEMENTARY READING

BETTELHEIM, BRUNO, "Growing Up Female," *Harper's Magazine,* October, 1962, pp. 120–128.

COTTON, DOROTHY W., *The Case for the Working Mother.* Stein and Day, New York, 1965.

DUVALL, EVELYN MILLIS and HILL, REUBEN, *When You Marry.* Association Press, New York, 1962.

GIANOPULOS, ARTIE and MITCHELL, HOWARD, E., "Marital Disagreement in Working Wife Marriages as a Function of Husband's Attitude Toward Wife's Employment," *Marriage and Family Living,* Vol. 19, No. 4, pp. 373–378, November, 1957.

GLUECK, S. and GLUECK, E., "Working Mothers and Delinquency," *Mental Hygiene,* New York, Vol. 41, 1957, pp. 327–352.

HEILBRONER, ROBERT L., "No Room at the Bottom," *Saturday Review,* February 19, 1966.

HOFFMAN, LOIS WLADIS, "Effects of Maternal Employment on the Child, *Sourcebook in Marriage and the Family,* Marvin B. Sussman, ed. Houghton Mifflin Co., Boston, 1963.

WHITMARSH, RUTH, "Adjustment Problems of Adolescent Daughters of Employed Mothers," *Journal of Home Economics,* Vol. 57, No. 3 (March, 1965), pp. 201–204.

Joseph Farris, *Look*

*"It's happened! There's a monthly installment due every day!"*

## 24
## Financial Values and Goals in Marriage

Money, in our highly technical and urban society, has become the measure of value. The "things" that money buys have become the status symbols. The worth of the individual is measured by his securities instead of his sincerities. We are oriented to the future. By the future, we mean tomorrow . . . tomorrow we will make the big deal, get the promotion, go to

270

a better job. We search for happiness. When we are pressed for our definition of happiness or the instrumentalities by which it is achieved, we think
usually of income, social status, a beautiful wife or a handsome husband,
brilliant children, a 24-foot boat or a Thunderbird.

Hopefully this is not a description of you, but it does describe thousands and thousands of people. With these values and goals in operation,
the individuals often find themselves in the straits depicted by the cartoons.
Putting a longer pole on the mail box won't deter the bills—just incon-
venience the mailman. The strait jacket imposed by having to meet a daily
installment often leads people to a loan shark or to full dependence in
money management. With these concerns in mind, it is important to consider the management of money. You should manage it; it should not
manage you.

271

## MARRIAGE AND THE USE OF MONEY

As mentioned in Chapter 21, money problems are among the most common in marriage. There is never enough money to satisfy all desires, and unless the couple learns to cooperate in the spending of it, there is trouble.

Our expectations, values, attitudes, family background, training, religious beliefs, and physical environment all affect our use of money. To help explain this phenomenon, study the case of Lisa and Mark and their attitudes and training in the area of money management.

*Lisa says:*
1. Whenever I needed money I always asked Daddy and he gave it to me. Daddy is so generous.

2. It is so important to wear the latest fashions in clothes.

3. One must give at least 15 percent of his income to the church of his choice.

4. It's important to remember family birthdays with something really nice.

5. Laundry and major cleaning tasks should be done by hired help. This is not woman's work.

6. An automobile should be an economy model. One should spend most of his money on household items and attractive interesting recreational activities.

7. "Save for a Rainy Day" is an old-fashioned motto.

8. The new houses in Joy Park are so neat and they advertise just $450 down.

*Mark says:*
1. Whenever I needed money, I earned it. I had a paper route at age 9.

2. Clothes should be durable, clean, and comfortable.

3. Our family attended church on special holidays.

4. Our family didn't pay much attention to birthdays.

5. Mom always did all the work around the house. She could hang wallpaper or upholster a chair.

6. I'd really like to have a new, big, safe car.

7. As a newly married couple it will be fun to spend our evenings at home or with friends.

8. I'd like to save so that in five or six years we could make a substantial downpayment on a well-built sturdy house.

Obviously, Lisa and Mark have many differences in the area of money management. If these differences are to lead to a happy marriage, they will have to learn to:

1. Consider each other's wishes with patience, understanding, and thoughtfulness.
2. Communicate reasons (relating to their values and goals) for buying certain items.
3. Make joint decisions.
4. Use their own talents to add to the income.
5. Appreciate their differences in background and training.
6. Compromise preconceived ideas on how a husband or wife should handle money.
7. Understand the differences in the values of men and women in regard to the use of money.
8. Make money work for them.
9. Fuse their aims in the spending of money.
10. Avoid becoming competitors for the use of the money.
11. Recognize that the security and stability shown in regularity and steadiness of employment, rather than income level, are important in marital happiness.

## INFLUENCES ON THE USE OF MONEY

Lisa and Mark illustrate the importance of individual *values and expectations* on the use of money. The *occupational demands* of the family members, particularly those of the breadwinner, dictate some of the items on the budget. For example, a doctor or a college professor may need to buy books or to attend professional meetings at his own expense; the salesman may find it necessary to play golf and to belong to a country club in order to have the proper business contacts; the craftsman, truck driver, or electrician may have to spend a certain amount for union dues. Clothing expenditures are also greatly influenced by the occupations of the family members.

*Social pressures* can also influence the cost of living. If the family lives among and associates with other families of like income and interests, it is difficult to resist the influence of the social group. If attending the children's theatre is done by all children in the group, it is difficult to deny the children in the family the same experience. If weekend outings for couples are a part of the club recreation, there is subtle pressure on the couple to participate.

*Psychological needs* often help determine the use of money. For example, a husband and wife may fail to achieve the recognition they need and therefore entertain frequently in order to compensate and be accepted in the "right circles." They may find it necessary to bowl, play poker, belong to a certain club, or join the group in the corner tavern for the same reason. Some couples satisfy their need for status (resulting from a feeling of inferiority or insecurity) by being sure that their children are given all the advantages they were denied or were ineligible to achieve.

Whether the need is to compensate for insecurity, lack of status, or for some other lack in their lives, these attempts to satisfy do affect spending in some families. It is impossible to indicate all the forms such action may take, and it is important that we understand rather than pass judgment upon a family's concept of its needs.

Of a quite different dimension in controlling money are the factors arising out of the psychological needs of the individual. Just as the family may have a need for security or status, so can the individual. Individual psychological needs are sometimes met through the use or the hoarding of money. The husband who must constantly prove to himself, his wife, and

*"Under our full-security plan you pay one monthly premium and we provide all your needs—insurance, housing, food, clothing, education, entertainment, a new car every three years, and burial service."*

Dave Gerard, *The Saturday Review*

274

his children that he is the dominant figure in the family can do so by holding a tight rein on the family's expenditures. The wife may demand that she control the finances and may arbitrarily dole out a small allowance to her husband because she resents his nominal headship in the family.

The changes in the needs of the family members as the family moves through the life cycle also influence the use of money. The new family spends more for major appliances, furniture, and other items that constitute the foundation for a family, whereas the family in the child-rearing state may spend more for educational pursuits, medical bills, and insurance.

## UNIQUE FINANCIAL DIFFICULTIES OF TEEN-AGE MARRIAGES

All marriages have the factors discussed above to a larger or smaller degree. However, teen-agers undertaking marriage have certain special financial difficulties. Among the sources of such problems which have been pointed out are (1) the financial resources with which teen-age marriages often are undertaken and (2) the rapid onset of parental responsibilities typical of teen-age marriages.[1]

However, other sources of financial problems need to be pointed out. These are the expectations and attitudes which teen-agers take with them into marriage. Teen-agers seem to expect that married life automatically will bring all the facilities and equipment which were found in their parents' homes. Philip Cateora, in a study of high school juniors and seniors in Texas, found that most teen-agers expected their first home after marriage to be well supplied with appliances. The high expectations coupled with the low incomes typical of most teen-age families perhaps explain the heavy involvement of many young families in installment debt.[2]

In 1962, about 57 percent of the spending units[3] with young heads had installment debts for personal loans as well as auto and consumer goods purchases. A major portion of the spending units with young heads which had installment debts had committed themselves deeply. Almost half of the spending units with young heads (18–24 years) which had installment debts had 20 percent or more of their previous year's income committed to installment payments. The large fixed payments

[1] J. Joel Moss, "Young Families: A Description," *Journal of Home Economics,* Vol. 53 (December, 1961), p. 830.

[2] Philip R. Cateora, "An Analysis of the Teen-Age Market," *Studies in Marketing,* No. 7 (Austin, Texas, Bureau of Business Research, University of Texas, 1963).

[3] The "spending unit" is the unit of inquiry used in many surveys of consumer finances. It is defined as "all persons living together who pool their incomes."

which these families had to pay left little flexibility in their budgets for emergencies or unexpected expenses.[4]

Cars, which may be a source of problems for many teen-agers before marriage, may continue to be a source of problems after marriage. Many adolescent boys continue their attachment to their cars after marriage and this may result in expenses which are a serious drain on the budgets of teen-age couples. In addition to its more utilitarian functions, a car often has symbolic importance to the young male. Hyman Weiland has pointed out that adolescent males may desire a car not so much for itself, but rather as a symbol of adult masculinity.[5]

Thus, even after marriage, the husband may wish to indulge these car needs, even though the wife may place a higher value on some other use of the money spent. In most families, the decision about buying a car is left principally to the husband, even though some conflict may arise over the impact of the purchase on the family budget. It appears that in many of these cases, the wife agrees to the purchase simply to keep her husband happy. According to Rainwater, Coleman, and Handel, this appears to be the case in working-class households.[6]

The percentage of families having cars is only slightly smaller for young families than for somewhat older or middle-aged families. In 1961, slightly over 60 percent of the spending units with young heads (18–24 years) had cars. Despite their low incomes, spending units with young heads are active in the car market. About 30 percent of them buy cars in a given year.[7]

This percentage is only slightly smaller than that for higher income, older families. Most of the purchases of the spending units with young heads are, not surprisingly, used cars rather than new ones.

Financing the ownership and operation of a car is a major item of expense in the budgets of young families. The amount spent for auto transportation is the third biggest item of expense (after housing and food) in the budget of young urban families with heads under age 25. The 1960–61 Bureau of Labor Statistics Survey of Consumer Expenditures found that the average young urban family (head under age 25) allo-

[4] Robert O. Herrmann, "Expectations and Attitudes As a Source of Financial Problems in Teen-Age Marriages," *Journal of Marriage and the Family,* Vol. 27, No. 1 (February, 1965), pp. 90–91.

[5] Hyman Weiland, "The Adolescent and the Automobile," *Chicago Review,* Vol. 9 (Fall, 1955), pp. 61–64.

[6] Lee Rainwater, Richard P. Coleman, and Gerald Handel, *Workingman's Wife* (New York, MacFadden, 1962), pp. 191–192.

[7] George Katona, and others, *1961 Survey of Consumer Finances,* Monograph No. 32 (Ann Arber, Survey Research Center, University of Michigan, 1962), pp. 38–41.

cated 17.3 percent of its expenditures to auto transportation. The average expenditure for the purchase and operation of a car in these families was $757 per year. Since this figure is an average for all households, including ones which did not own cars, the actual expenditures of the car-owning families probably substantially exceeded $750.[8] These large outlays for car expenses interfere with the accumulation of the household goods needed by beginning families and the building of much needed savings.

The optimistic expectations of teen-agers about their first home after marriage and the high priority assigned to car ownership can be potential sources of financial problems for teen-agers entering marriage. Without adequate financial counseling, these expectations and attitudes can become problems for newly married couples.

## HANDLING MONEY

*Credit* in any form costs money. When you borrow money, you must pay interest on the money borrowed. Rates may range from 6 to 30 percent and more for the use of cash or installment credit. The most common forms of credit are charge accounts, installment plans and loans. Charge accounts mainly offer convenience, but they may encourage careless buying. Installment plans and loans differ in the conditions under which they are set up, and the buyer should consider carefully how much extra he will pay for the privilege of an extended payment plan. *Contracts must be read very carefully.* The advantages and disadvantages of credit are listed below:

ADVANTAGES

1. Credit increases buying power.
2. Some appliances may pay for themselves in the length of time required to save the money. For example, a vacuum cleaner may help maintain the lustre of a carpet and thereby make professional cleaning bills unnecessary.
3. Necessary items can be had now.

DISADVANTAGES

1. Credit purchases create a debt.
2. The fees for the credit increase the cost of the item being purchased.
3. Buying power is restricted while the family pays off the debt.

*Savings* help a family to be self-supporting when unusual circumstances arise. They enable a family to make purchases without the additional cost

---

[8] *U.S. Bureau of Labor Statistics, Consumer Expenditures and Income, Urban United States,* 1960–61, Report No. 237–38 (April, 1964), p. 12.

of credit. A good savings program allows the money in the savings to earn additional money.

A *budget* is a financial statement of estimated income and expenses for a period of time. It is a plan for spending. A budget can give direction to your spending and it also can help you see where the money is being spent. Budgets can help families reach financial goals and help them receive value for their money.

To make a trial plan or budget, follow these five steps:

1. What is your total income?     $_____

2. What are the fixed expenses?     $_____

3. What are the flexible expenses?     $_____

4. Total items 2 and 3.     $_____

5. Deduct item 4 from item 1.     $_____

This is the amount left as savings for goals.

The basis for health and life insurance is to protect the family against the loss of income and to build up savings that can be used in an emer-

278

gency, for a special purpose, or to supplement income after the policy-holder's retirement.

There are four basic types of life insurance policies:

1.  A *straight life policy* provides lifetime protection. This is the most widely used of all types of ordinary life insurance and costs less annually than any other kind of lifetime protection. The low cost is based on the fact that the premiums are paid throughout the policy-holder's lifetime, and he is likely to live to a ripe old age. Whenever he does die, however, the benefits of the policy will be immediately available to his beneficiary.

    As the premiums are paid over the years, the straight life policy accumulates a cash value the policyholder may use. For example, the head of a household may borrow up to the cash value of his life insurance to help with expenses for college.

2.  A *limited payment life policy,* like straight life insurance, provides lifetime protection. However, premiums are paid only during a specified period of time. Since fewer premiums are called for on a limited payment policy than on the average straight life policy, each premium is larger.

    Many people buy a limited payment life policy which will be all paid up at the age of 65, so that they will not have to pay any premiums out of their retirement income, which is likely to be lower. Limited payment life polices also accumulate cash values.

3.  A *term insurance policy* offers only temporary protection for a stated number of years (or term) that the policy is in effect and usually does not accumulate any cash value. Should the policyholder die during the term, the full amount of the policy will be paid to his beneficiary. If he does not die during the term, the insurance protection ends when the term expires.

    If a term policy has a convertible provision, it may be exchanged for another type of insurance policy without a medical examination. A term policy may be renewed before it expires without a medical examination, if there is a renewable provision in the contract. Upon renewal, the policyholder will pay a higher premium because he is older.

    The premium is usually lower than for other kinds of policies because the risk is for a short period of time.

    Term insurance is designed to meet temporary needs, rather than for use in a family's permanent protection program. Many families use it, for example, while the children are growing up or while there is a mortgage or loan to pay, or until they are able to convert it to a program of lifetime protection.

4. An *endowment policy,* more than any other life insurance policy, puts the emphasis on savings. Its purpose is to accumulate a certain amount of money in a certain period of time, while at the same time providing life insurance during that period. If the policyholder lives, the whole amount of the policy is paid to him when the endowment matures or comes due, often 20 years after it was taken out.[9]

## TO PROMOTE UNDERSTANDING OF THIS CHAPTER

1. Define the following terms:

   credit          straight life policy          term policy
   budget          endowment policy

2. What factors cause money problems in marriage?

3. What affects an individual's use of money?

4. Write five situations for class discussion that you think Mark and Lisa may experience.

5. Differences in the use of money are solved by _____.

6. The use of money is influenced by _____.

7. How do teen-age marriages differ in their financial problems?

8. Write a paper on some aspect of money management. Possible titles:

   a. "The love of money, the root of all evil."
   b. "Two can live as cheaply as one."
   c. "Saving Goals."
   d. "Differences in male and female money values."
   e. "Money Discussions Before Marriage."

9. Collect actual budget expenses from three young married couples. Compare their costs of living.

10. Interview an auto salesman and find out at least three ways by which an automobile may be financed. What would be the sum of all payments on a $2500 auto bought by each plan?

---

[9] "Money Management for the Young Adult," Educational Division, Institute of Life Insurance, 277 Park Ave., New York 10017, p. 20.

## SUPPLEMENTARY READING

BOWMAN, HENRY A., *Marriage for Moderns.* McGraw-Hill, Inc., New York, 1965.

BUTTERFIELD, O. M., *Planning for Marriage.* D. Van Nostrand Company, Inc., Princeton, N.J., 1956.

DUVALL, EVELYN MILLIS and HILL, REUBEN, *When You Marry.* Association Press, New York, 1962.

FITZSIMMONS, CLEO, and WHITE, NELL, *Management for You.* J. B. Lippincott Co., Philadelphia, 1964.

HERRMANN, ROBERT O., "Expectations and Attitudes As a Source of Financial Problems in Teen-Age Marriage," *Journal of Marriage and the Family,* Vol. 27, No. 1, February, 1965, pp. 89–90.

KOOS, EARL LEMON, *Marriage.* Holt, Rinehart and Winston, Inc., New York, 1960.

LANDIS, PAUL H., *Making the Most of Marriage.* Appleton-Century-Crofts, Inc., New York, 1960.

"Money Management for the Young Adult," Educational Division, Institute of Life Insurance. New York, 10017.

MOSS, J. JOEL, "Young Families: A Description," *Journal of Home Economics,* Vol. 53, December, 1961.

STARR, MARY CATHERINE, Management for Better Living, 2d ed. revised. D. C. Heath & Co., Boston, 1963.

© 1953 The Curtis Publishing Company

*"Let's wait awhile. Maybe it'll taste better cold."*

# 25
# Happy and Unhappy Marriages

"A successful marriage is a dynamic, growing relationship in which the personalities of both partners continue to develop."[1]

Whether or not the cartoonists have portrayed successful marriages depends upon the tastes and expectations of the couples involved. The husband who smilingly suggests that the food may taste better cold may not be using sarcasm but instead may be showing sympathy for his wife's culinary experiments.

A successful marriage is not synonymous with words like happy, ideal, satisfactory or perfect. Happiness is subjective and individual; it depends

[1] Henry A. Bowman, *Marriage for Moderns* (New York, McGraw-Hill Book Company, Inc., 1965), p. 306.

*"You never did that before we were married!"*

upon the degree to which the relationship approaches the expectations of the two partners. An ideal marriage is the marriage that each one most desires; it makes the nearest approach to perfection and implies that each partner is satisfied with his lot. Further, no marriage is perfect.

A successful marriage is happy, but one can conceive of a happy marriage that is not successful because the standards of the couple are low and their relationship does not meet the criteria set up by society.

To help you consider the question of what is a successful marriage, the following standards of marital success are presented.

Mr. and Mrs. Joe Harris at 48 N. Lincoln Street might view their marriage as successful if:

1. they have developed the ability to communicate effectively with each other and have reached a pattern of affectionate responses that are mutually satisfying.

2. they can look back on their twenty years together and see many family objectives accomplished, and yet look forward to future accomplishments.

283

3. the wife has sufficient outside interests, so she is not threatened by the developing independence of the children now that they are entering their teens and will soon graduate from high school.

4. as a couple, they have enough outside, or social, participation to make them happy in their permanent, monogamous marriage.

5. they have developed an economically sound family unit.

Bob and Joan Green, newlyweds, in Apartment 5, 46 Fenway Avenue might view their marriage as successful if:

1. they are beginning to define their roles in marriage to their mutual satisfaction.

2. their love for each other is growing and developing in this new experience of marriage.

3. their development as a couple leaves room for respect of the rights and needs of the individual.

4. they are developing a common philosophy on economics so that they can feel mutually secure in each other's ability to handle the family finances.

5. they are creating the foundation of a home where the atmosphere would nurture children.

Mr. and Mrs. Roland Smith at 42 South Rocky Lane might view their marriage as successful if:

1. the husband keeps his position and supports the family.

2. they do no physical harm to each other.

3. the children do not come into conflict with the law.

4. the wife keeps the home reasonably comfortable.

Our culture, and the community, views marriage as successful if the couple has a permanent relationship. In other words, if the couple stays together, the community assumes that the marriage is working well. From the community view, the family that has permanence and participates in the welfare of other families in the community is most successful.

As you can see by the sketches above, however, individuals have different standards for the success of their marriages, and as you would expect, there is no one pattern of marriage that is essential for a satisfying union. There is reason to believe that the choice of a marital partner represents the merging of many needs and motives. When a person approaches marriage, he is likely to select a person who seems to meet his needs on both an unconscious and a conscious level. If the couple drawn by Ed Reed has a

Cartoon by Ed Reed

Reproduced by permission of the Register and Tribune Syndicate

satisfactory marriage, Edward's wife may really want to be told to shut-up. The quality of satisfaction in a marriage is closely related to the meeting of each other's needs. Whether the marriage can weather the adjustment necessary when children arrive depends to a large extent on how each partner has been able to develop into a more independent individual, to readjust to the changed configuration of the family, and yet to maintain needs that the other partner could meet to some satisfactory degree.

# THE IN-LAW NAMED MOST DIFFICULT BY 1,337 PERSONS

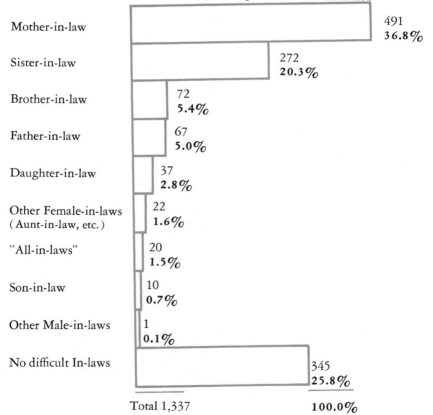

Number and percent of times mentioned

| | | |
|---|---|---|
| Mother-in-law | | 491  36.8% |
| Sister-in-law | | 272  20.3% |
| Brother-in-law | 72  5.4% | |
| Father-in-law | 67  5.0% | |
| Daughter-in-law | 37  2.8% | |
| Other Female-in-laws (Aunt-in-law, etc.) | 22  1.6% | |
| "All-in-laws" | 20  1.5% | |
| Son-in-law | 10  0.7% | |
| Other Male-in-laws | 1  0.1% | |
| No difficult In-laws | | 345  25.8% |
| Total 1,337 | | 100.0% |

From *In-Laws: Pro and Con* by Evelyn M. Duvall; Association Press, New York

286

Problems of many different kinds may be cited as the immediate cause of marital difficulties—money, sexual adjustment, in-laws, children, infidelity, and so on. However, the problems most frequently complained about fall within the broad category of lack of consideration by one spouse for the other. The lack of consideration may be in the handling of money—selfishness about money or failure to support; it may be in the area of affection and sex—failure to respond or perform adequately sexually or undue demand or withholding; it may be in the area of work or recreation—overactivity which leaves out the spouse or laziness in meeting responsibilities; it may be ineffectual communication or complete absence of an attempt to let the partner know what is going on. But essentially, the basic complaint is that a person fails to consider his spouse's feelings, needs, values, and goals, or acts in disregard of them.

Failure to meet the other partner's preconceived ideas of how a husband or wife should act, and failure to agree with his standards of behavior or value systems, i.e., the idea that the other is "different," with "different" interpreted as "undesirable," may cause misunderstanding and difficulty. Any difference from one partner's preconceived ideas of how his spouse should function in marriage may be regarded as a failure to perform satisfactorily or in a socially acceptable way and may be considered an affront by the other partner.

Basic for adjustment to different temperaments, desires, values, and ideals is an acceptance by each partner of the right of the other person to be different and a willingness to work out a compromise in terms of the long-range welfare of the marital unit—rather than a demand that one's own expectations and happiness come first.

Jealousy, not founded on fact, is the outward manifestation of a deep insecurity of the jealous partner in his or her sexual role and in his or her concept of self, especially in the capacity to evoke and keep the affection and fidelity of the other partner. Often this leads to attempts to limit or control the behavior of the partner with inevitable hostility, doubt, and fear in the jealous spouse, so that a destructive spiral may be set up between the partners.

A wife's *overdependence on her parents* may provoke frustration for her husband, who may feel that decisions are never made by himself and his wife, but by the wife and her parents. If this situation continues, anger is aroused because the wife seems to care more for her parents than for her husband and the marriage. A similar situation may arise between a husband and his parents. If a marriage is to be successful, *it is essential that the partners separate themselves from the child role in relation to their par-*

Specific reason reported
Number       Percent

| Number / Percent | Specific reason reported |
|---|---|
| 112<br>**14.9%** | They do not meddle, interfere, nor butt into my life, etc. |
| 38<br>**5.1%** | We overlook differences; respect each other's rights; etc. |
| 36<br>**4.8%** | They are mature, have outside interests, are independent, etc. |
| 33<br>**4.4%** | They are congenial; are tolerant of our differences; etc. |
| 29<br>**3.9%** | They come only when invited, do not abuse hospitality, etc. |
| 9<br>**1.2%** | They are not demanding or possessive; want us to be free |

Total Mutual | 257
Respect mentions | **34.3%**

From *In-Laws: Pro and Con* by Evelyn M. Duvall; Association Press, New York *ents* and accept an independent, adult role, both in their marriage and with their parents.

However, it is also important for the small nuclear family to have connections with the larger kinship groups and for each partner to have some willingness to accept and adjust to, and at times even to implement, the need of the other to maintain adult contact with the larger family groups.

Mothers-in-law head the list of difficult in-laws. More wives than husbands dislike their mothers-in-law. Generally, younger women more frequently than older ones find their mothers-in-law the most difficult in-law.

The main complaints against the mothers-in-law in the study by Duvall were their meddlesomeness, possessiveness, nagging, indifference, and thoughtlessness. Thus the complaints reach a wide range from too close to too far in communication.

However, the in-law problem can be alleviated if the persons concerned try to develop acceptance and mutual respect.

*Sexual problems* range from those caused by ignorance or thoughtlessness to those arising from unconscious neurotic attitudes or conflicts. One set of problems stems from overly rigid attitudes above love-making or perfectionistic expectations as to sexual response. Each couple has to discover from experimentation and experience the forms and patterns of foreplay that are most enjoyable and effective for them. Men sometimes have to learn that women are generally not as easily or quickly aroused as they themselves are. Physical stimulation is more important for women while psychic stimulation is often sufficient for men. The woman, on her part, may have to learn that she may be active in initiating and taking part in lovemaking and that, in general, her acceptance of her own sexuality and of her sexual partner may well be as important for him as his for her. Both partners will respect the aesthetic sensitivities of the other but, if necessary, will make an effort to overcome the sorts of prudishness and inhibition that represent a carryover from early masturbation guilt or other attitudes not properly attached to adult sexuality. Both partners will also do well to avoid "orgasm worship," that is, thinking that intercourse must end in a complete orgasm for each. The criteria for sexual gratification are overall pleasure followed by relaxation, and whatever leads to these is "good technique." An overemphasis upon physical gratification at the expense of closeness, tenderness, and manifestations of mutual acceptance leads to problems of sexual adjustment in marriage. It helps to remember that sexual intercourse is a psychosexual relationship, not simply a physical one.

Difficulties arise when one partner is interested in intercourse and the other is not. Couples often attempt intercourse when unduly tired, preoccupied or distraught. Gratifying sexual intercourse under such circumstances can be a comfort and a source of renewed hope, but the percentage

289

of failures is bound to be high. Unvoiced fears of pregnancy, the presence of children in the same or adjoining room, or any other situation that precludes complete privacy and abandon tend to interfere with sexual happiness. Most young couples require time and patience to overcome early attitudes of shame, fear, and guilt with respect to seeing, touching, and otherwise enjoying each other's bodies, in learning and creating together the optimum conditions for mutual physical enjoyment, and in working out the most satisfactory total emotional and physical interaction that spells psychosexual gratification.

*Infidelity* is most commonly the result of a search for something—sexual gratification, companionship, a sense of acceptance, and so on—not found in the marriage. Infidelity may be a sign of a psychological upset. The definition for a psychological upset may imply anything from a spiteful reaction during a quarrel to deep conflicts. The following examples suggest the range of possibilities: (1) Husband and wife quarrel, husband goes to a bar and picks up a prostitute. (2) A couple has a child. The husband cannot tolerate his wife's devotion to the infant so he turns to another woman. (3) Husband and wife are approaching middle age, are (perhaps unconsciously) threatened by declining sexual attractiveness and prowess, and (one or both) start having affairs to prove that nothing has changed (4) After a few years of marriage, the wife becomes a "golf widow" or "business widow" and so turns to someone else for attention, admiration, and sexual gratification. (5) Unconsciously one or both marital partners have married spouses who can be admired, adored and respected, but with whom sexuality is (again unconsciously) felt as gross, dirty, and forbidden; sex is therefore enjoyable only with a degraded love object, "a prostitute type." Psychological upset exists in all of these situations.

## QUARRELING

The innocent croquet game may lead to a family quarrel. Richard Brinsley Sheridan in *The Rivals* said, "The quarrel is a very pretty quarrel as it stands; we should only spoil it by trying to explain it." This may be true for some quarrels. However, quarreling can be a destructive or constructive force in a relationship depending upon the techniques and tactics employed. Chapter 6 discussed conflict in individual choice. This discussion of quarreling takes the individual conflicts and relates them to decisions that the couple must make as one.

*Constructive quarreling* brings the couple closer together. The quarrel has helped them see each other's point of view and they are made more aware of their definite opinions on the particular problem. The quarrel clears the air and dispels the tension that was building up. It defines the

290

issues more clearly. The quarrel helps the partners to see each other as real human beings and helps dispel the "halo effect" or the romantic illusion with which they were encumbered. Their mutual respect and understanding grow because of the outcome of the quarrel.

*The destructive quarrel* widens the gap between the couple. It dissolves in unkind words, hurt feelings, and an attack upon the psychological or physical frailties of the partners. The quarrel does not stay on the subject, but degrades into name-calling and the debunking of relatives and friends. The subject of the quarrel is lost, but the quarrel leaves deep wounds.

Butterfield, in *Planning for Marriage,* suggests some rules for the prevention of quarreling. Yet he cautions against the problem of rule-following without judgment. With this in mind, the rules are quoted for your consideration.

1. Be sure you understand the other person's point of view. Many arguments get well along and both contestants are highly overheated before they discover that they are talking about two different things.

2. Look for all possible points of agreement.

3. Do not start an argument you ought not to win. It is possible to win an argument and lose a marriage.

4. Avoid all forms of pressure tactics, such as (1) shouting the other person down, (2) using force or striking the other person, (3) being completely silent and denying the other person the satisfaction of a decent reply, (4) "pulling one's rank" on the other person, (5) withholding one's physical love.

5. Consider alternatives.

6. Be hopeful.

Few arguments are so important that they demand an immediate and complete solution on the spot. Many an argument at night is tangled with fatigue and the emotional stresses of the day. Tomorrow morning the issues may be crystal clear or they may seem insignificant and even childish.


## TO PROMOTE UNDERSTANDING OF THIS CHAPTER

1. Happiness in marriage is subjective and individual because _____.

2. Might a marriage be successful for one partner and not for another? Explain your answer.

3. Which criteria of marital success do you consider most important? Why?

4. Write a case study of an unhappy or happily married man or woman for class discussion.

5. How might the launching of the adolescent child affect an unhappy marriage? A happy marriage?

6. What are the frequent problems that cause marital difficulties?

7. Why is the husband's mother the most difficult in-law?

8. How can the in-law problem be alleviated?

9. What are the main causes of sexual adjustment problems in marriage?

10. What are the main causes of infidelity?

11. Define a constructive quarrel and a destructive quarrel.

12. Write a sketch of a quarrel. Which rules are applied or abused by the couple in conflict?

## SUPPLEMENTARY READING

BOWMAN, HENRY A., *Marriage for Moderns,* 5th ed. McGraw-Hill, Inc., New York, 1965.

BUTTERFIELD, OLIVER M., *Planning for Marriage.* D. Van Nostrand Company, Princeton, 1956, pp. 111–119.

———— *Sexual Harmony in Marriage.* New York, Emerson Books, 1955.

CLEMENS, ALPHONSE H., *Design for Successful Marriage,* 2nd ed. Prentice-Hall, Inc., Englewood Cliffs, N.J., 1964.

DUVALL, EVELYN MILLIS, *In-Laws Pro and Con.* Association Press, New York, 1964.

———— and HILL, REUBEN L., *Being Married.* Association Press, New York, 1960.

ELLIS, ALBERT and ABARBENEL, ALBERT, *The Encyclopedia of Sexual Behavior.* Hawthorn Books, New York, 1961.

MUDD, EMILY H. and KRICH, ARON, *Man and Wife, A Source Book on Family Attitudes, Sex Behavior, and Marriage Counseling.* W. W. Norton and Co., Inc., New York, 1957.

STONE, HANNAH M. and ABRAHAM A., *Marriage Manual,* Rev. ed. Simon and Schuster, Inc., New York, 1952.

TERMAN, LEWIS M. et al, *Psychological Factors in Marital Happiness.* McGraw-Hill, Inc., New York, 1938.

*"Oops! We're too late!"*

# 26
# The Family and Crises

Webster's dictionary defines a crisis as a crucial time . . . the decisive moment or turning point in a situation. The decisive moments, the turning points in our lives, vary according to our experiences and the way we view situations. The cartoon above and the one on the following page may portray a crisis for some and a humorous situation for others. In other words, we view them with the same mixed emotions as shown by Busino's audience at the play. What is a crisis for you may be just an annoyance for me. On the other hand, the situation which is of major concern to me may go unnoticed by you.

*"I understand this play opened to mixed reviews."*

## FAMILY CRISES

There are four main kinds of crises that families face. These are loss of a member, addition of a member, loss of status or of face, and a combination of loss or addition of a member plus loss of status.

Dismemberment (loss of a member) may be brought about by death, hospitalization, or separation for business reasons or military service. Accession (the addition of a member) is characterized by birth, adoption, moving of a relative into a family home, return of a deserter, the remarriage of a parent, or a reunion after a long period of separation. Demoralization (loss of status or face) can be a part of a disgrace such as alcoholism, drug addiction, crime, or delinquency. It could also be brought about by progressive dissension, infidelity, and nonsupport. Demoralization plus dismemberment or accession is defined by situations such as suicide or homicide, imprisonment, illegitimacy, divorce, desertion, or annulment.

This chapter will not try to deal with all of the major crises. It will only discuss some of those that are more commonly faced in our culture. We must remember, however, that what may precipitate a major crisis in one marriage may be handled adequately by the partners in another. The first year of marriage is a year of new adjustments for both partners and, depending upon their maturity and temperament, may be completed without undue stress. On the other hand, these new adjustments may foment serious problems. The largest number of divorces is reported in the first year of marriage, the next largest numbers in the third and fifth years. Adjustment to the role of parent, in addition to that of husband and wife, imposes additional strain. How severe the strain and whether the birth of a child may be disrupting to the marriage depend upon the couple's marital stability and their readiness for the responsibilities of parenthood.

## DEATH (DISMEMBERMENT)

Death is a constitutive part of life. It is another life experience. The democracy of death will eventually include us all.

294

Death can mean different things to different people. Its specific meaning depends on the nature and fortunes of a person's development and his cultural setting. To many, death represents a teacher of transcendental truths incomprehensible during life. For others, death is a friend who brings an end to pain through peaceful sleep. Still others visualize it as an adventure—a great, new, oncoming experience. And there are those who see it as the great destroyer who is to be fought to the bitter end.

Attitudes toward death are the result of many interweaving factors. Some of the more significant variables seem to be the age of the person, religious orientation, psychological maturity, and level of threat. For example, it is apparent that the thought of death may mean one thing at the age of twenty, another thing at the age of forty, and something quite different at eighty. Or, consider the aspect of the temporal nearness or distance of personal death. It is wholly conceivable that a person's perception of the world and attitudes about death might not be quite the same tomorrow as they are today, if meanwhile he were informed that he had a spreading cancer. Likewise, a person who knows that he is suffering from a

*"He took it with him."*

disease that will lead to death and remains in his everyday environment with its regular duties and problems is quite unlike the person who is immobilized and awaiting death in a hospital bed. The type or kind of person one is may sometimes be more important than the threat of death itself in determining the individual's reaction.

Our life receives one of its principal directions, if not its main one, from what death means to us. The kind of immortality we seek has a major impact on the kind of life we lead, whether the immortality is biological (children), social (work accomplishments that testify to our existence and live on in the thoughts of the living), or transcendental (beliefs that this life is but the precondition for the "true" life yet to come).

There is also, of course, the outlook of the Roman poet, Horace, which highlights personal pleasures and gratifications. His philosophy implies that since this life is the only one we have, let's "live it up." Others with a similar philosophic view feel that if we do have only this one chance at living, then life must be utilized to its utmost to give it full value and meaning. Religion is another factor that guides us to live in such a manner as to be judged favorably in the hereafter. Religion also gives direction, value, and meaning to this life.

People ordinarily become conscious of thoughts about death and dying in the following major situations: (1) they personally become seriously ill, (2) someone in their immediate family becomes seriously ill or dies, (3) friends develop a serious illness or die, (4) they join the armed forces or are involved in a war situation, (5) they are personally involved in an accident of some consequence, or (6) disastrous public accidents are reported in the newspaper or over radio or television.

*Grief* is the state of pain, discomfort, and often mental and physical impairment that in most persons follows the loss of a loved one. It is marked by the painful feelings of sorrow, loss of appetite and sleep, a sense of excessive fatigue, and a general state of mood depression. While sorrow is the pain and misery attending the state of grieving, grief itself is an active state of adapting to the loss of a dear one by a special kind of psychological work.

Much can be done to help the mourning person to readaptation to life after a severe loss. It seems important to have an opportunity to express the deep emotion that is part of mourning and to have a chance to review the experiences and activities which were previously shared with a lost person. The eulogy and traditional ceremony are often helpful in bringing together friends and relatives to discuss aspects of the lost person's life and to give the mourners a chance to express their feelings without embarrassment. The real work of adaptation, however, usually starts later when the survivor finds himself alone in his efforts to cope with the new situation. Con-

296

tinued friendly contact and more opportunities for talking about the loss are then helpful.

The loss that precipitates mourning and grieving is most commonly the death of a person important in one's life. However, it may also be the loss of another person who has jilted or disappointed one or it may be loss by geographical removal of another individual. Finally, leaving home and parents at the end of school or even leaving one's place of work for another may often be followed by unrecognized forms of grieving and mourning that go under the names of homesickness and promotional depression.

The United States Bureau of the Census reports that in 1960 there were nearly eight million widows in the United States, an increase of more than 17 percent since 1950.

A woman younger than her husband is very likely to be left a widow. Only if a wife is five years older than her husband are the odds even against her becoming a widow. Among women between thirty-five and forty-five who have been married, 4.5 percent are widows. If we make further allowance for the fact that, as a rule, men are two or more years older than their wives, the unavoidable conclusion is that many women have to face years of widowhood without either a provider or an object for their whole-hearted attention.

There are common elements in the experiences of wives when their husbands die. This does not mean that all women share identical reactions to this loss, nor that these reactions will be of the same order or degree of intensity. Much will depend on the specific situation, the nature of the marital relationship, available resources for assistance, and the personality of the wife.

The initial response to a husband's death is frequently a kind of numbness or paralysis. The widow is unable to integrate what has happened. This numbness is an expression of the struggle against accepting the finality of the loss. Initially, her insulation is a healthy protection against the deep pain and difficult reality.

This numbness ultimately wears off; reality and pain seep in and a variety of new feelings may appear. There is often physical pain, a tightness in the throat, a choking or empty feeling, and insomnia. Common physical manifestations include extreme exhaustion and loss of appetite.

Accompanying these physical reactions is a range of emotional responses such as (1) restlessness, with a need for activity that has no purpose, (2) inconsistency, with a feeling of being driven in many directions, (3) irritability, with no apparent provocation, and (4) an accompanying sense of resignation, as though nothing mattered. Everything appears distorted, out of focus. There is often a relentless preoccupation with the image of the husband and a withdrawal from the usual patterns of living. Impatience with other people is common, despite a dread of being alone; a sense of isolation is experienced even among friends and relatives. The widow may accuse herself of negligence and berate herself for not having been a more devoted wife—expressions of a strong sense of guilt and self-pity.

## ACCESSION—BIRTH OR ADOPTION

Ordinarily we think about the parent-child relationships in terms of the influence of the parents on the child. But the child can also have an effect on his parents, and at no time is this impact likely to be greater than at the very beginning of the child's life. Harold Feldman and his co-workers at Cornell University have been studying the behavior and attitudes of married couples before and after the arrival of the first child. In general, they find that childless couples report a higher level of marital satisfaction and talk more with each other about personal feelings and common interests. In contrast, couples with a young child experience fewer stimulating exchanges of ideas, fewer gay times, fewer moments of laughter, and additional feelings of resentment. Inasmuch as the couples were matched on age and length of marriage, the differences could not have been due to changes associated with either of these factors. Feldman concludes that the arrival of a child typically brings about a blunting of emotional expression and a lowering of the level of verbal communication between the spouses.

Such findings bring home the fact that the arrival of a first child involves a period of tension and anxiety for the parents. At the same time, the strain is not without its rewards. The couples in Feldman's research, representing all stages of the family cycle, rated the "first year with an infant" as the most satisfying stage in married life, superior even to the stage "before the children arrive." The least satisfying period was when children were "gone from home" and next to that "having teen-agers." Clearly child-rearing is replete both with problems and rewards. The wise parent does well to be prepared for the former and let the latter catch him by surprise.

## ALCOHOLISM (DEMORALIZATION)

A 1965 nationwide survey by the Social Research Group of George Washington University, which was based on a weighted sample of 2746 subjects, indicated that 68 percent of all American adults—77 percent of the men and 60 percent of the women—drink at least occasionally. While the proportion of men drinkers in the adult population has remained about constant in the past 20 years, the proportion of women drinkers has risen.

Out of all adults, the survey classified 56 percent as infrequent-to-moderate drinkers and 12 percent as heavy drinkers. The latter are not necessarily alcoholics, but they do include the problem drinkers. They are more apt to be men than women (a four-to-one ratio).[1]

Estimates of the number of alcoholics in the United States are among the most publicized statistics. According to the Rutgers Center of Alcohol Studies, the number may be between four million and five million—approximately four percent of the total adult population.[2]

Individual variation makes it impossible to present a complete list of the signs and symptoms uniformly characterizing the early stages of problem drinking. However, demoralization of the individual and his family occur when the individual exhibits some of the following types of behavior: (1) the need to drink before facing certain situations, (2) frequent drinking sprees, (3) a steady increase in intake, (4) solitary drinking, (5) early morning drinking, (6) Monday morning absenteeism, (7) frequent disputes about drinking, and (8) the occurrence of what are termed blackouts.

For a drinker, a blackout is not "passing out" but a period of time in which, while remaining otherwise fully conscious, he undergoes a loss of memory. He walks, talks, and acts, but does not remember any of his words or actions. Such blackouts may represent one of the early signs of the more serious forms of alcoholism.

Alcoholism may be present without blackouts, however, and without any of the other popularly accepted symptoms of addictive drinking. Many alcoholics do not go on drinking sprees, or drink alone, or drink in the morning, or miss work on Monday, yet they are considered alcoholics.

In general, an individual may be considered an alcoholic if he continues to drink even though his drinking consistently causes physical illness—headache, gastric distress, or hangover—or consistently causes trouble with his wife, employer, or the police.

Among the most demoralizing effects charged against excessive drinking are unhappy marriages, broken homes, impoverished families, and deprived or displaced children. The cost to public and private agencies for support of families ravaged by alcoholism has been put at many millions of dollars a year. The cost in human suffering and loss of status and face is incalculable.

It should, however, be understood that when excessive drinking is involved in these social catastrophes, it may not necessarily be the primary

---

[1] Ira H. Cisin, paper presented before the American Association for the Advancement of Science, Washington, D.C., December, 1966.

[2] Vera Efron and Mark Keller, *Selected Statistical Tables on the Consumption of Alcohol, 1850–1962 and on Alcoholism, 1930–1960,* Rutgers Center of Alcohol Studies, New Brunswick, N.J., 1963.

cause. In many broken marriages, the complaint is heard, "Everything was all right until my husband started drinking too much." But perceptive marriage counselors have asked, "If everything was all right, then why did he start drinking excessively?"

It is clear that not only does the alcoholic affect his family, but the family also affects the alcoholic and the severity of his illness. Solutions to such tangled relationships usually pose problems that can be resolved only if the biological, psychological, and sociological aspects of the specific situations are placed in balance for each member of the family.

Research has shown that for people who use alcohol to a significant degree, the lowest incidence of alcoholism is associated with certain habits and attitudes:

1. The children are exposed to alcohol early in life, within a strong family or religious group. Whatever the beverage, it is served in very diluted form and in small quantities, with consequent low blood-alcohol levels.

2. The beverage is considered mainly as a food and usually consumed with meals.

3. Parents present a constant example of moderate drinking.

4. No moral importance is attached to drinking. It is considered neither a virtue nor a sin.

5. Drinking is not viewed as a proof of adulthood or virility.

6. Abstinence is socially acceptable. It is no more rude or ungracious to decline a drink than to decline a piece of bread.

7. Excessive drinking or intoxication is not socially acceptable. It is not considered stylish, comical, or tolerable.

8. Finally, and perhaps most important, there is a wide and usually complete agreement among members of the group on what might be called the ground rules of drinking.[3]

## DIVORCE (DEMORALIZATION PLUS DISMEMBERMENT)

There are essentially two forms of divorce: (1) an absolute legal dissolution of the marriage bond and (2) a judicial separation of man and wife, or termination of cohabitation, without dissolution of the marriage bond.

[3] *Alcohol and Alcoholism,* National Institute of Mental Health, Public Health Service Publication No. 1640, Superintendent of Documents, U.S. Government Printing Office, Washington, D.C., p. 28.

The census reports for 1960 recorded 2,814,000 divorced persons in the United States: 1,106,000 men, 1,708,000 women.

Although divorce rates are lower in lower income groups, this does not offer a true picture of the amount of family disorganization or marital disharmony existing within these families. The cost of divorce undoubtedly affects the rate of divorce in the lower income group. In many instances where cost is prohibitive and there is a desire on the part of one or both parties to escape the unhappiness of the marital bond, either separation by mutual agreement or desertion by one partner takes place. Permanent desertion has been characterized as "the poor man's divorce." Deserted wives (and wives are more often deserted than husbands) frequently are handicapped both by lack of legal knowledge and by the lack of financial means for obtaining a divorce. In consequence, we have no way of knowing the extent of desertion, whereas divorce statistics are available for most states and for the country as a whole.

The fact that divorce laws have become more lenient may have some slight bearing on the divorce rate, but marriage and divorce are part of a

*"Drop whatever you're doing. We're going out to dinner . . ."*

very complicated and changing cultural pattern. The functions and expectations of marriage are changing, calling for new and untried adjustments. Separation and divorce may seem to many to be forms of adjustment of conflicting wants and values.

Marriage today, as contrasted with marriage some fifty years ago, has as its primary values mutual love and affection, including sexual satisfaction, equality of the partners, and freedom for personal development and happiness. Anything that disturbs the mutual sympathy and love between husband and wife creates serious tensions. If happiness is not attained, the marriage is regarded as a failure. Since marriage for love has become the basic pattern in our country, unhappiness in marriage is often blamed on a faulty choice of mate, rather than on faulty adjustment between the two partners. Divorce or separation, with choice of another partner, may be seen as a possible solution. Essentially, marriage is a vulnerable human relationship composed of the feelings, attitudes, values, behaviors, and demands that flow back and forth between the partners. Each acts as both cause and effect within this relationship. The difficulty that disrupts the relationship lies in a destructive interaction between the two partners. The focus of their difficulty may be in a mother-in-law, sexual incompatibility,

*"Try to look happy—it's my first wife!"*

money, and so on, but the basic problem is the failure of each to meet the other's emotional needs to a satisfactory degree.

Loneliness is probably the most painful fear for both man and woman. Marriage is the most intimate of relationships and embraces more facets of an individual's personality than do other adult relationships. Loss of this relationship, by and large, therefore, represents a loss of a great number of human satisfactions. Failure in a human relationship, in our culture, carries with it some stigma of shame for the failure and some guilt and question about oneself and one's adequacy. For the woman, there may be loss of adequate support and the necessity, once more, to earn her own living and to help in the support of her own children. Usually the woman is responsible for the day-to-day rearing of the children, and this imposes a dual burden. She is again faced with the possibility of competing in the marriage market. In addition to loneliness and the lack of home care, a man may face complicated problems in the financial field. It is more expensive to support two domiciles. Should he marry again, he may be faced with supporting two families, neither adequately. If he remains unmarried, his opportunity for building a sustained and satisfying emotional relationship is limited. His relationship to his children must, of necessity, be piecemeal and unsatisfying. In many instances a man is unduly and unfairly treated by the divorce laws.

## FACING CRISES

There is no pat answer to the problem of facing crises, whether they involve one individual or many families. Yet, some help for facing a crisis may come from taking time to consider the following:

1. Try to face and accept the reality of the situation.

2. Try to deal with the emotional upheaval that ensues.

3. Try to determine what was good in the past and how it can be used in the present by thinking through needs and wishes, resources and capacities, choices, and alternatives.

## TO PROMOTE UNDERSTANDING OF THIS CHAPTER

1. List as many crises as you can that a family might face.

2. Define a crisis in your own terms.

3. What are the main kinds of crises? Does the list you made for question 1 fit these four categories?

4. What are the two forms of divorce?
5. What are the main causes of divorce?
6. What are the fears of an individual facing a divorce?
7. What is your philosophy of death?
8. Do you think that one's philosophy of death influences his life? Explain your answer.
9. What influences one's attitudes toward death?
10. What is grief?
11. How would you help a friend adjust to his grief?
12. What factors contribute to the demoralizing crises caused by alcohol?
13. Choose a crisis and then analyze how you would face it. Some suggestions of crises are loss of money, loss of a father or a mother, loss of a boyfriend or girlfriend, illegitimate birth, failure in school, lack of a date for the prom, indulgence in drugs, and so on.

## SUPPLEMENTARY READING

*Alcohol and Alcoholism,* National Institute of Mental Health, Public Health Service Publication No. 1640, Superintendent of Documents, U.S. Government Printing Office, Washington, D.C., p. 28.

BERNARD, JESSIE, *Remarriage: A Study of Marriage.* Holt, Rinehart, and Winston, Inc., New York, 1956.

BOGUE, DONALD J., *Skid Row in American Cities.* University of Chicago Press, Chicago, 1963.

CESIN, IRA H., Paper presented before American Association for the Advancement of Science, Washington, D.C., December, 1966.

CHEIN, ISIDOR, and others, *The Road to H.* Basic Books, Inc., New York, 1964.

COIN, ARTHUR H., *The Cured Alcoholic.* John Day Company, New York, 1964.

DESPERT, J. LOUIS, *Children of Divorce.* Doubleday & Co., Inc., New York, 1953.

DUVALL, EVELYN M. and HILL, REUBEN L., *Being Married.* Association Press, New York, 1960.

EFRON, VERA and KELLER, MARK, *Selected Statistical Tables on the Consumption of Alcohol, 1850–1962 and on Alcoholism, 1930–*

1960. Rutgers Center of Alcohol Studies, New Brunswick, N.J., 1963.

FELDMAN, HAROLD, Unpublished Paper, given before the American Psychological Association, Fall 1968.

GLICK, PAUL, *American Families*. John Wiley & Sons, Inc., New York, 1957.

GOODE, WILLIAM J., *After Divorce*. Free Press of Glencoe, Glencoe, Ill., 1956.

JACKSON, EDGAR N., *Understanding Grief*. Abingdon Press, Nashville, Tenn., 1957.

MYERS, FREDERICK W. H., *Human Personality and Its Survival of Bodily Death*, 2 vols. David McKay Co., New York, reprinted 1954.

MYRDAL, ALVA and KLEIN, VIOLA, *Women's Two Roles*. Humanities Press, New York, 1962.

STRAUS, ROBERT and GERARD, DONALD, *Drinking in College*. Yale University Press, New Haven, Conn., 1953.

*". . . and that's me entering the church for the wedding!"*

# 27
# The Unmarried

Comedians and cartoonists use the conflicts and problems of marriage and the joys of bachelorhood as subjects for reams of material. The bridegroom is often portrayed as reluctant. The bachelor has complete freedom to play poker with the boys and to come and go as he wishes. He is seen as a free agent who is identified with the idea of a life of "fun and games." However, although attitudes are starting to change, even today the bachelor girl is stereotyped as the "old maid."

The psychological problem of the unmarried in our society is a serious one. It is, for example, known that men tend to die at an earlier age than

*"My arms are getting tired!"*

women, men traditionally marry women who are somewhat younger than themselves, and the estimated number of women in our population who have never married or who are presently divorced or widowed runs as high as eight million. Many individuals are therefore bound to experience disappointment with respect to a major goal in their lives, and the statistics that exhibit higher rates of suicide, alcoholism, and earlier deaths among both single men and single women are of concern to society.

Within the culture and at various points in the individual's development, the idea of the worth and value of marriage is reinforced. Parents often become anxious when their children do not "date" and subtly communicate their anxiety, frequently nonverbally. One's marital status sometimes is a consideration in a job promotion, and advertisers attempt to sell soap, deodorant, mouthwash, and hair tonic by associating them with one's attractiveness to the opposite sex. The prospect of remaining unmarried, even for the individual who does so as a matter of choice, can evoke

307

anxiety and fear. For many persons, the prospect of living one's life alone without the guarantee of physical and psychological closeness to another is depressing.

The situation for an unmarried woman is more difficult both psychologically and socially than for a single man. According to the mores of our culture, the woman's role is a passive one; the man is expected to take the initiative in the relationships between the sexes. A difficult dilemma is posed for the unmarried woman; she faces the frustration resulting from passively hoping that she will be noticed by men who will then make the proper social overtures to her. If she takes too active a course, she risks social disapproval for taking the initiative, risks the disapproval of the man or men she hopes to impress, and most importantly, risks her own disapproval of herself for violating a deeply-ingrained social rule of the game of man-woman relationships. Some women successfully interest men through appearance and behavior carefully planned and carried out for the purpose of taking the initiative without appearing to do so. Such maneuverings are not always successful, however, and for many women, the duplicity and the skills required are so alien to their own concepts of proper role behavior that they cannot engage in this form of competition.

Not only does the unmarried woman frequently have personal feelings of devaluation and of being unfulfilled and deprived of the opportunity for motherhood, but our society tends to reenforce such devaluation. Rarely is it assumed that the unmarried woman has chosen to remain single because she has not found a man with whom she has wanted to participate in a love relationship. Jokes that feature the spinster lady or the old maid reflect this devaluation of the role of the unmarried woman. Thus, for many women, attracting a husband constitutes a signal achievement, a mark of feminine adequacy, and a public statement that social expectations have been fulfilled.

However, a certain percentage of our population, either through choice or circumstance, will not marry. Another percentage will marry and then conclude that they can live a more harmonious life as a single person, and a third group will not marry but not through their own choice.

Some of the circumstances which lead to the single state include the fact that in our culture there is a larger number of women than men of marriageable age who want to marry. It is estimated that there are six million females in the United States over 14 years old. Although many of these women would choose to marry, they will not. Who these will be depends on many factors some of which are not directly associated with personality.

A woman's vocation or geographic location can affect her chances for marriage. For example, teachers and city-dwelling women meet fewer acceptable mates than do business women and women in rural areas. The

308

*"Lately, after I get to the top, I find myself saying, 'So what?'!"*

more education the woman has, the less likely she is to marry, mainly because the number of eligible males decreases as her standards become higher. Seventy-two percent of college women marry as compared to ninety per cent for the population as a whole. Some individuals who want to marry perceive these patterns in our culture and plan their lives so that they will operate to favor their plans.

## SOCIETY'S CONCEPT OF THE SINGLE PERSON

Marriage not only represents a valued social institution in our culture; it also confers a valued status upon its members. The roles of husband and wife carry a degree of prestige and are a source of self-esteem. Although one out of every seven girls in our society will never marry, both the expectation and the hope of most men and women is that they will marry and remain married. Thus, it might be argued that no one in our culture chooses to remain unmarried and that a conscious decision of this sort is really dictated by unconscious feelings of guilt about sexuality, or of fear and hatred toward the opposite sex, or a deep insecurity with respect to oneself. The choice of the celibate life is made in face of powerful social forces, and such a choice is applauded in our culture only if there is a sense of renunciation for the sake of great artistic, social, or religious purpose. In general, if one is not married to a spouse, one is expected to be married to a cause.

## INDIVIDUALS WHO SHOULD NOT MARRY

It is easy to assert that certain persons should never marry. In practice, however, most authorities are reluctant to be categorical. In most states, for example, marriage licenses will not be issued to actively syphilitic individuals, but this is a temporary rather than permanent obstacle to marriage. After being cured the individual can reapply for a license. Hereditary feeblemindedness and "incurable" insanity or epilepsy are reasons for legal sterilization in many states, but the legal "capacity to give consent" may be all that is required for marriage. One may, therefore, distinguish between those who should not have children from those who should not marry at all, but legal definitions in either area are most difficult because of actual or potential threats to civil liberties.

Considering the probable fate of the marriage and the social consequences, most authorities recommend that the following should not marry: (1) persons with inherited degenerative diseases, (2) feebleminded people who require institutional care, (3) chronic epileptics who need constant supervision, (4) persons who have chronic or recurrent mental illnesses, (5) confirmed homosexuals, (6) chronic, severe alcoholics, (7) persons of adult years who have never achieved and show no promise of emotional and intellectual emancipation from parents or parent-substitutes, (8) those who, for whatever reason, cannot tolerate the restrictions of marriage, and (9) individuals so dedicated to causes or careers as to preclude the kinds of emotional commitment to another person usually required for marriage.

## ADJUSTMENT TO SINGLEHOOD

We have discussed the difficulties that single men and women encounter. These difficulties should not lead us to think that they are denied the possibility for meaningful relationships with others, challenging work, or full and rewarding lives. Because of the uneven distribution of men and women of marriageable age, many persons, apparently well qualified for marriage, do not marry.

There are several things one needs to watch if he is to be happy though unmarried. Too many unmarried people become peculiar, warped, and eccentric personalities because they resigned themselves too soon to a life of isolation, loneliness, and negativism.

First, one needs to choose some creative career in life and become enthusiastic about it. The unenthusiastic person is pretty much of a dud, whether single or married. Special enthusiasm for a vocation or avocation is one of the most realistic antidotes for the anguish of loneliness.

Second, one should discover some hobby or volunteer work that gives the promise of satisfying some deep interests and of becoming a mental, if not a source of physical, relaxation and enthusiasm. This second adjustment is beneficial to the development of self-identity and latent talents.

Third, one should hold on to one's friends, even though they may marry and become absorbed in their own family interests. The children of friends can become interesting. Their growth, advancement, successes, and failures can be a part of a family friend's life. A friend of similar sex is valuable for the sharing of hopes, jokes, speculations, and recreational activities. The companionship of kindred minds expels loneliness.

Fourth, a single person should become generally more intelligent about sex. One ought to have a general understanding of the nature of sexual drives in individuals and in one's self so that he can manage sex instead of feeling that it is driving him.

Fifth, one should continue learning. No one is ever too wise or too old to stop his education. This is doubly true of single people. Those who are married and have families will have education thrust upon them.

Finally, the single man or girl should not fall into the error of considering himself a martyr, freak, or misfit because he is still single. It is well to remember that many people face half or more of their total lives as single persons. Most people have from eight to fifteen years of single living after they have reached adolescence. Many others, through no fault of their own, find that they must survive as single people because of widowhood, separation, or divorce. If a person is ever tempted to think that the world has passed him by, he should be smart enough not to show it. Such thoughts will show in his attitudes and behavior, and people will begin to avoid his company.

In any case, if a person remains single, he should face the facts, maintain his friendships and interests but not force them to the saturation point, avoid self-pity, make use of his opportunities, and never think of himself as inferior or peculiar. Being an "old maid" or an "old bachelor" is a state of mind rather than a legal status. There are well-adjusted single persons; there are married "old maids" and "old bachelors." Insofar as certain qualities are necessary for success in marriage, the individual is faced with the two alternatives of marrying or not marrying; and his choice should be based, at least in part, on the personality traits he exhibits combined with his interest in marriage. If he feels that remaining single is the way to greater happiness in life, he should by all means remain single. He should not marry against his will just because there is social pressure exerted.

## UNMARRIED PARENTS

In 1964, for each 1000 unmarried women, 23.4 illegitimate babies were born. In 1965, the latest year for which illegitimacy records are available, illegitimate births reached 291,200.

As you see, the problem of illegitimacy is not concentrated in young women. Actually, teen-age girls are less likely to have babies out of wedlock than older women. Unwed mothers are not a homogeneous group as to age, cultural values, economic status, education, and religious and moral background. Births out of wedlock occur among women of all ages within the child-bearing range. Forty percent of the reported births out of wedlock were to women under 19 years of age.

In the discussion of unmarried parents, the focus will be on the 20 to 29 percent of the children born out of wedlock who live with their mothers. An unmarried mother who is planning for herself and her child

| ILLEGITIMATE LIVE BIRTHS, BY AGE AND COLOR OF MOTHER: 1940–1965[1] | | | | | | | | | |
|---|---|---|---|---|---|---|---|---|---|
| Age and color | 1940 | 1945 | 1950 | 1955 | 1960 | 1962 | 1963 | 1964 | 1965 |
| Total | 89.5 | 117.4 | 141.6 | 183.3 | 224.3 | 245.1 | 259.4 | 275.7 | 291.2 |
| Rates[2] | 7.1 | 10.1 | 14.1 | 19.3 | 21.8 | 21.5 | 22.5 | 23.4 | 23.4 |
| By age of mother: | | | | | | | | | |
| Under 15 years | 2.1 | 2.5 | 3.2 | 3.9 | 4.6 | 5.1 | 5.4 | 5.8 | 6.1 |
| 15 to 19 years | 40.5 | 49.2 | 56.0 | 68.9 | 87.1 | 94.4 | 101.8 | 111.4 | 123.1 |
| 20 to 24 years | 27.2 | 39.3 | 43.1 | 55.7 | 68.0 | 77.3 | 82.6 | 87.9 | 90.7 |
| 25 to 29 years | 10.5 | 14.1 | 20.9 | 28.0 | 32.1 | 34.0 | 35.4 | 36.4 | 36.8 |
| 30 to 34 years | 5.2 | 7.1 | 10.8 | 16.1 | 18.9 | 19.8 | 19.8 | 19.5 | 19.6 |
| 35 to 39 years | 3.0 | 4.0 | 6.0 | 8.3 | 10.6 | 11.1 | 10.9 | 11.1 | 11.4 |
| 40 and over | 1.0 | 1.2 | 1.7 | 2.4 | 3.0 | 3.2 | 3.5 | 3.6 | 3.7 |
| By color of mother: | | | | | | | | | |
| White | 40.3 | 56.4 | 53.5 | 64.2 | 82.5 | 92.6[3] | 102.2[3] | 114.3 | 123.7 |
| Nonwhite | 49.2 | 60.9 | 88.1 | 119.2 | 141.8 | 146.7[3] | 150.7[3] | 161.3 | 167.5 |

*Statistical Abstract of the United States*, U.S. Bureau of the Census, Washington, D.C., 1967. p. 51.

[1] Prior to 1960, excludes Alaska and Hawaii. Includes estimates for states in which legitimacy data were not reported. No estimates included for misstatements on birth records or failures to register births. Beginning in 1960, based on a 50 per cent sample of live births in the reporting states.

[2] Rate per 1,000 unmarried (never married, widowed, and divorced) women aged 15–44 years enumerated as of April 1 for 1940 and 1950 and estimated as of July 1 for all other years.

[3] Figures by color exclude data for residents of New Jersey.

may do one of four things: (1) return to her own home with the baby, (2) set herself up independently with the baby in this case, usually with the choice of self-support or of requesting public assistance, (3) place the baby in a foster home for a temporary or an indefinite period, or (4) surrender the baby for adoption.[1]

In middle-class circles, the first alternative is almost certainly doomed to failure unless a girl's family and community can honestly accept both her and the child without shock, critical judgment, or recrimination. Otherwise, there are almost insuperable obstacles to their finding a secure and unbiased place for themselves. Rarely is the fact of the child's illegitimacy permanently forgotten.

The woman who attempts to make her own way independently with the child faces problems just as great. The practical difficulty of arranging good and consistent care for her child while she works to support both of them is enormous. They face the same problem of acceptance in the community, and this may mean facing all the practical obstacles and complications with little outside help or support. While a mother may avoid the hurdle of securing reliable, outside care for her child by seeking public assistance and remaining at home to take care of her child herself she increases the difficulties of winning public acceptance by that very fact.

Boarding-home placement has the inestimable asset for the woman of postponing any active decision about the child. The degree of self-delusion becomes apparent only as an unmarried mother seeks to prolong temporary placement into the total period of the child's growing up.

Adoption is in and of itself no magic key. It is an opportunity, the best life chance for both mother and child in the great majority of cases. For the child, it is as good or as bad as the kind of adoptive parents selected.

Clark E. Vincent studied 105 unwed mothers. For those who kept their children, he found these characteristics:

1. They had less favorable intra-family relationships.

2. They came from the lower socio-economic families.

3. They tended to come from broken homes.

4. They came from unhappy or mother-dominated homes.

5. They had less self-confidence and experiences in heterosexual relations.

6. They appeared to be either relatively isolated from or rebellious against the traditional sex mores and the stigma attached to deviant sexual behavior.

[1] O. M. Butterfield, *Planning for Marriage* (Princeton, D. Van Nostrand Company, Inc., 1956), pp. 315–321.

Most important for basic understanding is the fact that the unwed mothers who keep their children reflect a desperate need for at least one primary relationship in which they are needed and loved by someone whose dependence on them makes it safe to receive and return love in their own way.

A minority of unwed mothers who keep their children have favorable personality profiles and family-life experiences and are motivated to keep their children as (1) an extension of positive, meaningful relationship with sexual mates they love and (2) an expression of their capacity and desires to love and rear their children.

## THE UNMARRIED FATHER

The adolescent unmarried father needs help badly but he is usually ignored. In the rush of attention precipitated by the girl's pregnancy, the boy has been pretty much shoved aside by most of the adults concerned. In most cases, he, like the girl, has been in a family background and an early life which has held more conflict than love, more fear, loneliness, and uncertainty than security and stability. Like the girl, he has been seeking an answer for himself, some assurances of being wanted or being important to someone, a place for himself. Like the girl, he is confused, frightened, and often feels guilty about what has happened. Only a fortunate few have parents who can at this critical point give sympathetic understanding and wise guidance. More often, the boy's parents respond with anger, condemnation, and more rejection, or they insist, in defiance of the facts, that their boy has been a victim, is not responsible for the girl's pregnancy, and seek frantically to dissociate him from the whole situation. This latter attitude arises most often, of course, when there is a question of support for the girl and baby since the financial responsibility devolves upon the parents rather than the boy.

## TO PROMOTE UNDERSTANDING OF THIS CHAPTER

1. What are the causes of the psychological problems of the unmarried in our society?

2. Why is it more difficult for an unmarried woman than an unmarried man?

3. Who should not marry in our society? What are the many factors against marriage for these groups?

4. Write a description of a single person who is well adjusted.

5. Write a description of a married "old maid" or "old bachelor."

6. Write a paper on the topic, "Our society should change its attitude toward the unmarried because . . ." or "Society's concept of the unmarried should remain the same because . . ."

7. What advice would you give an unwed parent?

8. What are some of the problems of the unwed father?

9. Describe some possible characteristics of the unwed mother who keeps her child with her.

10. Unwed parents are . . .

## SUPPLEMENTARY READING

BERNARD, JESSIE, *Remarriage; A Study of Marriage.* Holt, Rinehart and Winston, Inc., New York, 1956.

BOWMAN, HENRY A., *Marriage for Moderns,* 5th ed. McGraw-Hill Book Company, Inc., New York, 1965.

BUTTERFIELD, O. M., *Planning for Marriage.* D. Van Nostrand Co., Inc., Princeton, N.J., 1956.

EDLIN, SARA B., *The Unmarried Mother in Our Society.* Farrar, Straus and Co., New York, 1954.

GLICK, PAUL, *American Families.* John Wiley & Sons, Inc., New York, 1957.

HOLMES, ARNOLD W., *The Family Problems Handbook.* Prentice-Hall, Englewood Cliffs, N.J., 1952.

MOUSTAKAS, CLARK E., *Loneliness.* Prentice-Hall, Inc., Englewood Cliffs, N.J., 1961.

REDL, FRITZ and WINEMAN, DAVID, *Controls From Within.* The Free Press of Glencoe, Glencoe, Ill., 1954.

VINCENT, CLARK E., *Unmarried Mothers.* The Free Press of Glencoe, Inc., Glencoe, Ill., 1961.

YOUNG, LEONTINE, *Out of Wedlock.* McGraw-Hill Book Co., Inc., New York, 1945.

# Unit 4

## Understanding Ourselves in the Intra-Relationships of the Family

# 28
# Reproduction

Being born is one of the greatest events of our lives. Birth and the birth process are miracles to behold. Children are helped to understand reproduction by observing the reproductive process as their pets reproduce their young. However, the transfer from animal reproduction to human repro-

318

duction is not made unless the child feels free to ask many questions at different times during his own development.

Children learn about reproduction in steps and from time to time just as they learn to talk, read, and describe their names and addresses. Adults expect the latter to be a long-term learning process but many times relegate sex education and knowledge about reproduction to one formal talk, movie or special assembly. Sex education needs to be a continuing process just as in the learning of other concepts. Sex education should begin in infancy and continue on through marriage and parenthood. Because of the importance of the relationship between the parents during pregnancy, because both of the parents, father and mother, need to understand reproduction and each of the stages of pregnancy, and because knowledge of the reproductive system in general is basic to male-female relations, this chapter is included.

## REPRODUCTIVE ORGANS

In order to understand better the process of reproduction, one needs to be able to name and to define the functions of the reproductive organs. The male reproductive organs consist of the testes, the prostate gland, the urethra, and the penis. The female reproductive system consists of the ovaries, the Fallopian tubes, the uterus, the vagina, and the breasts. These organs compose the reproductive systems that produce the gametes (matured sex cells) which unite to form the new individual. Thus, our human race goes on because human bodies have systems which enable two cells, the sperm from the man and the ovum from the woman, to unite, form a new life, and bring it into the world.

A female gamete, or ovum (ova is the plural form of this word), commonly called an egg, is globular and about 1/100 to 1/200 of an inch in diameter. Sperms (spermatozoa), or male gametes, are extremely minute and are shaped roughly like tadpoles. Each sperm has an oval head approximately 1/5000 of an inch long, a middle section, and a comparatively long tail, making the total length about 1/500 inch. Ova are nonmobile; that is, they cannot move by their own power. Sperms, on the other hand, are able to propel themselves by lashing their tails in very much the same way as a tadpole swims. They can move approximately an inch in five or six minutes.

Sperms are formed or produced in minute tubes within the testes (testicles), two oval-shaped organs suspended in the scrotum. The immature sperms pass from the tubules in each testis into the corresponding epididymis and from there into the vas deferens. During sexual stimulation, the spongy interior of the penis becomes engorged with blood, causing the or-

319

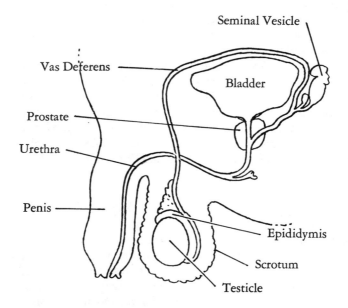

gan to increase both in size and in rigidity (erection) and enabling it to enter the vagina. At the climax of sexual excitement, sperms are mixed with the secretions of several glands including the seminal vesicles and the prostate gland. The whitish, viscous mixture (called semen or seminal fluid) passes, as a result of muscular contraction through the urethra and thus out of the male body.

Seminal fluid is ejaculated (discharged) during sexual intercourse. It may also be discharged as a result of self-stimulation and periodically is discharged spontaneously during sleep (called seminal emissions or nocturnal emissions) when there has been no sexual excitement.

*Sperms* are produced in great numbers. In a single ejaculation of seminal fluid (about one teaspoonful) there are normally 200 to 300 million sperms. Once discharged into the vagina the sperms tend to move in all directions.

*Ova* are produced in the ovaries, two almond-shaped organs situated on either side of the uterus. The ovaries are 1 to 2 inches long and in life are reddish gray in color. The formation of ova in the ovaries begins in prenatal life. Many ova degenerate during the life of a woman and new ova

320

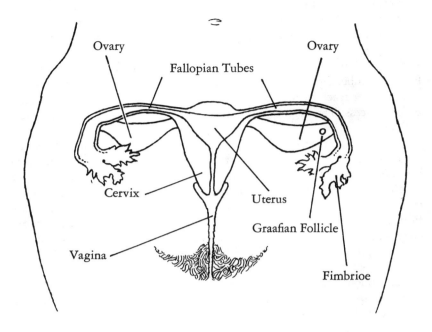

are produced. Ova mature one at a time in response to certain hormones which are produced by the anterior lobe of the pituitary gland. During the maturing process, the ovum migrates toward the surface of the ovary and there becomes surrounded by a fluid which eventually bulges out the surface tissue of the ovary forming a bubble about the size of half a small cherry. This is called the Graafian follicle. This follicle then ruptures or breaks and the ovum is discharged. This release of the ovum is termed ovulation and in the normal, mature woman occurs once in approximately twenty-eight days.

After the ovum leaves the ovary, its life is subject to as much conjecture as is the life of sperms. There is no direct connection between ovaries and Fallopian tubes. The ends of the tubes, in close conjunction with the ovaries, divide into fingerlike projections (fimbrioe) which, at the time of ovulation, are activated to come into even closer contact than usual with the ovary. Both fimbrial and the interior surface of the tubes are lined with tiny hairlike protuberances (cilia), which have the capacity to move with a whiplike motion. They move more vigorously toward the uterus than toward the ovaries on the return stroke. Thus a current is set up and the

321

ovum, which has been released, starts its trip toward the uterus. The ovum is moved along by the cilia, much as a ball might roll over a carpet if the fibers could move so as to push the ball. The ovum takes from three to seven days to move from the ovary through the Fallopian tubes into the uterus.

Fertilization is the union of one sperm with the ovum. It occurs in the Fallopian tube. Of all the sperms that enter the vagina, only a very small fraction ever reach the ovum, and only one sperm is involved in the fertilization process. The zygote (the fertilized egg) is the beginning of a new individual.

Each gamete (mature sex cell) has twenty-three chromosomes. Chromosomes are tiny bodies composed of genes. The genes are determiners of hereditary traits. An individual has twenty-three pairs of chromosomes or 46 chromosomes. Thus, when a sperm meets the ovum, its head penetrates the latter's outer wall and fuses with the nucleus of the egg, establishing the twenty-three pairs (or 46) chromosomes. The tail of the sperm drops off. When one sperm has penetrated the ovum, all other sperms are repelled. At the time of fertilization, the new individual's sex and hereditary traits are determined.

Conception occurs in human beings only through insemination (entrance of sperms into the female genital tract). Insemination by normal means is called coitus or sexual intercourse.

## THE DEVELOPMENT OF THE HUMAN EMBRYO

After fertilization has taken place, the zygote (the united sperm and ovum) continues its movement through the Fallopian tube to the uterus. Before it reaches the uterus, it has already begun to divide, first into two cells, then four, eight, sixteen, thirty-two, and so on. This early stage of cell division does not cause any increase in size. For a period of time the zygote remains free in the uterus. After several days, it embeds itself in the wall of the uterus, which, through the action of certain hormones, has been prepared for this implantation. *Nidation* is the term used for the process of implantation.

The stages of the development of the human embryo are pictured and described on pages 323–325. The photographs were taken the same distance from the specimens to help you get an orientation to the size at the various stages of growth. No attempt is made to describe all of the physiology. This discussion is included to help you better understand the stages and their importance to the developing individual. The photographs are of the specimens of the human fetuses on display at the Museum of Science and Industry, Chicago, Illinois.

*Approximate Age— 6 weeks*

The embryo is less than ½ inch long at the end of the first six weeks. The heart and the brain are among the first organs to form.

*Approximate Age—9 weeks*

At two months, the embryo is about 1¼ inches long. The organs have continued to develop and have assumed their permanent functions. Tiny budlike projections that will form the limbs are noticeable, but fingers and toes are not yet completely formed. The face has begun to look human. Genital organs have appeared. The male genital organs are developed first. In a female, the organs are developed more slowly. However, if the embryo is aborted at this stage and carefully examined, its sex can be determined.

*Approximate Age—10 weeks*

The embryo is now called a fetus. The fetus at three months weighs about one ounce and is less than three inches long. Arms, legs, hands, fingers, toes, and ears are formed. Nails have begun to develop. The fetus appears human but has a head that is very large in proportion to the rest of the body. Vocal cords are formed. Teeth have begun to develop in sockets in the jawbones.

*Approximate Age—11 weeks and 6 days*

At four and one-half months, the fetus is 6 to 8 inches long or about one-half its length at birth. It weighs 5 or 6 ounces. One can hear the heartbeat through a stethoscope. Eyebrows and eyelashes have appeared. The skin is reddish and somewhat transparent. However, the skin ridges, which will make foot and fingerprints possible, have already formed.

*Approximate Age—15 weeks*

At five months fetal movements may be clearly felt by the mother. Head hair has appeared. Nails are well formed. The fetus weighs nearly one pound and is 8 to 12 inches long. Vernix caseosa covers the surface of the body. This vernix caseosa is a mixture of fatty secretion and dead skin cells which forms a cheesy covering. If born at this time, the fetus usually cannot survive except for a few moments.

*Approximate Age—18 weeks and 3 days*

The fetus may live for a few hours if born at six months. He weighs 2 pounds and is about 14 inches tall.

324

*Approximate Age—20 weeks and 4 days*

The fetus measures about fifteen inches in length and weighs approximately two and a half pounds after seven months. If born at this time, it has perhaps a one in ten chance of survival. The widespread notion that infants born at the seventh month are more likely to survive than those born at the eighth month is quite incorrect.

*Approximate Age—26 weeks and 4 days*

As if to improve its appearance before making its debut into the world, the fetus uses the last two months for growing and filling out. With good care infants born at the end of the eighth month have better than even chances of survival, possibly as high as two chances out of three.

*Approximate Age—31 weeks and 2 days*

The full term fetus weighs, on the average, about seven pounds if a girl and seven and one-half pounds if a boy; its length is approximately twenty inches. Its skin is now its natural color and thickly coated with the cheesy vernix. The fine down hair which previously covered its body has largely disappeared. The fingernails are firm and protrude beyond the ends of the fingers. The breasts in both boys and girls are often firm and protruding due to the fact that the same substance which causes the mother's breasts to enlarge during pregnancy passes through the placenta and stimulates development of fetal breasts. This enlargement disappears within a few days of the birth.

The length of pregnancy varies greatly; it may range between such wide extremes as 240 days and 300 days and yet be entirely normal in every respect. The average duration, counting from the time of conception, is nine and a half lunar months; that is, thirty-eight weeks or 266 days. Counting from the first day of the last menstrual period, its average length is ten lunar months or forty weeks or 280 days. These average figures mean very little, however. It would appear that some children require a longer time, others a shorter time in the uterus for full development. The time-honored method, used to predict the time of birth, is to count back three calendar months from the first day of the last menstrual period and add seven days. This would give a rough estimate. For example, if the last period began on April 14, we would count back three months to January 14, and add seven days. Thus the baby's birth would be around January 21.

Being pregnant is a natural and normal condition. A pregnant woman should consider herself capable of doing her daily tasks and recreation the same as before becoming pregnant. However, she should not become overtired nor assume strenuous new activity to which she is unaccustomed.

A well-balanced diet is always important for the well-being of an individual. The diet during pregnancy should provide foods from the four major food groups. The *quantity of food* eaten should remain the same as before pregnancy, provided that that quantity was adequate for the body build and activity. However, the diet should optimally contain increased amounts of protein, vitamins, and mineral salts—especially calcium—in order to feed the developing fetus. This can and should be done without increasing the caloric intake. If the pregnant woman has a voracious appetite, the only certain recommendation to meet this situation is self-restraint. She should eat only three meals a day and avoid snacks, especially those composed of fatty foods and sweets.

During the first three and one-half months of pregnancy the weight is usually stationary and may show a slight loss. During the latter two-thirds of the period of pregnancy, there is a steady gain. The average increase in weight during pregnancy is twenty-four pounds. The main part of this weight increase is understandable when one considers the following:

| | |
|---|---|
| Baby | 7 pounds |
| Amniotic fluid | 1½ pounds |
| Afterbirth (placenta) | 1 pound |
| Increase in weight of uterus | 2 pounds |
| Increase in weight of breasts | 1½ pounds |
| Increase in blood | 1 pound |
| | 14 pounds |

The remaining ten pounds represents, in part, general accumulation of fat and the increased amount of fluid which tissues tend to retain at this time. Thus, gains between twenty and twenty-four pounds are natural and in keeping with good health. An increase in weight of thirty pounds or more is undesirable on several counts. First, these extra pounds represent unnecessary weight for the muscles of the legs and back to carry about, and this suddenly imposed strain is a common cause of backache and pain in the legs. Second, many complications of pregnancy and labor are associated with excessive increments in weight. Third, additions of fat are likely to be permanent acquisitions which can be removed only by the most rigorous dieting.

## EMOTIONS AFFECTING PREGNANCY

An emotionally well-adjusted woman does not suffer excessively from the nausea and cramps which are alleged to be typical of pregnancy. This does not deny the fact that pregnancy will have its difficult moments for the woman, but rather it reminds us that the way she reacts to these disturbances will depend upon the nature of her emotional make-up. Some people have difficulties taking even such minor physical upsets as a cold or a headache in their stride. The well-adjusted person tends to make little of them, whereas the poorly-adjusted person unwittingly exploits these minor disturbances for all they are worth. Since illness in our culture is an acceptable excuse, there is a strong tendency for some people to use illness for emotional gains. It is not uncommon for many women to act in this fashion during their pregnancies. Because the physical burden of pregnancy is theirs alone, many women will act as though special privileges are in order. Little do they realize that their own deep misgivings about wanting to be a mother are forcing them to retreat into illness.

When a person is getting what he wants, the satisfactions he enjoys have a beneficial effect on his health. Thus, a woman who eagerly awaits the birth of her child, may develop a glow and beauty greater than she ever enjoyed before. In such cases, her deep enthusiasm for the child she is going to bear is enough to remove the marks of strain, anxiety, and doubt which normally affect her appearance. On the other hand, the woman who has an overprotective attitude toward her child even before his birth can focus this tendency on herself by pampering. This focus may seriously limit her activities and swamp her with excessive self-concern. The growth of this anxiety may enhance the difficulties of her pregnancy and affect her appearance. Thus, instead of developing a warm and enthusiastic glow, such a mother-to-be may give the appearance of being somewhat harried by the whole thing.

The husband can play a leading role in helping his wife make a good emotional adjustment to pregnancy. His task is simply to reinforce the desire for children. He must be enthusiastic, relaxed, and reassuring about the pregnancy. As they discuss the plans for and the problems of parenthood, his attitude should express the connection of faith in their joint ability to meet these problems successfully. It is during the pregnancy that the parent-child relationship is conceived.

## TO PROMOTE UNDERSTANDING OF THIS CHAPTER

1. Name and define the function of the reproductive organs of each sex.

2. Define the following terms:

   | | | | | |
   |---|---|---|---|---|
   | gametes | ova | embryo | sperm | nidation |
   | fertilization | zygote | fetus | semen | |

3. When does the embryo emerge into a fetus? What developments make it appropriate to change the name?

4. How do the first three months of the embryo compare to the last three months?

5. If a child is born prematurely, which month gives it the best chance for survival?

6. What is the average length of pregnancy?

7. What is the main part of the weight increase during pregnancy?

8. Why should a pregnant woman be conscious of diet and calories?

9. How do emotions affect pregnancy?

10. What is the role of the husband during pregnancy?

## SUPPLEMENTARY READING

GIBBARD, P. H., POMEROY, W. B., MARTIN, C. E. and CHRISTENSON, C. V., *Pregnancy, Birth and Abortion*. Holler-Harper, New York, 1958.

GRUENBERG, SIDONIE M., *The Wonderful Story of How You Were Born*. Doubleday & Co., New York, 1952.

MAGOUN, F. ALEXANDER, *Love and Marriage*, rev. ed. Harper and Row, New York, 1956.

NOVAK, EDMUND R., and JONES, GEORGEANNA S., ed., *Textbook of Gynecology* 6th ed. Williams and Wilkins Co., Baltimore, Md., 1961.

Hoest © 1965 The Curtis Publishing Company

*"Let me get this straight . . . neither one of you wants custody of the children?"*

# 29
# Family Planning

One of the basic reasons for family planning is shown in the cartoon. Children need to be born to parents who are willing to rear them to adulthood, not to parents who are only willing to beget them. Most parents would not make the statement summarized by the lawyer, but many act toward their children in a way that suggests that they subscribe to it.

The basic principle that underlines the importance of family planning is the simple statement that everyone has a psychological "breaking point." Efficient and comfortable functioning of families cannot exist when that breaking point is passed for any member. Families are subject to many different kinds of stresses and each family feels them differently, depending upon the personalities living together and their reaction to each other, their physical conditions, their financial resources, and their emotional stability.

If the world were large enough to provide food for an unlimited population, and if everyone had the resources to get a sufficient share of this food, and if everyone could manage a complicated household with many members, then we wouldn't have to be concerned if all women produced all the children they were capable of producing in the ages from thirteen to fifty. This, however, is not the case, and most families have to plan carefully how many mouths can be fed, how many bodies can be clothed, and how many persons can be sheltered. In the more developed societies, an additional consideration must be how many can be educated to the level demanded by modern industrial societies. The strain of seeing children inadequately fed, improperly clothed, and shelterless is certainly an enormous stress on parents, even those whose sensibilities may have been dulled by years of chronic frustration of hopes for improvement in their lives.

Buffeted by poverty and famine and too often unable to control their economic situation, it would appear wise if parents could limit the number of children with whom they must share their inadequate supplies. If family size could be controlled, fewer children would die before maturity and the health of survivors would be more robust. Parents could provide better because their own health would be improved as a result of getting a larger share of the family's food supply.

In the privileged countries, the issues may be less acute physically and the specter faced may be far from starvation or disease. However, in these countries, the fact that parents may be unable to supply needed and appropriate education adds another type of strain. Parents may also not be able to supply the emotional or psychological needs necessary in a large family.

Raising a family successfully requires a certain level of emotional maturity. Not all persons are equally endowed emotionally, intellectually, or in management skills. The parents may be able to manage a family of two or three or four children but might break under the strain of trying to manage a home with six or more. Many mothers and fathers realize that they are approaching their breaking points but may not know how to limit the number of children and are thus more or less forced into intolerable stress situations. Furthermore, the intensity of the care and training any mother can supply to her brood must be fractioned each time another individual is added. Parental care appears to be related to the mental health of the offspring and to the development of their talents.

In short, family planning is important so that individuals will not find themselves in situations of intolerable stress, so that children will have healthful places in which to be nurtured and to mature, and so that popula-

330

tions will not need to kill others in order to have enough space and food to survive and to live in reasonable security and comfort.

## TERMS FOR FAMILY PLANNING

The regulation of the number of offspring, the time at which they are born, and the period which elapses between pregnancies is the process of family planning. Ordinarily this process is designated *birth control*. The term is objectionable to some people because for them it has connotations of abortion and sterilization. Abortion and sterilization are not generally acceptable in the United States at the present.

*Contraception* is another commonly employed term. The term *prevenception* has been suggested by some as a substitute for contraception, since it connotes the prevention of conception rather than something working against conception (contra-ception).

Contraception and prevenception are means used to prevent conception, that is, to prevent the meeting of egg and sperm. This may be accomplished by keeping them apart with a mechanical barrier until egg and sperms are no longer able to unite, by employing chemicals to inactivate the sperms, or by refraining from coitus or engaging in it only at certain periods when the sperms and egg are least likely to unite. In any case, the end result is the same—namely, sperms and egg do not unite to produce a new individual.

Contraception is a tool for family planning. Ideally, a contraceptive method allows a couple to avoid having children at inopportune times, to avoid having more children than they want, and space children sufficiently to permit the woman to maintain good health and to give birth to healthy babies. In short, contraception or prevenception allows parenthood by choice rather than parenthood by chance.

The term birth control is much in the news today. The term appears in discussion of religion, declining morality, the fight against poverty, population explosion, food and water shortages, air and water pollution, and so on. Some may argue that some forms of contraception interfere with nature and are therefore morally wrong. But numerous other interferences with nature are generally accepted when they lead to the well-being of humans, as, for example, pasteurization, vaccination, and surgery.

The same natural processes that imbue man with reproductive powers also imbue him with intelligence. He must use his intelligence to improve his lot and that of his children on this increasingly restricted and crowded planet. Family planning, by whatever means the individual married couple is able to accept, is becoming an increasingly important part of man's use of intelligently controlled and applied knowledge for human betterment.

331

The prescription of contraceptives is a problem to be handled by physicians on the basis of individual examination and needs. It is not something to be dealt with in a general discussion. No two couples are identical as to principles, anatomy, attitudes, or goals. Thus a particular couple should see their physician to be sure that they are making an appropriate choice for them. However, the method should fulfill the following criteria:

1.  It should be relatively effective. No method is entirely foolproof.

2.  It should be relatively easy to use, simple, and readily understood.

3.  It should be readily available and relatively inexpensive.

4.  It should be aesthetically acceptable to both parties and repugnant to neither.

5.  It should permit normal, satisfactory, successful sexual adjustment.

6.  It should have no harmful results. The contraceptive should contain or entail no chemical or mechanical irritant that may give rise to infection or poisoning.

7.  It should be temporary, in the sense that its use may be terminated at will.

### EFFECTS OF CONTRACEPTION

Some say that information about contraception would lead individuals inevitably to more widespread immorality. This insults the intelligence of human beings. It contradicts all that we have studied about values, goals, philosophy, religion, love, and the psychological and physiological basis of integrity and self-respect. Most people are moral because they want to be. Man should not be led or directed by fear, but by reason. Individuals should take the time to think about, discuss, and understand their own beliefs concerning morality. Young unmarried persons are not on the alert for opportunities to be immoral without unpleasant consequences. There are some, of course, but these persons will probably be immoral in any event.

The probable result, if reliable contraceptive information were more widespread, would be that sincere young couples could marry with more of a chance to solidify and establish themselves as an understanding family unit. Couples could develop a stronger basic relationship before adding the responsibility of children. Instead of having children before they were ready, child-bearing could be postponed for a year or two while they prepared themselves financially, emotionally, and socially as an established family unit. More widespread knowledge of contraception could decrease

332

the number of criminal abortions, unwanted children, and families that break up because of too many burdens too soon.

## DECISIONS FOR FAMILY PLANNING

Parenthood should be a dignified and voluntary function rather than the blind acceptance of biological chance. The marriage partners should establish themselves as a working unit and learn to appreciate each other as individuals with joint family goals. As students of human development have explored the factors contributing to personality growth, they have increasingly emphasized the need of the child for a home environment that provides emotional security and affection and is free from conflict. The child absorbs the attitudes, aspirations, joys, anxieties, and tensions he feels in his home, and will tend to give out what he receives. If he is raised in an emotionally secure home, he will tend to be an emotionally secure child; if he is raised in a home which lacks happiness and affords little emotional security, he may in time tend to be unhappy and insecure. Further, as studies of adjustment in marriage show, there is at least an unconscious tendency for the individual to repeat in his own marriage the major characteristics he found in his parental family.

The important question, then, is whether or not the couple can provide such an atmosphere of affection and security. The couple certainly cannot supply it for a child until they have supplied it to each other. If there are serious maladjustments in their relationship, it is not unlikely that these will be reflected in any children they may have. If they themselves are well adjusted, and there are no hereditary or physical obstacles to parenthood, there seems no reason to doubt their suitability as parents. The decision to have or not have children cannot always be arrived at in the first year of marriage. Adjustment in marriage is the result of a process that requires both time and effort. Some couples adjust well to each other in marriage but have personalities and values that are not compatible with the demands of child-rearing. The value of a child lies not in his economic contribution to his parents, but in the enriched living that his presence in the family brings to his parents and that they in turn contribute to him.

The decision to have children is not a simple one. In the first place, the couple needs a period of time in which to make the necessary postwedding adjustments. Those who must face all the adjustments required by pregnancy at the same time that they face the adjustments required by their first years of living together are unduly handicapped in attempting either.

A couple is ready to have a child only when both really want it and have faced all the ramifications in their relationships which will result from its coming. For all but the most affluent, child-rearing involves sacrifices—

of time, freedom, money, and aspirations. It is worthwhile, certainly, but it demands the giving up of many things. Unless *both* husband and wife are ready to make these sacrifices, and want to make them, numerous difficulties are sure to present themselves. When, for example, the wife is very anxious to have a child and the husband agrees only because he thinks it will make his wife happy, there is no way of predicting accurately the reception the child will receive from its father. Its presence may stimulate affection permanently, which is all to the good; it may stimulate affection which is temporary and later changes to resentment—to the detriment of the father-child relationship; it may arouse resentment immediately. Both of the latter situations can only mean insecurity for the child and strained husband-wife relations for the parents.

There is no wisdom in deciding to have a child in order to hold a marriage together. The wife, or husband, or both, who believe that waning affections can thus be restored, or that a child can be "the moral equivalent" of other needs the marriage has been unable to fulfill, is expecting more from a child's presence in the family than seems wise. It is true that children do cement husband-wife relationships, and do enrich the lives of both, but only when these relationships are good to begin with and the child is genuinely wanted.

## PRO AND CON

The facts of family planning must be presented and reviewed objectively. Indeed, it is only fitting and proper that each married couple consider seriously both the positive and the negative aspects of planning for their children.

If couples wish to control conception, it is absolutely necessary for them to agree on the method to be used. Birth control places the decision whether and when to have a baby directly upon the parents themselves. This is a different kind of responsibility from that of simply letting a pregnancy "happen." Indeed, it may be too much of a burden for some couples who find it difficult to agree even on trivial things.

Conception control may also increase psychological problems if it is at odds with the religious doctrines of the couple. It may even create an antireligious feeling among couples who disagree with their church's announced views.

Family planning gives the young couple the needed time for adjustment to each other. The average young married couple know much less about each other at the beginning of marriage than couples in an earlier American era did. Most young couples must mature as husband and wife before they can attain the basic prerequisites of parenthood. However, the time

334

required for working out initial marital adjustments varies with each couple, so that it is impossible to generalize.

On the other hand, it is important that couples not wait too long before having children. If too comfortable and rigid a routine is established, there is a danger that the couple will not want to disrupt their isolated, adult serenity with a baby. Such couples might be worse off in the long run than those who have children very soon after marriage.

Family planning is also warranted by economic considerations today. Most people now need more education than their forebears had, not only because technology requires greater skills but because marriage itself demands a higher standard of living. Furthermore, a college-educated wife should work for a while after graduation to apply her education in the world of work so that she can better understand her potential in the post-child rearing years.

In addition, couples need money in order to have children. Finances may be a limiting factor in family planning, but they should not be an eliminating factor. Financial difficulties are less often real than fancied. In one sense, who can ever afford to have children? For example, is it valid for a couple to say they cannot afford a child because they need a new car? Standards of living change. Thus, couples who rationalize that they cannot now afford to have children may find that their standard of living increases every year. After a few years they may still contend that they are not able to afford children. In postponing children for financial reasons, there is a great danger that the period of postponement may never end.

By planning their family, the couple can better prepare themselves for parenthood and the responsibilities of parenthood. The techniques of good parents do not come naturally. Too many people learn too late that they should not have avoided courses in child development and child psychology that might have better prepared them for understanding and training their own children. Furthermore, except for those few couples who have been adequately prepared, parenthood is one of the most serious crises of young married life. The haphazard experience in child care that some young people get within their own families is of questionable value. The oldest child in a larger group is frequently given some responsibility for the care of younger ones; however, this experience seldom gives insight into proper child-care methods. In fact, many adults who have had this experience frequently appear worse off than if they had had no experience at all.

Some people have little desire for children of their own. For them, parenthood would result probably only in despair and frustration. Such people should probably avoid having any children, for a marriage with no children may be better adjusted than a marriage with unwanted children. Interest in children and the desire to have additional offspring seem to diminish as the family increases. Numerous studies indicate that after the first two or three children are born, parents wish for fewer than they had first estimated as their ideal family size.

This discussion, however, must not be misinterpreted as suggesting that today's married couples do not desire children, for surveys disclose otherwise. Today's young couples want children as much or more than ever, but they want them at the time and in the number that seems best for total family happiness.

## TO PROMOTE UNDERSTANDING OF THIS CHAPTER

1. What are the reasons for family planning?

2. What are the terms used in discussing family planning?

3. Write an essay titled either "Contraception is Interfering with Nature" or "Contraception is Improving Upon Nature."

4. Some say that contraception would lead people to more immorality. Do you agree with this statement? If so, why? If not, why not?

5. What decisions should a couple make before deciding to have children?

6. Dick and Pat are feeling bored with each other and their life together. They think that if they could have a baby, life would become more interesting. What would be your advice? Upon what do you base your answer?

7. What responsibilities do parents have toward children today?

8. Why is family planning important in privileged countries?

## SUPPLEMENTARY READING

BABER, RAY E., *Marriage and the Family*. McGraw-Hill Book Co., New York, 1953.

BECKER, HOWARD, and HILL, REUBEN, *Family Marriage and Parenthood*. D. C. Heath and Co., Boston, 1955.

BOSSARD, JAMES H. S., *Parent and Child*. University of Pennsylvania Press, Philadelphia, 1953.

DICKINSON, R. L., *Techniques of Conception Control*. The Williams and Wilkins Co., Baltimore, 1950.

DRIEKURS, RUDOLPH, *The Challenge of Marriage*. Duell, Sloane and Pearce, New York, 1946.

KANE, JOHN J., *Marriage and the Family: A Catholic Approach*. The Dryden Press, Inc., New York, 1952.

MANN, DAVID, WOODWARD, LUTHER E., and JOSEPH, NATHAN, *Educating Expectant Parents*. Visiting Nurse Service of New York, New York, 1961.

RAINWATER, LEE, *And The Poor Get Children*. Quadrangle Books, Chicago, 1960.

―――― *Family Design*. Aldine Publishing Company, Chicago, 1964.

...saying *"Hello"*

FROM OUR HOUSE TO YOUR HOUSE !

The Andersons
(Fred, Janet, Marla, Karen
and Baby Mike)

# 30
# Involuntary Childlessness

Much is said and written about the effects of childlessness upon the couple concerned. In our culture, children are highly valued, their pictures appear on the Christmas greetings of the family, and the activities of the family are oriented around the children and their needs. Without doubt, children, when they are wanted, enrich marriage and a couple's life together. When they are not wanted, both parents and children are likely to

338

suffer. The effects of being without them are relative to the personalities of the couple, their attitudes, desires, hopes, and interests. No broad statement to the effect that childlessness warps and distorts the personality of a marriage is warranted. In the case of some couples it does; in that of others it does not.

Unfortunately, there are persons who develop feelings of inferiority when they find that they must remain involuntarily childless because of some physiological malfunction. There is no logical reason for feeling inferior because of low fertility anymore than there is for feeling inferior because one has brown eyes, small feet, large ears, high blood pressure, or any other physical condition over which one has no control.

## PHYSICAL CAUSES OF STERILITY

The physical causes of sterility in women include the following: (1) absence, defect, or disease of the sex glands (ovaries), (2) failure of the ovaries to develop normal germ cells (ova), (3) blockage of the tubes so that the ova fail to reach the womb (uterus), (4) absence, defect, or disease of the uterus, precluding nourishment and development of a fertilized ovum, (5) blockage of the entrance to the uterus (cervix) preventing male germ cells (sperm) from reaching the ovum, or (6) absence, defect, or disease of the vagina sufficient to destroy the sperm, or block their entrance into the uterus.

Physical causes of sterility in men include: (1) absence, defect, or disease of the sex glands (testes), (2) absence or blockage (due to defect or disease) of the minute tubes that carry germ cells (spermatozoa) from the testes to the penis, (3) blockage (due to defect or disease) of the tube (urethra) through which sperm must pass into the woman's vagina. In both men and women, diseases or deficiencies involving the whole organism may cause or contribute to sterility. Severe vitamin deficiencies, for example, or endocrine (hormonal) disorders, or such debilitating conditions as malnutrition, tuberculosis, and so on can be responsible.

The most common physical cause for sterility, of course, is failure of sexual partners to have intercourse at a time when impregnation can occur. The reasons may be psychological, but physical action is involved.

## PSYCHOLOGICAL CAUSES OF STERILITY

The psychological causes of sterility are many, varied, and debatable. Consider, for example, why one or both partners consciously or unconsiously avoid sexual intercourse. Reasons range from an entirely conscious aversion to the partner, to deeply unconscious fear or guilt about sex,

339

pregnancy, or parenthood. There are women whose sexual desire is greatest close to or during menstruation, when impregnation is least likely to occur. Such a paradoxical situation might indicate a wish for sexual gratification without conception. Spasm of the Fallopian tubes precluding pregnancy can occur in women who nevertheless enjoy frequent sexual intercourse. Comparable emotional conflicts in men can cause avoidance or bad timing in intercourse. Two common forms of sterility in men and women, whether from physical or psychological causes, are impotence and frigidity. Impotence of a man is the incapacity for sexual intercourse. Frigidity in a woman is an abnormal aversion to sexual intercourse.

## INCIDENCE OF STERILITY

It used to be assumed that a barren marriage was attributable to the wife, and among some people this attitude still persists. Some authorities state, however, that in 30 to 50 percent of such marriages, the cause can be traced to the husband; others assert that the ratio is about fifty-fifty. Evaluation of a sterile marriage must include both husband and wife.

In considering sterility according to various groups, it is again useful to distinguish fecundity from fertility, that is, the potentiality for having children from the actuality of having them. It is estimated the fecundity is about the same the world over. Healthy couples anywhere would have an average of ten or eleven children if they were sexually active without contraception throughout the childbearing period of life. This potential does not vary significantly with race, class, or creed.

Factors that influence fertility—that is, the actual number of offspring —are those that determine the frequency of sexual intercourse, the length of exposure to childbearing (early or late marriage, for example), the use of contraceptive plans or devices, and the health of the marital partners. Age is the most important determinant in the frequency of sexual intercourse. The chances of pregnancy fall off rapidly after the age of thirty. Statistically, the period of greatest fertility is under twenty, with the period between twenty and twenty-five a close second. Some authorities believe that the length of marriage before impregnation is attempted may be an even more important factor than age. In any event, the longer a married couple postpones trying to have children, the less are their chances of having them or, at least, having as many as they desire.

Psychological effects of sterility are multiform. Some couples are easily and happily reconciled to being childless; others react with varying degrees of regret, resignation, and sorrowful acceptance. Still others suffer moderate to severe feelings of social stigma, inferiority, or deprivation. A given individual sometimes feels guilty or ashamed because of the conscious or unconscious assumption—perhaps mistaken—that the present infertility is his or her fault. The "fault" is often regarded as a punishment for childhood masturbation, premarital sex relations, or marital infidelity. The sense of guilt or worry often obscures the medical problem. Just as often, perhaps, there are silent (or not so silent) suspicions of the marital partner and consequent added strains within the marriage.

Social effects of sterility vary with the culture. If regarded as a stigma, it can lead to withdrawal and isolation. Sterility remains a reason for divorce in some parts of the world.

## TREATMENTS FOR STERILITY

A premarital medical examination may reveal the possibility of sterility. If there are physical conditions or emotional conflicts that will make pregnancy difficult or impossible, the prospective husband and wife should face and deal with them as soon as possible. The most beneficial result may be educational; complete and accurate knowledge about sexual intercourse and conception will often foster positive and confident attitudes that lessen the chances of sterility.

Sterility sometimes vanishes when a couple faces the problem and decides to do something about it. In an astonishing number of cases, pregnancy follows making the appointment with a gynecologist or clinic, or occurs during the medical "workup" itself. It is common for pregnancy to occur following an adoption or the decision to adopt. In such cases, of course, psychological factors have been the important ones preventing conception.

Of all couples coming to sterility clinics, from 25 to 35 percent eventually become fertile. In one study of one hundred couples, the causes of sterility were physical in about 40 percent of the cases, psychological in about 30 percent, and a mixture in about 30 percent. Of the total, 27 percent achieved pregnancy—80 percent of these within one year, and 100 percent within four years. It is, from this analysis, worth seeking treatment. In some cases the cure is spontaneous; in others, there will be no cure. Whatever the outcome, it is best to face the problem and then make decisions on the basis of the diagnostic facts rather than on one's suppositions and concerns.

## ADOPTION

Adoption is the voluntary act of taking a child of other parents as one's own child. According to statistics published by the United States Department of Health, Education, and Welfare, 142,000 petitions for adoption were filed in 1965. The great increase in the number of adoptions over the past decades may be attributed to a variety of factors. First, the great value placed on children in our society has given rise to the feeling that a childless couple is "incomplete" as a family unit. Second, changed social attitudes have made adoption much more acceptable; it is associated with far greater frankness and enjoyment, nowadays, than with the former degree of secrecy and shame.

In selecting from among the adoptive homes for children under their care, agencies nowadays give the greatest weight to those personal qualities that make for "capacity for parenthood." As a general rule, the capacity for warm, mature love for a child as an individual in his own right by each parent and by both as a unit, plus a compatible, stable marriage, are accepted as the mental health prerequisites for any adoption, whatever the age of the adopted child. In addition, adoption agencies give high priority to the applicants' adaptability, flexibility, and their ability to cope with the unpredictable vicissitudes of life.

Agencies do not look for some single personality stereotype or hypothetical paragon of perfection among adoptive applicants. They know there are multiple patterns and styles of life through which basically positive human experience may be lived. Similarly, aside from protecting the child against foreseeable extreme economic deprivation, children are placed with adoptive parents who cover a very wide range, financially; the same is true socially and educationally.

Eligibility requirements as to the couple's religion vary among different denominational, nonsectarian, and tax-supported agencies. The agencies in turn are subject to widely differing laws and their interpretations in various parts of the country. According to the Child Welfare League of America the natural mother has the right to determine the religion in which she wishes her child to be reared, and "placement of children should not be restricted, in general, to homes with formal church affiliations." These principles differ, in certain respects, however, from those held by the Roman Catholic agencies whose statement, also included in the published "Standards," regards the religious status of the adoptive couple as "the weightiest, although not the sole element . . . among the several important factors . . . in successful adoption."

In addition to the fundamental attributes for all parents which are conducive to the child's healthy growth and development, and which agencies seek for the children they place, there are some psychological qualifications specific to adoptive parenthood. Perhaps the most important of these relates to the couple's inner ability for successfully transposing their parental urge from the biologically conceived child they desired to the adopted child as an accepted substitute. For the wish to adopt is ultimately rooted in the

342

reproductive drive, with its associated parental feelings. Adoptive applicants cannot therefore demand of themselves, nor do agencies expect, that adoption must represent their primary choice. If, however, their feelings cannot move on to the adopted child comfortably and completely enough, with minimal persistent anxiety and conflict, this does not detract from their worthwhileness as people, nor signify maladjustment per se, but it does jeopardize the mental health outcome of the adoption. Such adoptions should not take place since the parent-child relationships, and hence the child's development, will be bound to suffer. Various unresolved emotional problems around their inability to bear children may obstruct a couple's sufficient deep-down acceptance of adoption for a satisfying experience by the child and by themselves. The child is too prone, for example, to represent a constant proof of painful defeat and deficiency.

There is more latitude about age limits in the placement of older children. Not infrequently older couples may decide to adopt a child after their own children are grown and have left home. These placements are with older parents who are experienced and "know what to expect," so that, in general, they can be more relaxed in dealing with the special problems that

| Year | Total Number Children Adopted | By Relatives | By Non-Relatives | Total Non-Relatives Placed by Social Agencies |
|------|------|------|------|------|
| ADOPTIONS BY TYPE: 1952 TO 1965[1] | | | | |
| 1952 | 85 | 43 | 42 | 24 |
| 1953 | 90 | 44 | 46 | 25 |
| 1954 | 90 | 43 | 47 | 26 |
| 1955 | 93 | 45 | 48 | 27 |
| 1956 | 93 | 46 | 47 | 27 |
| 1957 | 91 | 44 | 47 | 28 |
| 1958 | 96 | 46 | 50 | 30 |
| 1959 | 102 | 50 | 52 | 32 |
| 1960 | 107 | 49 | 58 | 34 |
| 1961 | 114 | 52 | 62 | 38 |
| 1962 | 121 | 58 | 63 | 40 |
| 1963 | 127 | 60 | 67 | 44 |
| 1964 | 135 | 63 | 72 | 48 |
| 1965 | 142 | 65 | 77 | 53 |
| Total | 1486 | 708 | 778 | 476 |

*Statistical Abstract of the United States,* U.S. Bureau of the Census, Washington, D.C., 1967, p. 309.

[1] In thousands. Includes Puerto Rico and Virgin Islands. Based on reports from state departments of public welfare with estimates added for non-reporting states, the number of which varied from year to year. Prior to 1957, represents number of adoption petitions filed; thereafter, number of petitions granted.

older children may bring to the new adjustment. Also, because their self-confidence as parents has been firmly established already, they can better tolerate with understanding, and need not take personally, such typical reactions of older children as provocative misbehavior to test the reliability of parental love. Because they are not dependent on the adopted child for the totality of their parental fulfillment, such parents have less need to overtax a child with expectations beyond his capacity, which could be a source of mutual unhappiness. Many deeply satisfying relationships are experienced by these older couples and older children who "adopt each other."

Couples who have already adopted one or two babies may be considered ineligible for more, according to the current policies of most agencies. This limitation, however, does not apply for the hard-to-place children with special needs—that is, children of mixed racial background, older children, sibling groups placed together, and children with physical or mental handicaps.

On the whole, agencies feel that adoptive parents should be approximately the same age as the biological parents. If a childless couple well into middle age, for example, were to adopt an infant, no matter how exemplary their other attributes as potential parents, their relationship with the child would be at a disadvantage in several ways. Some lack of rapport would be likely to stem from this spread of years between the child and themselves, increasing as the age difference between them increased, with respect to attitudes, interests, and approaches to life. Also, such a couple has gone past the life epoch when the necessary energy and endurance for taking care of a young child is usually available, without overexertion, so that it may impair the child-parent interactions. Furthermore, a husband and wife's good adjustment to childlessness, evolved over the years as a "twosome," may be thrown off balance by belated conversion, through the advent of a child, into a threesome, even though originally their lives might have been happier with children. Moreover, childless couples well along in life are likely to have become "set in their ways," without the desirable degree of flexibility for coping with a young child. They may, therefore, lose patience with him too quickly, or tend to impose excessive restrictions before he is really able to control his behavior.

The factor of age is also pertinent with respect to the adoptive parents' life expectancy in relation to the age of the child they adopt. Authorized agencies strive to protect the children they place as much as possible against risks of losing their parents for a second time, due to death or incapacitating illness. They require, therefore, that applicants be examined by their own physician, or a physician working in conjunction with the agency, who submits a report of their medical history and his findings.

344

## THE ADOPTION AGENCY

Adopting parents should arrange for the adoption through a first-rate child placing agency. It is foolish and risky to deal directly with the child's true parents or with just a third person who is inexperienced. It leaves the way open for blackmail or for the true parents to change their minds and to try to get their child back. The law stands in the way of this but the cost and unpleasantness of the lawsuits could ruin the happiness of the family and the security of the child. To protect the child, the good adoption agency keeps the two sets of parents involved in the adoption from ever knowing each other and keeps them from ever making any kind of trouble for each other.

Practices vary among agencies with respect to charging fees for services to adoptive applicants. Ability to pay a fee is definitely not regarded as a proper criterion of applicant acceptability and should in no way affect the choice of the most suitable home for each child. A good many agencies never charge any fee. Others have a sliding scale based on ability to pay in relation to income, or have a set fee with provision for reducing or waiving it when indicated. For couples who can afford it, the payment of a fee

enables them to share responsibility for the cost of the agency service and is often welcomed as a kind of equivalent for the medical and hospital expenses of natural childbirth. All agencies are nonprofit, however, and their expenses far exceed whatever may be collected as fees. Independent adoptions, however, may involve heavy expenses; of course, the sky is the limit for blackmarket baby "sales."

Inquiries as to existent agencies in any particular community or area may be directed to the State Department of Public Welfare through its Child Welfare Division, since this department in most states has responsibility for the licensing, standard setting, and supervision of adoption services by public and voluntary agencies.

### ANNOUNCEMENT OF ADOPTION

Parents should from the beginning let the fact that the child is adopted come openly, but casually, into their conversations with each other, with the child, and with their acquaintances. This allows the child to ask questions as he grows and begins to understand. If the parents make extensive efforts to conceal the child's origin, the child may sense that his identity or his adoption is something to be ashamed of or to hide.

Attempts are no longer made to keep adoption a secret. In fact, the custom of announcing the birth of a baby is extending to adoptive parents who, often nowadays, send out announcements of the arrival of an adopted child. Changing cultural attitudes toward adoption are investing it with positive connotations. Agency selection of an adoptive couple may be regarded as a socially valued tribute to their qualities as parents. By the same token, the adopted child is no longer pictured as a homeless waif, at the mercy of anyone who will provide him with food and shelter. Rather, he, too, may be recognized as privileged; his parents were particularly eager to assume the responsibilities of parenthood, and were handpicked by an exacting agency for their child-rearing abilities.

The adopted child will not, of course, be impervious to the problems and conflicts in his relationships with others that will typically arise at various stages of life. However, having been adopted need not make him any more vulnerable to such difficulties.

The fact that an individual has been adopted may, at times, be used as a screen for various unacceptable feelings that arise in the complex area of human relationships. Children or adults who were adopted, like everyone else, share the general range of human failings. Clearly, however, they should be judged on the basis of their own good qualities as human beings, rather than being judged on the basis of life circumstances that were beyond their control.

346

## TO PROMOTE UNDERSTANDING OF THIS CHAPTER

1. Define the following terms:

   | | | |
   |---|---|---|
   | sterility | impotence | frigidity |
   | fertility | fecundity | adoption |

2. What are the effects of involuntary childlessness?
3. What are the physical causes of sterility?
4. What are the main psychological causes of sterility in men? in women?
5. Who is responsible for a barren marriage?
6. What are the factors that influence fertility?
7. Why do people adopt children?
8. What is the main characteristic that an adoption agency searches for in a couple?
9. What psychological qualifications must adoptive parents have?
10. Are adoption agencies concerned with age? Why or why not?
11. Why is it important to check the agency before adopting a child?
12. How should the family announce the adoption of a child?
13. Should one tell a child that he is adopted? Why? Why not?

## SUPPLEMENTARY READING

EATON, J. W. and MAYER, ROBERT J., *Man's Capacity to Reproduce.* Free Press of Glencoe, Glencoe, Ill., 1954.

ELLIS, ALBERT, and ABARBENEL, ALBERT, *The Encyclopedia of Sexual Behavior.* Hawthorne Books, New York, 1961.

LeSHAW, EDA J., *You and Your Adopted Child.* Public Affairs Pamphlet, No. 274, New York, New York, 1958.

MAAS, HENRY and ENGLER, RICHARD E., *Children in Need of Parents.* Columbia University Press, New York, 1959.

MUDD, EMILY H. and KRIEL, ARON, *Man and Wife, A Source Book on Family Attitudes, Sex Behavior, and Marriage Counseling.* W. W. Norton and Co., Inc., New York, 1957.

REEVES, KATHERINE, *Children: Their Ways and Wants.* The Educational Publishing Corp., Darien, Conn., 1959.

ROSE, PETER I., *They and We.* Random House, Inc., New York, 1964.

*"Strontium 90."*

# 31
# A Birthright

Everyone should have the right to be well-born. "Well-born" does not mean that one should be born with the so-called "silver spoon" or with monetary resources. The golden birthright provides the optimum chance for each baby to develop his full potential for both physical and psychological well-being.

Air and water pollution, the effect of strontium 90, and the threat of nuclear war are of world concern. These threats must be handled individually and collectively by the world community to insure the safety of all

348

*"—and they lived happily ever after. . . . Now be a good boy and go to sleep, and don't forget, Daddy loves you. . . ."*

people living now and all children yet unborn. However, the golden birthright also includes being born to parents who want a baby, being born to a household that has love and trust to share with a new life, and being born to parents who realize the basic needs of a new life. These are the birthrights that this chapter will discuss.

## PRENATAL CARE

The most important and most crucial time for the baby is in the first ninety days of pregnancy. His birthrights need to be considered from the time the ovum and the sperm unite. The earliest stages of pregnancy are the most dangerous ones for the baby. Often this is the time when the mother doesn't even realize that she is pregnant. During these very early weeks the baby's principal organs are formed. For better or for worse, all

349

of the components for the new human being are present in the baby at this very early time.

Pregnancy does not begin when the first menstrual period is missed. It begins about two important weeks before. Therefore, it is possible for a woman to be pregnant without knowing it. The importance that is attached to this fact is that a woman should begin taking care of the couple's baby as soon as they are married.

More and more doctors are now treating all married women as if they were pregnant, at least during the last two-thirds of the menstrual cycle. Everything they do should take into consideration the baby-that-might-be, because, if that baby really is, he is in the most crucial weeks of his life. Remember, by the end of the third month, the baby is completely formed. He has a brain and a heart that beats. He is either off to a good start—or he isn't.

The prospective parents (anyone who wishes to have a family) can do some practical things to help insure a healthy, happy baby.

First they should bear in mind that it is dangerous to marry a close relative. To do so increases the risk of compounding the errors in heredity.

Second, the newly married couple should select a family physician. It is important for both husband and wife to realize that in the event of pregnancy, prenatal care is extremely important. If there is a family history of defects or if there are possible complications such as Rh incompatibility, the doctor would then be alerted. The husband and wife should know their Rh blood group. In addition, medical help should be readily available to avoid a premature birth because premature babies are more prone to defects.

Third, every mother should be sure to tell her doctor if she thinks she is pregnant and she should take only the medicines he prescribes. Indiscriminate self-dosing from the medicine chest is dangerous. Some drugs can harm unborn babies. "Pep-pills," tranquilizers, sleeping pills, and pain killers are all medicines. Their effect on an embryo early in pregnancy might be disastrous.

Dr. Virginia Apgar discusses some of these drugs. She writes:

In the possibly harmful category are many of the tranquilizers that some people take casually. Reserpine (Serpasil) has been shown in animal experiments to increase infant mortality. When rats are given meprobamate (Miltown, Equanil), their offspring are slow learners.

There are some drugs that are even more definitely in the potentially harmful category. They are *known* to have caused damage or even death to unborn babies at least on rare occasions. Iodides, which are commonly used in cough medicines, can produce goiters in babies before they are born. These babies whose thyroids get mixed up may also be mentally retarded. The long-acting sulfa drugs prescribed for some stubborn infections can produce nerve deafness in the unborn child. We also know that the embryo cannot excrete tetracycline. If this common antibiotic is given to the mother, it is deposited in the bones of the baby, where it may slow down growth. And it can also cause discoloration of his teeth. Chloramphicol, another antibiotic, can cause jaundice and possible brain damage. Excessive amounts of vitamin K can have the same effect, and excessive vitamin D may cause bone damage.

Of course, we must strike a commonsense balance between caution and the need to treat an illness. However, I think the time is rapidly coming when any woman planning to have children will take no more medicine than is necessary to preserve her life or health.[1]

Fourth, certain virus diseases such as rubella (German measles) can cause birth defects. The pregnant mother should make every effort to avoid contact with these diseases.

Fifth, abdominal X-rays should be avoided during early weeks of pregnancy. Doctors usually prescribe X-rays of the abdomen only in the first ten days after the beginning of the menstrual period.

Sixth, excessive smoking during pregnancy should be avoided, for this practice is associated with subnormal birth weight. Recent studies indicate that the more cigarettes a mother smokes during her pregnancy, the less her baby will weigh. The average weight loss is half a pound. For the baby under five pounds this half pound is very important because it is related to survival.

Seventh, age should be considered. Many studies have been made on the age of the mother and its correlation to the well-being of the baby. Although no absolute statements can be made, the following possibilities are reported: (1) the best childbearing years seem to be in the 25 to 34 age bracket, (2) teen-age mothers run a somewhat greater risk of having premature babies and babies who may be retarded, and (3) mothers over 35 also run more risk of having defective off-spring.

Eighth, spacing is important, too. When the babies are only a year apart, there are more complications of pregnancy, more premature babies, and more babies who do not live. On the average, a full two years between babies seems to be needed to produce the healthiest children.

Ninth, diet affects growth. It is important for girls to acquire proper eating habits early in life. These are conducive not only to their own good health but to that of their children. Because the teen-age diet is so crucial

---

[1] Virginia Apgar, "New Ways to Save Your Unborn Child," *Ladies Home Journal,* Vol. 83 (August, 1966), p. 46. Copyright 1966, The Curtis Publishing Company.

in this respect, it is imperative to impress this upon girls from 13–19. This is vital to their health and that of their children and yet this is just the time when food fads instead of balanced meals may be desired.

The pregnant woman should have a diet that contains increased amounts of protein, vitamins, and mineral salts—especially calcium—in order to feed the developing fetus. A deficient diet may cause a maldeveloped baby or a premature birth, with the consequent danger to the baby's physical and mental health.

Finally, there comes a time when the question is not when one should have a baby, but if. According to some studies, the risk of mental retardation for the third and fourth child is greater than for the first and second. With the fifth pregnancy, that risk doubles. With six or more children, even though a mother is still under 35, the risk is three to five times as great.

In fact, the idyll of a houseful of healthy, strong children has been attacked as a myth in a number of recent studies. One shows that the larger the family, the smaller the children in height, weight, and chest circumference; the larger the family, the lower their scores on memory and I.Q. tests. This general tendency was not influenced by the educational level of the family. One investigator, Dr. Wagner H. Bridger of New York, says that he finds the most vigorous children come from small families with a large span of time between births.

In short, medically speaking, there is an ideal time to have babies and an ideal time to stop.

## SYMPTOMS OF PREGNANCY

The physical symptoms of pregnancy are, of course, noticed by the woman, but the husband should be made aware of these physical symptoms too. The wife needs his understanding and acceptance during this change in their lives. The cessation of menstruation is the earliest and one of the most important symptoms of pregnancy. However, not until the date of the expected period has been passed by ten days or more can any reliance be put on this symptom. The breasts become larger, firmer, and more tender. A sensation of stretching fullness accompanied by tingling both in the breasts and nipples often develops, and in many instances a feeling of throbbing is also experienced. Frequent urination is an early symptom. This is attributed to the fact that the growing uterus stretches the base of the bladder so that a sensation results identical with that felt when the bladder wall is stretched with urine. Nausea is of no diagnostic value because many women suffer no nausea at all. When this "morning sickness" occurs it usually makes its appearance about two weeks after the first missed menstrual period. However, this is a symptom of many other conditions, such as ordinary indigestion. The combination of all of these symptoms is a basis for assuming that conception has taken place.

## THE EFFECT OF PREGNANCY ON THE
## MARRIAGE RELATIONSHIP

Pregnancy can be a rewarding experience if the marital partners support each other in facing the developments and the psychological challenges of their more complicated individual and joint roles. Many jokes and cartoons depict the husband during the pregnancy and the delivery as an awkward nuisance. This portrayal is humorous, but not necessarily accurate. A sympathetic and loving husband is of prime importance to the pregnant wife. She has an increased need for love and attention. She turns to her husband for increased demonstrations of affection and reassurance that even with her changing appearance she is still acceptable and lovable in his eyes. Besides turning to their husbands, some women also turn to their mothers, and some prefer the latter to the former. This preference for the mother over the husband may be due to the woman's realization that what she craves is a nurturing type of love that she has received in the past from her mother, rather than the erotic kind of love she associates with her husband. Moreover, as she prepares for the maternal role, she identifies with her mother and usually feels a closer bond to her than in the past.

This situation need not lead to any special problem, since both husband and mother are likely to understand and accept their new roles. Occasionally, where the previous relationship between the woman and her family has been disturbed, her mother may resent the extra demands upon her affection and may be rejecting, or the husband may feel jealous because he sees himself being passed over by his wife. The increased dependence of the woman on her mother may also lead to difficulties after the birth of the baby, either because the grandmother may be tempted to play too central a role in its care or because she may feel rejected when the daughter's dependence upon her changes rather suddenly to a wish for independence in taking care of the child.

Thus, the husband and wife need to realize that pregnancy and especially the first pregnancy can complicate their relationship. They are stimulated to plan jointly for the coming baby and for their future roles as parents. On the other hand, psychological changes in the expectant mother interfere with her previous relationship with her husband, and the close link between the partners begins to open up to include the baby—at first purely in fantasy, and later in actuality. The changes have a maturing effect on both husband and wife, as individuals and as a couple. At the beginning

353

of pregnancy, the partners achieve a greater intimacy and a feeling that their love for each other has been concretely consummated. Later on they progress to the even higher stage of satisfaction of their needs for generativity, as they envisage their joint responsibility for bringing a new life into the world.

It is common for the prevailing mood of the woman to change during pregnancy. Some women feel better during pregnancy than at any other time. Others feel unusually depressed throughout pregnancy. Sudden unexplainable mood swings are not uncommon, even in women who usually are emotionally stable.

These mood changes are not related to whether the woman wanted to become pregnant or not. Physicians believe that they are influenced both by the biochemical changes, especially the complicated alterations in hormones (the secretions of the ductless glands), and by the psychological reactions to pregnancy (the preparation for the coming baby and for the assumption of the maternal role). Some of the common changes observed are a tendency to become angry at slight provocation, laugh and cry easily, and have rapid changes in mood as a result of minor external stimulation.

Introversion and passivity are the chief characteristic emotional changes of pregnancy. These changes usually begin during the second or third month and gradually increase in intensity reaching a peak around the seventh or eighth month. The woman, who previously may have been an active outgoing person and whose role as wife and mother has been one of nurturance and giving, gradually or suddenly becomes turned in on herself, feels passive and lazy, and wants to be cared for instead of caring for others. The emphasis is on the increased need for demonstrations of love and affection.

Changes in sexual desire and performance occur in many women at various phases of pregnancy. Some women have increased desire, and it is not uncommon to find women who experience orgasm only during pregnancy. A diminution of sexual desire is common toward the middle of pregnancy.

These changes, as mentioned above, may possibly be due to complicated changes in the pregnant woman's hormones. They are more likely, however, to be due to psychological factors. Sexual desire in the wife may previously have been impaired by fear of pregnancy, which is now removed, or by her feelings of doubt about her femininity, which are now reduced because conception has proved that she is fertile. In some cultures, women proudly exhibit the external signs of their pregnancies, and men regard these as signs of beauty. In these cultures, the woman's awareness of the physical changes of pregnancy may stimulate her sexual desire. In other cultures, women feel less beautiful during pregnancy, and sexual desire

354

may therefore be inhibited by feelings of shame or modesty or by the fear that their husbands will turn away from them. Sexual desire and performance may also be inhibited by the unfounded fear that intercourse will harm the fetus by pressure on the abdomen or by trauma to the uterus.

## THE DANGER SIGNALS IN PREGNANCY

Good obstetrical care is important for both mother and child. Thus, at the first hint of pregnancy, the couple should visit their physician. Only the physician's careful examination can reassure the parents that the pregnancy is progressing normally. Sometimes, between visits to her doctor, the expectant mother may notice certain changes in her condition which the physician should be aware of at once. Often these findings observed by the mother-to-be are of no significance; however, the physician should be notified without delay so that he may make an examination and evaluate their importance. The following symptoms demand immediate report to the obstetrician:

1. Vaginal bleeding, no matter how slight
2. Swelling of the face or fingers
3. Severe, continuous headache
4. Dimness or blurring of vision
5. Pain in the abdomen
6. Persistent vomiting
7. Chills and fever
8. Sudden escape of water from the vagina

Although these symptoms sound formidable, their significance depends entirely on the circumstances under which they occur. Even the development of several of them may be quite in keeping with the normal state of affairs and is not necessarily a cause for concern. For instance, the onset of normal labor is often heralded by a very slight amount of bleeding, recurrent pain in the abdomen and a discharge of water from the vagina. In the main, however, these symptoms deserve particular attention because they often constitute warning signs of the three most common complications of pregnancy, namely miscarriage, toxemia, and pyelitis.[2]

[2] Nicholson J. Eastman, *Expectant Motherhood,* 4th ed. (Boston, Little, Brown and Company, 1963), pp. 111–112. Copyright 1940, 1947, Copyright 1957 by Nicholson J. Eastman. Copyright 1963 by Nicholson J. Eastman and Loretta R. Eastman.

A miscarriage or abortion is the premature expulsion of the fetus. There is "criminal abortion" (meaning that it was effected illegally without justification), and "therapeutic abortion" (meaning that it was produced ethically because of some grave maternal disease which made continuation of the pregnancy hazardous). There is the natural miscarriage or abortion when nature expels a defective embryo. Miscarriage can also occur from some types of infection, certain diseases (such as syphilis), vitamin deficiency, glandular dysfunction, accident, poisoning, or anything that causes the death of the fetus. It is also thought that psychological factors, such as severe emotional shock, can cause natural miscarriage.

Natural miscarriages, it is estimated, terminate about one in every ten pregnancies. The second and third months are the most dangerous in terms of the possibility of a miscarriage. These miscarriages are nature's way of extinguishing an embryo which is imperfect. Since imperfectly formed embryos are almost always aborted early in pregnancy, the likelihood of a full-term child's being defective is only 5 out of every 100 births.

Toxemia (blood poisoning) is exhibited by an increase in blood pressure, albumin in the urine, swelling of the face and fingers, and an increase in weight. Toxemia is detrimental to the mother and baby.

Pyelitis is an inflammation of the ureter, the funnel-like portion of the kidney which conveys the urine from the kidney to the tube leading to the bladder. When the flow of urine through the kidney, pelvis, and ureter is not brisk, stagnation is prone to ensue with consequent inflammation. The characteristic symptoms of pyelitis are chills, fever, and pain in one thigh or the other, most frequently the right.

## ATTITUDES

It is important to develop positive attitudes about childbirth itself and the child's birthright. Birth is a physical and emotional crisis for baby, mother, and family. The mother's emotions and her experience of pain during labor are determined to some extent by what she has been taught to expect. Education of the parents for childbirth can be a very positive influence.

Labor, the work which the mother does in giving birth, consists of three stages. The first stage, the opening of the cervix, is accomplished by muscles which are not under voluntary control. The confident, secure mother can probably help the process by relaxing. The second stage, pushing the baby out, is partially involuntary and partially controllable by the mother. Education and positive attitudes can prepare the mother to help herself and her baby. The third stage, a brief process, is the expelling of the placenta. The duration of labor varies considerably with each pregnancy, but the average length of time is seven hours for the first baby and four hours for additional offspring.

Directly connected with the mother's fear or confidence, tension or relaxation, pain or easiness in giving birth, is her confidence in herself and the help she is receiving.

The crowning emotional experience is, of course, the joy of receiving her baby, the result of the mother's labor and the conjugal love between the new parents. The child's birthright is to have been born to parents who want and welcome him and who appreciate him as a person in his own right.

## TO PROMOTE UNDERSTANDING OF THIS CHAPTER

1. What is the golden birthright?
2. What is the most crucial and important time in the life of a baby?
3. When should a married couple start considering their child's birthright?
4. What practical things can a couple do to help ensure a healthy, happy baby?
5. What should be considered in the spacing of children? In the age of the mother?
6. What are the symptoms of pregnancy?
7. How does pregnancy affect the marriage relationship?
8. What are some of the basic needs of the mother-to-be?
9. What are some of the duties of the father-to-be?
10. What are some of the psychological and sexual changes that may take place in pregnancy?
11. What are some of the danger signals during pregnancy?
12. Define the following terms:

    obstetrician      therapeutic abortion     fetus
    miscarriage       criminal abortion        toxemia

13. Write an attitude analysis about parenthood.

## SUPPLEMENTARY READING

APGAR, VIRGINIA, "New Ways to Save Your Unborn Child." *Ladies Home Journal,* Vol. 83, August 1966, p. 46.

Duvall, Evelyn Millis, *Family Development,* 3rd ed. J. B. Lippincott Co., New York, 1967.

Eastman, Nicholson J., *Expectant Motherhood,* 4th ed. Little, Brown and Company, Boston, 1963.

Newton, Niles, *Maternal Emotions.* Harper and Row, New York, 1955.

Constantin Alajalov © 1955 The Curtis Publishing Company

# 32
# Needs of Babies

The delight and pride shown on Daddy's face and the joy Mother is receiving from baby's "conversation" with Daddy indicate that this baby's basic needs will be met. Daddy appears to be willing to try his hand in the kitchen and will no doubt continue to cooperate when mother and baby come home. Baby doesn't need a spotless home or an expert in formula measuring and bath temperatures. These things are easy to do reasonably well. Baby, however, does need some one who appreciates him, gives him security, and encourages him to develop.

## UNDERSTANDING BABY

A baby is not an unconscious little organism that simply eats and sleeps. He is a seeking, reacting human being with a capacity to learn and an ability to be deeply influenced for good or ill. Baby wants and needs to be securely held. He wants to be played with and talked to right from the start. Fortunately, most mothers quite naturally hold their babies, play with them, and talk to them. They enjoy these activities. It is interesting that scientists are finding new proof that these actions are a vital part of mothering. Mothering is defined here as tender, loving care and is as important coming from Daddy as from Mother.

The newborn baby can see and is interested in what he sees. For example, infants under five days old will stare longer at a patterned surface than a plain one because it is more stimulating. By the end of the third week of life, a baby smiles a "social smile" in response to a human voice. An investigator who studied babies' smiles states that while babies will sometimes smile at the sound of a bird whistle or a rattle, the human voice is the sound that brings the most smiles.

*There is in life no blessing like affection and adoration.*

Donald G. Westlake

A baby's sense of touch and temperature is even better developed than his sight and hearing. The sense of comfort and well-being is made much easier when the baby is held and fondled. Studies of children who do not get much holding—for example, babies in some orphanages—show that such children do not sleep or eat well. Being held and fondled in infancy helps a baby learn to relate to other persons.

One of the first things a baby has to learn is that his parent is separate from him. He has to learn there is a "me" and a "not-me." There is warmth, comfort, and food that goes away and returns. Playing peek-a-boo helps the baby realize mother or daddy disappear and then reappear.

At about eight weeks of age, a baby is old enough to start worrying. Scientists think that at this age the sight and hearing of an infant have become keen enough so that he knows one person from another. He suddenly realizes that there is more than one "not-me." Are all the "not-me's" warm and loving? He isn't sure. If a stranger picks him up, he's likely to cry. Psychologists call this reaction "stranger anxiety."

Somewhat later, the baby develops another worry, "separation anxiety." From six months to eighteen months is a crucial period during which the baby is really afraid of losing his mother or the person with whom he has had the closest communication. Perhaps it is at this time that the baby has really identified his mother as the most important "not-me" in his life, and he understands that he would have a difficult time without her or the person who cares for him. If anything happens to make him believe that he has lost his mother, he may suffer a mental depression severe enough to have a continued effect throughout his life. Psychologists are now recommending that children not be adopted into strange homes or moved from one foster home to another during this period. For example, if a couple wishes to adopt a child who is in this age span, they should be encouraged to leave him in the orphanage until he has passed through this stage. It is vitally important to emphasize the need for allaying the separation anxiety in babies from six to eighteen months. The mother who is going through some emotional problem may enhance this anxiety in the baby if her problem causes her to be detached and absent either physically or psychologically. This is a period when a mother particularly needs the reassurance of her husband and the knowledge that her marriage is sound so that she doesn't transfer anxiety to the child.

Security and stimulation—these are the two gifts that a baby continues to need. As he begins to babble and coo, he needs a verbal response from his mother. He learns that human beings like to make sounds to each other —that there is a pattern of give-and-take in making sounds. He must learn that pattern before he can begin to learn that sounds have meanings. A baby who has never been talked to never learns to talk.

When a baby is encouraged to reach for a rattle, he is learning. One recent study has shown that babies who have had this kind of coaching learn to grasp objects six weeks sooner than do babies who are not as well-handled. When a baby is held in a standing position, he is being stimulated to learn to stand and walk.

The attitudes that a baby develops toward food are also learned. These attitudes may affect his lifelong physical well-being. Experts in nutrition view the United States as an overweight nation, and they say that the trouble goes back to infancy. Pediatricians tell mothers that a healthy baby gains about seven ounces a week. Some mothers consider it a personal triumph if they can make their babies gain eight or ten ounces a week. But the year-old baby dimpled with fat should no longer be cause for maternal pride. Experts now know that the overweight baby has been victimized in several ways. First, he has been force-fed so that he has lost his innate ability to know when he is full and is ready to stop. He has been trained to overeat.

Secondly, the overweight baby has probably learned to accept food as a substitute for emotional satisfaction. Every time he cries or frets, his mother pops a bottle of milk or some other food into his mouth. Yet he may be crying or fretting because he is lonely or bored. Food, a bottle, or a pacifier should not take the place of holding and cuddling.

Of course, the baby who does *not* gain at a normal rate is in trouble, too. Pediatricians call this condition "failure to thrive," and it is a signal to look for the source of trouble. It may be trouble not solved by merely juggling the feeding formula. Such babies may have malformations of the heart or of the digestive tract that can be corrected by surgery. Or they may have metabolic disorders that require prompt treatment.

There is an increasing alertness to the inborn errors of metabolism. In a recent study of 2,000 mentally-retarded children, it was shown that 21 percent of them suffered metabolic disorders. Two of these disorders, phenylketonuria (P.K.U.) and galactosemia are currently in the news because new tests make it possible to detect them in the first few weeks of life. The P.K.U. child cannot metabolize one of the common amino acids in protein. Children suffering from either of these disorders need special diets and medical care if they are to develop normally.

## EVALUATING THE DEVELOPMENT OF A BABY

Regular medical (which includes developmental) observation of a baby under one year of age should be performed at monthly intervals in order to evaluate his progress. Babies develop at their own individual rates. Each baby who is healthy has his own developmental pattern. It is unfair to the

362

baby to compare him with other babies of the same age except in a very general way. However, his growth and development should be measured against themselves. A baby should progress steadily from stage to stage in accordance with his own growth pattern. In addition to the developmental observations, visits to the pediatrician or family doctor provide opportunities to immunize the baby against potentially hazardous diseases such as poliomyelitis (infantile paralysis), whooping cough, diphtheria, tetanus (lock jaw), measles, and smallpox.

The basic evaluations of physical growth are noted in the baby's weight gain and growth in length. The baby will usually triple his birth weight in the first year and grow to one and one-half times his birth length. Regular measurements of the growth of the head are made during physical examinations. This is an indirect measurement of the growth and development of the brain.

Further evaluations of the growth and development of the brain and central nervous system are made from observations of the behavior of the infant and the testing of his reflexes. Observations of the time of responsive smiling, control of head movements, eye and hand coordination, sitting, crawling, standing, walking, and social responsiveness are all helpful in evaluating the general progress of the baby. These observations have been recorded systematically by observers of child development so that more detailed studies may be made if there is any indication that further observations are needed. These more systematic observations must be done by professionally-trained workers who are familiar with the circumstances under which the tests should be conducted and the proper interpretation of the results.

## LINES OF COMMUNICATION IN INFANCY

The number of bodily contacts of the child with his mother and others who care for him runs into thousands. To pick up an infant, hold, feed, bathe, and play with him mean far more than just physical manipulation. In connection with each event there is a special communication between the adult and the child. As the result of this communication, an interpersonal relationship is established.

The adult brings to these interpersonal relationships his own emotions, moods, and mannerisms. Physical contact is the most successful means of attaining emotional intimacy with a child, provided, of course, the adult has the capacity for it.

Many, perhaps most, of the experiences that occur in a child's contacts with people early in life are infused with feeling. The child has much at stake. He is desperately hungry, for example, even though he was well fed only a few hours before. Emotion is bound to come into play when something for which a child is eager is supplied or withheld. Even when his physical needs are cared for, the child is pleased to have company and disappointed when the company leaves him. Meanwhile, many of the child's own undertakings are accompanied by eagerness or annoyance and an obligato of sounds with emotional overtones as he cries, coos, trills, smiles, gurgles, yawns, sighs, and belches.

As all of this occurs, the adult in the company of an infant is communicating something from within himself as he deals with the child. With the older child, what the adult says or does may clearly show that he has a human touch, that he is unsure of himself, or that he is plodding through his job in a mechanical way.

However, when the baby is quite young there are subtler interchanges that take place. There is a kind of emotional linkage involving emotional contagion or communion between the baby and other significant people (the mother, the father, or the nurse). This emotional linkage is called empathy. Communication exists between the child and the significant adult

*The first duty to children is to make them happy.*

Vivienne

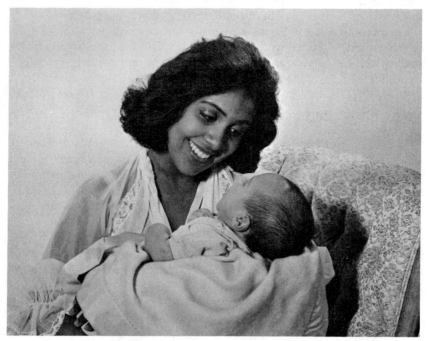

through empathy before the child is mature enough to perceive overt expressions of emotion, such as smiling, paleness, or a worried look. Empathy endures throughout life. But the time of its greatest importance is in later infancy and early childhood—perhaps from the age of six months to twenty-seven months.

This concept of emotional communication between an adult and an infant is shown by many signs and symbols. There are studies which indicate that babies in the care of mothers who are obviously anxious cry more than the babies of mothers who are not so obviously anxious. Such studies support the view that a mother's emotional state affects her child. However, to make a conclusive test, it would be necessary to study not only the characteristics of mothers but also those of children, since some babies are more serene or cry more than others regardless of who is caring for them. The idea that there are subtle communications between babies and adults agrees with observations in everyday life where it appears that babies are definitely more fretful or at ease with some people than with others. Hospital workers have maintained, for example, that some nurses seem to have a soothing effect on babies. The same babies tend to fuss and cry when in the care of other nurses. The actions of a nurse who likes children and welcomes them into her arms may differ from those of another well-trained nurse in ways that are perceptible to a baby even though the actions may be too subtle to be measured.

A study by MacFarland, Allen, and Honzik in 1954 found that major benefits accrued to young children when their mothers were helped to be more understanding and at ease with themselves so that they were freer to handle wisely the rearing of their children. This necessity for self-understanding, being at ease with oneself, and having a kind of inner freedom places the emphasis on the parent as a person. It underscores the position that self-knowledge and a healthy attitude of self-acceptance are more basic to the parent's role than a set of practical rules or an intellectual notion as to whether a parent should be strict or lenient, permissive, or authoritarian. Self-understanding is as important for parenthood as for the individual acceptance as discussed in Unit 1.

## FEEDING PRACTICES AND CHILD BEHAVIOR

Advice to parents about the feeding of infants shifts drastically. In the 1930's, for example, most advice-giving articles recommended strict feeding schedules, in contrast to the present predominance of recommendations for self-regulatory ("on demand") feeding. Recommendations have been based upon differing viewpoints concerning the effects of various feeding methods on many aspects of the child's behavior and the development of his personality. Careful studies of feeding practices have found that breast versus bottle feeding has no demonstrable effect on such behavior as aggression, dependency, feeding problems, thumb-sucking, bed wetting, or disturbance over toilet training. Researchers are not in complete agreement, but some find the mothers who breast feed feel no warmer toward their children nor more competent in child care, nor are they any happier about having children. In the past, parents with more education tended to prefer bottle feeding for their children. In recent years, this group has moved toward a greater preference for breast feeding while those with lesser education are giving it up. From a clinical viewpoint, breast feeding, when possible, would seem preferable inasmuch as it provides a food uniquely suited for the infant under comfortable feeding conditions.

Although most mothers now follow a rather permissive feeding schedule for their babies, about one-fifth still schedule feedings rather rigidly. These latter mothers tend to be somewhat more anxious about child care, but the fact that their babies are fed on a rigid schedule does not seem to affect the development of their children's personalities. The occurrence of feeding problems similarly is unrelated to scheduled versus "self-demand" feeding practices.

Observations suggest that breast feeding and a flexible or rigid handling of the feeding schedule are not the important factors per se; the mother's attitude toward the child as expressed in the total feeding situation is more important than any one isolated factor in the manner of feeding. Similar overt procedures in feeding can have psychologically different meanings, depending on the attitude of the mother. Again, these observations underscore the importance of self-knowledge, self-acceptance, and self-confidence on the part of the parent, in order that feeding be one of the warm experiences of a total parent-baby relationship.

## MATERNAL BEHAVIOR AND DEPENDENCY IN CHILDREN

Dependency is displayed by a child in his attempts to secure the presence and nurturance of another person. Degree of dependence is estimated by how hard a child tries to obtain the company and attention of someone else, usually his mother. Children use many different modes of dependent behavior, including crying, following, cuddling, smiling, talking, showing accomplishments, shouting, and asking for help. Dependent behavior has been classified into five types: seeking help, seeking physical contact, seeking proximity, seeking attention, and seeking recognition.

As children grow, their dependency behavior changes in its relation to mutuality. As the child or person matures, he gives more nurturance. Still dependent on others for company and nurturance, he can give as he accepts. The objects of dependency relationships also change. Dependent in the beginning on his mother, the child comes to depend upon other family members, then peers, teachers, other adults, eventually a husband or wife and, perhaps, finally children.

Many studies have dealt with the effects of mothers' behavior on dependency in children. The availability of the mother has a bearing on the young child's seeking of contact. Two- and three-year-old boys sought more affectionate contact with their female nursery school teachers when they (the children) came from large families where children were spaced close together. There is some agreement that frustration and punishment in infancy and preschool years are associated with dependency in the preschool period. Evidence comes from studies which correlated mothers' feeding practices and discipline practices with later behavior in their children. The preschool child's dependency tended to be greater if his mother used withdrawal of love to discipline him, showed signs of rejection, punished parent-directed aggression, and was demonstrative with affection. There is agreement in the literature that maternal rejection is associated with dependency in children. Research suggests that frustration and punishment in early childhood may affect adult dependency behavior.

Overprotection also has been related to child dependency. Very indulgent, protective mothers tended to have children who expressed their dependency in negative, aggressive ways, while dominating, protective mothers' children tended to be passive and submissive in their dependency.

*No affection is so purely angelic as the love of a father to a daughter.*

Leo de Wys, Inc.

367

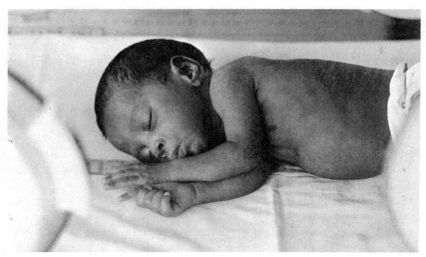

*A new born baby is a blank page on which can be written his history.*

A certain amount of protection and nurturance is essential for a child's existence and health. Parents are faced with many decisions as to how to give their children enough response, help, contact, proximity, attention, recognition, and encouragement toward independent effort without forcing or dominating him.[1]

## CHARACTERISTICS OF BABYHOOD

The newborn baby's activity is related to the state of his stomach. He needs frequent feedings and usually settles on a 3 to 4 hour schedule. His sense of taste gives a positive response to mild and sweet solutions. However, sour, bitter, or strongly salty tastes receive a negative response. He appears to be relatively insensitive to pain. It is difficult to determine how soon or how deeply an infant feels pain as compared to an adult, but it is undoubtedly true that an adult's pain is frequently more intense because of past experiences. If pain stimulation could be stripped of tensions and fears that grow out of past experiences, many agonies experienced by older people would probably be less severe.

It is interesting to observe how the infant's apparent insensibility to certain pains is reflected in medical practice. Circumcisions performed

[1] J. C. Finney, "Some Maternal Influences on Children's Personality and Character." *Genetic Psychology Monographs,* Vol. 63, 1963, pp. 199–278.

368

*Curiosity in children shows their appetite for knowledge.*

without anesthetic upon a child under two weeks of age and other forms of surgical treatment do not customarily produce signs of suffering as acute as one would expect if an older person were to receive similar treatment. However, one cannot be certain that the absence of outward signs denotes a similar absence of feeling.

For the infant, crying is one of the most important accomplishments. Crying, for the young child, has a vastly complex set of functions and meanings. Through his crying, the child expresses his needs, wants, discomfort, and in time, his desire for company, wish to be noticed, hurts and bruises, annoyances, impatience, and grief. Crying becomes not merely a sign of distress but also a kind of self-assertion. Crying serves the child as a means of calling his friends to his side. Very early in life (although not intentionally at first) crying becomes a weapon which the infant can use as a protest against those who ignore, neglect, or abuse him.

At birth, babies do not show clear-cut patterns of fear and anger. These patterns are learned and the learning starts immediately. Individual babies differ widely in their maturity at birth. The differences in maturity vary as much as the differences in personalities which they exhibit. Some babies are mobile and active while others are placid and serene.

By six months, a baby discriminates between familiar persons and strangers. He is very conscious of strange places and faces. He recognizes his mother's voice and wants to join her if he hears her talking in an adjacent room. He may be able to sit alone. When he is placed on the floor,

369

his knees go into a creeping position. If he is held erect, he can stand firmly with help. His eyes and hands are beginning to function together and he is able to reach for toys and grasp them. Moreover, he reaches a block or a toy promptly on sight. A baby of this age likes to bang toys. He also enjoys throwing them on the floor and looking after them when they have fallen from the high chair or from his mother's lap. He inspects all objects and may put them into his mouth. Children, however, vary in their need to mouth objects.

By nine months, the child stands alone by pulling himself up with the help of furniture and the sides of his crib. He enjoys motor activity such as sitting and playing, creeping, leaning far forward, and standing upright after he has pulled himself up. He enjoys playing with toys which can be pulled about because he can now grasp things by their handles and can pluck a string and give it a tug.

The nine-month-old is a very social being. He is responsive to demonstrations and teaching. He learns nursery tricks like pat-a-cake and bye-bye and says "mama," "papa," "dada," or other articulate vocalizations. Making lip noises and vocalizing at a high pitch are part of his daily enjoyment. Playing in the bath, high chair, play pen, or crib is a delightful pastime. Individuality is beginning to take form. The young child is becoming more discriminating, more perceptive of small variations in sight and

*The chief pleasure in eating is in yourself.*

Major Morris

370

sound and more sensitive to his surroundings. There is also the beginning of a show of temper that may be either a way of resistance or a mode of communication.

The year-old child is learning to walk and is seldom quiet when awake. He has a variable appetite and begins to show signs of definite food likes and dislikes. He can use a spoon and wants to feed himself. Sometimes he plays at meals and enjoys feeling the different food textures. He has learned to drop objects on purpose and enjoys seeing the way different foods land. He listens to words and tries to imitate. However, most of his talk is still gibberish. His social status in the family is good because he is an actor and a show-off. He responds to music. He also laughs at strange and different sounds made by others. He makes friends very quickly. Usually he designates his friends by bringing them some of his toys to play with or by asking them to read a book to him. He is too young to play with other children but enjoys playing around them. The child who is one year old is capable of showing fear, anger, affection, jealousy, anxiety, and sympathy.

At fifteen months, a child discards creeping for toddling. Walking is a favorite activity. Usually, while walking, a child carries things in either hand. He doesn't settle down in any one place for long—he seems to feel a need to exercise his newly-formed powers almost to excess. Emptying

*Happiness and companionship are the atmosphere in which all good affections grow.*

George W. Martin D.P.I.

371

*It is a profound mistake to think that everything has been discovered.*

H. Armstrong Roberts

the wastepaper basket and overturning it many times are among his realm of endless activities. This mobility calls for close supervision from others. This age is a very demanding one. The child usually wants to be at his mother's heels instead of being cooped up in a playpen or crib. He also wants to be held up so he can see what mother is doing.

By eighteen months, the child has gained general body control. He can walk upstairs with help, climb into an adult's chair, seat himself on a child's chair, and move with a hurried gait. Pushing chairs around, throwing balls, and pulling wheeled toys as he walks are enjoyable feats. He can point to pictures he recognizes and can recognize photographs of the family members. He distinguishes between *you* and *me* and is capable of proclaiming *mine*. He enjoys errands of fetching and carrying. His vocabulary may be about ten words. He gestures to enhance understanding.

The above descriptions are based on average children. Some children will perform at an older level of achievement while others will perform at a younger level. Some children mature faster than others and within this growth sequence there are spurts of growth and periods of quiescence. Each individual is unique in his pattern and rate of development. Each individual also differs from every other individual in his inherent poten-

372

*Independence is united to the idea of dignity and virtue.*

John D. Burns, Jr. D.P.I.

tialities. Therefore, each child should be treated as an individual and given the most effective environment possible to grow toward his fullest potential.

## TO PROMOTE UNDERSTANDING OF THIS CHAPTER

1. What are the basic psychological needs of a new baby?
2. Define "mothering." Must a child have his natural mother with him to be well-mothered?
3. What is the degree of sensory development in the very young baby?
4. What is the importance of being held and fondled in infancy?
5. When does a baby begin to worry? What does he worry about?
6. What is separation anxiety? How should one cope with it?
7. What are the two most important gifts that a baby continues to need all through life?
8. How do one's attitudes toward food in babyhood affect his life?
9. Describe one of the inborn errors of metabolism in babies.

10. How is the development of a baby evaluated?

11. How does an infant communicate?

12. What is empathy? How is empathy shown?

13. What are the most important factors in the feeding practices of children?

14. How does the behavior of the mother affect the dependency in the children?

15. If children develop at their own individual rate of growth, why is it important to study the average characteristics at each age?

## SUPPLEMENTARY READING

BEHRENS, M. L., "Child Rearing and the Character Structure of the Mother." *Child Development*, Vol. 25, 1954, pp. 225–328.

FINNEY, J. C., "Some Maternal Influences on Children's Personality and Character." *Genetic Psychology Monographs,* Vol. 63, 1963, pp. 199–278.

HARTUP, W. W., "Dependence and Independence," in H. W. Stevenson, J. Kagan, and C. SPIKER, ed., *Child Psychology, The Sixty-second Yearbook of the Study of Education.* University of Chicago, Chicago, 1963.

ILG, F. L., and AMES, L. B., *Child Behavior.* Harper and Row, New York, 1955.

JERSILD, ARTHUR T., *Child Psychology,* 5th ed. Prentice-Hall, Inc., Englewood Cliffs, N.J., 1960.

MACFARLAND, J., ALLEN, L., and HONZIK, M. P., *A Developmental Study of the Behavior Problems of Normal Children Between Twenty-One Months and Fourteen Years.* University of California Press, Berkeley, 1954.

SMART, MOLLIE S., and SMART, RUSSELL C., *Children Development and Relationships.* The Macmillan Company, New York, 1967.

SEARS, R. R., MACCOBY, ELEANOR E., and LEVIN, H., *Patterns of Child Rearing.* Harper and Row, New York, 1957.

THOMPSON, GEORGE G., *Child Psychology.* Houghton Mifflin Co., Boston, 1952.

WHITING, J. W. M. and CHILD, I. L., *Child Training and Personality.* Yale University, New Haven, Conn., 1953.

374

# 33
# Characteristics of Ages and Stages

The children in the doctor's office display a range of ages and exhibit various stages of development. The previous chapter concerned itself with the needs of babies. The baby here in the waiting room is content in his mother's arms. We'll assume that his contentment continues and not concern ourselves with his needs. Instead we will place the emphasis upon the other ages pictured—the ages that are patiently, hesitantly, impatiently, and actively waiting for the nurse to beckon. The great joy of the ages and stages of children is that the negative, climbing two-year old that visits the doctor this year will be the patient, contented, seated-on-stool three-year-old next year. Mother should not be too concerned nor too smug for with the passing of time each stage, enjoyable or unenjoyable, moves on to another new phase of development.

## THE TODDLER

The child between sixteen months and three years is a toddler. The toddler is moving rapidly away from babyhood and into childhood. The central theme of development during toddlerhood is autonomy: becoming aware of himself as a person among other people and wanting to do things for himself. The toddler demonstrates his beginning autonomy—and his drive for more of it—in every field; that is, in the mastery of his own body (in walking, climbing, jumping, and in controlling his muscles), in the mastery of objects (the toddler typically wants to push his stroller instead of riding in it, he wants to put on and remove his own clothes although he is not very adept at doing so, and in social relationships (he learns language, he begins to refuse parental commands, requests and offers of help).

*Experience is a good school.*

Henry Monroe D.P.I.

376

*Autonomy* is defined as a self-governing state that is without outside control. During toddlerhood, the push toward autonomy is begun. However, it is by no means absolute and continuous. At first the child vacillates between dependence and independence. This pattern of behavior will persist in various guises well into adolescence. The toddler, out on a walk, may plunge off in pursuit of a squirrel, or dash into an empty building, only to stop short, return to his mother, and want to be carried. He may strike out on his own to explore the wonders of a large department store and then burst into tears when he finds that the hand he is reaching for is that of a stranger. When trying some new feat such as jumping from a step, he will make a great show of boldness but still cling tightly to an adult's hand. He is only beginning to try himself out, and it will be some time before he can shift his emotional base from parents to contemporaries and, finally, have a secure anchorage in a sense of his own identity.

This self-governing state which is called the sense of autonomy has in it the control of impulses and thus the development of conscience. As a child takes over the wishes and demands of parents and accepts them as his own, he is developing a conscience. When his conscience isn't strong enough, his impulses take over. For example, the child says, "no, no," but goes ahead and does what he is tempted to do if his parent isn't there to help him.

If his conscience becomes so strong that he can't stand his guilt feelings, he chooses ways to relieve these feelings and to control his impulses. Four of these ways are described below:

1. He blames someone else. Sometimes the child adopts a make-believe friend, sister, or brother and when food is spilled, toys scattered or an object broken, he blames his imaginary friend.

2. He attacks the person that is frustrating him. This can result in real guilt feelings if the child is allowed to attack his mother. He desperately needs his mother to love him and would usually worry about losing her love if he attacks her. One way for the parent to handle it would be to say, "I know you want to hit me but I can't let you do that. Here, hit your punching clown."

3. He shames himself. Most children shame themselves to control their impulses and hate this feeling of shame which they heap on themselves. When an adult adds to this load by shaming a child it can be very damaging. An "I am bad, I am unworthy" feeling can result. The feeling can result in extreme shyness.

4. He becomes disgusted or loathes an impulse. Disgust and loathing can be related to any impulse such as climbing, getting hands dirty or

377

playing with food. When he feels that the impulse is bad, he can't stand any expression of it. This often carries over into adult life; a child that was trained to be fastidious in her play may be an adult who cannot make pies because the rolling of the dough is too messy. Finger painting frees some children from a disgust of getting dirty or messy.

Some children who have guilty feelings use fantasy. These fantasies are often extreme and ridiculous. For example, a child who is angry at his mother, feels guilty because he is angry, and who is also worried about losing her love can momentarily wish that she would get killed. Then, upon looking for her, he becomes frantic if he can't find her immediately.

When the conscience is developing, the child starts to take responsibility for his environment. Instead of just reacting to circumstances, he has come to feel responsible for the circumstances. The trouble is that he starts out feeling *totally* responsible for what happens to him and for the external factors in his life. Only gradually does he sort out what he *is* responsible for from all that he *feels* responsible for.

When a child is tired, hungry, or ill, he usually cannot control his impulses and needs kind, *firm* help. We should remember that most adults can't control themselves, either, under these circumstances. Thus to help the child, the parent, in his manner of handling, can say, "I know you can't decide for yourself right now, so I am going to help you."

Impulses are much stronger in some children than in others. Those with strong impulses are harder to help and are harder on parents. Progress is made when there is free energy available. If a child is *too frustrated,* he hasn't energy to learn new things. Speech is acquired during this time. If a child acquires a hostile conscience, it is harder for him to start talking. This compounds the situation because delayed speech prevents the child from getting rid of feelings. It is important to remember that the child's orientation is "a tooth for a tooth."

*Love and aggression* are two of the instinctual drives that are operating in the young child. This is a difficult time for the young child because he wants both the love of the parent and autonomy at the same time. Parents who have a tendency to give the impression that if the child controls his instinctual drives and impulses, they will love him, make it difficult for the child to solve this conflict between love and aggression. The child should have love, regardless of his behavior. The parent can give this by saying "I don't like what you are doing, but I like you." In other words, the parent can dislike the act, but not the child. The child sees praise as a form of love.

These drives function during toilet training. The child gets satisfaction when he knows that when he can delay or inhibit his impulses, he receives both parent's love and control of self. In toilet training, the parent is asking the child to give up the pleasure of eliminating where and how he wants to. Before the child can do this, he needs to have voluntary control of sphincter (about 18 months) and anal muscles (about 10 months). In toilet training, the parent should give the child plenty of time to gain control and to take major responsibility for himself. Some children who experience pleasant feelings with the operating of anus and sphincter muscles will enjoy eliminating. They are the children who like to go behind chairs or in the closet to sit and enjoy it. Urine and feces are a part of the child. Disgust with them can give a young child the feeling that part of him is bad. Organs of elimination and of sex are so related that confusion and feelings of badness can spread to sex organs. Severe toilet training often results in damaging feelings about sex.

As the toddler develops his sense of autonomy, he needs to be given opportunities for a free choice. This free choice should be given gradually and should also be a well-guided experience. For example, the toddler may have a choice between two or three alternatives. After a nap, he may choose from among three or four suitable playsuits. He may choose to help himself to a drink of water or to a cookie. He should have an opportunity to make some independent decisions. This gives him an identity with himself as a person and an opportunity to be in charge of his impulses. However, these free choices need to be ones that he can successfully manage. If instead of a free choice, he has to perform to the letter of

*"Should I cry? Or should I be quiet and brave?"*

George W. Martin D.P.I.

379

parental or adult decisions, he may develop a feeling that there is only one way to perform. This may create compulsive behavior.

Once the first crucial developmental conflict has, in principle, been solved, the baby knows of himself as distinct from other persons and from objects. When he has thus learned a good deal about his immediate surroundings, he will begin to feel himself as a person in his own right—someone capable of acting on his own impulse and purpose, choosing between opposing suggestion and command, following directions, and influencing what happens to him rather than being altogether dependent on the dictates of other people and of circumstances. The feelings of adequacy and of well-being in later life depend upon the development and maintenance of a sense of autonomy. Feelings of self-worth and of counting for something in this world are essential aspects of healthy personality functioning at any age. For the good of the child and for the world, we need the balance of love and aggression to be tipped in favor of love.

## EARLY CHILDHOOD

Early childhood is usually thought of as the ages of three, four, and five years. This is the time for plans and ideas. This is the age that wakes up before you do and decides that this is the day for scrambled eggs—and they scramble all over the kitchen. This is the age to ask questions, ob-

*Every noble acquisition is attended with its risks . . . especially at three.*

Henry Monroe D.P.I.

380

serve, and make-believe. The child at this age needs to try things out. All he requests is the material he needs to work with and the time to carry out his ideas in play.

The child's large muscles are developing rapidly. Thus, he needs opportunities to run, climb, slide, and jump so that he can gain control over these muscles and develop his coordination. However, his motor skills are developing unevenly, and he may perform extremely well in one skill and very poorly in another.

At three the child will probably speak in sentences and use words as tools of thought such as, "I don't like this hat" or "My doll is hungry." The next year, he asks many questions, recognizes the relationship between things, and displays an active tendency to state an idea and to generalize from it. A four-year-old child may say as many as 1500 to 2500 words.

At five, the child usually talks without infantile speech. He can tell a long story—and frequently does. Often he talks so incessantly that his mother finds it a trial when she is trying to do something else. When he is in this age, his mother may wonder whether the gift of speech is such a blessing after all! There is evidence of a close relationship between language and intelligence. Studies show that bright children generally talk earlier and develop more mature vocabularies than children of lesser intelligence. However, environment has a role to play in this development.

*"Hello! I'm the doctor. Let me look at your throat"*

Bill Anderson

381

*Popular leaders can be distinguished on the playground.*

And girls, generally, are ahead of boys in language development, up to maturity.

Friendly contacts between children become more pronounced between the ages of three and five. During these years, children form their first friendships, generally, but not exclusively, with others of their own sex. Friendship patterns change markedly with age. Between the ages of three and four, the number of friends increases; after this age, the primary change is in the closeness of attachment to a few particular children.

A socially-oriented and responsive preschool child seeks out companions and has a variety of contacts with them. In the course of learning the modes of social interaction, such a child has both satisfying and frustrating experiences, and, consequently, exhibits social responses that seem to be contradictory. For example, preschool friends who have played together in their own neighborhood are more likely to argue with each

382

other in school than with children who are new acquaintances. Highly aggressive nursery school children are also most sympathetic with their classmates, responding most readily to their distresses. The child who grabs a toy from a playmate at one moment may rush to comfort a crying, unhappy child the next.

Popular children and leaders can be distinguished during early childhood. Some children are continually being sought out as playmates; others are consistently shunned and avoided by their peers. Some youngsters ordinarily assume a dominant role, while others are usually passive followers.

The average child in this age span, in a social situation, is involved in some sort of conflict every five minutes. Boys tend to participate in more conflicts and make more attacks, whereas girls tend to argue more. These sex differences are more pronounced among the older children in this age group. Perhaps this reflects their more firmly established sex-typing of behavior.

In general, the interactions of these youngsters are more characteristically cooperative and friendly than unfriendly, hostile, or competitive.

*Nature pleases, attracts, delights particularly at five.*

William Ziegler

Even the most highly aggressive three- to five-year-old children actually make more friendly than aggressive responses. Aggressiveness, incidentally, tends to be a fairly stable characteristic. The frequency of a child's conflicts during this age is a reliable indicator of his proneness to conflict in school.

Competitiveness appears as early as the ages of three or four, according to the findings of one study in which pairs of children were given a pile of blocks and each one was instructed to compete to build something prettier or bigger than his companions. Those between the ages of four and six compete with considerable intensity, grabbing materials from each other, disregarding the other child's feelings and intentions, and refusing to give help or materials. By this age, competitive motives are strong enough to produce improvement in performance when a child is competing with someone else. As children advance in age, they become acutely aware of the culture's prevalent attitudes toward, and consistent rewards for, competition; hence, they adopt competitive values and motivations.

Boys seem to compete more than girls, and lower-middle-class children are more competitive than those from the upper-middle class. Highly competitive children often come from democratic, freedom-giving homes, but they are likely to have histories of conflicts with siblings. During this preschool period, competition and aggression appear to be relatively independent; that is, the most competitive children are not ordinarily the most aggressive. Among older children and adults, these motives are likely to be more closely associated.

## MIDDLE CHILDHOOD

The years from six to twelve compose the period of middle childhood. These are the years when it matters so much for youngsters to be good at something. Much of their real sense of know-how grows on the play fields. This is the age for collections, hobbies, and enthusiasms, gang loyalty, sloppiness, and noise. These young people are busy with secret clubs and social organizations.

In one sense, the peer-group affiliation of these middle years, the immersion in being a child, looks like a detour on the road to maturity. It however, is a necessary and valuable stage in the process of finding one's own identity. During the preschool years, the child has acquired a first identity from his parents—an identity that is in effect an identification. Now, with this much of a foundation, he is ready to begin the quest for an independent existence. As he has grown in stature, he has been able to see his parents more realistically; he knows their frailties and imperfections, and realizes—although still dimly—that he has to find stability in himself. This "detour," then, is an essential moving away from the parents in which a genuine and separate identity can be formed. But the new identity toward which the school child is moving differs from that of the preschool child in more than the matter of independence. Most significantly, he is becoming less egocentric and more detached from his own viewpoint. He is more aware of himself in objective terms, according to the labels that society attaches to him: male or female, age six to twelve, poor or rich, and so forth.

The gang, too, has its set of labels by which it knows the child and he knows himself. The gang is quick to seize on any idiosyncrasy of appearance, manner, skill, or whatever, and thereafter treat the child in terms of this trait. The stereotype by which the gang identifies the child is often expressed in his nickname: "Skinny," "Fatso," "Four-eyes," "Mouse," "Dopey," "Limpy,"—the total frankness, especially of boys, often startles adults. Most children wear their nicknames, even opprobrious ones, proudly, as a badge of their belonging. Any recognition, even if only contempt, is better than being ignored. Even the outcast or scapegoat would rather have the gang persecute him than ignore him, and even the label "Stinky" means that he has an identity in the eyes of others. Now, the child's view of himself comes not only out of a feeling that he is loved and accepted by his family, but also from a sense of adequacy and com-

*To be amiable is to be satisfied with oneself and others.*

Major Morris

petence that he can do the things that are demanded of him. He knows that he has a role to play. All this further implies that he is becoming capable of criticizing and viewing himself and his achievements through the eyes and according to the standards of others.

The developmental danger of the gang age lies in the failure of the child to go on to relative independence of the group and group standards. Some children who meet persistent rejection by the group may feel isolated and unworthy, and, failing to find group acceptance and group support, return to an identification with adults. It is worth noting that the "good boy" or the "good girl," who may appear to adults as a model for childhood, may be missing out on an important part of experience and heading for trouble. Such a child's estrangement from his peer group may be made worse by adult acceptance, as he gets to be known as a "goody-goody," "Mama's boy," or "teacher's pet."

Other children, still less visibly to the casual eye, run the risk of so complete an identification with or absorption in the group that they acquire little ability to think for themselves without recourse to group opinion. They feel threatened and disoriented if obliged to take a stand without knowing the "right" way of thinking. It is, of course, perfectly normal to experience some discomfort and anxiety when one is ignorant of or in conflict with the standards of the group, but a mature identity permits us to know what our own opinions are and to stand by them confidently, even in opposition of the group.

At this age, a child must make an idea his own before he accepts it. He will not take it merely on adult say so. Most adults sound fatuous to the school-age children they try to influence. They should, however, continue to discuss their notions of conduct and morals, for the child continues to identify with the important adults in his life even as he resists them. The child may seem deliberately deaf to parental lectures. He may, also, seem casually deaf to conversations directed over his head. However, even when he apparently is not attentive, he is hearing and learning a variety of facts, opinions, and attitudes.

## EARLY ADOLESCENCE

The next stages are early adolescence, later adolescence, and young adulthood. Since these were discussed in the first three units, we shall omit them here. However, we shall describe early adolescence as a time when the sense of identity is beginning. Young people are wondering "Who am I really?" This age goes to extremes at times, particularly in words. The early adolescent has big ideas and very sensitive feelings. They are saying: "I want to like myself." "I want others to like me." "I want to be like others." "I want to like others." The early adolescent needs patience and a sense of confidence from others. The adults in the lives of adolescents should keep all of their requests, demands, and reminders to a minimum but when discipline is necessary they should stand by their decisions and hold firm.

## CHANGING NEEDS

Since part of the ages and stages are in Unit One, we shall briefly sketch how needs change with growth. The significant people in the infant's life are the members of his immediate family, especially his mother. In his social contacts, he prefers either solitude or one or two people at a time. He requires nurturing care and the response to this care is as a receiving, amoral person.

Significant people for the preschool child are two or three playmates and family. He will play beside a friend, but not with him. This is called parallel play. He requires constant supervision. His response to others is one of exchanging. "I'll let you use my airplane if I can play with your car." His character type is expedient.

The school child needs his family and many companions. He enjoys group games and active play. He requires guidance and if the guidance is properly given he is a very sharing and conforming individual.

*A companion not a playmate nor an adversary.*

Courtesy Gerber Products Company

387

The adolescent needs many friends of his own age. It is important for him to have contact with boy-girl activities. He needs encouragement in independence. When he receives this, he is a very accommodating individual.

A wide variety of significant people is required by the adult. He needs affirmation through interdependence and many forms of contacts. When these needs are satisfied, he is a very cooperative individual.

## TO PROMOTE UNDERSTANDING OF THIS CHAPTER

1. What is the central theme of development during toddlerhood?
2. What are the characteristics of a toddler?
3. What is autonomy?
4. How does a child develop a conscience?
5. How does a child relieve his guilt feelings?
6. What is the function of fantasy in the development of a child?
7. Impulses are stronger in some children than in others. How should one handle a child with strong impulses?
8. How can one help the child solve the conflict between love and aggression?
9. How do the instinctual drives of love and aggression function during toilet training?
10. What are the characteristics of early childhood?
11. What effect does competitiveness have on early childhood?
12. In middle childhood, the developmental emphasis is on achievement. How is it accomplished? What kinds of achievements are important?
13. How does the child in the 6–12 age span view his parents?
14. What are the developmental dangers of the gang age?
15. What are the characteristics of early adolescents?

## SUPPLEMENTARY READING

BERNSTEIN, B., "Language and Social Class." *British Journal of Sociology*, Vol. 2, 1960, pp. 271–276.

DINKMEYER, DON, *Child Development: The Emerging Self*. Prentice-Hall, Inc., Englewood Cliffs, N.J., 1965.

JERSILD, ARTHUR T., *Child Psychology,* 5th ed. Prentice-Hall, Inc., Englewood Cliffs, N.J., 1960.

MCCANDLESS, B. R., *Children and Adolescents: Behavior and Development.* Holt, Rinehart and Winston, New York, 1961.

MILLER, D. R., and SWANSON, GUY E., *Inner-Conflict and Defense.* Holt, Rinehart and Winston, New York, 1960.

—————— *The Changing American Parent.* John Wiley & Sons, New York, 1958.

SCHUEY, REBEKAH, WOODS, ELIZABETH, and YOUNG, ESTHER, *Learning About Children.* J. B. Lippincott Co., Philadelphia, 1964.

SEARS, R. R., MACCOBY, ELEANOR E., and LEVIN, H., *Patterns of Child Rearing.* Row, Peterson, Evanston, Ill., 1957.

SMART, MOLLIE S., and SMART, RUSSELL C., *Children Development and Relationships.* The Macmillan Co., New York, 1967.

SPOCK, BENJAMIN, *Baby and Child Care.* Pocket Books, Inc., New York, 1959.

TEMPLIN, MILDRED C., *Certain Language Skills in Children.* University of Minnesota Press, Minneapolis, 1957.

© 1963 The Curtis Publishing Company

*"Is it a girl or bunk beds?"*

## 34
# Fears of Children

A new baby can cause a child to feel that he has lost his place in his parents' hearts and home. The question, "Is it a girl or bunk beds?" indicates that little sister's arrival was discussed and that some planning for the baby was made by big brother. A new baby or a new experience, whether it be school or swallowing gargle, can contribute to the fears and anxieties of childhood. The task of coping with anxieties and fears is a part of the daily job of all children. This task continues into adulthood.

390

*"Hi ho, hi ho, it's off to school we go!"*

## DEFINITIONS OF FEAR AND ANXIETY

Fear is an emotional reaction to an external danger, real or imagined, before which we feel helpless or inadequate. It is a painful feeling consisting of certain physiological changes, the awareness of these changes, and the particular mental sensations that give to fear its special quality.

Anxiety, like fear, is an emotional reaction to danger. The emotional reaction, the painful feeling, is the same as in fear. The difference is in the nature of the danger. In fear, the danger is external and known; in anxiety, the danger is internal and usually unknown or unconscious.

The amount of fear we experience at any given time depends on the nature of the danger and our ability to meet it. The fear may be mild, met with alertness, heightened awareness, and sharpened perception; moderate, met with rapid heartbeat, perspiring and weakness; or severe, met with

1
"Help! Swallowed
the gargle!"

2
"Mom, help!"

3
"I swallowed the
gargle, help!"

4
"Glug! Swallowed
the gargle, Mom!"

5
"Help! I ..."

6

panic and disorganization of thought and behavior. Unless the fear para-
lyzes us, we try to act to diminish it. This may range from the primitive
instinctive fight or flight action to more complex planned attempts to avoid,
control, master, modify, or otherwise cope with the danger.

Anxiety, the internal danger, is thought to develop from fears that as
children we could not express. As children, we may have had certain sexual and aggressive impulses, wishes, thoughts or feelings that we were
afraid to express. Correctly or not we may have had the impression that
their expression would result in our being deserted, unloved, or punished.
In order to diminish our fear, we automatically used an internal action similar to fleeing an external danger. Both the dangerous impulse and the
assumed threat became unconscious and the fear disappeared.

Subsequently, however, if either the unconscious impulse or the unconscious threat is reactivated with sufficient intensity, the old danger returns
and we experience anxiety as a response to it. Although it is clear what is
causing fear, anxiety has a quality of indefiniteness and a lack of object
inasmuch as its cause is internal and unconscious. Fear signals a danger in
the external world while anxiety signals a danger in the inner world of the
person, a danger of which he is unaware.

*"I've been thinking things over.*
*I'm afraid we're people."*

## CAUSES OF FEAR

In the first months of life, the infant reacts to outer stimuli, such as loud noises, or inner stimuli, such as hunger, with diffuse emotional spells that are assumed to be painful. As time passes, he learns that certain stimuli or situations will bring on such a painful state of physiological tension. He learns to fear and avoid such stimuli. Hunger is difficult to avoid. However, the child learns that he suffers more often from hunger pangs in the absence of his mother than in her presence. Thus, this physiological tension is translated into a fear of his mother's absence. The child fears that if his mother is not present, hunger will become intolerable.

These are the beginnings of what we fear in adulthood. From being oblivious, as in infancy, to most external dangers, we come to know what is dangerous in the physical world. In the psychological realm, matters are more complicated. Each development stage has its own major fear. We proceed from the fear of mother's absence, to the fear of the withdrawal of mother's loving care, to the fear of the withdrawal of love, to the fear of physical injury, to the fear of punishment, and finally to the fear of our own conscience.

393

# DEVELOPMENT OF FEAR

| Age in Years | Fear | Possible Aids |
|---|---|---|
| 1–2½ | separation from mother | 1. Children from infancy who have been around different people and who have been allowed to develop independence and outgoingness are less apt to develop such fears. |
| | | 2. Let the child gradually get thoroughly used to the person who is going to take care of him. If his mother reappears after a short period, he is reassured that she will always come back. |
| | | 3. If the mother acts hesitant or guilty every time she leaves his side or if she hurries into his room at night, her anxiety reinforces his fear that there is great danger in being apart from her. |
| | | 4. To avoid a two-year-old child's fears, be careful about drastic changes. |
| 2 | terrified of going to bed | 1. The child may be afraid of his mother's disapproval if he wets or soils the bed. He may feel that if he wets, his mother won't love him so much and will therefore be more likely to go away. |
| | | 2. Reassure the frightened 2-year-old by sitting by his bed as he goes to sleep. |
| | | 3. Do not be overprotective. |
| 3–4 | the dark | 1. Try to reassure him by words and by your manner. |
| | | 2. Don't make fun of him or try to argue him out of his fear. |
| | | 3. Avoid scary movies or TV programs and cruel fairy tales. |
| | | 4. Never threaten a child with bogeymen or policemen or the devil. |
| | | 5. Arrange a full outgoing life with other children every day. The more he is absorbed in games and plans, the less he will worry about his inner fears. |
| | death | 1. Realize that questions about death are apt to come up at this age. Make the explanation casual and suggest that death is a natural part of life. |
| | | 2. Remember to hug him, smile at him, and reassure him that you are going to be together for years and years yet. |

| Age in Years | Fear | Possible Aids |
|---|---|---|
| | dogs | 1. Don't drag him to a dog to reassure him. The more he is pulled, the more he is made to feel that he must pull in an opposite direction. |
| | becoming a cripple or being physically different | 1. A child at this age wants to know the reason for everything, worries easily, and applies dangers to himself. Give him opportunities to see that his body is similar to the bodies of children who are the same sex and age.<br>2. Give him reasons for the crippled people he may encounter. |
| 3–4–5 | of sex differences | 1. A normal child between 2½ and 3½ years of age is likely to wonder about things like bodily differences. If he isn't given a comforting explanation when he first gets curious, he's apt to come to worrisome conclusions.<br>2. Children should be made to feel comfortable about their sex differences, about their questions, and interest in handling the genitals.<br>3. Explain in a matter-of-fact manner that boys differ from girls, men differ from women, girls differ from women, and boys differ from men. If he feels your acceptance of his questions, he will ask many and thus dispel his worry. |
| 6–11 | loss of status in peer group | 1. Adults should not kiss a child of this age in public or treat him in an infantile way around his peers.<br>2. It is important for such a child to dress like, talk like, play like, and have the same allowance and privileges as the other average kids in the neighborhood. |
| 6–11 | going to school | 1. This often happens after a child has been absent for a few days because of an illness or accident, especially if the illness or the accident happened at school. If the child is freely allowed to stay home, his dread of returning to school usually gets stronger. It is increased by the fear that he is behind in his work. It usually works best for the parents to be very firm about getting him back to school promptly. They should not be dissuaded by his physical complaints or try to get the doctor to excuse him. |

Parents often develop unnecessary fears in their children by behaving in a frightening manner with use of threats that reinforce the child's ordinary fears, by being unduly punitive, and by reacting to danger with panic or denial. The future mental health of a child depends not only on the presence and severity of early fears but also on the child's solution of these fears. If the solution is a poor one, he may become anxious; if it is successful, he will become courageous, not timid.

Some fears are necessary for normal development for a child must learn what is dangerous. He must also develop a conscience. Nor can unnecessary fears be completely avoided even in the best parent-child relationship. They seem to be an invariable accompaniment of becoming civilized, resulting from the conflict between the child's impulses (love and hate), between the child's impulses and external controls and forces (parents and reality), and between the child's impulses and his internal controls (conscience) once these internal controls are established.

It is impossible to know everything about how children should be reared in order to avoid unnecessary fears. However, many simple fears can be subdued with reassurance and explanation. Sometimes fear expresses itself as something else, such as apathy, avoidance, or stubbornness. It is important to recognize and understand the underlying fear in order to help the child with it. If discipline is too lax, it will not help a child learn to tolerate small but increasing amounts of frustration and fear. If the discipline is too strict, it may lead to excessive fear in connection with learning controls.

It is important here to distinguish between what may be termed "healthy" fears and "morbid" fears. A child needs to learn early that some situations are dangerous and should be avoided. He must be aware of the fact that he may be harmed if he touches a hot stove, steps out into the middle of traffic, or puts himself into any other danger-producing situation. This is the development of reasonable caution and is not accompanied by inner or overt symptoms of the fear emotion. He also needs to learn to behave so that he does not harm someone else. Emotionalized fear results when or if the child finds himself in a dangerous situation that exists or is imagined to be productive of hurt but is not able to do anything about it. Morbid fears are irrational fears. They usually have little or no basis in fact but can cause considerable suffering on the part of the child. Because of the irrational nature of the fears, it is difficult for the child to express what he fears and to enlist aid from concerned adults. Adults are likely to negate his statement of fears by making light of them because of their irrational nature. Shadows, dragons, monsters or "boogie men" are seen as objects of laughter rather than concern.

# INFLUENCES OF FEAR UPON A CHILD

Responses to irrational fears

or

Responses to healthy fears

The following list explains the way that children react to healthy fears and morbid fears:

*INFLUENCES OF FEAR UPON A CHILD*

| RESPONSES TO HEALTHY FEARS | RESPONSES TO IRRATIONAL MORBID FEARS |
|---|---|
| Flight | Contrariness |
| Illness | Nightmares |
| Caution | Daydreams |
| Reduced Activity | Overaggressive Behavior |
| Stepped-up Activity | Psychosomatic Illness |
| Bragging | Withdrawal |
| Lying | |

Most children have a wide variety of ways to cope with both rational and irrational fears. Some children who experience rational fears during an activity that could be harmful, will simply put much effort into learning to avoid the danger, without having to leave the danger-involving activity itself. For example, the child learns to master ocean waves or a treacherous pony instead of having to develop anxious avoidances of such preoccupations altogether. For others, the most reasonable way out is simply a readiness to ask for help around the danger area. For other children, the emotional tie to a beloved person present at the time of danger or the exposure to a "secure" and acceptant group atmosphere may be all that is needed to allow them to cope with fears which might have kept them from entering the activity.

For fear with real danger elements and for irrational fears or anxieties from within, most children manage to use the defense mechanism of displacement and dramatic play, talking, or daydreams as a way to minimize their fear. Clinging to fantasies of power, force, indestructibility or omniscience, or acting out terrifying play behavior or bravado, they cope happily with what otherwise might become a state of panic or an anxiety attack.

## DEVELOPMENT REVISITED

In order to understand anxiety, guilt feelings, and fears both rational and irrational, we must keep in mind the developmental phases. When the development of the child is hindered or threatened, fears, guilt feelings, and anxieties can be the result.

Early psychoanalytic theory of the development of personality was derived through the study of adult's recall of their childhood years, but it led

398

to many investigations with infants and children as subjects in the areas of feeding, toilet training, identification, dependency, and the growth of conscience and guilt feelings.

After much research, Erikson suggested eight successive periods of development, each with its "psychosocial crises" to be resolved by the child before he can move to the next level.

1. Learning trust versus mistrust. During infancy, the child who is loved and nurtured becomes basically secure and optimistic. The child who is unloved becomes insecure and mistrustful.

2. Learning autonomy versus shame. The learning of bowel control is the prototype of many social lessons during the ages one to four, during which the child may develop either feelings of pride in accomplishment and self-control, or feelings of shame.

3. Learning initiative versus guilt. During the preschool years, the child learns to develop his social skills with other children, to cooperate, and to be able to lead as well as to follow. The child not able to do this feels guilty, clings to adults, and does not develop play skills and imagination.

4. Learning industry versus inferiority. The school child learns the techniques of self-discipline, more formal rules of living in his peer group, and the satisfaction of accomplishment. Failing to do this, he feels inadequate and inferior.

5. Learning identity versus identity confusion. During adolescence, a mature perspective of time and a sense of achievement develop in the successful person. Although most adolescents probably experiment with minor delinquency, are rebellious, and have feelings of self-doubt, the maturing young adult gradually learns, by trial and error, his stable social role. At this stage, the growing and developing youth looks for models to inspire him and for ideals to guide him.

6. Learning intimacy versus isolation. A successful basis for marriage and lasting friendships depends upon the development of the ability to experience real intimacy. The avoidance of such experiences may lead to isolation.

7. Learning generativity versus self-absorption. The successful adult lives productively, in his family as well as in his lifework. If the individual is unable to do this, he may become overly self-absorbed.

8. Learning personality integration versus despair. The mature adult, having successfully passed the earlier stages, develops independence and

399

security. The adult who remains at conflict on one or more of the lower levels is chronically dissatisfied and never at peace with himself.[1]

The successful growth of an individual through each of the above periods of development would eliminate many anxieties and fears. This is placed here for consideration and for comparison. It is important to remember two generalizations. They are (1) when an individual experiences satisfaction from the results of a particular pattern of behavior, he is likely to incorporate that pattern into his behavior, and (2) to the extent that an individual's developmental needs are met as they occur, he is free to move toward his full potential. If the basic needs of children are met, one can be unafraid in the handling of their fears.

## TO PROMOTE UNDERSTANDING OF THIS CHAPTER

1. Define fear and anxiety. Give an example of each.

2. The statements below depict either healthy or morbid fears. Indicate which is described.
   a. "I am afraid of snakes because their appearance surprises me."
   b. "I wish my brother were dead."
   c. "When there is thunder and lightning outside, my heart beats rapidly and the palms of my hands sweat."
   d. "When mother sits and reads, she is really wishing I'd go away."
   e. "If I don't say anything, my father won't spank me."

3. What are the causes of fear in infants?

4. If you were a nursery school teacher, how would you help a two-year-old child overcome his fear of separation?

5. Why is a two-year-old child often terrified of going to bed?

6. Johnny is three years old. He wants a light on in his room while he goes to sleep. If you were his parent, what would you do about this request?

7. Mary Jane's grandfather died. Mary Jane is four years old. Her grandfather was someone very special to her. For the last two weeks since his death, she has been playing funeral with her dolls and teddy bears. If you were her parent, how would you handle this? Is this a healthy activity for Mary Jane?

[1] George Simpson, *People in Families* (The World Publishing Company, Cleveland, Ohio, 1966), p. 121.

8. Children worry about the natural differences between boys and girls. When a child asks a question about physical differences he is asking it as he would any question. Thus he needs an honest, direct, reassuring answer. How would you answer little Johnny who while watching his baby sister being diapered asks why she has no penis?

9. How would you deal with a four-year-old girl who became worried when she found out that the genitals of boys were different from her own genitals?

10. How do parents develop unnecessary fears in their children?

11. Why are some fears necessary?

12. Why is it important to recognize the way that a child is coping with a specific fear?

13. What kind of fears might develop if the first three developmental stages designated by Erikson are not successfully mastered?


## SUPPLEMENTARY READING

BALDWIN, ALFRED L., *Behavior and Development in Childhood*. Holt, Rinehart and Winston, New York, 1955.

CROW, LESTER D., and ALICE, *Child Development and Adjustment*. The Macmillan Company, New York, 1962.

ERIKSON, ERIK H., *Childhood and Society*. Holt, Rinehart and Winston, New York, 1955.

———— *Identity and the Life Cycle*. International Universities Press, New York, 1959.

ILG, F. L., and AMES, L. B., *Child Behavior*. Harper and Row, New York, 1955.

McCANDLESS, BOYD R., *Children and Adolescents*. Holt, Rinehart and Winston, New York, 1961.

SEARS, R. R., MACCOBY, ELEANOR E., and LEVIN H., *Patterns of Child-Rearing*. Harper and Row, New York, 1957.

SIMPSON, GEORGE, *People in Families*. The World Publishing Company, Cleveland, Ohio, 1966.

SMART, MOLLIE S. and SMART, RUSSELL C., *Child Development and Relationships*. The Macmillan Co., New York, 1967.

*What To Tell Your Children About Sex*. Child Study Association of America, Affiliated Publishers, New York, 1959.

*"Gosh, you're beautiful when you're angry."*

# 35
# Discipline

The disciplinarian is often rebuffed by the disciplinant with a question or a quip, as in the adjoining cartoons. In fact, some children learn very early how to break a disciplinary mood or how to skirt the real nucleus of the subject under discussion. To discipline is to train, to educate, or to bring under control. Educationally and psychologically, discipline is social control within a group; it includes all the forces that mold attitudes and inspire conduct.

*"Why do I drive you to distraction, mommy?"*

Children of all ages need to know the limits of their behavior. A child needs to feel that his parents will help him control himself. Children want parents to be firm and to help them become reasonable and thoughtful people. However, parents must be consistent and fair in their discipline. The parental mood should not influence the rules of discipline for a particular child. Parents should feel free to discipline their children while they are still feeling friendly toward them. For example, if a child wants to continue playing ball after his parents are exhausted, they should not hesitate to say pleasantly but precisely, "We're tired of playing ball. We're going to read the newspaper now, and you can read one of your books."

When a child is being rude, perhaps because he is jealous or frustrated, one should promptly stop him and insist upon politeness. A child knows when he has displeased or broken a rule, and he expects to be corrected. He

403

*"... and the flashlight!"*

© *Better Homes and Gardens*
Magazine

is more secure if he is disciplined and his conscience is cleared. But at the same time, the child should be helped to understand that we all get cross sometimes; all people sometimes become angry at those that they love best. The child should know that in spite of his angry feelings or his hostile actions he is still loved. It is only his behavior that is unacceptable. This realization helps him get over his anger and keeps him from feeling too guilty or frightened because of it. It is helpful to make a distinction between hostile feelings and hostile actions.

## EFFECTS OF TYPES OF DISCIPLINE

*The behavior of the child is a function of the balance between parental support and parental discipline.* This general principle is further complicated by the different effects of various types of discipline. In recent years, for example, several investigators working independently have shown that so-called "psychological" techniques of discipline (such as reasoning, appeals to guilt, showing disappointment) are more effective in bringing about desired social behavior in the child than more direct methods (such as physical punishment, scolding, or threats). In fact, a number of studies indicate that the more a child is spanked for being aggressive, the more aggressive he will be. However, one must be careful about jumping to conclusions from such findings, for researchers have not pinned down the direc-

404

tion of the relationship. Is it spanking that causes the aggressiveness, or the aggressiveness that brings on the spanking? Moreover, there are indications that a reliance on psychological techniques of discipline to the exclusion of more direct methods, such as spanking, may result in an "over-socialized" child lacking in spontaneity and initiative.

Such considerations may help to explain the differences in behavior observed in children of different sexes and from different social class levels. Psychological techniques of discipline, for instance, are more likely to be used with girls than with boys, and are more frequently employed in middle-class families than in working-class families. It is also a well-established fact that girls are generally more obedient, cooperative, and better socialized than boys at comparable age levels.

Systematic differences are observed not only in the techniques used, but in the occasions on which they are applied. For example, working-class parents tend to punish children more for the consequence of their action than for the underlying motive, whereas the reverse holds true for middle-class parents. Much work remains to be done, however, in exploring the relations between parental techniques of discipline, the occasions on which they are employed, the values in the name of which they are administered and the effect of all these factors on the behavior of the child. In the meantime, the clearest lesson one can draw from available research is that extreme reliance on any one type of discipline—be it physical punishment, reasoning, or withdrawal of parental companionship—is likely to have undesirable effects.

## DISCIPLINE AND DEPENDENCE

Biological as well as cultural and direct experimental factors cause dependence. A baby comes into the world in a condition of biological helplessness and would soon perish if his parents, especially his mother, did not care for him. He performs, at first, few purposeful skeletal body movements except sucking and those associated with excretion, and even these seem relatively unconditioned. His physical dependence upon his parents for food and care generates a related emotional dependence which at first is focused on the mother. This is especially true in American culture based upon a small family unit and may be contrasted with the more diffusely directed dependence in some so-called primitive cultures.

In our culture, the mother is the one most concerned in the development of the basic socialization of the child. As the baby grows through infancy, he gradually begins to recognize his mother as a separate person, realizes his dependence upon her, and comes to take refuge in her in time of trouble. She gives him solace and a sense of security. The father, too, serves to protect the child from the hazards and insecurities of a large and unknown world. If the young child's security is threatened, as by separation from his parents or their failure to respond to his needs, the child may become disturbed in a variety of ways. It is primarily through dependence upon and trust in the parents that it is possible for a child to grow and to adapt himself to the requirements of the world. Some degree of dependence is, therefore, essential in normal development.

Overdependency may result from the failure, unwillingness, or inability of the parents to promote the child's growth. The degree of dependence is conditioned by early affectionate relations with the parents, early training and discipline, and the parents' wisdom in permitting the child to exercise initiative, creativeness, and imagination consistent with his abilities. Parents with a need to dominate may use their children as objects for the expression of their need for superiority by controlling their children excessively. On the other hand, a failure to provide *loving discipline* may leave a child insecure and anxious. Children growing up in a healthy family environment make the transition from dependence to independence gradually.

Probably the best philosophy is one which recognizes that childhood with its varying degrees of dependence and independence is a significant and important time of life and that the child's expression of growing independence need not be accepted as final. It is important that a child be given the opportunity to grow, but at the same time, the child should recognize that the insights he reaches as a child will be amplified and enlarged as he grows up and this process of widening horizons need never cease in his life.

Dependence can be normal or abnormal. The kind of dependence is determined by biological factors such as sex and physical patterns, customs of child rearing, and attitudes and practices of education and training. The child's dependence upon a parent is conditioned by the parents' capacity for fostering growth, recognizing normal fluctuation in dependence needs, and giving *loving support and discipline*. When a child is deeply dependent upon the parent in an emotional relationship and yet feels unwanted, unloved, and rejected, he will suffer anxiety and may react to this in many ways. He may become permanently embittered, hostile, or fearful, may never be able to achieve independent status, and may cling to a parent or parent substitute even as an adult.

Abnormal dependency in adult life may be prevented by helping a child to learn gradually to assume responsibility and an independent way of life. These measures should be taken from birth. In the early years, the child depends upon his parents and should be allowed fully to satisfy his need to be secure. Some anxiety is inevitable for biological and for sociological reasons. However, in a loving, disciplined family, the child is usually able to

406

build adequate defenses. The child needs growing space so that he can become a person uniquely aware of his capacity for self-determination. He will show spontaneously his desires toward independence, and if given the opportunity, will take responsibility and be creative in terms of his ability at each stage in his growth. If parents are able and willing gradually to give up their control of the child, he will develop into a normal adult. Unfortunately, some parents are not sufficiently secure. They impose their own will upon the child by denying him room to grow. They become frightened if the child's behavior threatens them, and they blame the child rather than support him in his problems.

The process of becoming a more and more independent person is slow and gradual. The child needs discipline and then the gradual release from discipline as well as the parents' help and encouragement in this process. Gradual growth in independence is a continuing process from birth through adulthood. A person who has grown up in this way is better prepared to face the inevitable changes from early adulthood to old age.

## DISCIPLINE AND AGGRESSION

Aggression refers to the total amount of energy expended in activity striving to satisfy instinctual, or inborn, drives. In human beings, we prefer to speak of drives; in lower animals, aggression is seen as a way of dealing with instincts. The psychiatric meaning of aggression refers to forceful attacking action that can be either physical, verbal, symbolic, or all three.

There are aggressions that develop slowly and are in keeping with day-to-day problems and frustrations. This happens particularly during the growing phases of human development. These aggressions may be a reaction to too much discipline—or to too little. When there are excessive prohibitions, the young child may feel a need to mobilize constantly increasing amounts of aggressive energy to cope with his frustrations. Where there is a lack of organized discipline, the child may feel that he is being left on his own too much; he then becomes anxious. This anxiety can stimulate aggressions in order to provoke his elders into giving him more protection and guidance. Such aggressions are an expression of the child's sense of insecurity.

Aggressions may be rational or irrational. Rational aggressions are most often a response to actual situations in the life of a person and most often they are justifiable. The irrational aggressions usually result from some inner mental attitude that compels the individual to act aggressively.

Essentially, aggressions are caused by frustration or interference with a natural development of the instinctual drives. Since the life of a human, even in its earliest phases, encounters checks on its instinctual drives, frus-

407

tration is ever present. The quantity of frustration, the capacity for its tolerance, the amount of support given the child by his parents (or lack of it), and later on, the support given by others, contribute to the ultimate degree of aggressive feelings.

## DISCIPLINE AND PUNISHMENT

Unfortunately, many people equate discipline with punishment. Discipline, however, should be a scheme for regulating childrens' behavior, teaching them self-control through reward and punishment, and helping them to internalize moral standards.

From several studies about punishment as experienced by children, it was found that there are important sex differences as to who gives and who receives punishment. Fathers punish more than mothers, especially where boys are concerned. Fathers use physical punishment more than mothers, especially with boys. Boys receive more physical punishment, girls more verbal punishment.

When children distinguish between the power of their parents, they tend to see the father as more powerful. They report that punishment, particularly physical punishment, is more often given by the father. They see their mothers as nurturant, helpful, and lenient. It is not surprising, therefore, that children more often like their mothers better than their fathers.

An important element in the punishment used is the way in which it is given and the way in which it is received. Most parents agree that they have to impose punishment on their children, but they also agree that one has to give thought to what punishment is best. Many agree that there is a time for physical punishment, but that deprivation of privileges or curtailment of freedom are often more effective.

The type of discipline which tries to use the child's internal forces to induce his compliance seems to foster understanding and adoption of appropriate behavior. Using the child's internal forces means appealing to his need for affection, his self-esteem, and his concern for others. Psychological or love-oriented discipline uses the child's affectionate relationship with his parents. The importance of loving children and letting them know it cannot be stressed too strongly. Physical coercion and other forms of direct power assertion of parent over child promotes a moral orientation based on fear of external detection and punishment.

## DISCIPLINE AND LIFE

One of the most needed lessons for adulthood, for achievement, for happiness, and for growth toward maturity is the lesson of discipline. Man must discipline his behavior in terms of his own conduct and in terms of his actions toward other men.

Discipline is important in all facets of life. For example, one must use self-discipline in eating to avoid overweight. To practice a vocation successfully demands the strictest kind of discipline from the individual. For the artist, life is always a discipline, and no discipline is without pain. This is true even of dancing, which, of all the arts, is the most associated in people's minds with pleasure.

Self-discipline does not, in actuality, end with the self. History is replete with men and nations who thought they were self-disciplined but could not control themselves in their actions toward other men and other nations. Man's struggle for power over other men which leads to inhumanity and war is evident in every day's newspapers, whether the articles focus on crimes in the streets or crimes in war.

Discipline should be guidance in personal, national, and international growth. A young person should try to discipline himself in areas such as school work, responsibilities at home, and relationships with his peers. A person in a vocation should try to discipline himself with regard to doing the best and most creative work of which he is capable. The statesman in government should discipline himself in terms of dealing intelligently with world crises and enlisting the aid of intelligence, sensitivity, and peaceful alternatives rather than weapons and armed might in times of stress. In all of these cases, there should be a consistency between words and actions; individuals and nations should mean what they say. If these types of discipline could be inherent in personal and national transactions, many acts of aggression would not be committed.


## TO PROMOTE UNDERSTANDING OF THIS CHAPTER

1. What is discipline?

2. What is the value of discipline to children?

3. What are the psychological techniques of discipline? What are the physical techniques of discipline? What are the advantages and disadvantages of each type?

4. How does discipline differ among the social classes?

5. Should one rely on any one type of discipline? If so, why? If not why not?

6. What causes overdependency?

7. How is dependence related to the type of discipline?

8. What is aggression?

9. What is the relationship between aggression and discipline?

10. Should discipline be equated to punishment? How are they alike? How are they different?

11. What type of discipline seems to foster the greatest degree of understanding in the child?

12. What are some of the individual and social advantages of self-discipline? What might be some of the disadvantages?

## SUPPLEMENTARY READING

BARUCH, DOROTHY WALTER, *New Ways in Discipline.* McGraw-Hill Book Company, New York, 1949.

COMBS, ARTHUR W., *Perceiving, Behaving, Becoming.* National Education Association, Association for Supervision and Curriculum Development, Washington, D.C., 1962.

GARDNER, L. P., "An Analysis of Children's Attitudes Toward Fathers." *Journal of Genetic Psychology,* Vol. 70 (1947), pp. 3–28.

GINOTT, HAIM G., *Between Parent and Child.* The Macmillan Company, New York, 1968.

HYMES, JAMES L., JR., *Behavior and Misbehavior.* Prentice-Hall, Inc., Englewood Cliffs, N.J., 1955.

KAGAN, J., "The Child's Perception of the Parent." *Journal of Abnormal Social Psychology,* Vol. 53 (1956), pp. 257–258.

———— HOSKEN, B., and WATSON, S., "Child's Symbolic Conceptualization of Parents." *Child Development,* Vol. 32 (1961), pp. 625–636.

LANGDON, G., and STOUT, I. W., *The Discipline of Well-Adjusted Children.* John Day, New York, 1952.

RASMUSSEN, MARGARET, *Discipline.* Bulletin No. 99, Association for Childhood Education International, Washington, D.C., 1957.

ROSEN, B. C., "Social Class and the Child's Perception of the Parent." *Child Development,* Vol. 35 (1964), pp. 1147–1153.

Henry Martin, *The Saturday Review*

*"What do you think, Professor? Is it a laser, a maser, a quasar, or just a little ray of hope for all mankind?"*

# 36
# For All Mankind

The question asked in the cartoon is a reminder of the irony of the present stage of mankind. Man's ingenuity, effort, expertise, and resources are deployed in building an intercontinental missile system. Although man recognizes the problems of worldwide famine, disease, illiteracy, inequality, and poverty, he has thus far chosen to devote only a relatively small part of his ability, time, and resources to the task of alleviating them. If man's rather confused priorities were somehow shifted from learning how to destroy toward developing greater understanding and mutual respect, man's uncertainty regarding his life might be lessened. If much more of man's intelligence, devotion to research, and technological knowledge were applied to the problems of understanding man and his development, a series of breakthroughs which would illuminate and inspire man's whole concept of his own future might be produced.

All over the world, fewer and fewer people today seem to be quite sure about where they stand, what they expect, and above all, what they should believe. In some circles, this is called "Westernization," or modernization. This uncertainty is expressed psychologically by words such as alienation, anomie, and identity crisis. The jargon is limitless. This same uncertainty may be expressed socially in such phenomena as delinquency, rising rates of alcoholism, and drug addiction.

Yet, with all of his uncertainty as to his priorities, position, and meaning in life, man has been and continues to be somewhat reluctant to really work at a study of his own relationships. He has tended instead to chalk up his failures to "human nature." It seems that man has frequently found it easier to make the assumption that "human nature" is in some way a force which cannot possibly be controlled or improved. He has often found it easier to hide behind his "human nature" instead of trying to adapt himself to technological and social change.

Fear of change is, no doubt, in all of us, but it most afflicts the man who fears that any change must lead to loss of his wealth and status. When this fear becomes inordinate, he may, if he has political power, abrogate such things as civil rights and the rule of law, using the argument that he abrogates them only to preserve them. If such a man would say, "I do this because I am afraid," it would be bearable; when he says, "I do this because I am good and I know best," it becomes intolerable.

One of the prime reasons for rapid change is technological development. The main reason for the resultant personal and social distortion is man's inability to adjust to these technological advances with sufficient speed and success. Technological development is producing constant alterations in our physical environment and social relationships. These alterations, in turn, require individual reappraisals and reorientation to institutions and behaviors. Man has found it difficult to adjust and to continue adjusting to the changes technology has produced. Indeed, he has often found that just as he attempts change, technology advances further, making his new adjustment obsolete and meaningless. Technology has also brought mankind into more frequent and intimate contact with others whose discipline, values, and relationships differ widely. This has tended to rob us of a complacency in our rightness and in the universal applicability of our own way of life.

412

Medical technology, in particular, born of the most profoundly humane impulses, is possibly one of the causes of our difficulties. It not only preserves lives, but it lengthens them. Youth and age confront each other more numerously and dramatically than ever before. Extraordinary advances in heart and other organ transplants is requiring us to reassess our moral standards as well as the questions, "What is life? What is death?"

Does this suggest that we should try to restrain our technological development? Of course not. The weight of history is totally against such an action. Ever since man began using tools, there has been a steady accumulation of technical proficiency. Yet, what is lacking is the accompanying progress of intelligence and greater sensitivity in using this technological power.

We must, therefore, face accelerating technological growth as a basic fact in human societies. This is an age inappropriate to narrow views encompassing too simple ideologies and the espousal of unchangeable ways of life. Quantitative changes have produced qualitative changes. Whether one is optimistic or pessimistic, bold or cautious, a contemporary appraisal of our position suggests that this age requires, perhaps as never before, a realistic and actively creative imagination if we are not to let our technological advances outrun and destroy our sense of the worth of living. Man must keep his intelligence and sensitivity in front of technological developments, not miles behind them. Man is no longer victim of life; he is now master, and this may be the ultimate danger.

Man has a biological capacity to use his intelligence and sensitivity to adjust to and keep pace with the rapid advances of technology. Taking the long view, the human being has many very real assets for the task of flexible adaptation. First, man has relatively few behaviors that are genetically specific. As seen in Unit I, he is capable of changing himself if he seriously and conscientiously attempts change. Second, the human animal, as discussed in Unit 4, has a long infancy, during which he is capable of much learning. One does not have to look further than the exploratory behavior of young children to find that the urge to learn is inherent in the human organism. The eagerness young children exhibit in exploring new objects and in trying out new skills seems proof enough. Pre-adolescents, however, with their endless questions about how things work, and adolescents, with their discussions of sex and the meaning of life, provide even more evidence. At whatever level of development one considers, human beings manifest a burning curiosity, a tremendous urge to know. Third (and perhaps more magnificently), man has an incredible capacity for symbolizing. Man is still in the state of mind where the traditional attitudes born of his past wants and conflicts influence him more than the abundant, and so far largely unexploited, opportunities of the hopeful present. The note of hope and idealism in the world is tremendous, but it tends to be

413

drowned out by a jangle of qualification, compromise, and cynicism. Man must sustain the note of hope until it overpowers the voices of fear, cynicism, and reaction. He must gain enough confidence in himself and in others to turn his ideals and his potentiality into reality.

In the words of Carl Sandburg:

> One thing I know deep out of my time: youth when
> lighted and alive and given a sporting chance is
> strong for struggle and not afraid of any toils or
> punishments or dangers or deaths.
>
> What shall be the course of society and civiliza-
> tion across the next hundred years?
>
> For the answers read if you can the strange and
> baffling eyes of youth.
>
> Yes, for the answers, read if you can, the strange
> and baffling eyes of youth.[1]

Yet, consider also the following words of Mark Twain:

> Every man is in his own person the whole human race, with not a de-
> tail lacking. I am the whole human race without a detail lacking. I have
> studied the human race with diligence and strong interest all these years
> in my own person; in myself I find in big or little proportion every qual-
> ity and every defect that is findable in the mass of the race. I knew I
> should not find in any philosophy a single thought which had not passed
> through the heads of millions and millions of men before I was born; I
> knew I should not find a single original thought in any philosophy, and
> I knew I could not furnish one to the world myself, if I had five cen-
> turies to invent it in. Nietzsche published his book, and was at once pro-
> nounced crazy by the world—by a world which included tens of bright,
> sane men who believed exactly as Nietzsche believed but concealed the
> fact and scoffed at Nietzsche. What a coward every man is and how
> surely he will find it out if he will just let other people alone and sit
> down and examine himself. The human race is a race of cowards; and I
> am not only marching in that procession but carrying a banner.[2]

---

[1] Carl Sandburg, *Always the Young Strangers* (New York, Harcourt, Brace and World, 1953), p. 304.

[2] Prefatory note "September 4, 1907" by Mark Twain in *Mark Twain in Eruption,* edited by Bernard DeVoto. Copyright 1940 by the Mark Twain Company. Reprinted by permission of Harper & Row, Publishers.

414

In summary, we cannot avoid change or choices. We can only assume responsibility for our decisions and hope that they are made with intelligence and thoughtfulness. We must make every effort to see that we are educated in breadth and depth, both intelligently and socially. Social structures must exist; however, this does not mean that such structures are to be treated as immutable truths.

Finally, our metaphysical premises must be placed in the context of that worldwide universe of discourse into which our technology has led us. To face the fact that eternal truths may not exist, or at least that we do not yet know what they are, is perhaps man's greatest act of intellectual and moral courage.

## TO PROMOTE UNDERSTANDING OF THIS CHAPTER

1.  Why has man been reluctant to work at a study and investigation of his own relationships?

2.  What are some of the main reasons for rapid changes?

3.  How does man react to change?

4.  What are the assets that man has for the task of adopting to change?

5.  What are some examples of compromise and cynicism that you see in your personal world or the world at large today?

6.  Mark Twain said, "Every man is in his own person the whole human race, with not a detail lacking." What does this mean to you? Write an essay titled "I am the Whole Human Race" or "The Human Race: A Race of Cowards."

7.  How might we gain enough confidence in ourselves and in each other to turn our ideals and our potentiality into reality?

## SUPPLEMENTARY READING

ARDREY, ROBERT, *The Territorial Imperative*. Atheneum Publishers, New York, 1966.

KAGAN, J., and MOSS, H. A., *Birth to Maturity*. John Wiley and Sons, New York, 1963.

SANDBURG, CARL, *Always the Young Strangers*. Harcourt, Brace and World, New York, 1953.

THURBER, JAMES, *Thurber Country*. Simon and Schuster, Inc., New York, 1953.

*"A leaf has its own fascination moved by wind or colored by fall. But when it floats above your hands, slick in the water, a leaf has a special wonder."*

John Arms (photo). *The Christian Science Monitor* (legend)

# Index

Abortion, 331, 333, 356
  criminal, 356
  therapeutic, 356
*Absence of a Cello, The* (Wallach), 153
Accession as a family crisis, 294–298
Adjustability of maturity vs. that of youth, 222
Adjustment to frustration, 64–72
Adler, Alfred, 22, 143
Adolescence, 128–130
  definition of, 129–130
  a period of ambivalence, 128–129
  sexuality in, 134–137
  *See also* Adolescent, the
Adolescent, the
  goals of, 130–131
  relationship of, with parents, 131–134
  siblings and, 144
  value of his sharing in discussion of adult problems, 137
  *See also* Adolescence
Adoption, 313, 341–346
  announcement of, 346
  as a family crisis, 294, 298
  eligibility requirements for adoptive parents, 342–344
  of older children by older couples, 343–344
  period in infant's life to avoid in adopting, 361
  prerequisites for adoptive parents, 342
  society's attitude toward, 346
  statistics on, 341–342, 343
  *See also* Adoption agencies
Adoption agencies, 345–346
  importance of working through, 345
  practice of, re fees, 345–346
Adult models, effect of, on personality development, 22–23
Adultery, 196
Aged, the, *see* Old age

Aggression:
  causes of, 407–408
  definition of, 407
  rational vs. irrational, 407
  relationship of discipline to, 407
Aging:
  legal date for, 162
  a process, 161, 168
  *See also* Old age
Alcoholism, 60, 294, 298–300, 307
  attitudes which lead to lowest incidence of, 300
  the blackout, 299
  demoralizing effects of, 299
  marriage and, 310
  statistics on, 298–299
Alienation:
  avoidance of, 168
  fostered by planned communities, 168
  in our present-day society, 165–166
  vs. aloneness, 166
Alimony, 252
Allen, L., 365
Allport, Gordon, 13–14
Ambivalence, defined, 128
Ambivert, defined, 21
Amoral behavior:
  definition of, 30
  examples of, 32
  parents' responsibility for, 37
Anal stage of character development, 30, 38
Annulment, 294
Anspacher, Louis Kaufman, 228
Antibiotics, 351
Anxiety, 398
  as a warning signal, 54–55
  compared with fear, 391–392
Anxiety neurosis, 62
Apgar, (Dr.) Virginia, 350
Approach-approach conflict, 67
Approach-avoidance conflict, 67, 68–69
Aquinas, Thomas, 110
Aristotle, 109, 110
*Art and Skill of Getting Along with People, The* (Duvall), 155
*As You Like It,* 161

Attack approach to conflict, 74–75
Attention-getting behavior, 5
Attitudes, 87–94
  analysis of, 91–93
  definition of, 87
  development of, 91
  formation of, 88
  of youth vs. those of old age, 160–171
  principles of, 185–186
Augustine, 110
Autonomous nuclear family, 162
  characteristics of, 164
  reasons for dominance of, today, 165
  relations of aging parents and adult offspring in, 165
Autonomy, developing a sense of, 376–380, 399
Avoidance-avoidance conflict, 67, 68

Baby, the, 359–374
  anxieties of, 361
  basic needs of, 360, 361, 368
  communication of, with adults, 363–365
  dependency of, in relation to mother's behavior, 367
  development stages of, 368–373
  evaluating the development of, 362–363
  feeding practices in relation to child behavior, 365–366
  fondling of, 361
  immunization of, against disease, 363
  needs of, 359–374
  overweight, 362
  sense development of, 360–361
Balance (emotional), 54
  flexible, 54
  rigid, 54–55
Barnard College, 261
Basic needs, see Needs
Behavior, adjustive, 7
  basic principles of, 8–9
  definition of, 3
  determined by needs, 5–7

Freud's theory on, 17
  influence of physical characteristics on, 20–21
  maladjustive, 7–8
  relationship of, to group values, 118
  See also Behavior patterns; Moral behavior
Behavior patterns:
  determination of, 3
  direction of, 3
  relationship of, to basic needs, 3, 5
Bettelheim, Bruno, 248, 265, 267
Bible, the, 119
Biological needs, see Physiological needs
Birth:
  as a family crisis, 294, 298, 356
  effect of, on parents, 298
  importance of attitude toward, 356–357
  premature, 324–325, 350, 351, 352
  See also Reproduction
Birth control, 331–332, 334
  See also Family planning
Birth defects, causes of, 350–352
  See also Veneral diseases
Birthright, meaning of, 348–349, 356
Blackout (alcoholic), 299
Blood poisoning, see Toxemia
Blood tests:
  premarital, 234–235
  state requirements for (table), 223, 235
Body build, influence of, on behavior and personality, 20–21
Bohannon, E. W., 143
Boredom, 251
  as a cause of early marriage, 225
Bottle feeding vs. breast feeding, 366
"Breaking point" (psychological), 329, 330
Breast feeding vs. bottle feeding, 366
Breasts, the, 319, 325
Bridger, (Dr.) Wagner H., 352
Brothers and sisters, see Siblings
Brown, Oscar, Jr., 236, 237

Buddhism, 121
Budget, the, 278
Burchinal, Lee, 227, 266
Bureau of the Census, 225
Business corporations, *see* Corporations
"Business widow," 290
Busino, Orlando (cartoonist), 41
Butterfield, Oliver M., 291

Car ownership, among young families, 276–277
Careers:
    combination of, with marriage, 243, 244, 261–263, 310; with parenthood, 263–267
    importance of education to, 260–261
    vs. marriage, 256–257
Carter, Hugh, 224
Cateora, Philip, 275
Cerebral arteriosclerosis, 61
Certainties, basic, 109
Chancre, defined, 235
Chaplin, Charlie, 57
Character, definition of, 28
    *See also* Character development
Character development, 27–40
    family influence on, 36–38
    Freud's theory of, 38–39
    in childhood, 29
    stages of, 29–32, 38–39
        amoral, 30, 33
        anal, 38
        conforming, 31, 34–35
        expedient, 33–34
        irrationally-conscientious, 31, 35–36
        oedpial, 38–39
        oral, 38
        rational-altruistic, 31–32, 36
Character disorders, 60
Charge accounts, 277
Child, the, 375–389
    changing needs of, 387–388
    characteristics of the various ages and stages of, 375–389; toddler, 375–380; early childhood, 380–384; middle childhood,

384–386; early adolescence, 386–387
    developmental periods of, 398–400
    effect on, of mother's working, 264–265
    fears of, 390–398
    health of, affected by number in the family, 352
    *See also* Baby, the
Child molesters, 214
Child Welfare League of America, 342
Childbearing, 246
    best age for, 351
    planning the time for, 332
Childlessness (involuntary), 338–347
    causes of, 339–340
    effects of, on the couple, 338–339
    *See also* Sterility
Child-rearing, 246, 298, 333
Chloramphicol, 351
Christianity, 120, 121
Chromosomes, 322
Church, Joseph, 136
Church, the, current changes in, 101–103
Cilia, 321–322
Circumcision, 368
Classification, value of, 60–62
Coitus, 322
Coleman, Richard P., 276
"Common sense" of mankind, the, 109
Compensation, 17
    as a defense mechanism, 74, 77–78
Compromise:
    as an approach to conflict, 74, 75
    value of, 75
Conception, 322
    control of, pros and cons for, 334–336
    *See also* Contraception
Concessions, *see* Compromise
Conflict:
    approach-approach, 67
    approach-avoidance, 67, 68–69
    approaches to, 74–76
        compromise, 74, 75

fight, 74–75
flight, 74, 75–76
avoidance-avoidance, 67, 68
between love and hate in the child,
378, 396
dealing with, 70
double-approach-avoidance, 67, 69
frustration resulting from, 66–69
kinds of conflict situation, 67–69
personality vs. environment, 65,
73
value of, 70–71
Conforming, 154
dangers of, 154, 186
value of, 118
within the corporation, 154–155
Conforming behavior:
definition of, 31
example of, 34–35
parents' responsibility for, 37
See also Conforming
Conscience:
development of, in the child, 377,
396
formation of, 88
Freud's concept of, 18
Contraception, 235, 331–332
importance of knowledge of, 332–
333
relationship of, to morality, 332
Contraceptives, criteria for, 332
Contracts, importance of reading carefully, 277
Conversion, 17
Conversion hysteria, 62
Coping, 215–216
Cornell University, 298
Corporation, the:
conforming demands of, on executives, 153–155
effects of, on personal life of em-
ployee, 154–155
Cotton, Dorothy, 267
Courtship, 230, 236
See also Dating
Creativity, 118, 145
Credit:
advantages and disadvantages of,
277
installment plans of, 277

Criminal acts, 60, 294
Crises, see Family crises
Croce, Bennedeto, 121–122
Crying, 369
Cunningham, Glen, 77

Dating and dates, 186–191, 221, 230
dangers of steady dating, 224, 225
patterns of, 189
problems of, 190–191
reasons for, 188–189
Daydreaming, see Fantasy
Death, 294–298
as a family crisis, 294–298
as a part of life, 169, 294
attitudes toward, 169, 295–296
reactions to, 296–298
statistics on, 307
Defense mechanisms, 17, 21, 73–86
adjustive or maladjustive, 84
as learned forms of behavior, 84
compensation, 77, 78
dangers of, 84
daydreaming, 82
displacement, 83–84, 132
fantasy, 82
flight, 74, 75–76
general principles of, 84
identification, 79, 80
projection, 80
rationalization, 78–79
regression, 80–81
repression, 81
suppression, 81–82
usefulness of, 84
withdrawal, 82–83
Delinquency, 294
Delirium tremens, characteristics of,
61
Demoralization as a family crisis, 294,
298–303
Dependency, 366–368, 405–407
abnormal, 406
effects of mother's behavior on,
367
overdependency, 406
transition from, to independence,
406–407
types of, 366

Descartes, René, 110
Desertion, 294, 301
Determinism, defined, 22 ftnt.
Deviancy, 204–217
    definition of, 204
    desirable and undesirable kinds of,
        205
    feminine tendencies in boys, 206,
        207
    masculine tendencies in girls, 205,
        207
    privatism, 205, 206–207
    sexual, see Sexual deviations
    skepticism, 208
Diet, importance of, to the future
    mother, 351–352
Discipline, 402–410
    child's need of, 406
    effect of, on aggression, 407–408;
        on personality development,
        22–23
    effects of lack of, 406
    importance of self-discipline, 408–
        409
    techniques of, psychological vs. di-
        rect, 404–405
    types of, 408
    vs. punishment, 408
Dismemberment as a family crisis,
    294–298
Displacement as a defense mechanism,
    17, 83–84, 152
Dissociative reaction (a neurosis), 62
Divorce, 300–303, 341
    forms of, 300
    laws concerning, 301, 341
    possible effects of, 303
    relationship of, to age of marriage,
        220, 225; to length of engage-
        ment, 234; to length of mar-
        riage, 294
    statistics on, 301
"Don Juan" character, 39
Double approach-avoidance conflict,
    67, 69
Draft, the, effect of, on early marriage,
    227
Draft-card burnings, 208
Drinking, excessive, see Alcoholism
Drug addiction, 60, 294

Drugs:
    harmful during pregnancy, 350–
        351
    LSD, 97
    See also Drug addiction
Durant, Will, 111
Duvall, Evelyn Millis, 44 ftnt., 185
Duvall, Sylvanus M., 155, 156

Early marriages, see Youthful mar-
    riages
Ectomorphy, 20
Edison, Thomas, 82
Education:
    effect of level of, on careers, 260–
        261; on income, 224; on mar-
        riage, 225, 231
    importance of, in today's society,
        330, 335
Ego, the, 54
    Freud's concept of, 17–19
Ego-ideal, the, defined, 18
Embryo (human), see Human em-
    bryo
Emerson, Ralph Waldo, 121
Empathy, defined, 364
Employer-employee    relationships,
    150–152
Endomorphy, 20
Endowment policy, 280
Engagement, the, 233–234
Engle, T. L., 13
Environment:
    dependence of intellectual matu-
        rity on, 46
    influence of, on child, 31
Epicureanism, 111–112
Epididymis, 319
Epilepsy, 310
Equanil (drug), 350
Erection, 320
Erikson, Erik H., 399
Escape mechanisms, 77
    See also Defense mechanisms
Ethics:
    definition of, 196
    formulating one's own sex ethics,
        194, 196–197
    vs. moral codes, 196

Executive wife, the, 248
Exhibitionism, 214, 215
Expedient behavior:
    definition of, 30
    examples of, 33–34
    parents' responsibility for, 37
Extended family, 162, 163–164
Extrovert vs. introvert, Jung's theory
    of, 21–22

Face-saving, *see* Defense mechanisms
"Fairies," 214
Fallopian tubes, 319, 321, 322
Family:
    changes in, as it grows, 140
    James on, 117
    regulating the size of, 330
    relation of number of children in,
        to their health, 352
    sibling relationships in, 139–147
    *See also* Family crises; Family
        planning; Family structure
Family crises, 293–305
    accession, 298
    adoption, 298
    alcoholism, 298–300
    birth, 298
    death, 294–298
    demoralization, 298–303
    dismemberment, 294–298, 300–
        303
    divorce, 300–303
    how to face, 303
    kinds of, 294
Family life cycle, changing roles dur-
    ing, 246–247
Family planning, 329–337
    importance of, 329–331
    pros and cons of, 334–336
Family structure, 162–164
    types of, 162
Family-founding, 246
Fantasy and daydreaming, 74, 79, 82,
    378
Fear:
    a cause of early marriage, 226
    compared with anxiety, 391–392
    *See also* Fears in children

Fears in children, 390–401
    aids in overcoming, 394–395
    avoidance of, 396
    causes of, 393–395
    healthy vs. morbid, 396, 398
    physical reactions to, 391–392
    responses to, 398
Fecundity, 340
Feeblemindedness, laws concerning,
    310
Feeding the infant, 365, 366
    force-feeding, effects of, 362
Feldman, Harold, 298
Fertility, 340
    factors influencing, 340
    vs. fecundity, 340
Fertilization, 322
Fetishism, 214, 215
Fetus:
    development of, 323–325
    effect of mother's diet on, 326
    premature expulsion of, 356
Fight approach to conflict, 74–75
Fimbrioe, 321
"First-child problem," the, 232, 265,
    298
Flight as a defense mechanism, 74,
    75–76
Flight reactions:
    regression, 80
    repression, 81
Florence Crittenden Home, the, 197,
    199
Follicle, 321
"Forced" marriages, 227
Forgetting, 81
Foster homes, 313, 361
Freedom, responsibility of, 195
Freud, Sigmund, 17, 56, 134
    on humor, 57
    theory of character development,
        17, 30, 38–39
Friendship, Emerson on, 121
Frigidity, 340
Fromme, Allan, 221
Frottage, 215
"Fruits," 214
Frustration, 64–72
    caused by having to choose be-
        tween alternatives, 66–67

factors involved in, 65–66
*See also* Frustrating situations
Frustrating situations:
developing tolerance for, 70–71
value of, 71
*See also* Frustration
Frustration tolerance, 70–71

Galactosemia, 362
Gametes, 319, 322
Gandhi, Mahatma, 121
Gang age, the, 385–386
Genes, 322
Genital character, a, 30, 39
George Washington University, 298
German measles, 351
Glick, Paul C., 224–225
Glueck, S. and E., 265
Goals:
change of, 7
influence of, on behavior, 3, 5, 7
"Gold-bricking," 77
"Golden birthright," 348–349
Golding, William, 150
"Golf widow," 290
Gonorrhea, 195, 235
Goodenough, Florence, 143
Graafian follicle, 321
"Great truths, the," 109
Grief, 296–298
causes of, 297
helping someone adjust to, 296–297
reactions to, 296–298
vs. sorrow, 296
Guilt feelings, 398
child's ways of relieving, 377–378

Habit patterns, changing of, 23–24
Hallucinations, 61, 62
Handel, Gerald, 276
"Harvey" (play), 82
Havighurst, Robert, 29, 30, 37
"Hazel" (cartoon), 2
Healthy self, the, *see* Mental health
Hedonism, 112, 113
Heilbroner, Robert, 261

Hereditary traits, determination of, 322
Hero-worship, 79
Hill, Reuben L., 185
Hoffman, (Dr.) Lois, 264
Home, the, effect of, on personality development, 22–23
Home pattern, value of, 187
Homesickness, 81, 297
Homicide, 294
Homosexuality, 134, 214, 215
causes of, 215
laws governing, 215
marriage and, 310
Honeymoon, the, 235–236
Honzik, M. P., 365
Horace (Roman poet), 296
Hormones, 354
Human embryo, development of, 322–325
Humor:
as a sign of mental health, 56–59
Freud's theory on, 57
off-color, 58
sick, 58–59
uses of, 57
Hysterical character, a, 30, 39

Id, the, 54
Freud's concept of, 17–19
"Ideal mate," study of, 232–233
Idealism, false:
dangers of, 236
popular meaning of, 113
vs. materialism, 112–113
Idealization, 17
Idealized image, the, 18
Ideals (personal), 116–117
*See also* Values
Identification as a defense mechanism, 17, 74, 79–80
Illegitimacy, 294, 313
statistics on, 312
Illegitimate motherhood, 197–199, 205, 312–314
Illness as an excuse, 327
Immortality, varied ideas on, 296
Impotence, 340

Imprisonment, 294
Impulses in the child, handling of, 378
Individualism:
a need assumed in our culture, 5–6
rise of, 112
Individuality, 118
Infatuation, 187
vs. love, 179–181
Inferiority complex, Adler's theory on, 22
Infidelity (marital), 290, 294, 341
In-laws, 288, 289
*See also* Mothers-in-law
Insanity, 310
Insemination, 322
Installment buying, 232, 270–271, 275
Installment plans of credit, 277
Insurance, 278–280
Integration of the personality, 54
Interaction, defined, 4
Introjection, 88–89
definition of, 28–29, 88
Introvert vs. extrovert, Jung's theory of, 21–22
Iodides, effect of, 350
"Irrational," defined, 31
Irrationally-conscientious behavior:
definition of, 31
examples of, 35
parents' responsibility for, 37
values and limitations of, 35

James, William, 110, 112, 117
Jealousy:
among adults, 142
among siblings, 141–142
a cause of early marriage, 226
in marriage, 287
Job, the, social importance of, 148–150
*See also* Relationships in one's job; Work satisfaction
Judaism, 120, 121
Judeo-Christian tradition, 191, 194
Jung, Carl G., 21
theory of, 21–22

Kahn blood test, 235
Kant, Immanuel, 110, 121
Keniston, Kenneth, 206
Kenkel, William, 245
Kennedy, John F., 71
Key, Ted (cartoonist), 2
Kinsey Report, 136
Kirkpatrick, Clifford, 251
Koch, Helen, 143

Labor (in giving birth), 356–357
length of, 356–357
stages of, 356–357
Labor Force by Age and Sex (chart), 258
Laughter:
reasons for, 57
a universal phenomenon, 57
Leadership, 158
qualities of, 150–152
Leaky, Alice, 143
Learning to talk, 361, 370, 372, 381–382
Learning to walk, 371–372
Lee, Dorothy, 169
"Lesbians," 214
Lewin, Kurt, 67
Life insurance, types of policy, 279–280
Life-maintaining needs, *see* Physiological needs
Life space, defined, 67
Loans, 277
Loneliness, 303
antidotes for, 311
a cause of early marriage, 226
*Lord of the Flies, The* (Golding), 150
Loss of face as a family crisis, 294, 299
Loss of memory, 77
Love:
before marriage, 221
complexities of, 181–182
definition of, 173
developmental stages of, 174–179
intellectual, 182
"love at first sight," 179
marital, 220, 221

mature, 179, 188
requisites for maintenance of, 201
romantic, 181, 220–221
sexual, 182
vs. infatuation, 179–181
LSD, 97

MacFarland, J., 365
Make-believe, 76
Maladjustments, *see* Mental disorders
Manic depressive, the, 61
Man's responsibility to the future, 411–415
Maritain, Jacques, 111
Marital Status of Women in the Civilian Labor Force: 1940–1966 (chart), 259
Marriage, 220–292
  age for, 220
  combination of, with career, 243, 244, 261–269, 310
  causes of disenchantment after, 230–231
  financial values and goals in, 270–281
  "forced," 227
  happy or unhappy, 236, 282–292
  hasty, 236
  interclass marriages, 231
  interfaith marriages, 231
  international marriages, 231
  interracial marriages, 231
  license requirements for, 223–224, 310
  mate selection for, 230–234
  minimum age legally allowed for, 222–224
  money and, 270–281, 224–225, 231–232
  of college women, before graduation, 261, 309
  preparation for, 234–238
  problems in, 287–290
  readiness for, 221–224
  relationship of educational level to, 224–225
  roles in, 240–255
  sex and, 136–137

  successful, common between people of same basic background, 231–232
  successful vs. happy, 282–285
  to a close relative, dangers of, 350
  unhappy, 287–291
  unsuccessful, effects of, 227–228
  *See also* Mate, the; Youthful marriages
Marriage relationship during pregnancy, 353–355
Maslow, A. H., 8
Masochism, 214
Masturbation, 134, 289, 341
Mate, the
  choice of, 230–232
  ideal vs. actual, 232–233
Materialism:
  popular meaning of, 113
  vs. idealism, 112–113
Matriarchal extended family, 162, 164
Maturity:
  as a process, 32, 36, 42
  characteristics of, 31–32, 36
  chronological, 44, 45
  definition of, 42
  emotional, 45, 46–47
  growth toward, 41–52
  intellectual, 45, 46
  philosophical, 45, 48–49, 50
  physical, 44, 45
  sexual, 50
  social, 45, 48
  stages of, 42
  types of, 44–45
McKinney, Fred, 50
Mead, Margaret, 102
Median age, defined, 224 ftnt.
Menninger, William, 118
Mental disorders, 60–62
  classification of, 60–62
  marriage and, 310
Mental dynamisms, *see* Defense mechanisms
Mental health, 53–63
  characteristics of the mentally healthy person, 55
  humor as an indication of, 56–59
  maintenance of, 59–60

Mental illnesses, *see* Mental disorders
Mental retardation, 351, 352, 362
Meprobamate, 350
Mesomorphy, 20
Metabolism, inborn errors of, 362
Middle age, necessary adjustments of, 169
Milton, John, 41, 42
Miltown (drug), 350
Miscarriage, 355, 356
Mohammedanism, 121
Money:
    influences on the use of, 273–275
    relationship of, to family planning, 335; to marriage, 224–225, 231–232, 270–281, 287, 303
Moral behavior:
    contraception and, 332
    guided by one's ethics, 194
    sex codes and, 193–203
    sexual, 137, 194
Moral codes:
    as social instruments, 196
    definition of, 196
    in transition, 194–195
    value of, 196
    *See also* Sex codes
Morality, *see* Moral behavior
"Morning sickness," 352
Mothering, defined, 360
Mothers-in-law, 288, 289, 302
Mourning, 296–297
Museum of Science and Industry, Chicago, Ill., 322

Narcissism, 175
    in love before marriage, 221
Narcissistic character, the, 30, 38
Nationalism, 112
Necking, 187, 191
Needs:
    definition of, 3
    human vs. animal, 4
    *See also* Needs (human)
Needs (human):
    basic, 5–11
    conflict of, 8
    cultural, 5–6

difficulty in identification of, 5
effects of, 64
individual, 5–7
interaction of, 4–5
Maslow's classification of, 8–9
physiological, 3
psychological, 3–4
reduction of, 5
Neuroses, *see* Psychoneuroses
Nidation, 322
Nocturnal emissions, 320
Nomenclature, defined, 60
Nonsupport, 294
Nuclear family, the, 162, 164, 165

Obsessive-compulsive behavior, 30, 38, 39
    as a neurosis, 62
Obstetrician, 355
Oedipal stage of character development, 30, 38–39
Old age:
    making a satisfying old age, 168
    problems of, in our society, 160, 165–167
    a stage of aging, 168
Oral stage of character development, 30, 38
"Orgasm worship," 289
Ovaries, 319
Overcompensation, 77
Ovulation, 321
Ovum (pl., ova), 319, 320–322

Pain killers, 350
Parallel play, 387
Paranoia, 61, 80
Parent-child relationship, 328
    *See also* Parents
Parenthood:
    basic requirements for success of, 333–334
    combination of, with careers, 263–267
    importance of self-understanding to, 365

preparing for, 335–336
reversed roles in, 243
Parents:
  indirect compensation of, through children, 77–78
  influence of, on child's attitudes, 88–89; on child's choice of a mate, 233; on child's values, 22–23, 28–29, 36–38
  problems of aging parents and adult offspring, 165
  relationship of, to married children, 287–289
  tasks of, in relation to the adolescent, 131–134
  unmarried, 312–313
  See also Parenthood
Part-time work, 261
Patriarchal extended family, 162, 163
Peck, Robert, 29, 30, 37
"Pecking order," 155–158
  factors determining rank in, 156–158
Pedophiles, 214
Peeping Toms, 214
Peer group, defined, 31
Penis, 319
"Pep-pills," 350
Personal philosophy, 115–125
  a basis for social action, 109
  definition of, 91
  development of, 119, 122
  religion and, 96–97
  value of, 119–120
  values dependent on, 109–110
  vs. way of life, 122
Personality, 12–26
  as a positive force, 23
  changing of, 119
  definitions of, 13–14, 118
  development of, 12–26
  effect of sibling position on, 142–143
  Freud's theories on development of, 17–19
  ideal, 19
  improving of, 23–24
  influence of body build on, 20–21
  integration of, 54
  Sheldon's theory of types of, 20–21

types of, based on body types, 20–21
vs. popularity, 13–14
See also Character, Character development
Personality disorders, 60
Personality traits, classification of, 24
Petting, 187, 191
Phallic phase of development, 30, 39
Phenylketonuria (P.K.U.), 362
Philosophy, 107–114
  definitions of, 111
  levels of philosophical development, 107–108
  not directly affected by social change, 111
  varying views on what it is, 110
  See also Personal philosophy
Philosophy of life, see Personal philosophy
Physical attraction, role of, in mate selection, 187–188
Physiological needs (basic), 3
Pierce, C. S., 112
Pituitary gland, 321
Placenta, 325, 326, 356
Planned communities, unnaturalness of, 168–169
Plato, 110
Popularity vs. personality, 13–14
Power success style, 144, 145
Pragmatism, 112, 117
Pregnancy, 326–328
  activity during, 326
  danger signals in, 355–356
  diet during, 326, 351–352
  diseases dangerous to the embryo, 351
  drugs dangerous to the embryo, 350–351
  early, possible bad effects of, 224
  effect of, on marriage relationship, 353–355; on sexual desire, 354–355
  emotions affecting, 327–328
  factors influencing chance of, 340
  following sterility, 341
  length of, 326
  most crucial time of, 349–350
  premarital, 197–199

psychological effects of, on the expectant mother, 353–354
role of husband during, 328
symptoms of, 352–353
weight of mother during, 326–327
Premarital counseling, 234
Premarital examinations, 234–235, 341
Premarital pregnancy, 197–199
Premarital sex relations, 194–195, 341
a case study, 197–199
changing social attitude toward, 195
present-day trends in, 194–195
Premature births, 324–325, 350
among teen-age mothers, 351
caused by mother's deficient diet, 352
Prenatal care, 349–352
Prevenception, 331–332
"Primitive behavior," defined, 81
Privatism, 205–206
Privacy, need for, 6
*Profiles in Courage* (J. F. Kennedy), 71
Projection as a defense mechanism, 17, 80
Promotional depression, 297
Prostate gland, 319, 320
Psychoanalysis, functions of, 17
Psychoanalytic system of classifying character, 30, 38–39
Psychological needs, basic, 3–4, 59
Psychological upset, 290
Psychoneurosis, 60
types of, 62
Psychophysiologic disorders, 60
Psychoses, 60
characteristics of, 62
kinds of, 61–62
Psychosexual development, Freud's theory of, 38–39
Psychosocial systems of classifying character, 29, 36–38
Psychosomatic disorder, 60
Puberty, defined, 45
Publilius Syrys, 41
Punishment, 408
Pyelitis, 355, 356

Quarreling, 290–291
"Queers," 214

Rainwater, Lee, 276
Rational-altruistic behavior:
definition of, 31–32
example of, 36
parents' influence on, 37–38
Rationalization as a defense mechanism, 17, 71, 74, 78–79
Regression as a defense mechanism, 80–81
Reinterpretation as a defense mechanism, 74, 75
Relationships:
between attitudes of youth and those of old age, 160–171
employer-employee, 150–152
in the family, 139–147
in one's job, 149–158
to one's organization, 150
to one's employer, 150–152
to other people, 149
outside the family, 148–159
Religion, 95–106
changing ideas about, as one becomes older, 98–99
confusion of adolescents concerning, 99
current re-examination of, 101
definition of, 97
diverse views on value of, 97
philosophy of life and, 96–97, 296
religious values in relation to sex ethics, 197
social change and, 97
varying ideas about, 99–101
Repression as a defense mechanism, 81
Reproduction, 318–329
a basic need, 9
organs of, 319–322
process of, 319–328
Reserpine, 350
Rh incompatibility, 350
Richter, Mischa, 95
Rivalry between siblings, 140
*Rivals, The* (Sheridan), 290

Rockwell, Norman, 73, 74, 83
Role expectation in marriage, 240–255
Role practice, 79
Roles:
  as cultural products, 241
  as family life cycle brings changes, 246–247
  changes in:
    female, 243–244
    male, 242–243
  companion, 251
  deciding on, 253–254
  feminine role today, confusing, 247–251
  marital, 244–247
  married woman's, 251–252
  masculine role today, 252–253
  partner, 252
  reversed, 243
  traditional, 241, 247, 251, 254
  wife-and-mother, 251
Rubella (German measles), 351
Rutgers Center of Alcohol Studies, 299

Sadism, 214
Sandburg, Carl, 414
Santayana, George, 121
*Saturday Review,* 261
Savings, advantages of, 277–278
Schizophrenia, 61
School-age marriages, *see* Youthful marriages
Schwartz, Jane, 261
Scrotum, 319
Sears, R. R., 79
Self, the:
  concepts of, 14–16
  ideal self, 14, 15
  personal, 14, 15
  total, 15
Self theory, 14–16
Self-discipline, importance of, 408–409
Self-love, 175
Self-preservation, a basic need, 9
Self-reliance, 59

Semen (seminal fluid), 320
Seminal vesicles, 320
Senescence, *see* Aging
Separation (of man and wife), 300, 301, 302
"Separation anxiety," 361
Serpasil (drug), 350
Sewell, Amos, 12, 13
Sex:
  exploitation of, 137, 194
  importance of knowledge of, 311
  a life force, 136
  marriage and, 136–137, 287
  obsession with today, 194
  relationship of off-color humor to, 58
  *See also* Premarital sex relations
Sexual behavior, value standards for, 199–201
Sex cells (mature), *see* Gametes
Sex codes, 193–203
  developing one's own personal code, 195
  *See also* Moral codes
Sex differences, 134–136, 249–250
Sex education, a continuing process, 319
Sex ethics, 193, 196–197
  developing one's own, 194, 195
Sex orientation, 196
Sexual desire, 7, 134
  aroused by petting, 191
  effect of mass media on, 227; of pregnancy on, 354–355
  fear of, 226
Sexual deviation, 58, 60, 194, 213–216
  prevention of, 213–214
  types of, 214–215
  understanding of, 215–216
Sexual maturity, 50
Sexual morality, 137
  *See also* Moral behavior
Sexual problems, 289–290
Sexual satisfaction, relationship of, to marriage, 302
Sexuality:
  differences in, in boys and girls, 134–136
  in adolescence, 134–137

a part of one's whole personality, 136

relationship of, to love, 134–135

Shakespeare, 161

Sheldon, W. H., theory of personality types, 20–21

Sheridan, Richard Brinsley, 290

Siblings:
  adolescent's attitude toward, 144
  definition of, 58
  jealousy between, 141–142
  relationship between ordinal position of, and personality, 142–143
  relationships in the family, 139–147; outside the family, 145
  rivalry between, 140–141
  social learning among, 144–145

Sit-ins, 208

Sleeping pills, 350

Smoking during pregnancy, effects of, 351

Socrates, 93, 110

Sorrow vs. grief, 296

Spacing of children, 351

Sperm (pl., spermatozoa), 319, 320–322

Spinoza, Baruch, 110

Spirochete, defined, 235

Status, loss of, as a family crisis, 294, 299

Stealing, 60

Sterility:
  causes of
    physical, 235, 338
    psychological, 339–340
  effects of
    psychological, 340–341
    social, 341
  treatments for, 341

Sterilization, 331
  laws concerning, 310

Stoicism, 111–112

Stone, Joseph L., 136

"Stranger anxiety," 361

Strategic success style, defined, 144

Strauss, Anselm, 232

Strecker, E. A., 44

Stress, responses to, 54–55

Sublimation, 90

of sexual energies, 134

Suicide, 77, 294, 307

Sulfa drugs, 351

Superego, the, 54
  Freud's concept of, 17–19

Suppression as a defense mechanism, 81–82

Syphilis, 195, 235
  causes of, 235
  diagnoses of, 235
  effects of, 235, 356
  marriage and, 310
  symptoms of, 61, 235

Tact, value of, 82

Talmud, the, 119

Technological development, effect of, on mankind, 412–415

Teen-age marriages:
  financial difficulties of, 275–277
  premature births among, 351
  See also Youthful marriages

Temperament, relationship of body build to, 20

Term insurance, 279–280

Testes, 319

Testicles, 319

Tetracycline, 351

Thurber, James, 53

"Time" (song by Oscar Brown, Jr.), 236, 237, 238

Tissue needs, see Physiological needs

Toddler, the, 376–389

Toilet training, 378–379

Toman, Walter, 143

Toulouse-Lautrec, 77

Toxemia (blood poisoning), 355, 356

Tranquilizers, 350

Transvestism, 215

Twain, Mark, 414

"Unconscious," the, Freud's views on, 17

Unmarried, the, 306–315
  adjusting to singlehood, 310–312

attitude of our society toward, 308, 309–310
circumstances leading to a woman's being unmarried, 308–309
individuals who should not marry, 310
psychological problems of, 306–309
statistics on unmarried women, 309
unmarried fathers, 314–315
unmarried mothers, 312–314
unmarried parents, 312–314
*See also* Illegitimate motherhood
Urethra, 319, 320
Uterus, 319, 320–322

Vagina, 319, 320, 322
Values, 116–118
for society, 117
formation of, 120
importance of, 117–118
moral, 117
personal, 116–117
relationship of, to personality, 118
time-proven, 120
Vas deferens, 319
Venereal diseases, 194, 195, 235
effect of, on babies born of an infected mother, 235
*See also* Syphilis
Vernix caseosa, 324, 325
Vincent, Clark E., 313
Vitamin D, danger of excessive use of, 351
Vitamin K, danger of excessive use of, 351
Voyeurs, 214

Wallach, Ira, 153
Wants, *see* Needs
Wassermann blood test, 235

Way of life:
definition of, 91
vs. philosophy of life, 122
Weddings, 225, 233
Weiland, Hyman, 276
Whitman, Ardis, 101
Whitmarsh, Ruth, 265
Whyte, William, 245
Widowhood, 297–298
Will to power, as a primary motive, 22
Withdrawal as a defense mechanism, 70, 71, 74, 82–83
Wordsworth, William, 41, 42
Work satisfaction, 152–153
importance of, 152
Working mothers, 264–267
Working women, statistics on, 257–261
*See also* Working mothers
Wright brothers, the, 82

X rays during pregnancy, 351

Youth, present-day preoccupation with, 160, 165
Youthful marriages, 194
causes of:
emotional, 225–226
social, 226–227
dangers of, 227–228
divorce rate and, 220, 225
effect of, on education, 224–225
outdated idea of value of, 222
present trend toward, 225–228
relationship of, to number of children, 225
statistics on, 224
*See also* Marriage; Teen-age marriages

Zygote, 322

C D E F G H I J 7 6 5 4 3 2 1 0
Printed in the United States of America